Microsoft

MCSE

Exam 70-226

Designing Highly Available Web Solutions with Microsoft® Windows® 2000 Server Technologies

Training Kit

PUBLISHED BY
Microsoft Press
A Division of Microsoft Corporation
One Microsoft Way
Redmond, Washington 98052-6399

Library of Congress Cataloging-in-Publication Data

MCSE Training Kit : Designing Highly Available Web Solutions with Microsoft Windows 2000 Server Technologies / Microsoft Corporation.
      p. cm.
   Includes index.
   ISBN 0-7356-1425-3
    1. Electronic data processing personnel--Certification. 2. Microsoft software--Examinations--Study guides. 3. Computer networks--Examinations--Study guides. 4. Microsoft Windows (Computer file) I. Title.

QA76.3 .S4645 2001
005.4'4769--dc21   2001044144

Printed and bound in the United States of America.

1 2 3 4 5 6 7 8 9   QWT   6 5 4 3 2 1

Distributed in Canada by Penguin Books Canada Limited.

A CIP catalogue record for this book is available from the British Library.

Microsoft Press books are available through booksellers and distributors worldwide. For further information about international editions, contact your local Microsoft Corporation office or contact Microsoft Press International directly at fax (425) 706-7329. Visit our Web site at www.microsoft.com/mspress. Send comments to *tkinput@microsoft.com*.

Active Directory, ActiveX, BackOffice, FrontPage, JScript, Microsoft, Microsoft Press, NetMeeting, NetShow, Outlook, Visual Basic, Visual C++, Visual InterDev, Visual J++, Windows, and Windows NT are either registered trademarks or trademarks of Microsoft Corporation in the United States and/or other countries. Other product and company names mentioned herein may be the trademarks of their respective owners.

The example companies, organizations, products, domain names, e-mail addresses, logos, people, places, and events depicted herein are fictitious. No association with any real company, organization, product, domain name, e-mail address, logo, person, place, or event is intended or should be inferred.

Microsoft Press
Acquisitions Editor: Thomas Pohlmann
Project Editor: Kurt Stephan

nSight, Inc.
Project Editor: Susan H. McClung
Technical Editor: John Panzarella
Manuscript Editor: Joe Gustaitis
Desktop Publisher: Mary Beth McDaniel
Indexer: James Minkin
Proofreaders: Charlotte Maurer, Rebecca Merz, and Jan Cocker

Body Part No. X08-01112

Contents

About This Book

Welcome to *MCSE Training Kit—Designing Highly Available Web Solutions with Microsoft Windows 2000 Server Technologies*. This book guides you through the process of designing Web sites that are highly available. You'll learn how to design network topologies that support redundant components, connections, and services. You'll also learn how to incorporate various clustering technologies into your design, including the Windows 2000 Cluster service, Network Load Balancing (NLB), and Microsoft Application Center 2000. This book also discusses how to determine the capacity requirements for your system and how to integrate directory services and applications into your design. Finally, you'll learn how to plan your Web site's security, how to monitor and audit your system, and how to plan a disaster recovery strategy.

Note   For more information on becoming a Microsoft Certified Systems Engineer, see the section entitled "The Microsoft Certified Professional Program" later in this chapter.

Each chapter in this book is divided into lessons, activities, labs, and reviews. The lessons discuss the considerations that you should take into account when designing a specific aspect of your Web environment, and they provide a structure for evaluating the possible decisions that you must make when developing that design. The lessons also include examples of how the information within the lessons is applied. In addition, each lesson ends with a lesson summary. The activities and labs are designed to allow you to practice or demonstrate your understanding of the design objectives discussed in a chapter. The activities and labs include scenarios to help illustrate how your design decisions are applied to real-life situations. Each chapter ends with a set of review questions to test your knowledge of the chapter material.

The "Getting Started" section of this introduction provides important information about hardware and software requirements, the evaluation software included in this kit, and the electronic version of this book.

Intended Audience

This book was developed for information technology (IT) professionals who need to design, plan, implement, and support a Web environment that uses Windows 2000 and Internet Information Services (IIS) or who plan to take the related Microsoft Certified Professional Exam 70-226: *Designing Highly Available Web Solutions with Microsoft Windows 2000 Server Technologies.*

Prerequisites

This course requires that students meet the following prerequisites:

- A working knowledge of network technologies, particularly as they relate to a Web environment.

- A minimum of two years of experience implementing, administering, and configuring network operating systems and services, including Windows 2000 Server and IIS. (A minimum of one year of experience planning and designing highly available Web site infrastructures is recommended.)

- Work in multiserver, *n*-tier application environments that have some or all of the following characteristics:

  - Concurrent client connections that can exceed 1,000

  - Transactional applications

  - User databases, such as Lightweight Directory Access Protocol (LDAP) server or directory service

  - Internet security, such as firewalls, secure protocols, or proxy servers

  - High-availability services that can include NLB, Component Load Balancing (CLB), the Cluster service, and Application Center 2000

- Successful completion of the following core exams for the Microsoft Windows 2000 MCSE track is recommended: Exam 70-215: *Installing, Configuring, and Administering Microsoft Windows 2000 Server,* and Exam 70-216: *Implementing and Administering a Microsoft Windows 2000 Network Infrastructure.*

Reference Materials

You might find the following reference materials useful:

- Howard, Michael, Marc Levy, and Richard Waymire. *Designing Secure Web-Based Applications for Microsoft Windows 2000.* Redmond, Washington: Microsoft Press, 2000.

- Microsoft Corporation. *MCSE Training Kit—Designing Microsoft Windows 2000 Network Security.* Redmond, Washington: Microsoft Press, 2001.

- Microsoft Corporation. *MCSE Training Kit—Microsoft Windows 2000 Server*. Redmond, Washington: Microsoft Press, 2000.

- Microsoft Corporation. *Microsoft Application Center Resource Kit*. Redmond, Washington: Microsoft Press, 2001.

- Microsoft Corporation. *Microsoft Windows 2000 Server Resource Kit*. Redmond, Washington: Microsoft Press, 2000.

- Microsoft Corporation. *Microsoft SQL Server 2000 Resource Kit*. Redmond, Washington: Microsoft Press, 2001.

- Microsoft Corporation. *Microsoft Exchange 2000 Server Resource Kit*. Redmond, Washington: Microsoft Press, 2001.

- Microsoft product and technical information (including white papers, case studies, and background information) available at *http://www.microsoft.com/technet/*.

- Windows 2000 white papers, case studies, and background information available at *http://www.microsoft.com/windows/server*.

About The Supplemental Course Materials CD-ROM

The Supplemental Course Materials CD-ROM contains a fully searchable electronic version of this book. For information about using the electronic book (eBook), see the section "About the eBook" later in this introduction. The compact discs also contain evaluation copies of Microsoft Windows 2000 Advanced Server and Microsoft Application Center 2000.

Features of This Book

Each chapter opens with a "Before You Begin" section that prepares you for completing the chapter.

The chapters are then divided into lessons, activities, and labs.

The "Review" section at the end of the chapter allows you to test what you've learned in the chapter's lessons.

The Appendix, "Questions and Answers," contains all of the book's questions and corresponding answers.

Notes

Several types of Notes appear throughout the lessons.

- Notes marked **Tip** contain explanations of possible results or alternative methods.

- Notes marked **Important** contain information that is essential to completing a task.
- Notes marked **Note** contain supplemental information.
- Notes marked **Caution** contain warnings about possible loss of data.
- Notes marked **More Info** contain cross-references to other critical reference material.

Conventions

The following conventions are used throughout this book.

Notational Conventions

- Characters or commands that you type appear in **bold lowercase** type.
- *Italic* in syntax statements indicates placeholders for variable information. *Italic* is also used for book titles.
- Names of files and folders appear in all caps, except when you're to type them directly. Unless otherwise indicated, you can use all lowercase letters when you type a file name in a dialog box or at a command prompt.
- File name extensions appear in all lowercase.
- Acronyms appear in all uppercase.
- Monospace type represents code samples, examples of screen text, or entries that you might type at a command prompt or in initialization files.
- Square brackets [ ] are used in syntax statements to enclose optional items. For example, [*FILENAME*] in command syntax indicates that you can choose to type a file name with the command. Type only the information within the brackets, not the brackets themselves.
- Braces { } are used in syntax statements to enclose required items. Type only the information within the braces, not the braces themselves.
- Icons represent specific sections in the book as follows:

Icon	Represents
	Activities and labs. You should perform the activities and labs to give yourself an opportunity to use the skills being presented in the lesson.
	Chapter review questions. These questions at the end of each chapter allow you to test what you have learned in the lessons. You will find the answers to the review questions in the "Questions and Answers" Appendix at the end of the book.

Chapter and Appendix Overview

This self-paced training course combines notes, hands-on activities and labs, professional interviews and worksheets, and review questions to teach you how to design highly available Web solutions with Windows 2000 Server technologies. It's designed to be completed from beginning to end, but you can choose a customized track and complete only the sections that interest you. (See the next section, "Finding the Best Starting Point for You," for more information.) If you choose the customized track option, see the "Before You Begin" section in each chapter. Any labs or chapters that require preliminary work or study from preceding chapters refer to the appropriate chapters.

The book is divided into the following chapters:

- The "About This Book" section contains a self-paced training overview and introduces the components of this training. Read this section thoroughly to get the greatest educational value from this self-paced training and to plan which lessons you'll complete.

- Chapter 1, "Introduction to Designing Highly Available Web Solutions," introduces you to the concepts of designing a highly available Web site. The chapter describes many of the concepts essential to the design of a highly available Web site and provides information about designing these sites and determining an appropriate method of ensuring high availability.

- Chapter 2, "Network Infrastructure," describes how to design a network topology that includes redundant components, paths, and services. You'll also learn how to design a subnet addressing structure, Dynamic Host Configuration Protocol (DHCP) server environment, and a name resolution structure for a Transmission Control Protocol/Internet Protocol (TCP/IP) network.

- Chapter 3, "Server Configurations," describes how to design a server configuration that's fault-tolerant and how to ensure a safe environment for those servers so that they remain highly available. You'll also learn how to design a fault-tolerant data storage system.

- Chapter 4, "Microsoft Windows 2000 Cluster Service," introduces you to the components that make up the Cluster service in Windows 2000. The chapter describes how to plan a server cluster and how to choose a server cluster model.

- Chapter 5, "Network Load Balancing (NLB)," provides an overview of NLB, describes how the service works, and discusses NLB architecture. The chapter also describes the steps that you should follow when planning NLB clusters and how to choose a configuration model when setting up your NLB cluster.

- Chapter 6, "Microsoft Application Center 2000," provides you with an overview of Application Center and introduces you to the features in Application Center that allow you to create Web clusters and COM+ application clusters. You'll also learn what steps to take in planning these clusters and what factors to take into consideration when determining which type of clusters to implement.

- Chapter 7, "Capacity Planning," introduces you to several concepts that you should consider when planning your capacity requirements. The chapter also explains how to calculate the costs imposed on your system by each user and how to plan your site's network capacity.

- Chapter 8, "Directory Services," introduces you to the Active Directory service in Windows 2000 and describes how Active Directory replication works. You'll then learn about the steps that you should take when planning the Active Directory physical structure.

- Chapter 9, "Application Integration," explains how to determine where to place application components to work within a distributed topology and how to develop an application deployment and synchronization strategy. The chapter also describes the steps that you should follow when planning a database integration strategy and designing an Exchange integration strategy to provide browser-based messaging to your clients.

- Chapter 10, "Network Security," describes how to design authentication, authorization, and encryption strategies that protect your network from threats that might compromise your resources. The chapter also provides an overview of firewalls and helps you determine which firewall strategy you should use for your organization.

- Chapter 11, "Systems Monitoring and Disaster Recovery," provides information on how to design comprehensive plans to monitor and audit your systems in order to ensure adequate performance, availability, and security. The chapter also describes how to design a disaster recovery strategy that protects your network from loss of data and from machine failure.

- The Appendix, "Questions and Answers," lists all of the review questions from the book, showing the page number where the question appears and the answer.

- The Glossary provides a list of terms—along with their definitions—that are important to the concepts discussed in the book.

Finding the Best Starting Point For You

Because this book is self-paced, you can skip some lessons and visit them later. Use the following table to find the best starting point for you:

If You	Follow This Learning Path
Are preparing to take the Microsoft Certified Professional Exam 70-226: *Designing Highly Available Web Solutions with Microsoft Windows 2000 Server Technologies*	Read the "Getting Started" section. Then work through Chapters 1–11.
Want to review information about specific topics from the exam	Use the "Where to Find Specific Skills in This Book" section that follows this table.

Where to Find Specific Skills in This Book

The following tables provide a list of the skills measured on certification Exam 70-226: *Designing Highly Available Web Solutions with Microsoft Windows 2000 Server Technologies.* The table lists the skill and shows where in this book you'll find the lesson relating to that skill.

Note   Exam skills are subject to change without prior notice and at the sole discretion of Microsoft.

Skills Being Measured	Location in Book
Designing Cluster and Server Architectures for Web Solutions	
Design NLB solutions to improve availability, scalability, and fault tolerance. Considerations include the number of hosts, number of clusters, placement of servers, multicast versus unicast, failover strategy, priority, affinity, filtering, load weighting, and application types.	Chapter 5, Lessons 1–3
Design Cluster service cluster solutions to improve fault tolerance. Considerations include the number of nodes, placement of servers, cluster resource groups, failover and failback strategy, active/active, active/passive, application types, and dependencies.	Chapter 4, Lessons 1–3
Design Component Load Balancing (CLB) solutions to provide redundancy and load balancing of COM+ components. Considerations include the number of nodes, placement of servers, NLB, and CLB routing.	Chapter 6, Lessons 1–3
Design data storage for high availability. Considerations include redundant array of independent disks (RAID) and storage area networks.	Chapter 3, Lesson 2
Design a system management and monitoring strategy. Considerations include performance monitoring, event monitoring, services, data analysis, and Windows Management Instrumentation (WMI).	Chapter 11, Lessons 1–2
Design a disaster recovery strategy.	Chapter 11, Lesson 3

Skills Being Measured	Location in Book
Designing a Highly Available Network Infrastructure	
Design a TCP/IP network infrastructure. Considerations include subnet addressing, Domain Name System (DNS) hierarchy and naming, Dynamic Host Configuration Protocol (DHCP) server environment, and routed and switched environments.	Chapter 2, Lessons 1–4
Design a highly available network topology. Considerations include redundant paths, redundant services, and redundant components.	Chapter 2, Lesson 1
Plan server configurations. Considerations include network adapters, cluster communication, connectivity, and bandwidth.	Chapter 2, Lesson 1 Chapter 3, Lesson 1 Chapter 4, Lessons 1–3 Chapter 7, Lessons 1–3
Analyze and design end-to-end bandwidth requirements throughout an n-*tier environment.*	Chapter 7, Lessons 1–3
Planning Capacity Requirements	
Calculate network, server, and cluster capacity. Considerations include memory, CPU, cost, flexibility, manageability, application scalability, and client/server and server/server communications.	Chapter 7, Lessons 1–3
Design an upgrade strategy for networks, servers, and clusters. Considerations include scaling up and scaling out.	Chapter 7, Lesson 3
Calculate storage requirements. Considerations include placement, RAID level, and redundancy.	Chapter 7, Lesson 3
Design directory services. Considerations include Active Directory, LDAP, availability, authentication, and sizing.	Chapter 8, Lessons 1–2
Designing Security Strategies for Web Solutions	
Design an authentication strategy. Considerations include certificates, anonymous access, directory services, Kerberos, and Public Key Infrastructure (PKI).	Chapter 10, Lesson 1
Design an authorization strategy. Considerations include group membership, Internet Protocol (IP) blocking, access control lists, and Web content zones.	Chapter 10, Lesson 2

Skills Being Measured	Location in Book
Designing Security Strategies for Web Solutions	
Design an encryption strategy. Considerations include IPSec, Secure Sockets Layer (SSL), certificates, Encrypting File System (EFS), and Point-to-Point Tunneling Protocol (PPTP).	Chapter 10, Lesson 3
Design a firewall strategy. Considerations include packet filters, proxy servers, protocol settings, Network Address Translation (NAT), and perimeter networks (also known as DMZs).	Chapter 10, Lesson 4
Design a security auditing strategy. Considerations include intrusion detection, security, performance, denial of service, logging, and data risk assessments.	Chapter 11, Lessons 1–2

Designing Application and Service Infrastructures for Web Solutions	
Design a Microsoft Exchange messaging Web integration strategy. Considerations include browser access and Wireless Access Protocol (WAP) gateways.	Chapter 9, Lesson 3
Design a database Web integration strategy. Considerations include database access and authentication.	Chapter 9, Lesson 2
Design content and application topology. Considerations include scaling out, load balancing, fault tolerance, deploying and synchronizing Web applications, state management, service placement, and log shipping.	Chapter 5, Lessons 1–3 Chapter 6, Lessons 1–3 Chapter 9, Lessons 1–2
Design an n-tier, component-based topology. Considerations include component placement and CLB.	Chapter 6, Lessons 1–3
Design an application management and monitoring strategy. Considerations include detection and notification of application failure.	Chapter 11, Lessons 1–2

Getting Started

This self-paced training course contains activities and labs to help you learn about designing highly available Web solutions with Windows 2000 Server technologies.

Hardware and Software Requirements

No specific hardware or software is required to complete this course. However, you might find it useful to set up an environment that includes systems configured with Microsoft Windows 2000 Advanced Server, IIS, Microsoft Application Center 2000, and Microsoft SQL Server 2000 so you can test some of the design components that are discussed in this book.

Caution   The 120-day Evaluation Editions provided with this book aren't the full retail product and are provided only for the purposes of training and evaluation. Microsoft Technical Support doesn't support these evaluation editions. For additional support information regarding this book and the CD-ROMs (including answers to commonly asked questions about installation and use), visit the Microsoft Press Technical Support Web site at *http://www.microsoft.com/ mspress/support/.* You can also e-mail TKINPUT@MICROSOFT.COM or send a letter to Microsoft Press, Attn: Microsoft Press Technical Support, One Microsoft Way, Redmond, WA 98502-6399.

Setup Instructions

There are no setup requirements for this course because no hardware or software is required. However, if you do decide to test some of the designs discussed in this book, you should set up your systems according to the manufacturer's instructions.

The accompanying CD-ROMs contain Evaluation Editions of Microsoft Windows 2000 Advanced Server and Microsoft Application Center 2000.

▶   **To install the Windows 2000 Advanced Server Evaluation Edition:**

1. Insert the Microsoft Windows 2000 Advanced Server Evaluation Edition CD-ROM into your CD-ROM drive. If the starting menu does not appear automatically, go to step 2.

2. Select Run from the Start menu on your desktop, and type **D:\Setup.exe** (where D: is the name of your CD-ROM disk drive).

3. Follow the onscreen prompts to complete the installation.

▶   **To install the Application Center 2000 Evaluation Edition:**

1. Insert the Supplemental Course Materials CD-ROM into your CD-ROM drive. If the starting menu does not appear automatically, go to step 2.

2. Select Run from the Start menu on your desktop, and type **D:\Setup.exe** (where D: is the name of your CD-ROM disk drive).

3. Follow the onscreen prompts to complete the installation.

Caution   If your computers are part of a larger network, you *must* verify with your network administrator that the computer names, domain name, and other information used in setting up Windows 2000 Advanced Server, Application Center 2000, SQL Server 2000, or any other product don't conflict with network operations.

About the eBook

The CD-ROM also includes an electronic version of the book that you can view using Microsoft Internet Explorer 5 or later.

▶ **To use the eBook**

1. Insert the Supplemental Course Materials CD-ROM into your CD-ROM drive.

2. On the starting menu that appears, click eBook and follow the instructions, or select Run from the Start menu and type **D:\eBook\Autorun.exe** (where D is the name of your CD-ROM disk drive). This will install an icon for the eBook on your desktop.

3. Click OK to exit the Installation Wizard.

Note   You must have the Supplemental Course Materials CD-ROM inserted in your CD-ROM drive to run the eBook.

The Microsoft Certified Professional Program

The Microsoft Certified Professional (MCP) program provides the best method to prove your command of current Microsoft products and technologies. Microsoft, an industry leader in certification, is in the forefront of testing methodology. Our exams and corresponding certifications are developed to validate your mastery of critical competencies as you design and develop, or implement and support, solutions with Microsoft products and technologies. Computer professionals who become Microsoft certified are recognized as experts and are sought after industry-wide.

Note   Please refer to the MCP program Web site (*http://www.microsoft.com/trainingandservices/*) for the latest information on and status and availability of the certifications and examinations. The MCP program develops new exams continually and retires some exams periodically to keep credentials up to date. To help you plan your certification, new exam retirements are announced quarterly. Exams are retired in June and December. After an exam retires, candidates have at least 12 months to fulfill any upgrade requirements.

The MCP program offers eight certifications, based on specific areas of technical expertise:

- **Microsoft Certified Professional (MCP)**   Demonstrated in-depth knowledge of at least one Microsoft operating system. Candidates may pass additional Microsoft certification exams to further qualify their skills with Microsoft BackOffice products, development tools, or desktop programs.

- **Microsoft Certified Professional + Internet**   Qualified to install and configure server products, manage server resources, extend servers to run CGI scripts or ISAPI scripts, monitor and analyze performance, plan security, and troubleshoot problems.

- **Microsoft Certified Professional + Site Building**   Qualified to plan, build, maintain, and manage Web sites using Microsoft technologies and products. The credential is appropriate for people who manage sophisticated, interactive Web sites that include database connectivity, multimedia, and searchable content.

- **Microsoft Certified Systems Engineer (MCSE)**   Qualified to plan, implement, maintain, and support information systems in a wide range of computing environments with Microsoft Windows NT Server and the Microsoft BackOffice integrated family of server software.

- **Microsoft Certified Systems Engineer + Internet**   Qualified to enhance, deploy, and manage sophisticated intranet and Internet solutions based on Microsoft Windows 2000 Server software. In addition, MCSE + Internet-certified professionals are able to manage and analyze Web sites.

- **Microsoft Certified Database Administrator (MCDBA)**   Individuals who derive physical database designs, develop logical data models, create physical databases, create data services by using Transact-SQL, manage and maintain databases, configure and manage security, monitor and optimize databases, and install and configure Microsoft SQL Server.

- **Microsoft Certified Solution Developer (MCSD)**   Qualified to design and develop custom business solutions with Microsoft development tools, technologies, and platforms, including Microsoft Office and Microsoft BackOffice.

- **Microsoft Certified Trainer (MCT)**   Instructionally and technically qualified to deliver Microsoft Official Curriculum through a Microsoft Certified Technical Education Center (CTEC).

Microsoft Certification Benefits

Microsoft certification, one of the most comprehensive certification programs available for assessing and maintaining software-related skills, is a valuable measure of an individual's knowledge and expertise. Microsoft certification is awarded to individuals who have successfully demonstrated their ability to perform specific tasks and implement solutions with Microsoft products. Not only does this provide an objective measure for employers to consider; it also provides guidance for what an individual should know to be proficient. And as with any skills-assessment and benchmarking measure, certification brings a variety of benefits: to the individual and to employers and organizations.

Microsoft Certification Benefits for Individuals

As an MCP, you receive many benefits:

- Industry recognition of your knowledge and proficiency with Microsoft products and technologies.

- A Microsoft Developer Network (MSDN) subscription. MCPs receive rebates or discounts on a one-year subscription to the Microsoft Developer Network (*msdn.microsoft.com/subscriptions/*) during the first year of certification. (Fulfillment details will vary, depending on your location; please see your Welcome Kit.) The rebate or discount amount is U.S. $50 for MSDN Library.

- Access to technical and product information direct from Microsoft through a secured area of the MCP program Web site (go to *http://www.microsoft.com/trainingandservices/*, then expand the Certification node from the tree directory in the left margin, and then select the "For MCPs Only" link).

- Access to exclusive discounts on products and services from selected companies. Individuals who are certified can learn more about exclusive discounts by visiting the MCP secured Web site (go to *http://www.microsoft.com/trainingandservices/,* then expand the Certification node from the tree directory in the left margin, and then select the "For MCPs Only" link and select the "Other Benefits" link).

- MCP logo, certificate, transcript, wallet card, and lapel pin to identify you as an MCP to colleagues and clients. Electronic files of logos and transcripts may be downloaded from the MCP secured Web site (go to *http://www.microsoft.com/trainingandservices/,* then expand the Certification node from the tree directory in the left margin, and then select the "For MCPs Only" link) upon certification.

- Invitations to Microsoft conferences, technical training sessions, and special events.

- Free access to *Microsoft Certified Professional Magazine Online,* a career and professional development magazine. Secured content on the *Microsoft Certified Professional Magazine Online* Web site includes the current issue (available only to MCPs), additional online-only content and columns, an MCP-only database, and regular chats with Microsoft and other technical experts.

MCSEs receive an additional benefit:

- A 50 percent rebate or discount off the estimated retail price of a one-year subscription to *TechNet* or *TechNet Plus* during the first year of certification. (Fulfillment details will vary, depending on your location. Please see your Welcome Kit.) In addition, about 95 percent of the CD-ROM content is available free online at the *TechNet* Web site (*http://www.microsoft.com/technet/*).

Microsoft Certification Benefits for Employers and Organizations

Through certification, computer professionals can maximize the return on investment in Microsoft technology. Research shows that Microsoft certification provides organizations with

- Excellent return on training and certification investments by providing a standard method of determining training needs and measuring results
- Increased customer satisfaction and decreased support costs through improved service, increased productivity, and greater technical self-sufficiency
- A reliable benchmark for hiring, promoting, and career planning
- Recognition and rewards for productive employees by validating their expertise
- Retraining options for employees so they can work effectively with new technologies
- Assurance of quality when outsourcing computer services

To learn more about how certification can help your company, see these backgrounders, white papers, and case studies available at the MCP program Web site (go to *http://www.microsoft.com/trainingandservices/,* expand the Certification node from the tree directory in the left margin, and then select the "Case Studies" link):

- A white paper, MCSE Criterion Validity Study White Paper, Oct. 1998, that evaluates the MCSE certification (SysEngrCert.doc)
- Compaq Case Study (Compaq.doc)
- CrossTier.com Case Study (CrossTier.doc)
- Extreme Logic Case Study (Extreme Logic.doc)
- Financial Benefits to Supporters of Microsoft Professional Certification, IDC white paper (1998wpidc.doc)
- Lyondel Case Study (Lyondel.doc)
- Prudential Case Study (Prudentl.exe)
- Stellcom Case Study (Stellcom.doc)
- Unisys Case Study (Unisys.doc)

Requirements for Becoming a Microsoft Certified Professional (MCP)

The certification requirements differ for each certification and are specific to the products and job functions addressed by the certification.

To become an MCP, you must pass rigorous certification exams that provide a valid and reliable measure of technical proficiency and expertise. These exams are designed to test your expertise and ability to perform a role or task with a product, and they're developed with the input of professionals in the industry. Questions in the exams reflect how Microsoft products are used in actual organizations, giving them "real-world" relevance.

MCP candidates are required to pass one current Microsoft certification exam that provides a valid and reliable measure of technical proficiency and expertise (a current exam is any that has not been retired). Please note that Exam 70-058: *Networking Essentials* and Exam 70-240: *Microsoft Windows 2000 Accelerated Exam for MCPs Certified on Microsoft Windows NT 4.0* are exceptions to the one-exam requirement. Passing either of these exams alone will not certify an individual as an MCP.

MCP + Internet candidates are required to pass three exams that provide a valid and reliable measure of technical proficiency and expertise.

MCP + Site Building candidates are required to pass two exams that provide a valid and reliable measure of technical proficiency and expertise.

MCSD candidates are required to pass three core exams and one elective exam. The core technology exams require candidates to prove their competency with solution architecture, desktop applications development, and distributed applications development. The elective exam requires proof of expertise with Microsoft development tools.

MCSE candidates on the Windows 2000 track are required to pass five core exams and two elective exams that provide a valid and reliable measure of technical proficiency and expertise in solution design and implementation.

An MCSE + Internet candidate is required to pass seven operating system exams and two elective exams that provide a valid and reliable measure of technical proficiency and expertise.

MCDBA candidates need to pass three core exams and one elective exam that provide a valid and reliable measure of technical proficiency and expertise in implementation and administration of Microsoft SQL Server databases.

MCTs are required to meet instructional and technical requirements specific to each Microsoft Official Curriculum course they're certified to deliver. For more information about becoming an MCT, visit *http://www.microsoft.com/ trainingandservices/* (expand the Certification node from the tree directory in the left margin, and then select the "MCT" link) or contact a regional service center near you.

Technical Training for Computer Professionals

Technical training is available in a variety of ways, with self-paced training, online instruction, or instructor-led classes available at thousands of locations worldwide.

Self-Paced Training

For motivated learners who are ready for the challenge, self-paced instruction is the most flexible, cost-effective way to increase your knowledge and skills.

A full line of self-paced print and computer-based training materials is available direct from the source—Microsoft Press. Microsoft Official Curriculum courseware kits from Microsoft Press are designed for advanced computer system professionals and are available from Microsoft Press and the Microsoft Developer Division. Self-paced training kits from Microsoft Press feature print-based instructional materials, along with CD-ROM–based product software, multimedia presentations, lab exercises, and practice files. The Mastering Series provides in-depth, interactive training on CD-ROM for experienced developers. They're both great ways to prepare for MCP exams.

Online Training

For a more flexible alternative to instructor-led classes, turn to online instruction. It's as near as the Internet and it's ready whenever you are. Learn at your own pace and on your own schedule in a virtual classroom, often with easy access to an online instructor. Without ever leaving your desk, you can gain the expertise you need. Online instruction covers a variety of Microsoft products and technologies. It includes options ranging from Microsoft Official Curriculum to choices available nowhere else. It's training on demand, with access to learning resources 24 hours a day. Online training is available through Microsoft Certified Technical Education Centers.

Microsoft Certified Technical Education Centers

Microsoft Certified Technical Education Centers (CTECs) are the best source for instructor-led training that can help you prepare to become an MCP. The Microsoft CTEC program is a worldwide network of qualified technical training organizations that provide authorized delivery of Microsoft Official Curriculum courses by Microsoft Certified Trainers to computer professionals.

For a listing of CTEC locations in the United States and Canada, visit *http://www.microsoft.com/ctec/*.

Technical Support

Every effort has been made to ensure the accuracy of this book and the contents of the CD-ROMs. If you have comments, questions, or ideas regarding this book or the CD-ROMs, please send them to Microsoft Press using either of the following methods:

E-Mail

TKINPUT@MICROSOFT.COM

Postal Mail

Microsoft Press
Attn: *MCSE Training Kit—Designing Highly Available Web Solutions* Editor
One Microsoft Way
Redmond, WA 98052-6399

Microsoft Press provides corrections for books through the World Wide Web at the following address:

http://www.microsoft.com/mspress/support/

Please note that product support isn't offered through the above mail addresses. For further information regarding Microsoft software support options, please connect to *http://www.microsoft.com/support/* or call Microsoft Support Network Sales at (800) 936-3500.

Evaluation Edition Software Support

The Evaluation Editions of Microsoft Application Center 2000 and Microsoft Windows 2000 Advanced Server included with this book are unsupported by both Microsoft and Microsoft Press and shouldn't be used on primary work computers. For online support information relating to the full version of Application Center (which might also apply to the Evaluation Edition), you can connect to

http://support.microsoft.com/directory

For information about ordering the full version of any Microsoft software, please call Microsoft Sales at (800) 426-9400 or visit *http://www.microsoft.com.* Information about any issues relating to the use of this evaluation edition with this training kit is posted to the Support section of the Microsoft Press Web site at

http://www.microsoft.com/mspress/support/search.asp

CHAPTER 1

Introduction to Designing Highly Available Web Solutions

About This Chapter

Protecting business uptime is an important challenge to many businesses. In some cases businesses try to have a Web site available 24 hours a day, 7 days a week. If they can't deliver a Web site that's highly responsive and always available, customers will find companies that can. Keeping a system up at all times is a high priority, especially in cases involving high financial stakes. To provide an infrastructure that meets these requirements, the system architect must design a platform that's available, reliable, and scalable. The platform should also provide ease of implementation, interoperability, and a short turnaround time to market. The front-end systems, back-end systems, and the networking infrastructure should work in conjunction with one another to provide high-performing, reliable, and scalable Web sites to online customers. This chapter introduces many of the concepts essential to the design of highly available Web sites. Additionally, this chapter provides information about designing these sites and determining an appropriate method of ensuring high availability. Many of the concepts introduced here are discussed in more detail in subsequent chapters. The information is presented here in order to provide a cohesive introduction to designing highly available Web solutions.

Before You Begin

To complete the lessons in this chapter, you must have

- An understanding of basic design and administration concepts in Microsoft Windows 2000
- An understanding of basic design and administration concepts of network infrastructures
- A basic understanding of the concepts of high availability, fault tolerance, cluster technologies, redundant array of independent disks (RAID) implementations, load balancing, and storage area networks (SANs)

Lesson 1: Introduction to Highly Available Web Solutions

Because World Wide Web technologies are rapidly becoming the platform of choice for supporting enterprise-wide applications, the infrastructure required to develop and host applications has grown in scale and complexity. Server technology is particularly hard-pressed to keep up with the daily client demands for Web pages. One of the greatest concerns of vendors today is to make their products and services available 24 hours a day, 7 days a week. Providing this kind of service isn't only a business consideration, but also a matter of brand reputation. Businesses have spent millions of dollars to achieve the ideal of very high uptime. Even a small amount of downtime can cost a business a significant amount of revenue and damage its reputation. An outage can be caused by a variety of factors. The hardware, operating system, data storage, network, and management applications are some of the vulnerable areas that can lead to downtime. The system might not be resilient against disasters and faults in the system. To meet the demands of highly available Web sites, Microsoft Windows 2000 Advanced Server has been designed to address mission-critical needs. This lesson introduces you to Windows 2000 Advanced Server and provides an overview of some of the key terminology used in designing highly available Web solutions. In addition, this lesson provides an overview of the architectural changes that have occurred as networks have moved toward a Web computing model for business.

After this lesson, you will be able to

- Describe which features in Windows 2000 Advanced Server support high availability and scalability
- Define the key terminology used in designing highly available Web solutions
- Describe the Web computing model for business

Estimated lesson time: 25 minutes

Windows 2000 Advanced Server

The Microsoft Windows 2000 Server family currently includes Windows 2000 Server, Windows 2000 Advanced Server, and Windows 2000 Datacenter Server. Windows 2000 Server offers core functionality appropriate to small and medium-sized organizations that have numerous workgroups and branch offices and that need essential services, including file, print, communications, infrastructure, and Web. Windows 2000 Advanced Server is designed to meet mission-critical needs—such as large data warehouses, online transaction processing (OLTP), messaging, e-commerce, and Web hosting services—for medium-sized and large organizations and for Internet service providers (ISPs). Datacenter Server includes all the functionality of Advanced Server, but provides greater reliability and availability. Datacenter Server is the best platform for large-scale line-of-business and enterprise.com back-end usage.

Windows 2000 Advanced Server evolved from Microsoft Windows NT Server 4, Enterprise Edition. It provides an integrated and comprehensive clustering infrastructure for high availability and scalability of applications and services, including main memory support up to 8 gigabytes (GB) on Intel Page Address Extension (PAE) systems. Designed for demanding enterprise applications, Advanced Server supports new systems with up to eight-way symmetric multiprocessing (SMP). SMP enables any one of the multiple processors in a computer to run any operating system or application threads simultaneously with the other processors in the system. Windows Advanced Server is well suited to database-intensive work and provides high availability server services and load balancing for excellent system and application availability.

Windows 2000 Advanced Server includes the full feature set of Windows 2000 Server and adds the high availability and scalability required for enterprise and larger departmental solutions. Windows 2000 Advanced Server includes the following functionality to support high availability:

- Network Load Balancing (NLB)
- The Cluster service, based on the Microsoft Cluster Server service in Windows NT Server 4, Enterprise Edition
- Up to 8 GB main memory on Intel PAE systems
- Up to eight-way SMP

Note   If you're uncertain about whether you have an Intel PAE computer system, contact your hardware vendor.

Key Terminology

In various types of documentation, the terminology used to describe specific characteristics of networks and Web sites often differs from one source to the next. In this section several key terms are defined to help you understand how specific terminology is used within this book.

Availability

Availability is a measure (from 0 to 100 percent) of the fault tolerance of a computer and its programs. The goal of a highly available computer is to run 24 hours a day, 7 days a week (100 percent availability), which means that applications and services are operational and usable by clients most of the time. Availability measures whether a particular service is functioning properly. For example, a service with an availability of 99.999 percent is available (functioning properly) for all but 5.3 minutes of unplanned downtime a year.

You can use many different methods to increase the availability of your Web site. They range from using servers with fault-tolerant components (such as hot swappable drives, RAID controllers, redundant network interfaces, and hot swappable system boards) to load-balanced clustered solutions (such as Cisco Local Directors or Microsoft Application Center Server 2000) to failover clustered solutions (such as the Cluster service or Veritas Cluster Server). In the case of a completely redundant computer system, the software model for using the hardware is one in which the primary computer runs the application while the other computer idles, acting as a standby in case the primary system fails. The main drawbacks to redundant systems are increased hardware costs with no improvement in system throughput, and, in some cases, no protection from application failure.

You can make front-end systems at the Web tier highly available through the use of clustered servers that provide a single virtual Internet Protocol (IP) address to their clients. You can use load balancing to distribute the load across the clones. Building a failure-detection process into the load-balancing system increases the service's availability. A clone that's no longer offering a service can be automatically removed from the load-balanced set while the remaining clones continue to offer the service.

You can make back-end systems highly available through the use of *failover clustering*. In failover clustering, if one node fails, the other node takes ownership of its resources. Failover clustering assumes that an application can resume on another computer that's been given access to the failed system disk subsystem. The primary node will automatically failover to the secondary node when a clustered application, the operating system, or a hardware component of the primary node fails. The secondary node, which should be a replica of the primary node, must have access to the same data storage.

Failure

Failure is defined as a departure from expected behavior on an individual computer system or a network system of associated computers and applications. Failures can include behavior that simply moves outside of defined performance parameters. If the system's specified behavior includes time constraints, such as a requirement to complete processing in a specified amount of time, performance degradation beyond the specified threshold is considered a failure. For example, a system that must process a transaction within 2 seconds may be in a failed state if transaction processing degrades beyond this 2-second window.

Software, hardware, operator and procedural errors and environmental factors can each cause a system failure. A *single point of failure* is any component in your network environment that prevents network communication, data transfer, or application availability. Single points of failure can include hardware, software, or external factors, such as power supplied by a utility company. One recent survey indicates that although hardware component failure accounts for up to 30 percent of all system outages, operating system and application failures account for almost 35 percent of all unplanned downtime. Typical hardware components that may fail include computer cooling fans, disk-drive hardware, and power supplies. Minimizing single points of failure or eliminating them completely will increase a site's overall reliability.

Fault Tolerance

Fault tolerance is the ability of a system to continue functioning when part of the system fails. Fault tolerance combats problems such as disk failures, power outages, or corrupted operating systems, which can affect startup files, the operating system itself, or system files. Windows 2000 Server includes features that support certain types of fault tolerance.

For example, Windows 2000 supports two implementations of RAID: RAID-1 and RAID-5. RAID-1 provides fault tolerance through the use of *mirroring*. All data that is written to the primary volume is also written to a secondary volume, or *mirror*. If one disk fails, the system uses data from the other disk. RAID-5 provides fault tolerance by sharing data across all the disks in an array. The system generates a small amount of data, called *parity information,* which is used to reconstruct lost information in case a disk fails.

Note Although the data is always available and current in a fault-tolerant system, you still need to make tape backups to protect the information about your disk subsystem against user errors and natural disasters. Disk fault tolerance is not an alternative to a backup strategy with off-site storage.

Fault tolerance can also be achieved through hardware implementations of RAID. Many hardware RAID solutions provide power-redundancy, bus-redundancy, and cable-redundancy within a single cabinet and can track the state of each component in the hardware RAID firmware. The significance of these capabilities is that they provide data availability with multiple redundancies to protect against multiple points of failure. Hardware RAID solutions can also use an onboard processor and cache. Windows 2000 Advanced Server can use these disks as standard disk resources. Though more costly than the software RAID supported by Windows 2000 Server, hardware RAID is generally considered the superior solution.

Manageability

Manageability is the ability to make changes to the system easily. Management has many facets, but it can be loosely divided into the following disciplines:

- **Change and configuration management** System administration, state management, and software life cycle management
- **Security management** User access, authentication, and tracking
- **Performance management** Tracing, tuning, and modeling applications and networks; also service level provisioning
- **Problem management** Error isolation, diagnostics, trouble ticketing, and consolidated help facilities

- **Event management**   System information monitoring, consolidation, aggregation, and delivery
- **Batch/output management**   Job execution, scheduling dependency, submission control, and charge back
- **Storage management**   Storage hardware administration, data protection, and placement

Reliability

Reliability is a measure of the time that elapses between failures in a system. Hardware and software components have different failure characteristics. Although formulas based on historical data exist to predict hardware reliability, such formulas for predicting software reliability are harder to find.

Hardware components usually have what is known as an *exponential failure distribution,* which means that—under normal circumstances and after an initial phase—the longer a hardware component operates, the more frequently it will fail. Therefore, if you know when a component is likely to fail, you can estimate that component's reliability.

Scalability

Scalability is a measure of how easily a computer, service, or application can expand to meet increasing performance demands. For server clusters, scalability refers to the ability to incrementally add one or more systems to an existing cluster when the cluster's load exceeds its capabilities. The ability to "scale" is traditionally thought of as the ability to handle increased load over time with minimal intervention. Scalability is a critical component of Web-enabled applications because the nature of the Web is such that load can't be predicted (but must always be handled). Scalability is also a critical component of intranet applications because these applications must support an ever-growing business.

Scalability can also be defined as the capacity of an application to perform increasing work while sustaining acceptable performance levels. In order to scale, business Web sites split their architecture into two parts: front-end systems (client accessible) and back-end systems where long-term persistent data is stored or where business-processing systems are located. Load-balancing systems are used to distribute the work across systems at each tier.

The Web Computing Model for Business

When Internet technology, notably the Web, moved into the computing mainstream in the mid-1990s, the model for business computing changed dramatically. This shift (as shown in Figure 1.1) was centered on the industry's notion of client/server computing, which previously had been very complex, costly, and proprietary.

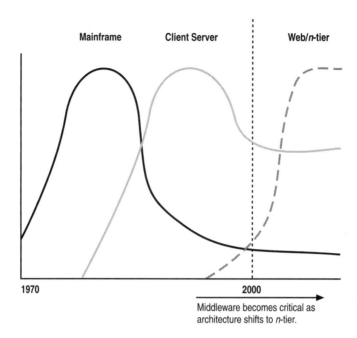

Mainframe   Client Server   Web/*n*-tier

1970   2000

Middleware becomes critical as
architecture shifts to *n*-tier.

Figure 1.1   Application architecture shifts since 1970

The Web model is characterized by loosely connected tiers of diverse collections
of information and applications that reside on a broad mix of hardware platforms.
This platform is flexible by design and not limited to one or two computing tiers.
The only real limits to application development in the Internet world are computer capacity and the application designer's imagination.

Because today's businesses are models of dynamic change—often growing
quickly and instituting rapid directional shifts—the Web model is ideally suited
for business computing. Web sites can grow exponentially with demand and provide a full range of services that can be tailored according to user requirements.
These services are often complex and need to be integrated with other services in
the organization.

Architectural Goals

An architecture that addresses business computing needs must meet the
following goals:

- **Scalability**   Enabling continuous growth to satisfy user demands and
  respond to business needs by providing near-linear, cost-effective scaling

- **Availability and reliability**   Ensuring that continuous services are in
  place to support business operations by using functional specialization and
  redundancy

- **Management** Providing management with ease of use and completeness to ensure that operations can keep pace with growth and reduce the total cost of ownership (TCO)
- **Security** Ensuring that adequate security is in place to protect the organization's assets, namely its infrastructure and data

Architectural Elements

The key architectural elements of an *n*-tier business Web site (as illustrated in Figure 1.2) are as follows:

- Clients
- Front-end systems
- Back-end systems

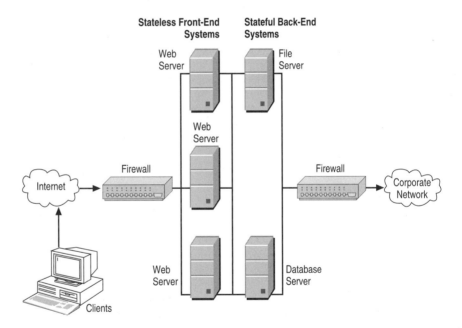

Figure 1.2   Architectural elements of an *n*-tier business Web site

The site architect and application developer must consider all these elements in the context of scalability and reliability, security, and management operations.

Figure 1.2 shows the split between the front-end and back-end systems as well as the firewall and network segmentation, which are key security elements in site architectures.

Clients

Clients issue service requests to the server that's hosting the application that the client is accessing. From the user's perspective, the only things visible are a Uniform Resource Locator (URL) that identifies a page on a site, hyperlinks for navigation once the page is retrieved, or forms that require completion. Neither the client nor the user has any idea of the inner workings of the server that satisfies the request.

Front-End Systems

Front-end systems consist of the collections of servers that provide core services, such as Hypertext Transfer Protocol/Hypertext Transfer Protocol Secure (HTTP/HTTPS) and File Transfer Protocol (FTP), to the clients. These servers host the Web pages that are requested and all usually run the same software. For efficiency's sake, it's not uncommon for these servers (known as *Web farms,* or *clusters*) to have access to common file shares, business-logic components, or database systems located on the back-end systems (or middle-tier systems in more extended models).

Front-end systems are typically described as *stateless* because they don't store any client information across sessions. If client information needs to persist between sessions, you can do that in several ways. The most common is through the use of cookies. Another technique involves writing client information into the HTTP header string of a Web page to be retrieved by the client. The last method is to store client information in a back-end database server. However, because the last technique can have significant performance implications you should use it judiciously. You can achieve scalability of the front-end systems by increasing the capacity of an individual server (scaling up) or by adding more servers (scaling out).

Back-End Systems

The back-end systems are the servers hosting the data stores that are used by the front-end systems. In some cases a back-end server doesn't store data but accesses it from a data source elsewhere in the corporate network. Data can be stored in flat files, inside other applications, or in database servers such as Microsoft SQL Server. Table 1.1 summarizes data and storage areas.

Table 1.1   Types of Data in Storage Areas

Type of Storage Areas	Example	Type of Data
File systems	File shares	Hypertext Markup Language (HTML) pages, images, executables, scripts, Component Object Model (COM) objects
Databases	SQL Server	Catalogs, customer information, logs, billing information, price lists
Applications	Ad insertion, SAP Agent	Banner ads, accounting information, inventory/stock information

Because of the data and state that back-end systems must maintain, they're described as *stateful* systems. As such, they present more challenges to scalability and availability.

Security Infrastructure

Securing the assets of today's businesses—with their mobile workers, business-to-business computer direct connections, and a revolving door to the Internet—is complex and costly. But not implementing computer security, or doing it poorly, can lead to an even more costly disaster.

At a high level, security domains—not to be confused with Internet or Windows NT/Windows 2000 domains—provide regions of consistent security with well-defined and protected interfaces between them. Large organizations may partition their computing environment into multiple domains, according to business division, geography, or physical network, to name but a few types. Security domains may be nested within one another or even overlap. There are as many security architectures as there are security mechanisms.

At a low level, the basic model for securing a single site involves setting up one or several perimeters to monitor and, if necessary, block incoming or outgoing network traffic. This perimeter defense (firewall) may consist of routers or specialized secure servers. Most organizations use a second firewall system, as shown in Figure 1.3. Security specialists refer to this area between the firewalls as the perimeter network.

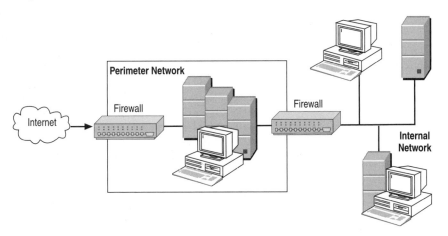

Figure 1.3 Using firewalls to establish a secure zone

Note that the configuration shown in Figure 1.3 is only a model; every organization builds its security architecture to meet its own requirements. In fact, some put their Web servers on the Internet side of the firewall because they've determined that the risk to, or cost of reconstructing, a Web server isn't high enough to warrant more protection. Another factor in this decision is the performance cost of providing more protection.

Management Infrastructure

Site management systems are often built on separate networks to ensure high availability and to avoid having a harmful impact on the application infrastructure. The core architectural elements of a management system are as follows:

- Management consoles serving as portals that allow administrators to access and manipulate managed servers

- Management servers (also called monitoring servers) that continuously monitor managed servers, receive alarms and notifications, log events and performance data, and serve as the first line of response to predetermined events

- Management agents, which are programs that perform management functions within the device on which they reside

As systems scale or their rate of change accelerates, the management and operation of a business Web site becomes critical in terms of reliability, availability, and scalability. Administrative simplicity, ease of configuration, and ongoing health/failure detection and performance monitoring become more important than application features and services.

Lesson Summary

Windows 2000 Advanced Server is designed to meet mission-critical needs and provides a comprehensive clustering infrastructure for high availability and scalability of applications and services. Availability is a measure (from 0 to 100 percent) of the fault tolerance of a computer and its programs. Failure is defined as a departure from expected behavior on an individual computer system or a network system of associated computers and applications. Fault tolerance is the ability of a system to continue functioning when part of the system fails. Manageability is the ability to make changes to the system easily. Reliability is a measure of the time that elapses between failures in a system. Scalability is a measure of how well a computer, service, or application can expand to meet increasing performance demands. To support availability, manageability, reliability, and scalability, the Web computing model has evolved into loosely connected tiers of diverse collections of information and applications that reside on a broad mix of hardware platforms. This platform is flexible by design and not limited to one or two computing tiers. The key architectural elements of an *n*-tier business Web site are clients, front-end systems, and back-end systems. At a high level, security domains provide regions of consistent security with well-defined and protected interfaces between them. The core architectural elements of a management system are management consoles, servers, and agents.

Lesson 2: Determining System Availability

It takes time and discipline to plan for high availability deployments. Successful deployments are invariably based on well-informed decision making in which how you go about a deployment is as important as the specific technologies you deploy. Many variables affect the availability of any system, such as hardware, system software, data, application technologies, and the environment. Furthermore, many of the factors critical to a successful deployment are managerial, organizational, and procedural. Each must come together in carefully thought out and correctly applied policies and procedures. This lesson explains how to measure system availability and what types of failures contribute to system downtime. The lesson also tells you how to create a checklist that allows you to monitor your site's availability.

After this lesson, you will be able to

- Use availability metrics to determine system availability

- Identify potential causes of downtime

- Describe the categories of information that should be included in a checklist to monitor your site's availability

Estimated lesson time: 20 minutes

Availability Metrics

When you build systems for high availability, you require them to perform necessary functions under stated conditions for specified periods. These systems need to behave predictably and reliably so that customers can build operating plans for the systems that are critical to the functioning of their businesses. To users and managers of information systems, application availability—not system availability—is paramount. Although there's no industry-wide standard for calculating availability, *mean time to failure (MTTF)* and *mean time to recovery (MTTR)* are the metrics most often cited. MTTF is the mean time until a device will fail, and MTTR is the mean time it takes to recover from a failure.

Mean Time to Failure and Mean Time to Recovery

Hardware components usually have what is known as an exponential failure distribution. Under normal circumstances and after an initial phase, the longer a hardware component operates, the more frequently it fails. Therefore, if you know the MTTF for a device, you might be able to predict when it will enter its failure mode. The historical statistical data of mechanical and electrical components fits the so-called bathtub curve, as shown in Figure 1.4.

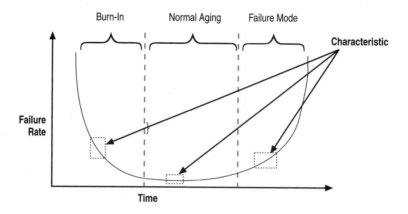

Figure 1.4   The bathtub curve

This model shows three distinguishable phases in a component's life cycle: burn-in, normal aging, and failure mode. Each phase is characterized by some signature or behavior, which varies from domain to domain. Failure rates are characteristically high during burn-in, but drop off rapidly. Devices seldom fail during the normal aging period. As the devices age, however, the failure rates rise dramatically but predictably.

You can use this observation in two ways. First, you can observe the characteristics of devices in the normal aging phase and look for indications that correlate with observed failure rates. Some hardware vendors do this and have devised mechanisms to measure the characteristics of devices that you can use with some success as failure predictors. Second, you can keep track of the actual failure rates of specific devices and replace them before they enter the expected failure mode. You usually use this strategy when the cost of a failed component can be catastrophic. It requires relatively long sample periods in order to capture statistically significant MTTF data.

Unfortunately, MTTF statistics are normally useful predictors only for components with an exponential failure distribution. Software and hardware components have different failure characteristics, which makes it difficult to manage or predict software failures. As a result, MTTF applies only to certain categories of software defects. For example, data dependent errors, such as those triggered by an anomalous input stream, require the input stream itself to be predictable in order for previous failure rates to act as predictors of future failure rates.

For systems that are fully recoverable, MTTR is an equally important quantity, since it correlates directly with system downtime. You can measure downtime by using the following formula:

Downtime = MTTR ÷ MTTF

For example, if you have a device with an MTTR of 2 hours and an MTTF of 2,000 hours, downtime will be 0.1 percent.

To calculate availability, you can use the following formula:

Availability = MTTF ÷ (MTTF + MTTR)

Again, if you have an MTTR of 2 and an MTTF of 2,000, your availability will be 99.9 percent.

As you can see, focusing exclusively on increasing MTTF without also taking MTTR into account won't maximize availability. This is due in part to the costs associated with designing hardware and software systems that never fail. Such systems tax current design methodologies and hardware technologies and are always extremely expensive to deploy and maintain.

Customers with high availability requirements should maximize MTTF by carefully designing and thoroughly testing both hardware and software and reduce MTTR by using failover mechanisms, such as clustering.

Rule of 9s

Availability depends on whether a service is operating properly. You can think of availability as a continuum ranging from 100 percent (a completely fault-tolerant site that never goes offline) to 0 percent (a site that's never available). All sites have some degree of availability. Today, many companies target "three 9s" availability (99.9 percent) for their Web sites, which means that there can be only approximately 8 hours and 45 minutes of unplanned downtime a year. Telephone companies in the United States typically target "five 9s," or 99.999 percent uptime (approximately 5 minutes and 15 seconds of unplanned downtime a year).

Table 1.2 shows these common classes of 9s and their associated availability percentages and related annual downtime.

Table 1.2   Rule of 9s

Availability Class	Availability Measurement	Annual Downtime
Two 9s	99 percent	3.7 days
Three 9s	99.9 percent	8.8 hours
Four 9s	99.99 percent	53 minutes
Five 9s	99.999 percent	5.3 minutes

Although any company might strive for additional uptime for its Web site, significant incremental hardware investment is required to get those extra "9s." However, maintaining even 99.9 percent uptime means downtime of 8.75 hours per year, which could result in a significant loss of revenue for a company that relies heavily on the revenue generated by its Web site.

Causes of Downtime

The high cost of downtime makes planning essential in environments that require high availability. The simplest model of downtime cost is based on the assumption that employees are made completely idle by outages, whether due to hardware, network, server, or application failure. In such a model, the cost of a service interruption is given by the sum of the labor costs of the idled employees combined with an estimate of the business lost due to the lack of service. Several factors cause system outages, such as software failures, hardware failures, network failures, operational failures, and environmental failures.

Software Failures

Identifying the cause of an outage can be complicated. For example, one company observed that about 20 percent of all the outages reported were attributed to operating system failures and 20 percent were attributed to application failures. However, a separate internal study of calls to Microsoft Product Service and Support found that most calls reporting apparent operating system failure turned out to be due to improper system configuration, defects in third-party device drivers, or system software.

It should also be noted that defects in virus protection software could cause system outages because they're implemented as kernel-level filter drivers. You can avoid many system outages attributed to software problems by using better operational procedures, such as carefully selecting the software that you allow to run on your servers.

Hardware Failures

Hardware failures occur most frequently in mechanical parts such as fans, disks, or removable storage media. Failure in one component may induce failure in another. For example, defective or insufficient cooling may induce memory failures or shorten the time to failure for a disk drive.

Other moving parts, such as mechanical and electromechanical components in the disk drive, are also among the most critical, although new storage techniques have dramatically enhanced the reliability of disk drives.

Market pressures have driven storage vendors to provide these improvements at commodity prices. In 1988 the MTTF rating for a commodity 100 MB disk was around 30,000 hours. Today the MTTF specification for a commodity 2 GB drive is 300,000 hours—about 34 years. In these demanding environments, hardware requires sufficient airflow and cooling equipment. System administrators are advised to use platforms capable of monitoring internal temperatures and generating Simple Network Management Protocol (SNMP) alarms when conditions exceed recommended ranges.

Random access memories allow for the use of parity bits to detect errors or the use of error correcting codes (ECC) to detect and correct single errors and to detect two-bit errors. The use of ECC memories for conventional and cache memories is as important to overall system reliability as the use of RAID.

Network Failures

With distributed systems, it's very important to realize that the underlying network's performance and reliability contribute significantly to the system's overall performance and reliability.

Changes in the topology and design of any layer of the protocol stack can affect the whole. To ensure robustness, it's necessary to evaluate all layers, although this holistic approach is rarely used. Instead, many businesses view the network as a black box with a well-defined interface and service level, totally ignoring the evidence of any coupling between system and network.

Operational Failures

Reliable deployments of Windows 2000–based systems require some procedures that may not be obvious to those migrating from more elaborate mainframe or minicomputer-based data centers or migrating their Information Technology (IT) operations from more informal personal computer environments. Customers can minimize or altogether avoid many of the problems identified so far by using disciplined operational procedures, such as regular, complete backups and avoidance of unnecessary changes to configuration and environment.

Environmental Failures

Statistics from one disaster-recovery study found that 27 percent of declared data-center disasters are recorded as due to power loss. In this study a declared disaster was defined as an incident in which there was actual loss of data in addition to loss of service. This figure includes power outages due to environmental disasters such as snowstorms, tornadoes, and hurricanes.

Availability Checklist

You can create a checklist to monitor your site's availability. Table 1.3 provides an overview of the types of information that you should include in your checklist. Many of these issues will be discussed in more detail in later chapters.

Table 1.3   Availability Checklist

Type of Information	Description
Bandwidth usage	Monitor how bandwidth is being used (peak and idle) and how usage increases (whether it increases, when it increases, and how long it increases).
Network availability	Monitor network availability by using Network Internet Control Message Protocol (ICMP) echo pings. ICMP is available from most network monitoring software.

(continued)

Table 1.3 *(continued)*

Type of Information	Description
System availability	Monitor normal and abnormal shutdowns of the operating system. Monitor normal operation and failover events of SQL Server. Monitor normal and abnormal shutdowns in Internet Information Server (IIS).
HTTP availability	Monitor HTTP requests issued internally, issued from ISP networks (such as AOL, Microsoft MSN, MCI, Sprint, and so on), and issued from different geographic locations (New York, San Francisco, London, Paris, Munich, Tokyo, Singapore, and so on).
Performance metrics	Use the following performance metrics to ensure availability: number of visits, latency of requests for set of operations and page groups, CPU utilization, disk storage, disk input/output (I/O), fiber channel loop bandwidth and performance, and memory.

Lesson Summary

The three distinguishable phases in a component's life cycle are burn-in, normal aging, and failure mode. Although there is no industry-wide standard for calculating availability, MTTF and MTTR are the metrics most often cited. You can determine downtime by using the formula MTTR ÷ MTTF. You can determine availability by using the formula MTTF ÷ (MTTF + MTTR). MTTF statistics are normally useful predictors only for components with an exponential failure distribution. As a result, MTTF applies only to certain categories of software defects. Customers who require high availability should maximize MTTF by carefully designing and thoroughly testing both hardware and software and reduce MTTR by using failover mechanisms such as clustering. All sites have some degree of availability. A specific number of 9s is sometimes used to describe a system's availability. For example, three 9s has an availability measurement of 99.9 percent and an annual downtime of 8.8 hours. Several factors cause system downtime, including software failures, hardware failures, network failures, operational failures, and environmental failures. You can create a checklist to monitor your site's availability. The checklist should include information about bandwidth usage, network availability, system availability, HTTP availability, and performance metrics.

Lesson 3: Ensuring System Availability

Hardware failure, data corruption, and physical site destruction all pose threats to a Web site that must be available nearly 100 percent of the time. You can enhance your site's availability by first identifying services that must be available and then identifying the points at which those services can fail. Increasing availability also means reducing the probability of failure. Decisions about how far to go to prevent failures are based on a combination of your company's tolerance for service outages, the budget, and your staff's expertise. System availability depends on the hardware and software you choose and the effectiveness of your operating procedures. This lesson introduces you to three fundamental strategies that you can use to design a highly available site: developing operational procedures, ensuring adequate capacity, and reducing the probability of failure.

After this lesson, you will be able to

- Identify three fundamental strategies that you can use to design a highly available Web site

Estimated lesson time: 20 minutes

Designing a Highly Available Web Site

You can design availability into a Web site by identifying services that must be available, determining where those services can fail, and then designing the services so that they continue to be available to customers even if a failure occurs. You can use three fundamental strategies to design a highly available site:

- Develop operational procedures that are well documented and appropriate for your goals and your staff's capabilities.
- Ensure that your site has enough capacity to handle processing loads.
- Reduce the probability of failure.

Developing Operational Procedures

One of the most effective means of ensuring site availability can also be inexpensive to implement. Creating well-documented and accurate standardized operational procedures is an effective means of ensuring site availability.

With the capacity of database systems often in the 100 GB range and higher, deploying proper data protection mechanisms is essential. This is becoming even more critical as databases approach the terabyte (TB) and some in the pentabyte (PB) size ranges. In particular, RAID systems can enhance both scalability and performance of disk systems, but such systems can simultaneously enhance data integrity. Because of the decreasing cost of disks compared to the increasing cost of downtime, redundant storage subsystems are even more attractive now than when they were introduced.

Consistent, detailed monitoring procedures are critical to deploying systems for high availability. First, you should restrict logical and physical access to servers. Second, you should monitor the system event log regularly in order to prevent failures and potential failures of systems from going undetected. Implementing an infrastructure that continuously monitors all of your systems and the entire network provides the best means of preventing and detecting system failures. Devices on the Hardware Compatibility List (HCL) are required to use the event log to record problems. Many systems designed for maximum reliability are able to continue operation with a single failure, such as a failed disk in a RAID-5 volume. A subsequent failure will cause an outage and even loss of data. You should set up automated procedures for alarm notification, such as pager notification of SNMP alarms.

Another way to avoid problems is to keep up with and understand the risks and benefits of system upgrades and service packs. Most large organizations establish their own testing organizations to qualify service packs and define baselines.

Operational procedures should include the following types of management:

- Change management
- Service-level management
- Problem management
- Capacity management
- Security management
- Availability management

Microsoft has created a knowledge base called the Enterprise Services frameworks (Microsoft Readiness Framework, Microsoft Solutions Framework, and Microsoft Operations Framework) to describe industry experience and best practices for such procedures. You can find more information online at *http://www.microsoft.com/technet/ecommerce/ecseries.asp*.

When you have a stable set of operational procedures, you can begin to explore ways to improve hardware and software availability. System availability doesn't depend only on how redundant your hardware and software systems are.

Ensuring Site Capacity

Site services can become unavailable if site traffic exceeds capacity and can become less reliable after operating for prolonged periods at peak load. You should scale your server farm to accommodate increased site traffic and to maintain site performance in a cost-effective manner. Capacity requirements are discussed in more detail in Chapter 7, "Capacity Planning."

Reducing the Probability of Failure

To design a highly available site, you should know what techniques you can use to help reduce failures. This section describes these techniques.

Application Failures

Use the following techniques to reduce possible application failures:

- Create a robust architecture based on redundant, load-balanced servers. (Note, however, that load-balanced clusters are different from Windows application clusters. Commerce Server 2000 components, such as List Manager and Direct Mailer, are not cluster aware.)

- Review code to avoid potential buffer overflows, infinite loops, code crashes, and openings for security attacks.

Climate Control Failures

Use the following techniques to reduce possible climate control failures:

- Maintain the temperature of your hardware within the manufacturer's specifications. Excessive heat can cause CPU meltdown, and excessive cold can cause failure of moving parts, such as fans and disk drives.

- Maintain humidity control. Excessive humidity can cause electrical short circuits that result from water condensing on circuit boards. Excessive dryness can cause static electricity discharges that damage components when you handle them.

Data Failures

Use the following techniques to reduce possible data failures:

- Conduct regular backups. In addition to regular backups, archive backups offsite. For example, to save space you can archive every fourth regular backup offsite. If your data becomes corrupted, you can restore the data from backups to the last point before the corruption occurred. If you also back up transaction logs, you can then apply the transaction logs to the restored database to bring it up to date.

- Replay transaction logs against a known valid database to maintain data. This technique, which is also known as *log shipping to a warm backup server,* is useful for maintaining a disaster-recovery site (a "hot site").

Note Microsoft SQL Server 2000 is the only version of SQL Server that supports log shipping.

- Deploy failover clusters for your back-end database servers. Two examples of failover clustering technologies are the Cluster service and Veritas Cluster Server, which also can be configured to provide load-balancing capabilities depending on the hardware platform you're using to host the cluster. Commerce Server uses data stores such as SQL Server and the Active Directory service. SQL Server provides access to data and services such as catalog search. SQL Server can use the Cluster service to provide redundancy. Active Directory provides access to profile data and can provide authentication services.

Active Directory uses data replication to provide redundancy. In general, clustering is more effective for dynamic (read/write) data and data replication is more effective for static (read-only) data.

- Minimize the probability and impact of a SQL Server failure by clustering SQL Server servers or by replicating data among SQL Server servers. If you're using Microsoft SQL Server 7, the full-text search feature is available only in a nonclustered configuration, so you must use a replication strategy for the product catalog. However, note that SQL Server 6.5 and 7 don't support high-availability configurations. Microsoft Data Access Components (MDAC) 2.6 is not supported for SQL Server 6.5 or SQL Server 7, when either release is in a failover cluster configuration. SQL Server 2000 is fully supported for high-availability configurations.

- Back up Active Directory stores (if you use Active Directory). You can back up the stores while Active Directory is online.

- Use at least two Active Directory domain controllers in each physical site, with a replication schedule appropriate to your requirements. Restoring a domain controller can be time-consuming and requires the domain controller to be offline. If you have peer domain controllers, you can minimize downtime if you must restore your site from backups.

Electrical Power Failures

Use the following techniques to reduce possible electrical power failures:

- Use an uninterruptible power supply (UPS) for all power connections. Because a UPS is typically battery-powered, it's useful only for outages that last for short periods. Be sure to use a UPS that has the same power rating as your equipment.

- Use power generators as secondary backups to the UPS. You can use generators for an indefinite period of time because they're fuel-powered (diesel or gasoline), and you can refuel them if necessary.

Network Failures

Use the following techniques to reduce possible network failures:

- Use multiple network interface cards (NICs), multiple routers, switches, local area networks (LANs), or firewalls.

- Contract with multiple ISPs or set up identical equipment in geographically dispersed locations.

Security Failures

Use the following techniques to reduce possible security failures:

- Contract an independent security audit firm to evaluate your environment.

- Deploy intrusion-detection tools.

- Deploy multiple firewalls.
- For the latest strategies and techniques for handling security issues, see *http://www.microsoft.com/windows2000/guide/server/features/securitysvcs.asp.*

Server Failures

Use the following techniques to reduce possible server failures:

- Deploy redundant, load-balanced servers. Single-IP solutions increase site capacity by distributing HTTP requests proportionally according to each server's capacity for handling the required load.
- Verify that users are referred only to operating servers when using a single IP address solution.

Hardware Failures

Use the following techniques to reduce possible hardware failures:

- Use hardware-implemented RAID-1, RAID-5, or RAID-10, dual disk controllers, and mirrored cache on the RAID controllers with integrated battery backup to minimize disk failures. Most hardware vendors now integrate an onboard RAID controller chip into the system board to provide some RAID support. Check with the hardware vendor to determine if your servers have this built-in feature and exactly what RAID capabilities are supported. Several excellent third-party solutions are available to reduce downtime related to disk failure.
- If you're implementing a Fibre Channel SAN, use redundant Fibre Channel host bus adapters, Fibre Channel hubs or fabric switches, and redundant disk array controllers for the Fibre Channel storage array. In the event of a failure of an adapter, hub, fiber cable, controller, switch, or some other component on the primary loop, the system will automatically switch over to the redundant or backup loop, providing an alternate path to the external storage array or SAN. When dealing with a Fibre Channel SAN, it is crucial to minimize or eliminate all single points of failure in the SAN. This will ensure that the SAN will have the best possible performance, availability, and overall integrity.
- Deploy other redundant hardware components.

Lesson Summary

You can use three fundamental strategies to design a highly available site: developing operational procedures that are well documented and appropriate for your goals and your staff's capabilities, ensuring that your site has enough capacity to handle processing loads, and reducing the probability of failure. Operational procedures should include change management, service-level management, problem management, capacity management, security management, and availability management. To design a highly available site, you should use techniques that can help reduce failures related to applications, climate control, data, electrical power, network, security, servers, and hardware.

Review

Answering the following questions will reinforce key information presented in this chapter. If you're unable to answer a question, review the appropriate lesson and then try the question again. Answers to the questions can be found in the appendix.

1. Define the following key terms: availability, failure, fault tolerance, manageability, reliability, and scalability.

2. What are the key architectural elements of an *n*-tier business Web site?

3. In the formula MTTR/MTTF, what do MTTR and MTTF refer to, how do they differ, and what's the purpose of this ratio?

4. What types of failures can cause system outages?

5. You're designing a highly available Web site. What are the three fundamental strategies that you should use?

6. You're designing a highly available Web site and you're specifically concerned about preventing application failures. What techniques should you use to reduce the chance of failures?

C H A P T E R   2

Network Infrastructure

About This Chapter

Because World Wide Web technologies are rapidly becoming the platform of choice for supporting enterprise-wide applications, the network infrastructure required to develop and host applications has grown in scale and complexity. One method that's used to ensure a highly available network design is to incorporate redundancy into the topology. *Redundancy* refers to the duplication of network components, paths, and services to provide fault tolerance and avoid any single points of failure in the network. A highly available network design must also take into consideration subnet addressing, the Dynamic Host Configuration Protocol (DHCP) server environment, and Domain Name System (DNS) hierarchy and naming. In this chapter you'll learn how to incorporate redundancy into the network topology and how to deal with issues concerning subnetting, DHCP, and DNS.

Before You Begin

To complete the lessons in this chapter, you must have

- A basic understanding of how redundancy is implemented in system and network designs
- Experience working with Internet Protocol (IP) addresses and subnets
- Experience administering DHCP and DNS services in Microsoft Windows 2000

Lesson 1: Designing a Highly Available Network Topology

One of the most effective ways to ensure a Web site's high availability is to use redundant hardware and software. Careful use of redundancy allows a data center or network system to tolerate failures of individual components and computers. A highly available topology eliminates any single point of failure. This type of topology will likely include redundant components, paths, and services. For example, a network design might include planning for redundant network interface cards (NICs), routers, and switches so that an individual component failure can occur without affecting a system's overall availability. In this lesson you'll learn how to design a network topology that includes redundant components, paths, and services.

After this lesson, you will be able to

- Describe the three types of redundancy—components, paths, and services— that you can incorporate into a network topology
- Design a highly available network topology that incorporates redundancy

Estimated lesson time: 30 minutes

Network Topology

In a complex system it's often possible to include redundant components, paths, and services to ensure a highly available network design.

Redundant Components

Redundant components can refer to hardware within a computer (such as hot swappable drives), completely duplicated computers, or network components outside a computer, such as routers, switches, and hubs. This section focuses on network components outside a computer. Duplicated computers are discussed later in this lesson (in the section entitled "Redundant Services"), and redundant components within a computer are discussed in Chapter 3, "Server Configurations."

Hubs and Switches

A *hub* is a network-enabled device joining communication lines at a central location, providing a common connection to all devices on the network. *Active* hubs require electrical power but are able to regenerate and retransmit network data. *Passive* hubs simply organize the wiring. When a hub receives a transmission, it broadcasts traffic to all ports.

A *switch* is a computer or other network-enabled device that controls routing and operation of a signal path. In clustering, a switch is used to connect the cluster host's network interface to a router or other source of incoming network connections. Rather than broadcasting the traffic to all ports, a switch establishes a direct path between two ports on the switch so that multiple pairs of ports can communicate without collisions. As the price of switches has decreased, their use has become more common in network topologies.

Multilayer switches provide the core network switching of many Web sites, particularly e-commerce sites. The switches can include the connectivity of Web, application, and database servers. As a result, they need to deliver high-performance Layer 2 and Layer 3 switching while supporting services that meet the requirements for availability, scalability, and security in a Web environment.

For example, multilayer switches must support high-speed interfaces, redundant power supplies, quality of service (QoS), virtual local area networks (VLANs), high port density, and rapid fault recovery. In addition, the switches must be able to carry a large number of user connections while providing Layer 3 forwarding at millions of packets per second (pps) in order to ensure that the switch isn't a performance bottleneck in the network architecture.

Network hubs and switches are very reliable, but they do fail. Consequently, using redundancy is very important. Figure 2.1 shows how redundant switches are used for each network segment.

Notice that the redundant switches provide redundant paths of network connectivity. Switches have the ability to aggregate any doubled-up connection, allowing for two connections with each section's hub. Each server and each clustered server has two NICs configured per local area network (LAN) segment by using the vendor's teaming solutions. Due to the redundancy, any one failure in any one item still allows the network segment to continue to function.

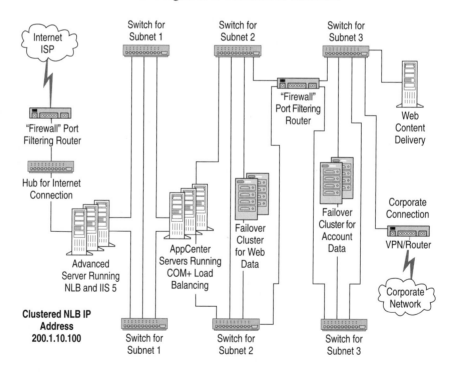

Figure 2.1   A multitiered network with redundant switches on each subnet

Routers

A *router* is a network device used to connect networks of different types, such as those using different architectures and protocols. Routers work at the network layer and can switch and route packets across multiple networks, which they do by exchanging protocol-specific information between separate networks. Routers determine the best path for sending data and filter broadcast traffic to the local segment.

Although routers don't fail very often, they can still fail. When they do, an entire Web site can become unavailable. Any single router that's placed between network segments represents a point of failure. Note that in Figure 2.1, the router that connects to the Internet and the router between subnet 2 and subnet 3 each represents a single point of failure. Having redundant routing capability at each single point of router failure is critical to a highly available network configuration.

In Figure 2.2, a second Internet connection has been added to the network topology. As a result, component redundancy is achieved through the second router and path redundancy is achieved through the second Internet connection.

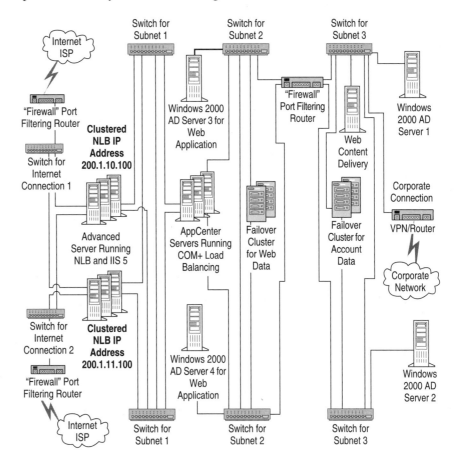

Figure 2.2   A network topology with a redundant Internet connection

Redundant Paths

You can implement redundant connectivity at several points in your network topology: within each LAN segment, at your connection to the Internet Service Provider (ISP), or through multiple sites.

LANs

A *LAN* is a communications network connecting a group of computers, printers, and other devices located within a relatively limited area (for example, a building). A LAN allows any connected device to interact with any other on the network. LANs allow users to share storage devices, printers, applications, data, and other network resources. In a multitiered network environment, LANs are often segmented into smaller units (subnets). You can use redundant switches in each subnet to provide redundant LAN connectivity, as shown in Figure 2.1.

ISPs

An *ISP* is an organization that provides individuals or companies access to the Internet and the Web. In most cases a network is connected to an ISP through a T1, DS3, OC3, or OC12 connection. To reduce the risk of a single route failure, many Web sites introduce a second connection to the Internet, as shown in Figure 2.2.

Multiple Sites

To ensure high availability, some organizations implement a live alternate site. This basically consists of setting up the same service at two locations. There are many ways to achieve this setup. Figure 2.3 demonstrates one way to split a Web service over two sites.

You can construct a multisite architecture in several ways. The architecture typically comprises a main Web site and one or more satellite sites that extend a company's service offerings. The satellite sites can contain a portion of the main site or its entire architecture. The key factors that determine your choice of architecture are the degrees of database synchronization desired between the sites and the amount of traffic that must be backhauled to a main site.

You can use a geographic load balancer (such as Cisco DistributedDirector) when a Web site is expanded to include geographically distributed sites. A geographic load balancer directs connection requests from clients to the site with the closest proximity based on information about the network topology. This process helps improve the response times of applications as seen by end users, especially when the geographic sites are widely distributed.

A geographic load balancer provides scalability to multiple sites and also delivers a high degree of availability by monitoring the state of each distributed e-commerce site. If a site is rendered inoperable, the geographic load balancer stops directing new client connections to the failed site.

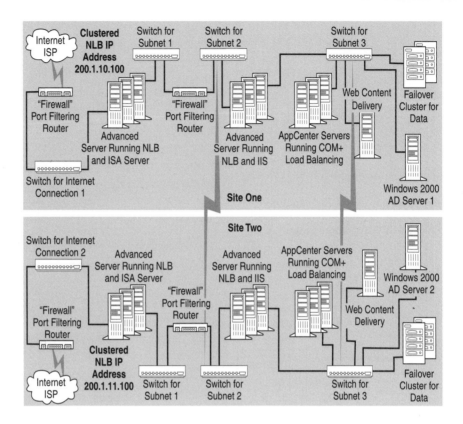

Figure 2.3 Multisite network architecture

The geographic load balancer's primary function is to play the role of an authoritative DNS server for the domain (for example, www.microsoft.com). A client who wants to access a Web site initiates a DNS request for the appropriate URL. The load balancer receives the DNS request and responds with the unique IP address of the site's data center that will provide the best service to the end user.

Redundant Services

An organization's Web applications typically perform such mission-critical tasks as e-commerce, financial transactions, and intranet applications. Businesses can lose millions of dollars when mission-critical applications aren't available, so it's important that these applications are available at all times.

An easy and effective way to achieve availability and reliability for your services is to use redundant servers. If you have more than one server implementing your site and one of them fails, the processing requests can be redirected to another server. This provides a highly available Web site.

You can use two methods of implementing redundant services on multiple computers: use backup servers or implement load balancing and clustering.

Backup Servers

One of the most common methods for restoring service is the use of backup systems. You can achieve high availability by using a hot standby with automated failover or by swapping the failed system with spare systems already configured for use.

Hot Standby   In situations where prolonged outages cause severe problems, hot standby systems provide a way to recover quickly. You use the standby system to replace a failed system quickly, or in some cases you use it as an source of spare parts. Should a system have a catastrophic failure, it might be possible to remove the drives from the failed system or use backup tapes to restore operations in a relatively short time. This scenario doesn't happen very frequently, but it does happen, in particular with CPU or motherboard component failures.

Hot standby systems are very expensive and complicated to manage, but their worth is measured by the reduced loss of service. One advantage to using standby equipment to recover from an outage is that the failed unit is available for a leisurely diagnostic to determine what failed. Getting to the root cause of the failure is extremely important to prevent repeated failures.

Standby equipment should be certified and running on a round-the-clock basis, just like the production equipment. You should monitor the equipment to make sure it's always operational. Keeping the equipment running is important. If it weren't running, you'd have no guarantees that it'll be available when it's needed.

Standby equipment is primarily used in data center operations where it has the highest return on its investment. However, in some cases where the costs of downtime are very high and clustering isn't a viable answer, standby systems can be used to provide reasonably fast recovery times in some cases. This is particularly true of process control, where loss of a computer can produce very expensive or dangerous results.

Spare Systems   Using spare systems to replace failed systems is another technique for rapidly restoring service. Sometimes the replacement system becomes the primary system. In other cases, the failed system is returned to operation as the primary system after it has been repaired. The spare system's success depends on using a cost-effective procedure to keep an adequate supply of spare systems and using standard configurations.

Load Balancing and Clustering

Load balancing and clustering provide access to resources on a group of servers in such a way that the workload can be shared among multiple servers. Numerous vendors supply hardware- and software-based load balancing and clustering solutions for enterprise networking, including round-robin DNS, load-balancing switches, and software-based solutions such as Windows 2000 Cluster service and Network Load Balancing (NLB).

DNS Round Robin   Round robin is a technique used by DNS servers to distribute the load for network resources. This technique rotates the order of the resource record (RR) data returned in a query answer when there are multiple RRs of the same type for a queried DNS domain name. For example, suppose a query is made against a computer that uses three IP addresses (10.0.0.1, 10.0.0.2, and 10.0.0.3), with each address specified in its own A-type RR. Table 2.1 illustrates how these client requests will be handled.

Table 2.1   Rotation of RRs

Client Request	IP Address Return Sequence
First	10.0.0.1, 10.0.0.2, 10.0.0.3
Second	10.0.0.2, 10.0.0.3, 10.0.0.1
Third	10.0.0.3, 10.0.0.1, 10.0.0.2

The rotation process continues until data from all of the same-type RRs for a name have been rotated to the top of the list returned in client query responses.

Although DNS round robin provides simple load balancing among Web servers as well as scalability and redundancy, it doesn't provide an extensive feature set for unified server management, content deployment and management, or health and performance monitoring. In the event of a failure, you have to remove the servers manually from the DNS tables.

The main advantage of round-robin DNS is that it requires no additional hardware—you just set up your DNS server properly and it works. However, several disadvantages prevent many sites from using round-robin DNS for load balancing:

- The caching feature of DNS prevents complete load balancing because not every request that comes in will get its address directly from our DNS server.

- You can solve the above problem by disabling caching, but doing so means that every resolution will have to be resolved by your servers, which is expensive and potentially slower for your users.

- The DNS server has no way of knowing if one or more of the servers in your Web farm is overloaded or out of service. So the round-robin scheme will send traffic to all servers in turn, even if some are overburdened or dead. This can affect a site's availability, although a browser user can hit the reload button to try again (and have a random chance of succeeding, assuming that caching doesn't occur).

Because of this last issue, round-robin DNS isn't used much (at least not by itself) for large or mission-critical Web farms. But you can use round-robin DNS for load balancing in a Web farm with two or three servers—or you can use it to balance load across two or three server clusters, each of which is load-balanced with one of the methods below. (The chances that an entire cluster will fail are quite small.)

Load-Balancing Switches   Load-balancing switches, such as Cisco LocalDirector, are hardware Internet scalability solutions that distribute TCP requests across multiple servers. Server load balancers help increase the scalability of an e-commerce site. Server load balancing works by distributing user requests among a group of servers that appear as a single virtual server to the end user. Its main function is to forward user traffic to the most available or the "best" server that can respond to the user. Server load balancers use sophisticated mechanisms to detect the best server. These mechanisms include finding the server with the fewest connections, the smallest load, or the fastest response times. They can also detect failed servers and automatically redirect users to the active servers. Ultimately, server load balancing helps maximize the use of servers and improves the response times to end users.

Hardware-based solutions use a specialized switch with additional software to manage request routing. For load balancing to take place, the switch first has to discover the IP addresses of all of the servers that it's connected to. The switch scans all the incoming packets directed to its IP address and rewrites them to contain a chosen server's IP address. Server selection depends on server availability and the particular load-balancing algorithm in use. The configuration shown in Figure 2.4 uses switches in combination with LocalDirector from Cisco Systems to distribute the load among three servers.

LocalDirector and similar third-party products provide more sophisticated mechanisms for delivering high performance load balancing solutions than round-robin DNS. These products are intelligent and feature-rich in the load-balancing arena—for example, they can transparently remove a server if it fails. However, they don't provide broad and robust Web farm management tools—and you'll need multiple switches to avoid making the switch a single point of failure for your entire Web application. Clustering is often less expensive than a load-balancing switch and avoids having a single point of failure.

Windows 2000 Clustering   A cluster is a collection of loosely coupled, independent servers that behave as a single system. Cluster members, or nodes, can be symmetric multiprocessing (SMP) systems if that level of computing power is required. The following features characterize clusters:

- **The ability to treat all the computers in the cluster as a single server**
  Application clients interact with a cluster as if it were a single server, and system administrators view the cluster in much the same way: as a single system image. The ease of cluster management depends on how a given clustering technology is implemented in addition to the toolset provided by the vendor.

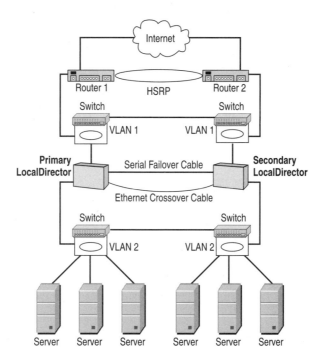

Figure 2.4   LocalDirector used in conjunction with switches

- **The ability to share the workload**   In a cluster some form of load balancing mechanism serves to distribute the load among the servers.

- **The ability to scale the cluster**   Whether clustering is implemented by using a group of standard servers or by using high-performance SMP servers, you can increase a cluster's processing capability in small incremental steps by adding another server.

- **The ability to provide a high level of availability**   Among the techniques used are fault tolerance, failover/failback, and isolation. These techniques are frequently used interchangeably—and incorrectly.

Clustering is a computer architecture that addresses several issues, including performance, availability, and scalability. As is the case with other architectures, the idea of clustering isn't new. What's new about it are its implementation and the platforms that can take advantage of this architecture.

Load balancing is one aspect of clustering. Microsoft's initial software-based load balancing solution was its Windows NT Load Balancing Service (WLBS), also known as Convoy. The essence of WLBS is a mapping of a shared virtual IP address (VIP) to the real IP addresses of the servers that are part of the load-balancing scheme. Network Load Balancing (NLB) is a Network Driver Interface Specification (NDIS) packet filter driver that sits above the network adapter's

NDIS driver and below the TCP/IP stack. Each server receives every packet for the VIP, and NLB decides on a packet-by-packet basis which packets should be processed by a given server. If another server should process the packet, the server running NLB discards the packet. If it determines that the packet should be processed locally, the packet is passed up to the TCP/IP stack.

Clustering is discussed in more detail in Chapter 4, "Microsoft Windows 2000 Cluster Service," Chapter 5, "Network Load Balancing (NLB)," and Chapter 6, "Microsoft Application Center 2000."

Making a Decision

When designing a highly available network topology, you can use redundancy to avoid any single point of failure. A highly available topology can include redundant components, redundant network paths, and redundant services. Table 2.2 provides a description of each strategy that you can use when designing redundancy into your network topology.

Table 2.2   Designing a Highly Available Network Topology

Strategy	Examples	Description
Redundant components	hubs switches routers	You should use redundant components to avoid any single point of failure. When a component fails, a backup component should be able to operate so that system availability isn't compromised. All components should be made redundant.
Redundant network paths	LANs ISPs multiple sites	Redundant network connections should exist at every level of the network, including connections within the LAN and the connections to the ISP. You can also implement redundant LAN and ISP connectivity through the use of multiple sites. Some organizations might choose to implement redundancy within the main site and then implement satellite sites to ensure further redundancy.
Redundant services	hot standby spare systems round-robin DNS load-balancing switches Windows Clustering	Of the examples provided here, clustering is considered the most efficient, manageable and cost-effective in terms of delivering high availability. You should implement clustering at all levels of a multitiered environment. Note that clustering is discussed in detail in later chapters. With the information provided in those chapters, you'll have a better understanding of how clustering is implemented and how you can use it to ensure high availability in your network topology.

Recommendations

When designing a highly available network infrastructure, you should use redundant components and network paths to avoid any single point of failure. You can achieve redundancy by implementing it within the LAN and to the ISP, by implementing multiple sites, or by combining both solutions. In addition, when designing a highly available network topology, you should implement clustering rather than round-robin DNS or load-balancing switches.

Example: Network Redundancy

The network topology shown in Figure 2.5 illustrates a design that uses redundant components and paths.

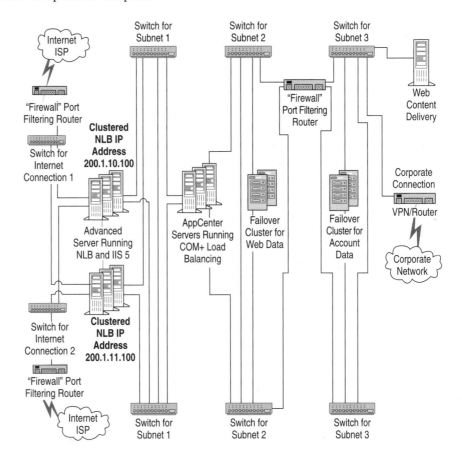

Figure 2.5   A network topology that uses redundant components and network paths

This network uses redundant routers and switches to provide redundant connections to the Internet. Should one connection fail, the redundant components and paths provide continued availability so that users aren't affected by any single point of failure. In addition, redundant switches and connections have been included for each subnet so that a path is always available in case of failure. Note that the network design uses clustering to ensure high availability, rather than round-robin DNS or load-balancing switches. Clustering is used at each layer of the network topology.

Lesson Summary

One of the most effective ways to ensure the high availability of a Web site is to use redundant hardware and software. In a complex system it's often possible to include redundant components, paths, and services to ensure a highly available network design. Redundant components can refer to hardware within a computer (such as hot swappable drives), completely duplicated computers, or network components outside a computer, such as routers, switches, and hubs. Although hubs, switches, and routers don't fail very often, they can still fail. Consequently, using redundancy is very important. You can also implement redundant connectivity at several points in your network topology: within each LAN segment, at your connection to the ISP, or through multiple sites. You can also achieve high availability for your services by using redundant servers. If you have more than one server implementing your site and one of the servers crashes, the processing requests can be redirected to another server. You can use two methods to implement redundant services on multiple computers: use backup servers and implement load balancing and clustering. When designing a highly available network infrastructure, you should use redundant components and network paths to avoid any single point of failure. In addition, when designing a highly available network topology, you should implement clustering rather than round-robin DNS or load-balancing switches.

Lesson 2: Designing a Subnet Addressing Structure for a TCP/IP Network

TCP/IP's success as the network protocol of the Internet is largely due to its ability to connect networks of different sizes and systems of different types. The Internet community originally defined five address classes: A through E. Microsoft TCP/IP supports classes A, B, and C. The classes have predefined sizes, each of which can be divided into smaller subnetworks, a process known as *subnetting*. Subnetting becomes necessary as you reconcile the logical address scheme of the Internet with the physical networks used by the real world. Subnetting allows you to partition a single TCP/IP network into a number of separate networks called *subnets*. By subnetting a multitiered Web network environment, you can enhance security and add bandwidth to your network, as well as increase your system's availability. In this lesson you'll learn how to design a subnetting structure for your multitiered Web environment in order to enhance security, add bandwidth, and increase availability.

After this lesson, you will be able to

- Describe subnets and the subnetting process
- Design a subnet addressing structure for a TCP/IP network

Estimated lesson time: 25 minutes

Subnetting a Multitiered Web Environment

Each TCP/IP host is identified by a logical IP address. The IP address is a network layer address and has no dependence on the Data-Link layer address (such as a Media Access Control [MAC] address of a network adapter). A unique IP address is required for each host and network component that uses TCP/IP to communicate.

The IP address identifies a system's location on the network in the same way a street address identifies a house on a city block. Just as a street address must identify a unique residence, an IP address must be globally unique and have a uniform format. Each IP address includes a network ID and a host ID.

The network ID identifies the TCP/IP hosts that are located on the same physical network. All hosts on the same physical network must be assigned the same network ID to communicate with one another. A network ID should adhere to the following guidelines:

- The network ID must be unique to the IP internetwork. If you plan on having a direct routed connection to the Internet, the network ID must be unique to the Internet. If you don't plan on connecting to the Internet, the local network ID must be unique to your private internetwork.
- The network ID can't begin with the number 127. The number 127 is reserved for internal loopback functions.

- All bits within the network ID can't be set to 1. All 1s in the network ID are reserved for use as an IP broadcast address.
- All bits within the network ID can't be set to 0. All 0s in the network ID are used to denote a specific host on the local network and aren't routed.

The host ID identifies a TCP/IP host within a network. The combination of IP network ID and IP host ID is an IP address. A host ID should adhere to the following guidelines:

- The host ID must be unique to the network ID.
- All bits within the host ID can't be set to 1 because this host ID is reserved as a broadcast address to send a packet to all hosts on a network.
- All bits in the host ID can't be set to 0 because this host ID is reserved to denote the IP network ID.

Subnets

The 32 bits of the IP address are apportioned between network IDs and host IDs, depending on how many networks and hosts per network are needed. However, it isn't always practical to have all possible network nodes on the same broadcast domain. All the hosts on the same physical network bounded by IP routers share the same broadcast traffic. For example, a class A network ID can contain more than 16 million hosts on the same network, which isn't a practical solution. As a result, most of the 16 million host addresses are unassignable and are wasted. Even a class B network with 65,000 hosts per network is impractical.

In an effort to create smaller broadcast domains and to better utilize the bits in the host ID, an IP network can be subdivided into smaller networks, each bounded by an IP router and assigned a new subnetted network ID, which is a subset of the original class-based network ID. This creates subnets, subdivisions of an IP network each with its own unique subnetted network ID. Subnetted network IDs are created by using bits from the host ID portion of the original class-based network ID.

For example, Figure 2.6 shows a class B network with a network ID of 139.12.0.0. The network can include up to 65,534 nodes. The network should be subnetted, but it should be done in such a way so that it neither affects the rest of the IP internetwork nor requires its reconfiguration.

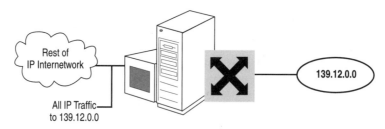

Figure 2.6   Network 139.12.0.0 before subnetting

Network 139.12.0.0 is subnetted by utilizing the first 8 host bits of the host ID (the third octet) for the new subnetted network ID. The subnetting of 139.12.0.0, as shown in Figure 2.7, creates separate networks with their own subnetted network IDs (139.12.1.0, 139.12.2.0, and 139.12.3.0). The router is aware of the separate subnetted network IDs and routes IP packets to the appropriate subnet.

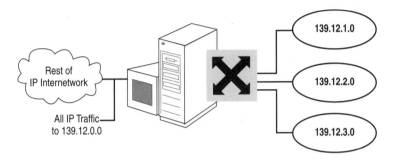

Figure 2.7   Network 139.12.0.0 after subnetting

Note that the rest of the IP internetwork still regards all the nodes on the three subnets as being on network 139.12.0.0. The other routers in the IP internetwork are unaware of the subnetting being done on network 139.12.0.0 and therefore require no reconfiguration.

A key element of subnetting is still missing. How does the router that's subdividing network 139.12.0.0 know how the network is being subdivided and which subnets are available on which router interfaces? To give the IP nodes this new level of awareness, they must be told exactly how to discern the new subnetted network ID regardless of Internet address classes. A subnet mask is used to tell an IP node how to extract a class-based or subnetted network ID.

Subnetting

Although the conceptual notion of subnetting by using host bits is straightforward, the actual mechanics of subnetting are a bit more complicated. Subnetting requires a three-step procedure:

1. Determine the number of host bits to be used for the subnetting.
2. Enumerate the new subnetted network IDs.
3. Enumerate the IP addresses for each new subnetted network ID.

Step 1: Determining the Number of Host Bits

The number of host bits being used for subnetting determines the possible number of subnets and hosts per subnet. Before you choose the number of host bits, you should have a good idea of the number of subnets and hosts you'll have in the future. Using more bits for the subnet mask than is required saves you the time of reassigning IP addresses in the future.

The more host bits you use, the more subnets (subnetted network IDs) you can have—but each subnet will have fewer hosts. Using too many host bits allows for growth in the number of subnets but limits the growth in the number of hosts. Using too few hosts allows for growth in the number of hosts but limits the growth in the number of subnets.

For example, Figure 2.8 illustrates the subnetting of up to the first 8 host bits of a class B host ID. If you choose 1 host bit for subnetting, you obtain two subnetted network IDs with 16,382 hosts per subnetted network ID. If you choose 8 host bits for subnetting, you obtain 256 subnetted network IDs with 254 hosts per subnetted network ID.

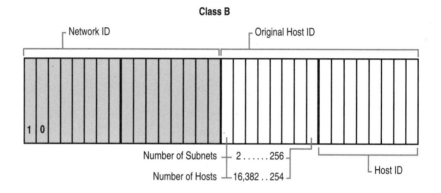

Figure 2.8   Subnetting a class B network ID

In practice, network administrators define a maximum number of nodes they want on a single network. Recall that all nodes on a single network share all the same broadcast traffic; they reside in the same broadcast domain. Therefore, growth in the number of subnets is favored over growth in the number of hosts per subnet.

Step 2: Enumerating Subnetted Network IDs
Based on the number of host bits you use for your subnetting, you must list the new subnetted network IDs. There are two main approaches:

- **Binary**   List all possible combinations of the host bits chosen for subnetting and convert each combination to dotted decimal notation.

- **Decimal**   Add a calculated increment value to each successive subnetted network ID and convert to dotted decimal notation.

Either method produces the same result: the enumerated list of subnetted network IDs.

Step 3: Enumerating IP Addresses for Each Subnetted Network ID

Based on the enumeration of the subnetted network IDs, you must now list the valid IP addresses for new subnetted network IDs. To list each IP address individually would be unnecessarily tedious. Instead, enumerate the IP addresses for each subnetted network ID by defining the range of IP addresses (the first and the last) for each subnetted network ID. There are two main approaches:

- **Binary**   Write down the first and last IP address for each subnetted network ID and convert to dotted decimal notation.

- **Decimal**   Add values incrementally, corresponding to the first and last IP addresses for each subnetted network ID and convert to dotted decimal notation.

Either method produces the same result: the range of IP addresses for each subnetted network ID.

Segmenting a Network into Subnets

All Web sites must be managed in such a way that adequate protections are provided for the confidentiality, privacy, integrity, and availability of information. Security is essential to the success of any business site. A business site uses multiple security domain segments. Systems with the same security needs are grouped into the same segment, and each segment is protected by a network filter or firewall, as shown in Figure 2.9. The three principal domain segments, each separated by a firewall, are as follows:

- the public network
- a perimeter network, where front ends and content servers are placed
- a secure network, where content is created or staged and secure data is managed and stored

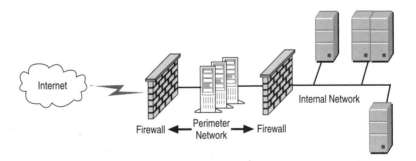

Figure 2.9   The three principal domain segments

Data networks internal to the perimeter network should be segregated for security, as well as to add bandwidth. Generally, each computer should be equipped with two or more NICs. You should adhere to the following guidelines when segmenting the perimeter network:

- Segregate different types of Internet traffic to different Web clusters. For example, Hypertext Transfer Protocol (HTTP) requests can be routed to one cluster and FTP requests can be routed to another cluster. You can then configure each cluster to reject traffic that's different from the type it's designed to service.

- Segregate Internet traffic from back-end traffic. This prevents direct access from the Internet to the internal network and permits filters to be configured for each NIC, thereby limiting traffic to only types appropriate for the server.

- Avoid IP forwarding in the Routing and Remote Access Service (RRAS) in Windows 2000 Server between the front-end servers. The only publicly accessible IP address is the virtual IP address used by the load-balanced front-end server cluster. Disabling IP forwarding is crucially important.

- Use non-routable network addresses for internal Web site networks.

- Implement a management network in order to segregate management from all other traffic. This also permits the configuration of NIC filters to restrict traffic to that NIC. Powerful management functions should then be restricted to the management network and be unable to traverse the service networks. It also eliminates management traffic from passing through firewalls, which further reduces vulnerabilities. Securing the management LAN itself is of crucial importance.

Making a Decision

When segmenting a network in order to support a secure, highly available Web environment, you can implement a multitiered strategy and use a separate network segment for the heartbeat LAN connection within each cluster and a network segment to act as the management network. Each of these strategies is outlined in Table 2.3.

Table 2.3   Segmenting Your Network

Strategy	Description
Multitiered network	A multitiered network should be divided into at least three basic domain segments that are each separated by a firewall: the public network; a perimeter network, where front ends and content servers are placed; and a secure network, where content is created or staged and secure data is managed and stored. In some cases the perimeter network is divided into smaller segments. The multitiered environment segregates Internet traffic from back-end traffic, preventing direct access from the Internet to the internal network.

Table 2.3 *(continued)*

Strategy	Description
Heartbeat LAN	The heartbeat LAN provides a segregated network segment in which servers within the same cluster can communicate with each other. Clustering is discussed in more detail later in this book.
Management network	A management network segregates management traffic from all other traffic. Although a separate segment isn't required, it's generally recommended to ensure a more secure environment.

Recommendations

To set up the most effective Web environment, you should implement all three of these strategies. A multitiered topology provides for a higher level of security, the heartbeat LAN segment is essential for clustering functionality, and the management network is strongly recommended because it eliminates management traffic through firewalls, which reduces vulnerabilities.

Example: A Subnetted Web Environment

The network topology shown in Figure 2.10 shows a highly available system. The design represents a large site and demonstrates both topological and component redundancy. Critical services can survive most failure modes short of a major disaster. Servers in each of the ISP 1 through ISP N groupings support each of the site's critical functions, so even the loss of an ISP will not take the site down. Providing nonstop service through most disaster scenarios requires replication of the entire site in multiple geographies (geoplex). Cisco's DistributedDirector is commonly used to support the geoplex. Unfortunately, site replication can more than double a site's cost and may introduce data consistency issues for Web applications.

The network design illustrates multiple connections for redundancy, labeled ISP 1 and ISP N. These should be provisioned from diverse (physically separate) networks. Servers on front-end networks are exposed to the Internet. Firewalls are essential security components that provide network isolation by filtering traffic by packet type as well as source and destination addresses. They form one boundary of a perimeter network depicted by the double-ended arrows. The first components in the path are Router/Firewalls, whose functions may be distinct or combined in single devices.

Front-End Network Segment

The front end provides the core Web services, such as HTTP/HTTPS, by using Microsoft Internet Information Server (IIS) to serve up Hypertext Markup Language (HTML) and ASP pages and Lightweight Directory Access Protocol (LDAP) servers to authenticate customers.

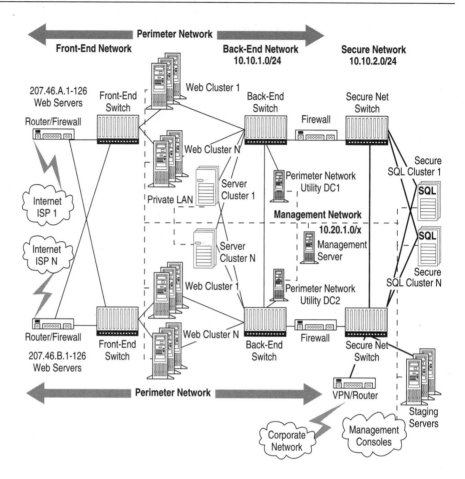

Figure 2.10   Web-based network topology with multiple segments

Each front-end server is specially hardened for security and connects to three networks:

- Front-end network (Internet access)
- Back-end network (access to perimeter network servers and, through inner firewalls, to the Secure Network)
- Management network (supports management and operations functions)

This network segregation improves security while increasing total available bandwidth and improving redundancy.

Note that the only publicly accessible IP addresses on any of the servers in this site are the virtual IP addresses, to which only the front-end servers can respond. IP filtering applied to Internet-facing NICs ensures that only the correct type and source of traffic for the functions supported can enter the front-end server. IP forwarding on the Web servers (through RRAS) has also been disabled between these networks.

Back-End Network Segment

The back-end network supports all perimeter network servers through use of a high-speed, private 10.10.1.*x* LAN. This architecture prevents direct network access from the Internet to the perimeter network servers, even if the firewall were to be breached, because Internet routers aren't permitted to forward designated ranges of IP addresses, including the 10.*x.x.x* range. As with the front-end network, redundant switches provide access to all front-end and back-end servers. All back-end switches share a common network, so back-end traffic loading can become problematic for active sites, especially if a separate management network isn't available for logging and other front-end management network traffic.

The major components on the back-end network are security-hardened server clusters that provide services for storing Web content and session state. File shares within the cluster support file storage services. Microsoft SQL Server running on the cluster provides database services. Each cluster server employs at least four NICs: one for each switch, one for the private heartbeat LAN (which should use another private network address, such as 192.168.10.*x*), and one for the management LAN. In addition to the servers' physical addresses, each cluster is assigned two virtual IP addresses (one for each NIC connected to the back-end switches).

Secure Network Segment

Another firewall forms the inner boundary of the perimeter network and isolates what we term the secure network from the back-end network. The firewall is configured to allow only required communications between permitted port and source/destination pairs. The secure network again comprises a private network (10.10.2.0 in this example), a pair of coupled switches, a variety of servers, and a device labeled VPN/Router that provides connectivity to the internal corporate network. The secure network is logically part of the corporate network. Servers on the secure network are often members of an internal corporate domain, so domain controllers and address and name servers are assumed to be internal.

Management Network Segment

A site management system is often built on a separate network to ensure high availability. Using a separate network for the management system also relieves the back-end network of the management traffic, which improves overall performance and response time. Sometimes, management and operations use the back-end network, but this isn't recommended for large, highly available sites.

Lesson Summary

The network ID identifies the TCP/IP hosts that are located on the same physical network. The host ID identifies a TCP/IP host within a network. The 32 bits of the IP address are apportioned between network IDs and host IDs, depending on how many networks and hosts per network are needed. To create smaller broadcast domains and to better utilize the bits in the host ID, you can subdivide an IP network into smaller networks, each bounded by an IP router and assigned a new subnetted network ID, which is a subset of the original class-based network ID. Subnetting requires a three-step procedure: determining the number of host bits to be used, enumerating the new subnetted network IDs, and enumerating the IP address of each new subnetted network ID. The three principal domain segments, each separated by a firewall, are the public network; a perimeter network, where front ends and content servers are placed; and a secure network, where content is created or staged and secure data is managed and stored. You can divide the perimeter network into smaller segments. In addition, it's generally recommended that you use a separate segment for a management network to ensure high availability and relieve the back-end management traffic. You should also use a heartbeat LAN for clustering.

Activity 2.1: Adding Redundancy to a Network Topology

Your company is a medium-sized retailer that sells children's clothes at storefront locations throughout Oregon and Washington. The company also mails out a printed catalog from which customers can place orders by phone or mail. Last year, you implemented a Web site whose sole purpose was to provide an online catalog to supplement the printed catalog. No transactions are conducted online. The network topology for the site is shown in Figure 2.11.

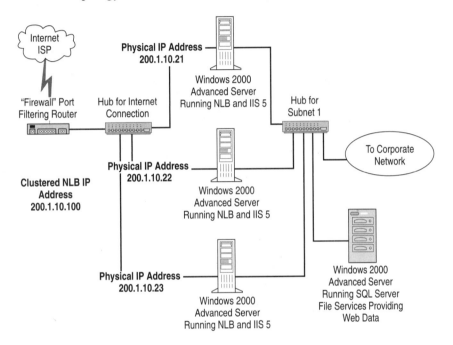

Figure 2.11   Web site serving as online catalog for retail operation

Your company now wants to implement an e-commerce site that supports online ordering and payments, so you must design a network topology that supports the availability, scalability, manageability, and security required to operate the site. You want to design a topology that uses redundancy to ensure that there are no single points of failure. You plan to add another subnet to support a middle tier and to use switches rather than hubs. Your site will be located in only one geographical location.

1. How should you design the network topology for the e-commerce site?

Lesson 3: Designing a DHCP Server Environment for a TCP/IP Network

Windows 2000 Server includes an enhanced implementation of DHCP. DHCP is an open industry standard that reduces the complexity of administering networks based on TCP/IP. Each host computer connected to a TCP/IP network must be assigned a unique IP address. DHCP frees network administrators from having to configure all of the computers by hand. DHCP can automatically configure a host while it's booting on a TCP/IP network, as well as change settings while the host is attached. All available IP addresses are stored in a central database along with associated configuration information, such as the subnet mask, gateways, and addresses of DNS servers. Without the dynamic assignment of IP configuration information, clients have to be configured one by one. IP addresses must be managed to avoid duplicate use. Changes must be applied to clients by hand. Configuration information isn't centralized; and it's difficult to get a view of all client configurations. This lesson provides an overview of DHCP and the DHCP lease process. The lesson also provides information on how to set up DHCP to be fault tolerant in order to enhance system availability.

After this lesson, you will be able to

- Describe the DHCP service in Windows 2000
- Design a fault-tolerant DHCP environment

Estimated lesson time: 25 minutes

Windows 2000 DHCP Service

DHCP was derived from the Internet standard Bootstrap Protocol (BOOTP), which allowed dynamic assignment of IP addresses (as well as remote booting of diskless work stations). In addition to supporting dynamic assignment of IP addresses, DHCP supplies all configuration data required by TCP/IP, plus additional data required for specific servers. Administrators can manually configure just one machine—the DHCP server. Whenever a new host is plugged into the network segment that's served by the DHCP server or an existing host is turned back on, the machine asks for a unique IP address.

When a DHCP server receives a request for an IP address, it selects the address from a pool of addresses defined in its database and offers the address—along with other IP configuration information—to the DHCP client. If the client accepts the offer, the DHCP server leases the IP addressing information to the client for a specified period.

DHCP Lease Process

The DHCP service allocates IP addressing information to client computers. The allocation of IP addressing information is called a *DHCP lease*. The DHCP lease process occurs when one of the following events occurs:

- TCP/IP is initialized for the first time on a DHCP client.
- A client requests a specific IP address and is denied, possibly because the DHCP server dropped the lease.
- A client previously leased an IP address but then released it and requires a new one. You can release a DHCP lease manually by typing **ipconfig /release** at a command prompt.

DHCP uses a four-phase process (DHCPDISCOVER, DHCPOFFER, DHCPREQUEST, and DHCPACK) to lease IP addressing information to a DHCP client for a specific period, as shown in Figure 2.12.

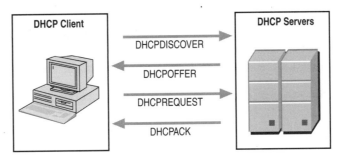

Figure 2.12   The DHCP lease process

DHCPDISCOVER

The first step in the DHCP lease process is DHCPDISCOVER. To begin the DHCP lease process, a client initializes a limited version of TCP/IP and broadcasts a DHCPDISCOVER message requesting the location of a DHCP server and IP addressing information. Because the client doesn't know the IP address of a DHCP server, the client uses 0.0.0.0 as the source address and 255.255.255.255 as the destination address. The DHCPDISCOVER message contains the client's hardware address and computer name so that the DHCP servers can determine which client sent the request.

DHCPOFFER

The second step in the DHCP lease process is DHCPOFFER. All DHCP servers that receive the IP lease request and that have a valid client configuration broadcast a DHCPOFFER message that includes the following information:

- The client's hardware address
- An offered IP address

- A subnet mask
- The length of the lease
- A server identifier (the IP address of the offering DHCP server)

The DHCP servers send a broadcasted message because the client doesn't yet have an IP address. The DHCP client selects the IP address from the first offer that it receives. The DHCP server issuing the IP address reserves the address so that it can't be offered to another DHCP client.

DHCPREQUEST

The third step in the DHCP lease process occurs after the client receives a DHCPOFFER from at least one DHCP server and selects an IP address. The client broadcasts a DHCPREQUEST message to all DHCP servers, indicating that it has accepted an offer. The DHCPREQUEST message includes the server identifier (IP address) of the server whose offer it accepted. All other DHCP servers then retract their offers and retain their IP addresses for the next IP lease request.

DHCPACK

The final step in a successful DHCP lease process occurs when the DHCP server issuing the accepted offer broadcasts a successful acknowledgment to the client in the form of a DHCPACK message. This message contains a valid lease for an IP address and possibly other configuration information.

When the DHCP client receives the acknowledgment, TCP/IP is completely initialized and the client is considered a bound DHCP client. Once bound, the client can use TCP/IP to communicate on the network.

DHCPNACK

If the DHCPREQUEST isn't successful, the DHCP server broadcasts a negative acknowledgement (DHCPNACK). A DHCP server broadcasts a DHCPNACK if one of the following conditions is met:

- The client is trying to lease its previous IP address and the IP address is no longer available.
- The IP address is invalid because the client computer has been moved to a different subnet.

When the client receives an unsuccessful acknowledgment, it autoconfigures its IP address by using Automatic Private IP Addressing (APIPA) and its class B subnet mask. Once it autoconfigures itself, it will continue to check for DHCP servers every 5 minutes until it finds one. Once that happens, the client releases the autoconfigured information and uses the IP addressing information issued by the DHCP server.

Note   If a computer has multiple network adapters bound to TCP/IP, the DHCP process occurs separately over each adapter. The DHCP service assigns a unique and valid IP address to each adapter in the computer bound to TCP/IP, if that adapter is configured as a DHCP client.

IP Lease Renewal and Release

All DHCP clients attempt to renew their lease when 50 percent of the lease time has expired. To renew its lease, a DHCP client sends a DHCPREQUEST message directly to the DHCP server from which it obtained the lease. If the DHCP server is available, it renews the lease and sends the client a DHCPACK message with the new lease time and any updated configuration parameters. The client updates its configuration when it receives the acknowledgment.

Note   Each time a DHCP client restarts, it attempts to lease the same IP address from the original DHCP server. If the lease request is unsuccessful and lease time is still available, the DHCP client continues to use the same IP address until the next attempt to renew the lease.

If a DHCP client can't renew its lease with the original DHCP server at the 50 percent interval, the client broadcasts a DHCPREQUEST to contact any available DHCP server when 87.5 percent of the lease time has expired. Any DHCP server can respond with a DHCPACK message (renewing the lease) or a DHCPNACK message (forcing the DHCP client to obtain a lease for a different IP address).

If the lease expires or a DHCPNACK message is received, the DHCP client must immediately discontinue using that IP address. The DHCP client then begins the DHCP lease process to lease a new IP address.

DHCP Scopes

You must define and activate a scope before DHCP clients can use the DHCP server for dynamic TCP/IP configurations. A DHCP scope is an administrative collection of IP addresses and TCP/IP configuration parameters that are available for lease to DHCP clients. The network administrator creates a scope for each logical or physical subnet.

A scope has the following properties:

- A scope name, assigned when the scope is created
- A range of possible IP addresses from which to include or exclude addresses used in DHCP lease offers
- A unique subnet mask, which determines the subnet for a given IP address
- Lease duration values

Each subnet can have a single DHCP scope with a single continuous range of IP addresses. To use several address ranges within a single scope or subnet, you must first define the scope and then set exclusion ranges.

DHCP Superscopes

A superscope allows a DHCP server to provide leases from more than one scope to clients on a single physical network. Before you can create a superscope, you must use DHCP Manager to define all the scopes you want to include in the superscope. Scopes added to a superscope are called *member scopes*. Superscopes can resolve DHCP service issues in various situations, including the following:

- When support is needed for DHCP clients on a single physical network segment—such as a single Ethernet LAN segment—and multiple logical IP networks are used. (When more than one logical IP network is used on a physical network, these configurations are also known as multinets.)

- When the available address pool for a currently active scope is nearly depleted and more computers need to be added to the physical network segment.

- When clients need to be migrated to a new scope.

- When support is needed for DHCP clients on the other side of BOOTP relay agents and the network on the other side of the relay agent has multiple logical subnets on one physical network.

Client Reservations

DHCP Manager allows you to reserve a specific IP address for a computer or for other IP addressable devices on the network. Reserving selected IP addresses for special-function devices on the network ensures that DHCP doesn't duplicate or reassign the address. Reservations can be useful for the following types of devices and computers:

- Other Windows 2000 Server computers on the network that require static IP addresses, such as WINS servers

- Any print servers that use TCP/IP print services

- UNIX clients or other clients that use IP addresses assigned by another TCP/IP configuration method

- Any DNS servers on the network, whether or not they're running Windows 2000

Each reservation requires a unique identifier for the device for which an address is reserved, which is the same as the MAC or physical address for the DHCP client. In the case of Ethernet, this address is a unique sequence of hexadecimal byte numbers that identifies the network adapter hardware for each network-connected device.

You can obtain MAC addresses on Windows 2000 clients by typing **ipconfig /all** at the command prompt of the client computer and viewing the Physical Address field. For Windows 95–based clients, you can run the WINIPCFG.EXE command prompt utility and view the Adapter Address field.

BOOTP/DHCP Relay Agents

BOOTP and DHCP rely on network broadcasts to communicate. Routers in normal routed environments don't automatically forward broadcasts from one interface to another, so a relay agent is needed to pass along this communication. A BOOTP/DHCP relay agent is either a router or a host computer configured to listen for BOOTP and DHCP broadcast messages and direct them to a specific DHCP server. Using relay agents eliminates the need to have a DHCP server on each physical network segment. Relay agents not only direct local DHCP client requests to remote DHCP servers but also return remote DHCP server responses to the DHCP clients.

RFC 2131–compliant routers (which supersede RFC 1542) contain relay agents that allow them to forward DHCP packets. Windows 2000 Server also comes with a DHCP relay agent that you can install and configure as a service.

Fault-Tolerant DHCP Configurations

One online DHCP server and one backup DHCP server can support a large number of clients, depending on hardware configurations and other issues. However, when you decide how many DHCP servers are necessary, you need to consider the location of routers on the network and whether you want a DHCP server in each subnet. You should also consider the transmission speed between each segment for which DHCP service is to be provided. With slower WAN links or dial-up links, you typically deploy a DHCP server on both sides of these links to service clients locally.

A network can have practical size constraints, based on the IP address class, such as the 254-node limit of Class C networks. In addition, server configuration issues, such as disk capacity and CPU speed, are critical. Before you install a DHCP server, identify the following information:

- The hardware and storage requirements for the DHCP server
- Which computers you can immediately configure as DHCP clients for dynamic TCP/IP configuration and which computers you should manually configure with static TCP/IP configuration parameters
- The DHCP option types and the option values that will be predefined for the DHCP clients

When setting up DHCP in your network, in most cases you should use the physical characteristics of your LAN or WAN infrastructure and not the logical groupings defined by Windows 2000 domains and your Active Directory service structure. When subnets are connected by routers that support BOOTP relay agents, you don't need DHCP servers on every subnet. Also, you can administer DHCP servers remotely from a computer running Windows 2000 and DHCP Manager.

Splitting Scopes

When you set up DHCP, you'll probably install more than one DHCP server so that the failure of any individual server doesn't prevent DHCP clients from starting. However, DHCP doesn't provide a way for DHCP servers to cooperate in ensuring that assigned addresses are unique. Therefore, you must divide the available address pool among the DHCP servers carefully to prevent duplicate address assignment.

For balancing DHCP server usage, use the 80/20 rule to divide scope addresses between DHCP servers. Figure 2.13 is an example of the 80/20 rule.

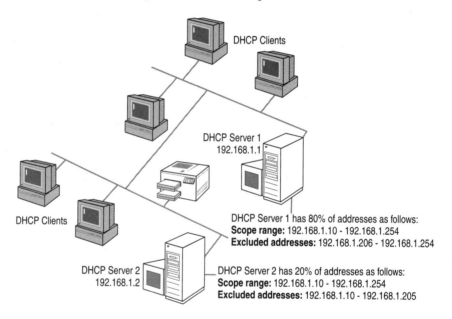

Figure 2.13   80/20 rule model

DHCP Server 1 is configured to lease most (about 80 percent) of the available addresses. DHCP Server 2 is configured to lease the remaining addresses (about 20 percent).

This scenario allows the local DHCP server (DHCP Server 1) to respond to requests from local DHCP clients most of the time. The remote or backup DHCP server (DHCP Server 2) assigns addresses to clients on the other subnet only when the local server isn't available or is out of addresses. You can use this same rule in a multiple-subnet scenario to ensure the availability of a DHCP server when a client requests a lease.

Backing Up the DHCP Database

By default, Windows 2000 backs up the DHCP database every 60 minutes. Windows 2000 stores the backup copies of the file in the %systemroot%\ System32\Dhcp\Backup\Jet\New folder.

You can change the default backup interval by changing the value (the number of minutes between backups) of the BackupInterval entry located in the registry under the following key:

```
HKEY_LOCAL_MACHINE\SYSTEM\CurrentControlSet\
    Services\DHCPServer\Parameters
```

By default, the DHCP service restores a corrupt DHCP database automatically when you restart the DHCP service. But you can manually restore the DHCP database file by editing the registry. First set the value for the RestoreFlag entry to 1, and then restart the DHCP service. The RestoreFlag entry is located in the registry under the following subkey:

```
HKEY_LOCAL_MACHINE\SYSTEM\CurrentControlSet\
    Services\DHCPServer\Parameters
```

Note   After the DHCP service restores the database, the server automatically changes the RestoreFlag parameter to the default value of 0.

You can also restore the DHCP database file manually by copying the contents of the %systemroot%\System32\Dhcp\Backup\Jet folder to the %systemroot%\System32\Dhcp folder and then restarting the DHCP service.

Clustering DHCP Servers

The Cluster service in Windows 2000 Advanced Server allows you to manage two servers as a single system. In Windows 2000 Datacenter Server, the Cluster service allows you to manage four servers as a single system. You can use the Cluster service for DHCP servers to provide higher availability, easier manageability, and greater scalability.

The Cluster service can automatically detect the failure of an application or server and quickly restart it on a surviving server with users experiencing only a short pause in service. With the Cluster service, administrators can quickly inspect the status of all cluster resources and easily move workloads around onto different servers within the cluster. This is useful for static load balancing and for performing rolling upgrades on the servers without taking important data and applications offline.

The Cluster service provides a virtual DHCP server so that if one of the clustered nodes crashes, the namespace and all the services are transparently reconstituted to the second node. This means no changes are visible to the client, which sees the same IP address for the clustered DHCP servers.

Without clustering, network administrators might split scopes between servers so that if one server goes down, a percentage of the available addresses remains available. However, clustering uses IP addresses more efficiently by eliminating the need to split scopes. A database stored on a remote disk tracks address assignment and other activity so that if the active cluster node goes down, the second node becomes the DHCP server and has complete knowledge of what's been assigned and access to the complete scope of addresses. Only one node at a time runs as a DHCP server, with the Windows 2000 clustering database providing transparent transition when needed.

Use the 80/20 rule when implementing clustered DHCP servers to provide additionally enhanced failover services. The combination of clustering DHCP servers and using the 80/20 rule to manage scopes between the clustered servers gives you an enhanced failover solution.

The Cluster service is discussed in more detail in Chapter 4, "Microsoft Windows 2000 Cluster Service."

Making a Decision

When designing a DHCP structure for your network environment, you can use three fault-tolerant strategies to ensure high availability: clustering, splitting scopes, and backing up the database. These strategies are outlined in Table 2.4.

Table 2.4   Designing a DHCP Structure

Strategy	Description
Clustering	The Cluster service allows you to manage two servers or four servers as a single system. You can use the Cluster service for DHCP servers to provide higher availability, easier manageability, and greater scalability. The Cluster service can automatically detect the failure of an application or server and quickly restart it on a surviving server; users would only experience a short pause in service. With the Cluster service, administrators can quickly inspect the status of all cluster resources and easily move workload around onto different servers within the cluster. This is useful for manual load balancing and for performing rolling updates on the servers without taking important data and applications offline. The Cluster service provides a virtual DHCP server so that if one of the clustered nodes fails, the namespace and all the services are transparently reconstituted to the second node. This means no changes for the client, which sees the same IP address for the clustered DHCP server.

Table 2.4   *(continued)*

Strategy	Description
Splitting scopes	Using more than one DHCP server on the same subnet and splitting scopes provides increased fault tolerance for servicing DHCP clients located on the subnet. With two DHCP servers, if one server goes down, the other server can be made to take its place and continue to lease new addresses or renew existing clients. However, clustering uses IP addresses more efficiently than splitting scopes. For the greatest degree of fault tolerance, you can use the 80/20 rule in addition to clustering to enable an enhanced failover solution.
Backing up the database	By default, Windows 2000 backs up the DHCP database every 60 minutes. If Windows 2000 detects a corrupt database when you restart the DHCP Server, the database is automatically restored from the copy that's been backed up. You can change the default backup interval by changing the value in the registry.

Recommendations

When designing a fault-tolerant DHCP structure for your network environment, you should use the Cluster service for the DHCP servers. You should also use the 80/20 rule along with clustering to provide an enhanced failover solution. In addition, you might choose to change the interval of how often the DHCP database is backed up, depending on network usage and DHCP configuration requirements.

Example: A DHCP Configuration

Figure 2.14 is a generic example of clustered DHCP servers. DHCP Server 1 is the active DHCP server, and DHCP Server 2 is the backup DHCP server.

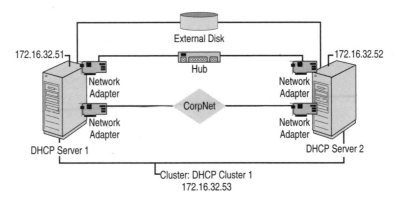

Figure 2.14   Clustered DHCP servers

The following information provides details about the DHCP configuration shown in Figure 2.14:

- DHCP Server 1 and DHCP Server 2 have Windows 2000 DHCP and the Cluster service installed.

- Each DHCP server has a unique server name and IP address.

- Each DHCP server has two network interfaces—one for the cluster identity and the connection to the enterprise network and the second for server-to-server communication. This latter connection is a private link used only for cluster communication. The network cable runs directly between the two servers and is usually referred to as a crossover for internal cluster communications (heartbeat).

- Both DHCP servers are configured with identical scopes. However, on Server 2, the scopes aren't activated because Server 2 isn't currently functioning as the active DHCP server. DHCP Server 2 can function as a hot spare, ready in the event of a shutdown of DHCP Server 1.

To facilitate clustering and the sharing of resources, the DHCP servers are connected to an external disk system that holds the DHCP database and log files. This allows DHCP Server 2 to access the DHCP database files if it needs to take over as the active DHCP server. The clustering service installed on each DHCP server prevents one server from trying to exclusively claim the external disk and prevent sharing of the disk system between the DHCP servers.

The cluster itself has a unique name and IP address so DHCP clients can use the cluster name and IP address to connect to the cluster and request DHCP services. This process prevents rejected DHCP client requests if one of the DHCP servers is turned off. For example, if the client is configured with a specific DHCP server name and IP address instead of the cluster address, the client won't receive DHCP services.

Lesson Summary

DHCP can automatically assign IP addressing information to a DHCP client. The allocation of IP addressing information is called a DHCP lease. DHCP uses a four-phase process (DHCPDISCOVER, DHCPOFFER, DHCPREQUEST, and DHCPACK) to lease IP addressing information to a DHCP client for a specific period. All DHCP clients attempt to renew their lease when 50 percent of the lease time has expired. A scope must be defined and activated before DHCP clients can use the DHCP server for dynamic TCP/IP configuration. DHCP

Manager allows you to reserve a specific IP address for a computer or other
IP addressable devices on the network. Depending on hardware configurations
and other issues, one online DHCP server and one backup DHCP server can support a large number of clients. You must carefully divide the available address
pool among the DHCP servers to prevent duplicate address assignment. For balancing DHCP server usage, use the 80/20 rule to divide scope addresses between
DHCP servers. By default, Windows 2000 backs up the DHCP database every 60
minutes. The Cluster service allows you to manage either two or four servers as a
single system. You can use the Cluster service for DHCP servers to provide
higher availability, easier manageability, and greater scalability. When designing
a fault-tolerant DHCP structure for your network environment, you should use
clustering for the DHCP servers and the 80/20 rule in conjunction with clustering
to provide an enhanced failover solution.

Lesson 4: Designing a Name Resolution Structure for a TCP/IP Network

DNS is a distributed database used in TCP/IP networks to translate computer names (host names) to IP addresses. DNS is most commonly associated with the Internet. However, private networks use DNS extensively to resolve computer host names and to locate computers within their local networks and the Internet. DNS name resolution is different from the name resolution provided by Windows Internet Naming Service (WINS). WINS resolves NetBIOS names to IP addresses, but DNS resolves IP hostnames to IP addresses. This lesson introduces you to DNS and the name resolution process used by Windows 2000. The lesson also provides information on how to design a DNS namespace for a network that supports Internet connectivity.

After this lesson, you will be able to
- Describe the DNS Service in Windows 2000
- Design a DNS hierarchy and naming structure for a Windows 2000 network connected to the Internet

Estimated lesson time: 25 minutes

DNS Hierarchy and Naming

DNS is the name service used in Windows 2000 networks. It is by design a highly reliable, hierarchical, distributed, and scalable database. Windows 2000 clients use DNS for name resolution and service location, including locating domain controllers for logon. DNS in Windows 2000 provides a unique DNS Server implementation that's fully interoperable with other standards-based implementations of DNS Server. You can integrate Windows 2000 DNS into Active Directory so that it uses the Windows 2000 multimaster replication engine.

DNS Structure

DNS is implemented as a hierarchical and distributed database containing various types of data, including host names and domain names. The names in a DNS database form a hierarchical tree structure called the *domain namespace*.

DNS Hierarchy

Domain names consist of individual labels separated by dots, such as mydomain.microsoft.com. A name such as mydomain.microsoft.com is referred to as a *fully qualified domain name* (FQDN). An FQDN uniquely identifies the host's position within the DNS hierarchical tree by specifying a list of names (separated by dots) on the path from the referenced host to the root. Figure 2.15 shows an example of a DNS tree with a host called mydomain located within the microsoft.com domain. The FQDN for the host would be mydomain.microsoft.com.

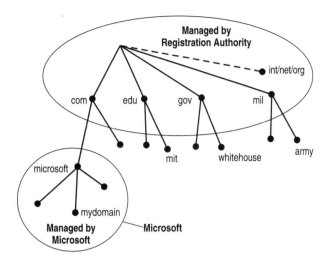

Figure 2.15 A DNS tree with a host named mydomain within the microsoft.com domain

DNS and the Internet

The Internet DNS is managed by a name registration authority on the Internet that's responsible for maintaining top-level domains that are assigned by organization and by country/region. These domain names follow the International Standard 3166. The existing abbreviations are listed in Table 2.5.

Table 2.5 Top-Level Domains

DNS Domain Name	Type of Organization
com	Commercial organizations
edu	Educational institutions
org	Nonprofit organizations
net	Networks (the backbone of the Internet)
gov	Nonmilitary government organizations
mil	Military government organizations
num	Phone numbers
arpa	Reverse DNS
xx	Two-letter country/region code

DNS Resource Records

A DNS database is made up of resource records (RRs). Each RR identifies a particular resource within the database. There are various types of RRs in DNS. Table 2.6 provides information on the structure of some of the common RRs. They're part of the Internet (IN) class of RRs.

Table 2.6 Common RRs

Description	TTL	Type	Data Options
Start of Authority	Default TTL is 60 minutes	SOA	Owner Name, Primary Name Server DNS Name, Serial Number, Refresh Interval, Retry Interval, Expire Time, Minimum TTL
Host	Zone (SOA) TTL	A	Owner Name (Host DNS Name), Host IP Address
Name Server	Zone (SOA) TTL	NS	Owner Name, Name Server DNS Name
Mail Exchanger	Zone (SOA) TTL	MX	Owner Name, Mail Exchange Server DNS Name, Preference Number
Canonical Name (an alias)	Zone (SOA) TTL	CNAME	Owner Name (Alias Name), Host DNS Name

DNS Zones

You can partition a DNS database into multiple zones. A *zone* is a portion of the DNS database that contains the RRs with the owner names that belong to the contiguous portion of the DNS namespace. Zone files are maintained on DNS servers. You can configure a single DNS server to host zero, one, or multiple zones.

Each zone is anchored at a specific domain name, which is referred to as the zone's *root domain*. A zone contains information about all names that end with the zone's root domain name. A DNS server is considered authoritative for a name if it loads the zone containing that name. The first record in any zone file is a Start of Authority (SOA) RR. The SOA RR identifies a primary DNS name server for the zone as the best source of information for the data within that zone and as an entity that processes the updates for the zone.

You can also delegate names within a zone to other zones. Delegation is a process of assigning responsibility for a portion of a DNS namespace to a separate entity. This separate entity could be another organization, department, or workgroup within your company. In technical terms, delegating means assigning authority over portions of your DNS namespace to other zones. Such delegation is represented by the NS record that specifies the delegated zone and the DNS name of the server that's authoritative for that zone. Delegating across multiple zones was part of the original design goal of DNS.

In Figure 2.16, the management of the microsoft.com domain is delegated across two zones: microsoft.com and mydomain.microsoft.com.

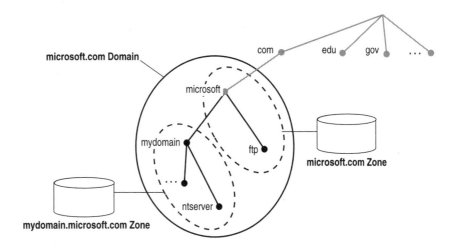

Figure 2.16 Delegating a domain across two zones

Note If multiple NS records exist for a delegated zone identifying multiple DNS servers available for querying, the Windows 2000 DNS server will be able to select the closest DNS server based on the round-trip intervals measured over time for every DNS server.

DNS Replication

Multiple zones can represent the same portion of a namespace. In this situation there are two types of zones: primary and secondary. A primary zone is one in which all updates for the records that belong to that zone are made. A secondary zone is represented by a read-only copy of the primary zone. The changes made to the primary zone file are then replicated to the secondary zone file.

A name server can host multiple zones. A server can therefore be primary for one zone (it has the master copy of the zone file) and secondary for another zone (it gets a read-only copy of the zone file).

The process of replicating a zone file to multiple name servers is called *zone transfer*. Zone transfer is achieved by copying the zone file information from the master server to the secondary server. A master server is the source of the zone information. The master server can be primary or secondary. If the master is primary, then the zone transfer comes directly from the source. If the master server is secondary, the file received from the master server by means of a zone transfer is a copy of the read-only zone file.

The zone transfer is initiated in one of the following ways:

- The master server sends a notification (RFC 1996) of a change in the zone to the secondary server.
- When the secondary server's DNS service starts or the secondary server's refresh interval (15 minutes by default) has expired, it will query the primary server for the changes.

DNS and Active Directory

You can't install Active Directory without having DNS on your network, because Active Directory uses DNS as its location service. However, you can install DNS without Active Directory. If you install DNS on a domain controller, you can also choose whether or not to use Active Directory to provide storage and replication for DNS. Using Active Directory for storage and replication provides the following benefits:

- Increased fault tolerance
- Security
- Easier management
- More efficient replication of large zones

In addition to storing zone files on DNS servers, you can store a primary zone in Active Directory. When you store a zone in Active Directory, zone data is stored as Active Directory objects and replicated as part of Active Directory replication.

Active Directory replication provides an advantage over standard DNS alone. With standard DNS, only the primary server for a zone can modify the zone. With Active Directory replication, all domain controllers for the domain can modify the zone and then replicate the changes to other domain controllers. This replication process is called *multimaster replication* because multiple domain controllers, or *masters*, can update the zone.

In multimaster replication, any domain controller can send or receive updates of information stored in Active Directory. Replication processing is performed on a per property basis, which means that only relevant changes are propagated. Replication processing differs from DNS full zone transfers, in which the entire zone is propagated. Replication processing also differs from incremental zone transfers, in which the server transfers all changes made since the last change. With Active Directory replication, however, only the final result of all changes to a record is sent.

When you store a primary zone in Active Directory, the zone information is replicated to all domain controllers within the Active Directory domain. Every DNS server running on a domain controller is then authoritative for that zone and can update it.

Although you can still perform standard zone transfers with Active Directory–integrated zones, Active Directory multimaster replication provides greater fault tolerance than using standard zone transfers alone. Standard zone transfers and updates rely on a single primary DNS server to update all the secondary servers. With Active Directory replication, however, there's no single point of failure for zone updates.

In an integrated zone, domain controllers for each of your Active Directory domains correspond in a direct one-to-one mapping to DNS servers. When you troubleshoot DNS and Active Directory replication problems, the same server computers are used in both topologies, which simplifies planning, deployment, and troubleshooting.

Using directory-integrated storage also simplifies dynamic updates for DNS clients that are running Windows 2000. When you configure a list of preferred and alternate DNS servers for each client, you can specify servers corresponding to domain controllers located near each client. If a client fails to update with its preferred server because the server is unavailable, the client can try an alternate server. When the preferred server becomes available, it loads the updated, directory-integrated zone that includes the updates that the client made.

If you're not using Active Directory, you need standard primary zones to create and manage zones in your DNS namespace. In this case a single-master update model applies, with one DNS server designated as the primary server for a zone. Only the primary server, as determined in the SOA record properties for the zone, can process an update to the zone. For this reason, make sure that this DNS server is reliable and available. Otherwise, clients can't update their A or PTR RRs.

Active Directory is discussed in more detail in Chapter 8, "Directory Services."

Internet Access

For your organization to be visible on the Internet, you must have an external namespace (public namespace) that anyone on the Internet can access. However, to help prevent malicious access to your network, you can use an internal namespace (private namespace) that only users within your organization can see, thus preventing unauthorized people from learning the names and IP addresses of the computers on your network.

If you plan to have both an internal and external namespace, you must configure your DNS servers to enable internal clients to resolve names in both namespaces. How you plan your namespace depends on the type of clients that you have.

Planning the Namespace

When planning your namespace, you must decide whether to use a private root and whether you want your internal and external namespaces to have the same domain name. Whether you can use a private root depends on the type of clients you have. You can use a private root only if each of your clients has one of the following:

- **Name exclusion list**   A list of DNS suffixes that are internal
- **Proxy autoconfiguration (PAC) file**   A list of DNS suffixes and exact names that are internal or external

If you have clients lacking both of these, the DNS server hosting your organization's top-level internal domain must forward queries to the Internet.

Table 2.7 shows whether you can use a private root, based on the your client's proxy capability.

Table 2.7   Using Private Roots

	No Proxy	Local Address Table (LAT)	Name Exclusion List	PAC File
Microsoft software with corresponding proxy capability	Generic Telnet	Windows Sockets Proxy (WSP) 1.x, WSP 2.x	WSP 1.x, WSP 2.x, and all versions of Internet Explorer	WSP 2.x, Internet Explorer 3.01 and later
Must you forward queries?	Yes	Yes	No, but you can if you want	No, but you can if you want
Can you use a private root?	No	No	Yes	Yes

To simplify name resolution for internal clients, use a different domain name for your internal and external namespaces. For example, you can use the name contoso-ext.com for your external namespace and contoso.com for your internal namespace. You can also use the name contoso.com for your external namespace and noam.contoso.com for your internal namespace. However, you should not make your external domain a subdomain of your internal domain; that is, in the context of this example, don't use contoso.com for your internal namespace and noam.contoso.com for your external namespace.

You can use the same name internally and externally, but doing so causes configuration problems and generally increases administrative overhead. If you want to use the same domain name internally and externally, you need to perform one of the following actions:

- Duplicate internally the public DNS zone of your organization.
- Duplicate internally the public DNS zone and all public servers (such as Web servers) that belong to your organization.
- Maintain a list (in the PAC file on each of your clients) of the public servers that belong to your organization.

Caution Make sure that the domain name for your internal namespace isn't used anywhere on the Internet. Otherwise you might have problems with ambiguity in the name resolution process.

Which action you need to perform to use the same domain name internally and externally varies. Table 2.8 shows whether you can use the same domain name for your internal and external namespaces, and if so, which method you must use, based on your client software proxy capability.

Table 2.8   Internal and External Namespaces

	No Proxy	LAT	Name Exclusion List	PAC file
Use different domain names	Yes	Yes	Yes	Possible (by using simple exclusion)
Use the same domain name; internally duplicating organization's public DNS namespace (records)	Yes	Yes (by populating LAT)	No	Possible (when a PAC file is used and duplicated external records aren't used)
Use the same domain name; internally duplicating organization's public DNS namespace and public servers	Yes	Yes	Yes	Yes
Use the same domain name; maintaining list of public servers in the PAC files.	No	No	No	Yes

Making a Decision

When you plan the DNS hierarchy and namespace for your network configuration, you must take into account two primary considerations when implementing an Internet connection to your network: whether you'll integrate DNS with Active Directory and whether you'll use separate domain names for your internal and external namespaces. Table 2.9 provides an overview of both of these considerations.

Table 2.9   DNS Hierarchy and Namespaces

Strategy	Description
Active Directory integration	If you install DNS on a domain controller, you can choose whether or not to use Active Directory to provide storage and replication for DNS. However, full Active Directory integration provides greater fault tolerance by supporting integrated storage and multimaster replication. If you don't use Active Directory integration, a standard primary zone becomes a single point of failure for dynamic updates and zone replication.

(continued)

Table 2.9   *(continued)*

Strategy	Description
Separate domain names	You can use the same name for your external and internal namespaces, or you can use different names. Using the same name causes configuration problems and increases administrative overhead. It's generally recommended that you use separate names.

Recommendations

The DNS Service should be fully integrated with Active Directory to provide a fault-tolerant name service for your network. In addition, you should use separate names for your external and internal namespaces in order to reduce configuration problems and decrease administrative overhead.

Example: A DNS Namespace

A company named Contoso has acquired a second company. The first organization, which has reserved the DNS domain names contoso-int.com and contoso-ext.com, has only proxy clients that support either exclusion lists or PACs. In contrast, the second organization, which has reserved the DNS domain names acquired01-int.com and acquired01-ext.com, has no such proxy clients. Both organizations use a different domain name for their internal and external namespaces.

The merged companies require a configuration that does the following:

- Exposes only the public part of the organization's namespace to the Internet
- Enables any computer within the organization to resolve any internal or external name
- Enables any computer within the organization to resolve any name from the Internet
- Allows each private namespace to be able to resolve any name from the other namespace

Figure 2.17 shows how the DNS domains should be configured in this scenario.

Configuring the External Namespace

In the external namespace, two zones exist: contoso-ext.com and acquired01-ext.com. The zones contain only the records (the names and delegations) that the companies want to expose to the outside world. The server named server.contoso-ext.com hosts the contoso-ext.com zone, and the server named server.acquired01-ext.com hosts the acquired01-ext.com zone. The names contoso-ext.com and acquired01-ext.com must be registered with an Internet name authority.

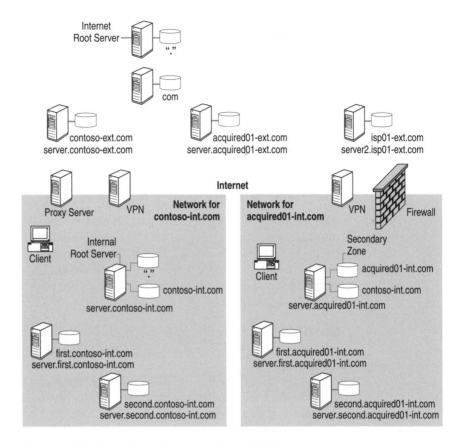

Figure 2.17   Example configuration of the DNS domains

Configuring the Internal Namespace

The internal namespace for the organization that hosts contoso-ext.com externally is contoso-int.com. Similarly, the internal namespace for the organization that hosts acquired01-ext.com externally is acquired01-int.com. The server named server.contoso-int.com hosts the contoso-int.com zone, and the server named server.acquired01-int.com hosts the acquired01-int.com zone. The names contoso-int.com and acquired01-int.com must be registered with an Internet name authority.

All the computers in contoso-int.com support either exclusion lists or PACs, and none of the computers in acquired01-int.com support exclusion lists or PACs.

Namespace Without Proxy Clients That Support Exclusion Lists or PACs

For a namespace in which none of the computers are proxy clients that support either exclusion lists or PACs (in this example, the namespace of acquired01-int.com), an organization must devote one or more DNS servers to maintain zones that contain all names from the internal namespace. Every DNS client must send DNS queries to one or more of these DNS servers. If a DNS server contains the zone for the top level of the organization's namespace (for example, acquired01-int.com), then it must forward those queries through a firewall to one or more DNS servers in the Internet namespace. All other DNS servers must forward queries to one or more DNS servers that contain the zone for the top level of the organization's namespace.

To make sure that any client within the organization can resolve any name from the merged organization, every DNS server containing the zone for the top level of the organization's namespace must also contain the zones that include all the internal and external names of the merged organization.

This solution places a significant load on the internal DNS servers that contain the organization's internal top-level zones. Most of the queries generated within the organization are forwarded to these servers, including queries for computers in the external namespace and in the merged organization's private namespace. Also, the servers must contain secondary copies of the merged organization's zones.

Namespace with Proxy Clients That Support Exclusion Lists or PACs

For a namespace in which all of the computers are proxy clients that support either exclusion lists or PACs (for example, the namespace of contoso-int.com), the private namespace can include a private root. One or more root servers can be in the internal namespace, and all other DNS servers must include the name and IP address of a root server in their root hints files.

To resolve internal and external names, every DNS client must submit all queries either to the internal DNS servers or to a proxy server, based on an exclusion list or PAC file. To make sure that every client within the organization can resolve every name from the merged organization, the private root zone must contain a delegation to the zone for the top level of the merged organization.

Using proxy clients and a private root simplifies DNS configuration because none of the DNS servers needs to include a secondary copy of the zone. However, this configuration requires you to create and manage exclusion lists or PAC files, which must be added to every proxy client in the network.

Lesson Summary

DNS is a distributed database used in TCP/IP networks to translate host names to IP addresses. DNS is implemented as a hierarchical and distributed database containing various types of data including host names and domain names. The names in a DNS database form a hierarchical tree structure called the domain namespace. A DNS database is made up of resource records that identify a particular resource within the database. A zone is a portion of the DNS database that contains the resource records with the owner names that belong to the contiguous portion of the DNS namespace. If you install DNS on a domain controller, you can also choose whether or not to use Active Directory to provide storage and replication for DNS. Full Active Directory integration provides greater fault tolerance by supporting integrated storage and multimaster replication. For your organization to be visible on the Internet, you must have an external namespace. When planning your namespace, you must decide whether you want your internal and external namespaces to have the same domain name. Using separate names for your external and internal namespaces reduces configuration problems and decreases administrative overhead.

Lab 2.1: Designing a Highly Available Network Infrastructure

Lab Objectives

After completing this lab, you'll be able to

- Design a network topology that incorporates redundant components and redundant network paths
- Design a subnet addressing structure for a TCP/IP network supporting a Web environment
- Design a DNS namespace for a Windows 2000 network that connects to the Internet

About This Lab

In this lab you'll have the opportunity to apply much of the information that you learned in this chapter by designing a highly available network topology. The lab is structured by first presenting a scenario that outlines the basic considerations that you'll need to take into account when you design the network infrastructure. The rest of the lab is divided into exercises, each of which focuses on a particular design element. The lab focuses primarily on redundant components and paths, network subnetting, and namespace design. It's only peripherally concerned with redundant services and the DHCP environment—with regard to how they apply to high availability—because the DHCP service and other services are made redundant though the use of clustering, which is discussed in greater detail in subsequent chapters. In addition, the lab doesn't incorporate DNS fault tolerance because that's implemented through Active Directory in order to ensure high availability. Active Directory is also discussed later in this book. As a result, the exercises are limited to the primary areas of focus, with the understanding that clustering solutions appear merely as *placeholders* at this phase of the design process and that clustering—along with Active Directory—will be incorporated into the network design later.

Before You Begin

Before you begin this lab, you must be able to

- Design a basic network topology
- Subnet a TCP/IP network
- Design a DNS namespace

Scenario: The Contoso Web Site

Contoso, Ltd., is a new company that plans to create a Web site that provides immunization and prophylaxis information to international travelers. The site will serve two purposes. The first is to provide general information about individual countries/regions in terms of immunization and prophylaxis requirements and recommendations. The information will include specific details about legal requirements, paperwork, drugs, side effects, diseases, and any other information related to health issues when traveling in different parts of the world. Initially, the site will target English-speaking travelers from around the world and will include any destination for which information can be obtained. Income will be generated through site advertisements. The site's second purpose is to provide a subscription-based service that maintains a record of where individuals have traveled, what immunizations and prophylaxis they received, and what risks they were exposed to. At any time, clients can know which vaccines or drugs they've taken and when. The information is also helpful if a person who develops symptoms after returning home needs to know what he or she may have been exposed to.

Because users must be able to access site information from any region in the world at any time of day, the site must be available around the clock. However, the company currently can support only one geographical location, so high availability must be designed into a single location and client records must be absolutely secure. The company has registered the name contoso.com with an Internet name authority.

You must design a network topology that meets the company's requirements. For the purpose of this lab, your main concern is the Web portion of the network topology. You can assume that the secure part of the corporate network will be a typical Ethernet topology that's connected to the Web topology through a router/firewall connection.

Exercise 1: Providing Redundant Components and Network Paths

Your first step in designing the network topology is to design a system that contains redundant components, paths, and services. As stated above, redundant services are implemented as clusters, so you need only to indicate their placement in the design. You plan to use a multitiered topology and create a perimeter network to support the Web portion of the network design. In addition, you plan to use switches rather then hubs within the perimeter network. You'll begin with a topology similar to the one in Figure 2.18.

You must now add redundancy to the network topology.

1. What network elements can you make redundant for this topology?

2. On a piece of paper, sketch a design that builds on the design in Figure 2.18. Be sure to incorporate any network elements that can be made redundant. How should you modify your design?

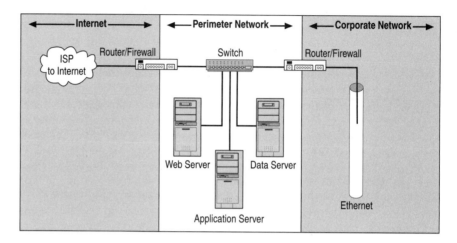

Figure 2.18   Basic network topology with a perimeter network

3. Suppose a computer in the application cluster tries to communicate with the data cluster. What possible LAN paths can that communication follow?

Exercise 2: Subnetting a TCP/IP Network

Once you've designed a redundant topology, you can now segment your network in order to create a multitiered environment. You don't necessarily have to wait to subnet your environment until after you've designed a redundant topology. You can create your subnetted structure before you design redundancy into the topology or as you're designing the redundant structure. The step is separated here in order to provide a better overview of the design process.

To subnet the network, you should determine how many network segments you'll use for the part of your network that isn't exposed to the Internet. Base your decision on the diagram illustrated in the answer to Exercise 1.

1. How many network segments will you use and where will you use them?

2. On your sketch of the network topology, label the four network segments and indicate the position of those segments. Your network topology should also indicate the position of the front-end network. How should you modify your design?

3. To which network segments do the Web clusters connect?

Exercise 3: Designing a Namespace

The next step in creating your network topology is to design the DNS namespace. The company has already registered the name contoso.com with an Internet name authority. You can choose to use the same name for your external and internal namespaces, or you can use different names.

1. How should you set up the internal and external namespaces?

2. You decide to use separate names for your external and internal namespaces: contoso.com for the external namespace and contoso-pvt.com for the internal namespace. On your sketch of the network topology, label how the namespaces are divided so the division between the two namespaces is clear. How should you modify your design?

3. Suppose that one of the servers in Web cluster 1 is named Web1. What would be the FQDN for that server?

4. Suppose that one of the servers in the application cluster is named App1. What would be the FQDN for that server?

Review

Answering the following questions will reinforce key information presented in this chapter. If you're unable to answer a question, review the appropriate lesson and then try the question again. Answers to the questions can be found in the appendix.

1. The network topology for your organization includes a Web component that provides information and online registration for your company's training facilities. Figure 2.19 shows the Web component of your network topology.

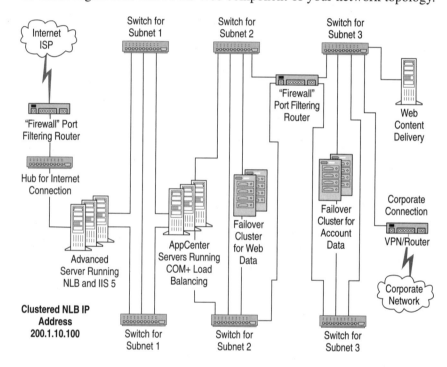

Figure 2.19   Network topology for multitiered Web site

Many users have been complaining that your site is often unavailable. You plan to modify the network topology to increase availability. What's the first step you should take?

2. When you subnet the network shown in Figure 2.19, you assign the network ID 10.10.1.0 to subnet 1, 10.10.2.0 to subnet 2, and 10.10.3.0 to subnet 3. What additional subnet should you add to this topology?

3. You're planning the configuration of the DHCP service for your network and want to ensure fault tolerance. However, you won't be implementing clustering. You set up a primary DHCP server and a backup DHCP server. How should you configure any scopes that you create?

4. Your company, Contoso, Ltd., plans to set up a Web site so customers can access services on the Internet. Until now, your company has had no Web presence. Your company has registered the name contoso.com with an Internet name authority and wants to use that name for both the internal and external namespaces. What actions must you perform to use the same name?

CHAPTER 3

Server Configurations

About This Chapter

When you design a highly available network, you should make server configurations part of the planning process in order to ensure that services continue to function in the event of a hardware or software failure or data corruption. You can make a server more available by using redundant and cold- or hot-swappable components and by providing an environment that safely houses the servers, their network connections, and other network components. You should also implement a data storage strategy that ensures against data loss and reduces the mean time between failures (MTBF) in the event of lost data. In this chapter you'll learn how to design a server configuration and data storage system that are fault-tolerant.

Before You Begin

To complete the lessons in this chapter, you must have

- A basic understanding of the hardware components in a computer

- An understanding of how to maintain hard disks and implement disk storage strategies such as redundant array of independent disks (RAID)

Lesson 1: Designing a Fault-Tolerant System

When designing a highly available network infrastructure, you must ensure that your Microsoft Windows 2000 Server computers remain available to the network. One way to ensure this availability is to use redundant components within the servers or to provide readily available backup components. Another way to ensure availability is to make certain that the environment in which the servers are located facilitates a highly available operation and that the servers have a supply of uninterruptible power. In this lesson you'll learn how to design a server configuration that's fault tolerant and how to ensure a safe environment for those servers so that they remain highly available.

After this lesson, you will be able to

- Plan a server configuration that uses redundant components to help ensure a highly available Web site
- Plan a server environment that protects the servers

Estimated lesson time: 30 minutes

Highly Available Configurations

Although it's important to be prepared for problems, you can take steps to protect against certain failures, such as disk failures, component problems, network problems, and power failures. You can implement hardware and software configurations to help reduce the likelihood of problems that result in costly downtime and recovery processes.

Computers running Windows 2000 Server have fault tolerance features built into the operating system. *Fault tolerance* is the ability of a computer or operating system to respond to a catastrophic event—a power outage or hardware failure, for example—so that no data is lost and that work in progress isn't corrupted. Although the term is often applied to disk subsystems, it also can refer to any piece of hardware that uses redundancy to ensure the system's availability. In a fully fault-tolerant system, every major component is made redundant. For example, such a system includes redundant disk controllers, power supplies, uninterruptible power supplies (UPSs), disk subsystems, and other redundant components. In such a system, every single point of failure is eliminated.

To ensure that your servers are configured to support high availability, you should use redundant and backup components and provide an environment that protects the servers.

Redundant Components

You can help to ensure a highly available network by using redundant components within your Windows 2000 Server computers or by having backup components on hand. This section provides information about many of the server components that you can make fault-tolerant.

NICs

A network interface card (NIC) is an adapter card that plugs into a computer's system bus and allows the computer to send and receive signals on a network. The NIC in most servers is a single point of failure. Fortunately, the NIC is typically very reliable and failures are rare; still, they do occur. You can install multiple NICs in a single server or configure a single NIC with multiple Internet Protocol (IP) addresses. This process is known as *multihoming* a computer. On a Transmission Control Protocol/Internet Protocol (TCP/IP) network, a multihomed machine has a separate IP address assigned to each of its interfaces. Multihoming is typically used to increase bandwidth by providing connectivity to several networks simultaneously.

Installing multiple NICs can also enhance the reliability of critical network servers. If you make a NIC fault tolerant by installing a redundant card, the redundant NIC, which is inactive, shares the device driver with the active NIC. If the device driver detects an unrecoverable error, the driver uses the redundant NIC without interrupting service.

In some cases you can configure each NIC into a subnet separate from the other NICs on the computer. Configuring multiple NICs into separate subnets can enhance both performance and availability. First, performance is improved by shortening the network routes between clients and servers. Second, availability is increased because clients may be able to find alternate routes to critical network services in the event of a failed network adapter.

Note You should take care to configure multiple NICs into separate subnets properly because some network services don't operate as expected on multihomed hosts.

By installing multiple NICs on separate network segments, administrators can significantly reduce downtime due to network outages of any single segment. For maximum reliability, you should configure the secondary NIC as a backup in case of failures on the primary NIC. In this case the secondary interface is kept in a hot standby mode. If the primary adapter fails, the standby adapter takes over.

In a clustered configuration, you can configure two network segments—one for normal network traffic and a second dedicated to the heartbeat signal used by cluster members to monitor the cluster's health.

Note Although this configuration works, other methods are more effective. For example, you can use a dedicated virtual local area network (VLAN) that supports heartbeat connections between cluster nodes. You can also use redundant direct connections (using cross-over cables) for the heartbeat.

When installing two NICs, make sure that you've run cabling from two separate hubs or switches. Make sure the network cables are color-coded or marked some other way to signify network A and B. This prevents the cables from being plugged into the wrong NIC. In addition, always use fixed IP addresses on these servers and don't use Dynamic Host Configuration Protocol (DHCP) to prevent an outage due to the failure of the DHCP server. This strategy can improve address resolution by Domain Name System (DNS) servers that don't handle the dynamic address assignment that DHCP provides.

Motherboard and CPU

Motherboards consist of electronics that can and do fail, although the motherboard and the central processing unit (CPU) are generally reliable computer components. You can't do very much to prevent a motherboard failure or CPU fault, except to run regular system checks to ensure that the components are functioning correctly. Some systems include built-in diagnostic tools that operate with Windows 2000.

Memory

The three major types of random access memory (RAM) that deal with error detection and correction are nonparity RAM, parity RAM, and error-correction coding (ECC) RAM.

- **Nonparity RAM**   If you use nonparity RAM, Windows 2000 has no way to detect memory problems and your computer might crash randomly. Nonparity RAM costs less than parity RAM, and parity RAM isn't available for all computers. If you don't have parity RAM in your computers, ask your vendor if it can be installed or if your computer supports it.

- **Parity RAM**   Parity RAM contains an extra bit that indicates whether a byte in the RAM is faulty. When parity RAM detects a parity difference, it signals the CPU through a nonmaskable interrupt (NMI). Depending on where and when detection happens, Windows 2000 determines if this is an input/output (I/O) board parity error, memory bus error, or some other kind of parity error. Windows 2000 can also report I/O channel parity errors from cards in slots. In these cases an error message is generated, and sometimes the computer stops. Parity memory isn't fault tolerant because even if it does detect a memory error, the memory can't correct it. Thus, the server halts operation—abruptly.

- **ECC RAM**   High-end systems often use ECC RAM, which can detect a two-bit failure and correct a single-bit failure in the system memory. With ECC RAM, Windows 2000 can continue to run in spite of a single-bit failure. Depending on the hardware design, there might or might not be a report of this corrective action. For maximum memory fault tolerance, choose advanced ECC memory whenever possible.

Be aware that even with ECC, memory chips do fail. Try to keep enough memory on hand to replace a computer's entire memory. If memory check errors become frequent, or the machine won't boot, replace all of the memory chips rather than spend time trying to figure out which one is bad. You can find the faulty chip at your leisure.

Cooling

Cooling is one of the most overlooked elements of a server. Should the cooling fan fail, the processors, hard drives, or controller cards might overheat and fail. If the computer feels extremely warm when you open the chassis, a cooling fan might have failed. Most servers have two or more fans to protect against overheating in this circumstance. Some servers also have thermal sensors to detect abnormal temperatures.

Power Supplies

Although power supplies are very reliable, they do fail. Most middle to high-end servers offer the option of multiple power supplies. If one of the power supplies should fail, another continues to provide power. When using dual power supplies, you should use two separate power feeds. Using two power feeds protects against a circuit breaker tripping or some other accidental event. Also, don't forget about external cabinets for RAID arrays or modem banks. If they have power supplies, check and see if dual supplies are available.

Disk Controllers

The disk controller, like other components, can be a single point of failure. If the controller fails, the data stored on the hard disks is not accessible until that controller is replaced, whether or not the disks themselves have been made fault-tolerant. Redundant controllers provide a level of fault tolerance that eliminates the single point of failure that exists when a system is configured with only one controller.

Storage

Storage strategies are based on the type and quantity of information that must be stored and the cost of equipment. If a particular computer isn't used to store data, the storage solution can be simple and inexpensive. However, if the computer will be used to store large amounts of data and to perform frequent database reads and writes, the storage strategy is more complicated. Consider the cost of any storage components when developing a strategy for storing the data that your organization needs. It doesn't make sense to spend more on the storage system than the expected cost recovery in which you may lose time and data. Storage strategies are discussed in more detail in Lesson 2, "Designing Data Storage for High Availability."

Environmental Concerns

When addressing environmental concerns, you must ensure that the network components, particularly servers, are protected from extremes in temperature and humidity. You must also keep them clean. In addition, you should provide a UPS and set up cables in a way that follows specific guidelines.

Temperature, Humidity, and Cleanliness

Computers perform best at a temperature of approximately 70° F (21° C). A long rack of computers can generate a huge amount of heat, which would raise the surrounding air temperature to unacceptable levels. For this reason, almost all computer rooms have some form of cooling or air conditioning. When adding servers to a computer room, be careful to make sure you won't exceed the room's cooling capacity. If the temperature greatly exceeds 70° F (21° C), you could have problems.

Humidity can be an important factor as well, provided it's high enough to create condensation or low enough to create static. Obviously, water condensing in a computer could cause that computer to fail. In addition, you don't want mold forming on the computers that could affect cooling or cause a short circuit. Too-dry air also can present a problem, as people near the computer can develop static in those conditions. A good static jolt can damage internal components or cause the computer to restart.

Cleanliness is very important for computers; dust and dirt can cause shorts and, in extreme conditions, fires. For computer-room computers, whenever the case is opened for any reason, a quick check should be made to determine if the unit needs cleaning. If it does, you should check all the units in the area.

You should check computers in office areas quarterly, or more often if they're in a dirty area. For computers on a plant floor or in other hazardous areas, an enclosure with air filtration and climate control is a necessity. You should clean the air filters on the cabinet according to the manufacturer's recommendation. At the same time, you should check and clean the computer and its cabinet if you need to.

Power

A computer won't run without power, and power grids aren't always that reliable. Consequently, backup power may be a necessity, to at least allow the computer to shut down in a controlled manner. There are two scopes of outages: the first is building or computer-room failure and the second is a regional outage.

In building power failures, particularly in a corporate computer center, it may be necessary to continue providing service to other buildings in the area or to areas geographically remote from the computer center. In this instance short outages can be survived by using UPS units. Standby generators can handle longer outages.

Most UPS devices are one of the following types:

- **Online UPS**   An online UPS is connected between the computer and the main power source that supplies power to your computer. The main power continuously charges the batteries that supply the power to the computer. Connecting it to the main power keeps its battery charged. This method provides power conditioning, which means that it removes spikes, surges, sags, and noise.

- **Standby UPS**   A device configured to provide either the main power or its own power source and to switch from one to the other as necessary. When main power is available, the UPS device connects the main power directly to the computer and monitors the main power voltage level. When the main power fails or the voltage falls below an acceptable level, the UPS device switches to its own power.

There are two strategies for using UPS: implementing one large unit or implementing many small units. Using a large UPS system to cover the entire computer room has the advantage of being easier to maintain and monitor. However, it's a big problem if it doesn't work. You should test the system regularly, preferably on weekends or holidays.

The other strategy is for every computer to have its own UPS. This tends to be more practical for computers outside of a computer room. The advantage of these systems is that they can interface directly with the computer to signal a shutdown warning when the battery power drops to a set point. The other advantage is that a breaker trip or some other isolated power outage won't shut down the computer. The disadvantage of these units is that maintenance is more involved because of the number of units, both from the point of view of record keeping and the physical replacement of batteries and testing of units.

When an area experiences a regional power outage, the UPS and generators may work fine but telecommunication links may fail. A regional failure can be very expensive if your company has distributed locations in the same region or your business is actively involved with e-commerce or the Internet. The best alternative in this case is to have another facility in a geographically separate location. This facility should duplicate as many server resources as is practical.

Cables

You need to consider what can fail in the connections between computers as well as within an individual computer. When working with cables, you should adhere to the following guidelines:

- Make sure cables are neat and orderly, either with a cable management system or tie wraps. Cables should never be loose in a cabinet; this could potentially result in accidental disconnects of cables.

- Use strain relief whenever possible to secure the cables to something the computer is connected to—with pull-out rack mounted equipment in particular. This way a tug on the cable won't pull the cable out of its socket.

- Make sure all cables are securely attached at both ends wherever possible.

- If you use multiple sources of power or network communications, try to route the cables feeding the cabinets from different points. This way, if one is severed, the other will likely still be functional.

- Label all cables at both ends if possible. Color-coding with tape or labels helps as well.
- Make sure rack-mounted pull-out equipment has enough slack in the cables and that the cables won't bind or be pinched or scraped.
- Don't plug dual power supplies into the same power strip or use the same power sources.
- Don't leave loose cables in cabinets.
- Make sure that cables can't be accidentally snagged on someone walking by or on a cart. All cables should be inside the cabinet.

Making a Decision

The level of fault tolerance that you can implement in your system often depends on the associated costs of implementing fault-tolerant components and on how much downtime can cost your business. Table 3.1 provides an overview of the issues involved in implementing fault tolerance into your server configurations.

Table 3.1   Implementing Fault Tolerance

Strategy	Description
Redundant NICs	Multiple NICs provide some fault tolerance for your network connections. However, if the NICs are on the same subnet, clients might not be able to find critical services if the primary NIC fails or the network path fails. Installing NICs on separate subnets allows clients to find alternative routes to the services.
Motherboard/CPU maintenance	In some systems, there is little you can do to avoid a motherboard failure or CPU fault, except to run regular system checks to ensure that the components are functioning correctly. However, some companies, such as Stratus and Marathon Technologies, provide fully fault-tolerant computer systems that include redundant system I/O boards and CPUs.
Fault-tolerant memory	Windows 2000 can't detect memory problems with nonparity RAM. Windows 2000 can detect problems with parity RAM but can't correct the error. With ECC RAM, Windows 2000 can detect and correct a one-bit failure and detect a two-bit failure.
Backup memory	Memory can fail. Enough backup memory should be kept on hand to replace all the memory in a computer should any of the memory fail.

Table 3.1 *(continued)*

Strategy	Description
Redundant cooling fans, power supplies, and disk controllers	Each server should have two or more fans to protect against the failure of a fan and at least two power supplies, each one using a power feed separate from the other. In addition, you can use multiple controllers to remove that point of failure.
Fault-tolerant storage	You should make storage fault-tolerant. Storage strategies are discussed in more detail in Lesson 2, "Designing Data Storage for High Availability."
Proper environment	You should maintain temperature, humidity, and cleanliness to ensure that servers don't risk failure.
Redundant power	UPS can be implemented on a large scale for a group of computers or implemented for individual computers. A large UPS is easier to maintain but is a major problem if it fails at a critical moment. Individual UPS systems require more maintenance but provide greater reliability. To protect against regional power failures, you should set up alternate sites in separate geographical areas.
Proper cable maintenance	You should properly maintain cables and make connections secure.

Recommendations

When configuring the server, use multiple NICs installed in separate subnets. In addition, use ECC RAM and keep enough memory on hand to replace all the memory in the computer. Each server should also have redundant cooling fans, power supplies, and disk controllers that support a fault-tolerant storage subsystem.

In addition to configuring a server with redundant components, pay careful attention to the environment in which they're to be located. Maintain temperature, humidity, and cleanliness to ensure that servers don't risk failure, and maintain cables according to recommended guidelines. Connect the servers to a UPS. If possible, each server should have its own UPS. To prepare for regional power failures, your network should, ideally, have at least one other facility in another geographical region.

Example: A Fault-Tolerant System

Organizations must determine how much money they want to invest in each server to provide fault tolerance. Figure 3.1 shows one way that you can configure a Windows 2000 Server computer.

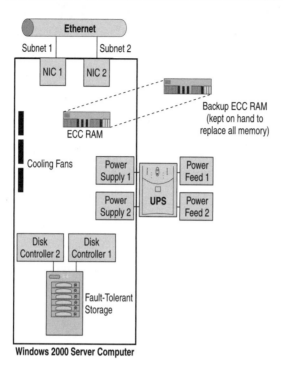

Figure 3.1   A Windows 2000 Server computer configured for fault tolerance

Lesson Summary

You can help to ensure a highly available network by using redundant components within your Windows 2000 Server computers or by having backup components on hand. In addition, you should use regular system checks to ensure that the components are functioning correctly. Installing multiple NICs in a computer can enhance the reliability of critical network servers. The three major types of RAM that deal with error detection and correction are nonparity RAM, parity RAM, and ECC RAM, which provides the greatest fault tolerance. You should keep enough backup ECC memory on hand to replace all the computer's memory. Each server should also include redundant cooling fans, power supplies, and disk controllers. When addressing environmental concerns, you must ensure that the network components are protected from extremes in temperature and humidity and that the server environment is kept clean. You should set up cables in a way that follows specific guidelines and provide a UPS.

Lesson 2: Designing Data Storage for High Availability

Fully fault-tolerant systems use fault-tolerant disk arrays, such as RAID, or storage area networks (SANs) to prevent the loss of data. In this lesson you'll learn how to design a fault-tolerant data storage system by using RAID or SANs.

After this lesson, you will be able to

- Design a data storage system that uses RAID to provide fault tolerance
- Incorporate a SAN into your data storage system to provide fault tolerance

Estimated lesson time: 30 minutes

Disk Fault Tolerance

One method you can use to protect data is RAID. RAID provides fault tolerance by implementing data redundancy. With data redundancy, a computer writes data to more than one disk, which protects the data in the event of a single hard disk failure. You can implement RAID fault tolerance as either a software or hardware solution. The software implementation is available in Windows 2000 Server.

Although the data is available and current in a fault-tolerant system, you should still make backups to protect the information on hard disks from erroneous deletions, fire, theft, or other disasters. Disk fault tolerance isn't an alternative to a backup strategy with offsite storage, which is the best insurance for recovering lost or damaged data.

If you experience the loss of a hard disk due to mechanical or electrical failure and haven't implemented fault tolerance, your only option for recovering the data on the failed drive is to replace the hard disk and restore your data from a backup. However, the loss of access to the data while you replace the hard disk and restore your data can translate into lost time and money.

To store large amounts of data, you can use a SAN to make data available in the event of a disaster. A SAN provides fault tolerance on a large scale.

Software Implementations of RAID

With software implementations of RAID, there's no fault tolerance following a failure until the fault is repaired. If a second fault occurs before the data lost from the first fault is regenerated, you can recover the data only by restoring it from a backup.

Windows 2000 Server supports two software implementations of RAID that provide fault tolerance: mirrored volumes (RAID-1) and striped volumes with parity (RAID-5). In Windows 2000, you can create new RAID volumes only on Windows 2000 dynamic disks.

Note When you upgrade Windows NT 4 to Windows 2000, any existing mirror sets or stripe sets with parity are retained. Windows 2000 provides limited support for these fault tolerance sets, allowing you to manage and delete them.

Mirrored Volumes (RAID-1)

A *mirrored volume* uses the Windows 2000 Server fault tolerance driver (FTDISK.SYS) to write the same data to a volume on each of two physical disks simultaneously, as shown in Figure 3.2. Each volume is considered a member of the mirrored volume. Implementing a mirrored volume helps to ensure the survival of data in the event that one member of the mirrored volume fails.

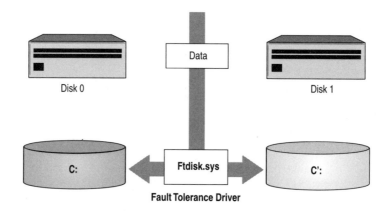

Figure 3.2   Mirrored volume

A mirrored volume can contain any partition, including the boot or system partition; however, both disks in a mirrored volume must be Windows 2000 dynamic disks.

Performance on Mirrored Volumes   Mirrored volumes can enhance read performance because the fault tolerance driver reads from both members of the volume at once. There can be a slight decrease in write performance because the fault tolerance driver must write to both members. When one member of a mirrored volume fails, performance returns to normal because the fault tolerance driver works with only a single partition.

Because disk space usage is only 50 percent (two members for one set of data), mirrored volumes can be expensive.

Caution   Deleting a mirrored volume will delete all the information stored on both disks.

Disk Duplexing

If the same disk controller controls both physical disks in a mirrored volume and the disk controller fails, neither member of the mirrored volume is accessible. You can install a second controller in the computer so that each disk in the mirrored volume has its own controller. This arrangement, called *disk duplexing*, can protect the mirrored volume against both controller failure and hard disk failure. Some hardware implementations of disk duplexing use two or more channels on a single disk controller card.

Disk duplexing reduces bus traffic and potentially improves read performance. Disk duplexing is a hardware enhancement to a Windows 2000 mirrored volume and requires no additional software configuration.

Striped Volumes with Parity (RAID-5)

Windows 2000 Server also supports fault tolerance through striped volumes with parity. *Parity* is a mathematical method of determining the number of odd and even bits in a number or series of numbers, which you can use to reconstruct data if one number in a sequence of numbers is lost.

In a RAID-5 volume, Windows 2000 achieves fault tolerance by adding a parity-information stripe to each disk partition in the volume, as shown in Figure 3.3. If a single disk fails, Windows 2000 can use the data and parity information on the remaining disks to reconstruct the data that was on the failed disk.

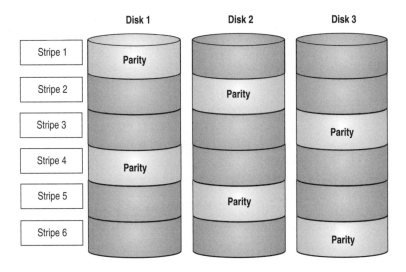

Figure 3.3   RAID-5 parity-information stripes

Because of the parity calculation, write operations on a RAID-5 volume are slower than on a mirrored volume. However, RAID-5 volumes provide better read performance than mirrored volumes, especially with multiple controllers, because data is distributed among multiple drives. If a disk fails, however, the read performance on a RAID-5 volume slows while Windows 2000 Server reconstructs the data for the failed disk by using parity information.

RAID-5 volumes have a cost advantage over mirrored volumes because disk usage is optimized. The more disks you have in the RAID-5 volume, the less the cost of the redundant data stripe. Table 3.2 shows how the amount of space required for the data stripe decreases with the addition of 2-gigabyte (GB) disks to the RAID-5 volume.

Table 3.2   RAID-5 Redundancy

Number of Disks	Disk Space Used	Available Disk Space	Redundancy
3	6 GB	4 GB	33 percent
4	8 GB	6 GB	25 percent
5	10 GB	8 GB	20 percent

RAID-5 volumes implement some software restrictions. First, RAID-5 volumes involve a minimum of 3 drives and a maximum of 32 drives. Second, a software-level RAID-5 volume can't contain the boot or system partition.

The Windows 2000 operating system isn't aware of RAID implementations in hardware. Therefore, the restrictions that apply to software-level RAID don't apply to hardware-level RAID configurations.

RAID-1 Volumes vs. RAID-5 Volumes

RAID-1 volumes and RAID-5 volumes provide different levels of fault tolerance. Deciding which option to implement depends on the level of protection you require and the cost of hardware. The major differences between RAID-1 and RAID-5 volumes are performance and cost. Table 3.3 describes some differences between software-level RAID-1 and RAID-5.

Table 3.3   Comparing RAID-1 and RAID-5

Mirrored Volumes (RAID-1)	Striped Volumes with Parity (RAID-5)
Supports file allocation table (FAT) and NT file system (NTFS)	Supports FAT and NTFS
Can protect system or boot partition	Can't protect system or boot partition
Requires two hard disks	Requires a minimum of 3 hard disks and allows a maximum of 32 hard disks
Has a higher cost per megabyte	Has a lower cost per megabyte
50 percent used for redundancy	Equivalent of one physical drive used for redundancy

Table 3.3 *(continued)*

Mirrored Volumes (RAID-1)	Striped Volumes with Parity (RAID-5)
Has good write performance	Has moderate write performance
Has good read performance	Has excellent read performance
Uses less system memory	Requires more system memory

Generally, mirrored volumes offer read and write performance comparable to that of single disks. RAID-5 volumes offer better read performance than mirrored volumes, especially with multiple controllers, because data is distributed among multiple drives. However, the need to calculate parity information requires more computer memory, which can slow write performance.

Mirroring uses only 50 percent of the available disk space, so it's more expensive in cost per MB than disks without mirroring. RAID-5 uses 33 percent of the available disk space for parity information when you use the minimum number of hard disks (three). With RAID-5, disk utilization improves as you increase the number of hard disks.

Hardware Implementations of RAID

In a hardware solution, the disk controller interface handles the creation and regeneration of redundant information. Some hardware vendors implement RAID data protection directly in their hardware, as with disk array controller cards. Because these methods are vendor specific and bypass the fault tolerance software drivers of the operating system, they offer performance improvements over software implementations of RAID. In addition, hardware implementations of RAID usually include extra features, such as additional fault-tolerant RAID configurations, hot swapping of failed hard disks, hot sparing for online failover, and dedicated cache memory for improved performance.

Note The level of RAID supported in a hardware implementation depends on the hardware manufacturer.

Consider the following points when deciding whether to use a software or hardware implementation of RAID:

- Hardware fault tolerance is more expensive than software fault tolerance.
- Hardware fault tolerance generally provides faster disk I/O than software fault tolerance.
- Hardware fault tolerance solutions might limit equipment options to a single vendor.
- Hardware fault tolerance solutions might implement hot swapping of hard disks to allow for replacement of a failed hard disk without shutting down the computer and hot sparing so that a failed disk is automatically replaced by an online spare.

With hardware RAID, mirrored volumes can be striped across multiple disks. This configuration is often referred to as RAID-10: RAID-1 mirroring and RAID-0 striping. Unlike RAID-0, RAID-10 is a fault-tolerant RAID configuration because each disk in the stripe is also mirrored. RAID-10 improves disk I/O by performing read and write operations across the stripe.

SANs

A *storage area network* (SAN) is an elaborate network comprised of one or more storage systems, each capable of providing terabytes of disk storage capacity at very high transfer rates. Most SANs use Fibre Channel technology and are capable of providing I/O throughputs in the gigabits-per-second (Gbps) range (100 to 200 megabytes per second [MBps] or higher). A SAN also allows for flexible configurations, is very scalable, and ensures high availability for mission-critical data storage.

SANs can improve performance for many applications that move large amounts of data between multiple servers over the network: Network resources are freed up for other transactions, and bulk data transfers are performed on the SAN at a much faster rate by utilizing the SAN Fibre Channel network. For example, before implementing SANs, one organization maintained a large sales database that performed five 70-GB transfers over the network per weekend and incurred 24 hours of planned downtime. With the SAN architecture, the same operation takes only two to three hours and the network isn't used.

Key elements common to different kinds of hardware-specific SANs include the following:

- **Externalized storage**   Storage that isn't installed for private single server access
- **Centralized storage**   Storage that can be centrally located, managed, and controlled
- **Remote clustering**   Storage that enables single server and multiserver access

The hardware components that make up a SAN are similar to those of a network with storage elements but vary depending on the type of SAN being implemented and the hardware vendor. Host servers require Fibre Channel interfaces, known as host bus adapters (HBAs), to interface with the SAN. Storage components such as tape drives, disk drives, RAID controllers, hubs, switches, storage processors, disk enclosures, and arrays make up the SAN itself.

In recent years there's been more and more interest in using SANs to provide fault-tolerant large-scale storage for both files and network applications. However, because of the large initial cost of implementing a SAN, they're generally used only in networks that need more than 100 to 200 GB of storage capacity.

You can use a SAN to centralize your data storage and simplify administration of backups and restores. SANs remove the storage function from general-purpose servers onto a high-speed network specifically designed for moving large amounts of data. This process provides the following advantages:

- Optimal server rack space created by moving disk arrays out of the rack
- Increased security created by storing data in a separate network not vulnerable to currently known types of attacks
- LAN-free backups provided by keeping backup traffic off the data network

If you can justify the cost, the SAN will allow you to build a storage solution with far greater scalability than multiple arrays. In addition, the cost of ownership is lower due to centralized management and higher availability of the storage within the SAN. For example, when you use a SAN with your Microsoft Exchange mailbox servers, you can back up and restore your mailbox data much faster, which in turn helps fulfill service level agreements (SLAs) and maximizes the number of users that one server can host.

Although a deployment can be expensive, a SAN solution could be preferable because the long-term total cost of ownership (TCO) might be lower than the cost of maintaining many small arrays. Consider the following advantages of a SAN solution:

- If you currently have multiple arrays managed by multiple administrators, centralized administration of all storage could allow administrators to be available for other tasks.
- No other single solution has the potential to offer the comprehensive and flexible reliability that a vendor-supported SAN provides.

Hardware vendors implement most SAN solutions. Find a SAN provider who will help you with the process of designing, installing, and maintaining your SAN and discuss your storage needs with them. They'll then be able to configure the SAN to offer you the best combination of performance, security, and storage group and tracking log distribution.

Before you invest in a SAN, calculate the cost of your current storage solution in terms of hardware and administrative resources and evaluate the company's need for dependable storage. Then calculate whether moving to a SAN would provide a greater overall cost and reliability benefit than maintaining multiple arrays would.

SANs Connectivity

In the past, SANs have been implemented by using a dedicated direct connection or a Fibre Channel–arbitrated loop. Newer Fibre Channel fabric switches provide much higher levels of throughput and allow administrators to design SANs that minimize or eliminate any single points of failure.

At minimum, a switched FC SAN includes the following:

- Interconnected switches or switches cascaded via E-ports
- Several switches at the edge—one switch for each LAN connected to the SAN
- An FC interface in each server, which is connected to its local SAN switch
- A switch for the SAN disk farm, which is connected to both core switches
- A switch for the SAN backup device, which is connected to both core switches

Note that each edge switch is connected to both core switches.

Eliminating Points of Failure

When implementing a SAN, double all devices except the core: use two Fibre Channel adapters in each server, two edge switches in each LAN, two edge switches for the SAN disk farm, and two edge switches for the SAN backup device.

Making a Decision

You might have to make several decisions when designing a fault-tolerant data storage system. First, you should decide whether to use RAID or a SAN. If you use RAID, you'll need to decide whether to use a hardware implementation or a software implementation. If you use a software implementation, you must decide whether to use RAID-1 or RAID-5. Table 3.4 describes each of these strategies.

Table 3.4   Storage Strategies

Strategy	Description
SAN/RAID	A SAN is a good strategy to use if you need more than 100 to 200 GB of storage capacity. Although the initial cost of implementing a SAN is large, the long-term TCO might be lower than RAID. In addition, the cost and management of the storage within the SAN can be kept to a minimum while providing high availability. If the cost of a SAN can't be justified, use a RAID configuration.
Hardware/software RAID	A hardware implementation can offer performance improvements over software implementations of RAID, and hardware can sometimes support hot swapping and hot sparing. However, a hardware implementation is more expensive than a software implementation, and your equipment options might be limited to a specific vendor. Software fault tolerance is cheaper, but if you have a drive failure, downtime is required to replace the failed drive.

Table 3.4 *(continued)*

Strategy	Description
RAID-1/RAID-5	RAID-5 volumes have a lower cost per MB and better read performance than RAID-1 volumes. However, RAID-1 volumes can protect system or boot partitions and have better write performance. You can eliminate any single point of failure when implementing RAID-1 by using disk duplexing.

Recommendations

If you need more than 100 to 200 GB of storage capacity and you can justify the expense, you should use a SAN to provide fault-tolerant storage. Otherwise, you should use RAID. A hardware implementation of RAID is preferable to a software implementation if you're willing to make the investment and if you can work within the limits of vendor specifications. If you decide to use a software implementation, use RAID-1 for applications that require high availability and don't require a lot of disk space. You should use RAID-5 for environments with mostly read operations and occasional write operations. When implementing RAID, use disk duplexing.

Example: RAID Configuration for Tailspin Toys

The Tailspin Toys company maintains a relational database that contains customer information. The database is stored on a dedicated Windows 2000 Server computer that's configured with SQL Server 2000. RAID-1 and RAID-5 are used to ensure fault tolerance. Figure 3.4 shows how the logical partitions, logical disks, and physical disks are set up on the server.

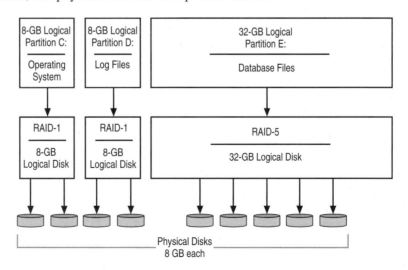

Figure 3.4 A fault-tolerant disk configuration in a Windows 2000 Server computer

The operating system is stored on one mirror set (partition C:), and the database log files are stored on a second mirror set (partition D:). Partition E: contains the database files. Partition D: is separate from Partition E: because the log files are write-intensive and RAID-1 is better suited to write-intensive operations. On the other hand, Partition E: contains the database files because RAID-5 is better suited for large sequential reads and large databases where reads occur more often than writes.

Lesson Summary

One method of protecting data is to use RAID. You can implement RAID fault tolerance as either a software or hardware solution. The software implementation is available in Windows 2000 Server. Windows 2000 supports RAID-1 and RAID-5. RAID-1 uses the fault tolerance driver (FTDISK.SYS) to write the same data to a volume on each of two physical disks simultaneously. You can install a second controller in the computer so that each disk in the mirrored volume has its own controller. In a RAID-5 volume, Windows 2000 achieves fault tolerance by adding a parity-information stripe to each disk partition in the volume. Generally, RAID-1 volumes offer read and write performance comparable to that of single disks. RAID-5 volumes offer better read performance than mirrored volumes, but poorer write performance. RAID-5 is also more inexpensive to implement than RAID-1. Some hardware vendors implement RAID data protection directly in their hardware, as with disk array controller cards. Hardware solutions are more expensive than software solutions, but performance is better and you can replace a disk without shutting down the computer. To store large amounts of data, you can use a SAN to make data available in the event of a disaster. A SAN provides fault-tolerant storage on a large scale. However, a SAN is expensive to implement. If you're storing more than 5 terabytes (TB) of data and you can justify the expense, you should use a SAN to provide fault-tolerant storage. Otherwise you should use RAID.

Lab 3.1: Planning RAID Configurations

Lab Objectives

After completing this lab, you'll be able to

- Design various RAID configurations to support fault-tolerant data storage

About This Lab

In this lab you'll design several RAID configurations. The configurations will provide fault tolerance for data storage systems in various types of Windows 2000 Server computers, including file servers, domain controllers, and database servers. Each exercise within the lab focuses on one type of server configuration.

Before You Begin

Before you begin this lab, you must be able to

- Configure RAID-1 and RAID-5 storage configurations in Windows 2000 Server

Scenario: Fault-Tolerant Storage for Lucerne Publishing

Lucerne Publishing is updating its network to implement fault tolerance in the data storage systems on various Windows 2000 Server computers. The company is upgrading four types of servers: two types of file servers, servers configured as domain controllers and DHCP and DNS servers, and database servers. You'll be using the software implementation of RAID that's available in Windows 2000 Server to provide fault tolerance. The upgrades will consist of implementing RAID-1, RAID-5, or both, on the four types of servers. You must design the RAID configuration for each type of server.

Exercise 1: Planning a File Server Configuration

Lucerne Publishing maintains a number of file servers on which users store various types of information. The file servers represent the greatest number of services in the network. You want to set up a fault-tolerant storage system on these servers, but you want to do it as inexpensively as possible. You plan to create two logical partitions: one for the operating system (partition C:) and one for the user data (partition D:). Partition C: should be 10 GB, and partition D: should be 30 GB. For this configuration, you'll use RAID-1 on two 10-GB hard disks and RAID-5 on four 10-GB hard disks.

On the diagram shown in Figure 3.5, you'll need to label the logical partitions, the logical disks, and the physical disks. You'll also be including the size of each partition and disk.

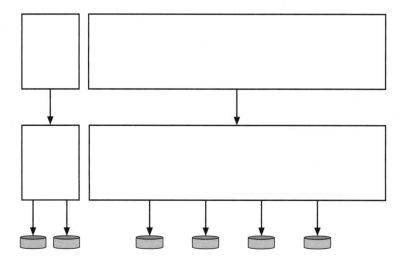

Figure 3.5   RAID configuration for a file server

The diagram should provide a conceptual overview of how RAID will be implemented in the file servers. For example, the box in the upper-left corner of the diagram might read, "10-GB logical partition C:—Operating system," and the box beneath that might read, "RAID-1—10-GB logical disk."

1. How should you label the rest of the diagram?

2. Why is there a difference in storage capacity between the logical disks and the physical disks?

Exercise 2: Planning a File Server and Operating System Configuration

The Lucerne Publishing network contains several additional file servers that must support a greater degree of fault tolerance than the basic file servers. For these specialized servers, the system partition must be protected and a small set of data files must be made highly available. You should also make the remaining user data fault tolerant using the most inexpensive method possible. To support this configuration, you plan to store the operating system on a 3-GB logical partition (partition C:), the highly available files on a 7-GB partition (partition D:), and the general user data on a 40-GB logical partition (partition E:). You plan to use RAID-1 and RAID-5 in combination with seven 10-GB hard disks.

On the diagram shown in Figure 3.6, you'll need to label the logical partitions, the logical disks, and the physical disks. You should also include the size of each partition and disk, their functions, and the RAID configuration used for each logical disk.

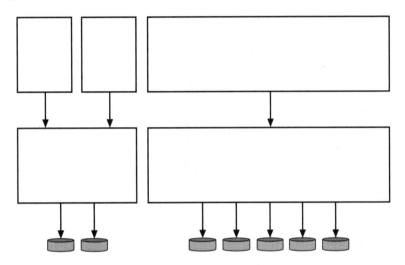

Figure 3.6   RAID configuration for a file server and operating system

1. How should you configure the data storage system for these servers?

2. Why is there a difference in storage capacity between the logical disk and the physical disks?

Exercise 3: Planning a Domain Controller and Services Configuration

The Lucerne Publishing network contains three Windows 2000 Server computers configured as domain controllers. The computers are also configured as DHCP and DNS servers. The servers must be highly available, although they don't require a large amount of disk space. You plan to implement a RAID-1 configuration that uses two 10-GB hard disks and two 5-GB logical partitions.

1. Draw a diagram that provides a conceptual overview of how RAID will be implemented on these servers. Label the logical partitions, the logical disk, and the physical disks. Include the size of each partition and disk and their functions.

Exercise 4: Planning a Relational Database Server Configuration

Lucerne Publishing maintains several database servers. The RAID configuration should support the high availability needs of the operating system, the write-intensive needs of the database log files, and the large sequential reads of the database files. You plan to create three logical partitions: one for the operating system (partition C:), one for the database log files (partition D:), and one for the database files (partition E:). Partitions C: and D: will each be 10 GB. Partition E: will be 40 GB. Your configuration will use RAID-1 and RAID-5 to support three logical disks and nine 10-GB physical disks.

1. How should you configure the data storage system for these servers?

2. How much storage would the RAID-5 logical disk support if another 10-GB hard disk were added to the configuration?

Review

Answering the following questions will reinforce key information presented in this chapter. If you're unable to answer a question, review the appropriate lesson and then try the question again. Answers to the questions can be found in the appendix.

1. You're designing a network infrastructure for the Baldwin Museum of Science, and you want to ensure that your servers are fault tolerant. One way that you plan to support fault tolerance is to use redundant components within your critical servers. What redundant components should you add to the servers?

2. Woodgrove Bank has been experiencing intermittent problems with their servers. The problems have included overheating, shorts, and unexpected restarts when an administrator touches one of the computers. Technicians have checked the computers, their components, and how they're configured and can't find an immediate cause of these problems. What other factors should be considered?

3. City Power & Light stores a great deal of data in order to maintain their operations. At any one time, their storage capacity can exceed 6 TB. You're designing a data storage system for the company, and you want to ensure that the system is fault tolerant, the data is centralized, and backup and restores are easy to administer. What type of storage would you recommend?

4. You're designing a data storage system for the Graphic Design Institute. The company maintains about 45 GB of data at any one time. The organization wants to ensure that the data storage system is fault tolerant, but they want to implement the least expensive solution available. Which storage solution would you recommend?

C H A P T E R   4

Microsoft Windows 2000 Cluster Service

About This Chapter

The Cluster service is one of two Microsoft Windows Clustering technologies available for the Windows 2000 family of server products. A server running Windows 2000 Advanced Server or Windows 2000 Datacenter Server and the Cluster service provides failover support for back-end applications and for services that require high availability and data integrity. These back-end applications include enterprise applications such as database, file server, Enterprise Resource Planning (ERP), and messaging systems. First designed for the Microsoft Windows NT Server 4 operating system, the Cluster service is substantially enhanced in the Windows 2000 Advanced Server and Datacenter Server operating systems. The Cluster service allows you to connect multiple servers into a cluster that provides high availability and easy manageability of data and programs running within the virtual server. In addition to the Cluster service, Windows Clustering includes Network Load Balancing (NLB), which supports highly available and scalable clusters for front-end applications and services such as Internet

or intranet sites, Web-based applications, media streaming, and Microsoft
Terminal Services. This chapter explains how to design Cluster service clusters
to improve fault tolerance in your network. NLB is discussed in Chapter 5,
"Network Load Balancing (NLB)."

Before You Begin

To complete the lessons in this chapter, you must have

- Experience administering Windows 2000 Advanced Server and designing
  Windows 2000 networks
- Knowledge about clustering technologies that are used to make services and
  applications highly available

Lesson 1: Introduction to Server Clusters

Windows 2000 Advanced Server and Windows 2000 Datacenter Server provide high availability by allowing a server in a cluster to take over and run a service or application that was running on another cluster member that failed. These services or applications are provided by means of *virtual servers*. To users, a virtual server appears as a single system. The cluster can provide any number of virtual servers, limited only by the capacity of the servers in the cluster and the storage available to provide the required performance. Administrators control the cluster servers as a single unit and can administer the cluster remotely. The Cluster service provides many benefits, including rolling upgrade support, improved use of hardware resources, greater availability, and ease of user access. This lesson will introduce you to the various components that make up clusters and the Cluster service.

After this lesson, you will be able to

- Identify the components and objects that make up the Cluster service
- Provide an overview of the server cluster architecture and how it's implemented in a Windows 2000 Server network

Estimated lesson time: 30 minutes

Overview of Server Clusters

A *server cluster* is a group of computers working together as a single system to ensure that mission-critical applications and resources remain available to clients. Each computer, known as a *node,* must be running Windows 2000 Advanced Server or Windows 2000 Datacenter Server. Every node is attached to one or more common storage devices used by every node in the cluster. Clustering allows users and administrators to access and manage the nodes as a single system rather than as separate computers.

The *Cluster service* is a Windows 2000 service that is made up of components on each node that perform cluster-specific activity. One of the primary activities is to manage *resources,* which are the hardware and software components within the cluster. The instrumentation mechanism that the Cluster service provides for managing resources is the resource dynamic-linked library (DLL). Resource DLLs define resource abstractions, communication interfaces, and management operations.

Note Windows NT Server 4, Enterprise Edition, supported a clustering technology named Microsoft Cluster Server, which provided much of the same functionality as the Cluster service in Windows 2000.

A resource is online when it's available and providing its service to the cluster. Resources include physical hardware devices, such as disk drives and network cards, and logical items, such as Internet Protocol (IP) addresses, applications, and application databases. Each node in the cluster has its own local resources. However, the cluster also has common resources, such as a common data storage array and private cluster network. Each node in the cluster can access these common resources. One special common resource is the *quorum resource,* a dedicated physical resource in the common cluster disk array that plays a critical role in cluster operations. It must be present for node operations—such as forming or joining a cluster—to occur.

Server Cluster Software

A server cluster runs several pieces of software that fall into two categories: the software that makes the cluster run (*clustering software*) and the software that you use to administer the cluster (*administrative software*). Table 4.1 describes each of these types of software.

Table 4.1   Clustering and Administrative Software on a Server Cluster

Type of Software	Description
Clustering	Clustering software enables a cluster's nodes to exchange specific messages that trigger the transfer of resource operations at the appropriate times. The two main pieces of clustering software are the Resource Monitor and the Cluster service.
Administrative	Administrators use cluster management applications to configure, control, and monitor clusters. Windows 2000 provides Cluster Administrator for this purpose. Any computer running Windows NT 4 Service Pack 3 or later, regardless of whether it's a cluster node, can install Cluster Administrator.

Server Cluster Components

Windows 2000 Advanced Server and Windows 2000 Datacenter Server use the server cluster components to create server clusters that provide high availability, easy manageability, and enhanced scalability. These components work together to manage the cluster objects. Figure 4.1 shows how the cluster components relate to applications of various types and to each other within a single cluster node.

Table 4.2 describes the components that are shown in Figure 4.1.

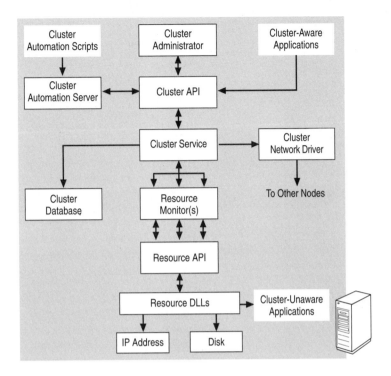

Figure 4.1   Components of the Cluster service

Table 4.2   Components of the Cluster Service

Component	Description
Cluster service	Manages all cluster-specific activity, including managing cluster objects and configurations, coordinating with other instances of the Cluster service, handling event notification, facilitating communication among components, and performing failover operations. One instance of the Cluster service is running on each node in a cluster.
Resource Monitor	Acts as an intermediary between the Cluster service and a resource DLL. The Resource Monitor transfers requests from the Cluster service to the appropriate DLL and delivers status and event information from the DLL to the Cluster service.

(continued)

Table 4.2   *(continued)*

Component	Description
Resource DLL	Manages cluster resources of a particular type. Each DLL can manage one or more resource types.
Cluster Administrator	Management application used to configure, control, and monitor clusters. Cluster Administrator allows you to manage cluster objects, establish resource groups, initiate failover, handle maintenance, and monitor cluster activity.
Cluster automation server	Exposes a set of 32-bit Component Object Model (COM) objects to any scripting language that supports automation. Cluster automation server enables object-oriented design and the use of high-level languages, simplifying the process of creating a cluster management application.
Cluster database	Resides in the Windows 2000 registry on each cluster node and is also known as the *cluster hive*. The cluster database contains information about all physical and logical elements in a cluster, including cluster objects, their properties, and configuration data. Each node's Cluster service maintains a consistent, updated image of the cluster database through global updates and periodic checkpointing. The quorum resource contains a copy of the cluster database as well.
Network and disk drivers	Monitors the status of all network paths between nodes, detects communication failure, and routes messages. Each node in the cluster runs an instance of the Cluster Network Driver.
Cluster application programming interface (API)	Acts as an interface to the Cluster Administrator, Cluster automation server, the Cluster service, and cluster-aware applications.
Resource API	Acts as an interface to any Resource Monitors and Resource DLLs.
IP Address and Disk	Two types of resources.

Server Cluster Objects

The Cluster service manages physical and logical units known as *cluster objects*. Each object is associated with the following attributes, controls, and functions:

- One or more properties, or attributes, that define the object and its behavior within the cluster

- A set of cluster control codes used to manipulate the object's properties

- A set of object management functions used to manage the object through the Cluster service

This section provides an overview of the objects managed by the Cluster service.

Networks

A *network* (sometimes called an *interconnect*) performs one of the following roles in a cluster:

- A private network that carries internal cluster communication
- A public network that provides client systems with access to cluster application services
- A public-and-private network that carries internal cluster communication and that provides client systems to cluster application services
- A network that is neither public nor private that carries traffic unrelated to cluster operation

Preventing Network Failure

The Cluster service uses all available private and public-and-private networks for internal communication. You should configure multiple networks as private or public-and-private to protect the cluster from a single network failure. If only one such network is available and it fails, the cluster nodes stop communicating with one another. When two nodes are unable to communicate, they're said to be *partitioned*. After two nodes become partitioned, the Cluster service automatically shuts down on one node to guarantee the consistency of application data and the cluster configuration. If the Cluster service were not shut down on one node, cluster resources could become unavailable to client systems.

Node-to-Node Communication

The Cluster service doesn't use public networks for internal communication, even if a public network is the only available network. For example, suppose a cluster has Network A configured as private and Network B configured as public, and Network A fails. Because Network B is public, the Cluster service doesn't use it, and the nodes stop communicating with each other.

Network Interfaces

A *network interface* is a card or other network adapter that connects a computer to a network. Windows 2000 Advanced Server and Windows 2000 Datacenter Server keep track of all network interfaces in a server cluster. As a result, you can view the state of all cluster network interfaces from a cluster management application, such as Cluster Administrator. Windows 2000 automatically detects the addition and removal of network interfaces.

Nodes

A *node* is a member of a server cluster. Windows 2000 Advanced Server supports two nodes in a cluster, and Windows 2000 Datacenter Server supports four nodes. Nodes must be either domain controllers or member servers authenticated by domain controllers. Nodes have their own resources, such as a hard disk and a dedicated network interface card (NIC) for private cluster network communication. Nodes in a cluster also share access to cluster resources on an external disk storage system called the *clustered disk*.

Every node is attached to one or more cluster storage devices, either directly or through Fibre Channel hubs or switches. Each cluster storage device contains multiple disks arranged in sets or arrays, and each set or array is configured as a specific RAID type. These sets of disks or arrays are typically known as logical unit numbers (LUNs). Usually, each LUN, or virtual disk, will have a specific Small Computer System Interface (SCSI) ID associated with it, and Windows 2000 will interpret each LUN as a physical disk in Disk Manager. The disks store all the cluster's configuration and resource data. Each disk can be owned by only one node at any one time, but ownership can be transferred between nodes. The result is that each node has access to all cluster configuration data.

All nodes in the cluster are grouped under a common name, the *cluster name*, which you use when accessing and managing the cluster.

Resource Groups

A *resource group* is a logical collection of cluster resources. Typically, a resource group is made up of logically related resources such as applications and their associated peripherals and data. However, it can contain cluster entities that are related only by administrative needs, such as an administrative collection of virtual server names and IP addresses. A resource group can be owned by only one node at a time, and individual resources within a group must exist on the node that currently owns the group. At any given instance, different servers in the cluster can't own different resources in the same resource group.

Each resource group has an associated cluster-wide policy that specifies which server the group prefers to run on and which server the group should move to in case of a failure. Each group also has a network service name and address to enable network clients to bind to the services provided by the resource group. In the event of a failure, resource groups, which will typically failover, are moved as atomic units from the failed node to an available node in the cluster.

Each resource in a group may depend on other resources in the cluster. Dependencies are relationships between resources that indicate which resources need to be started and be available before another resource can be started. For example, a database application might depend on the availability of a disk, IP address, and network name to be able to start and provide services to other applications and clients.

The scope of any identified dependency is limited to resources within the same resource group. Cluster-managed dependencies can't extend beyond the resource group, because resource groups are failed over, moved, and brought online and offline independently.

Three concepts important to the management of resource groups are virtual servers, failover, and failback. This section discusses these concepts and explains how they apply to resource groups.

Virtual Servers

One of the benefits of the Cluster service is that applications and services running on a server cluster can be exposed to users and workstations as virtual servers. To users and clients, connecting to an application or service running as a clustered virtual server appears to be the same process as connecting to a single physical server. In fact, any node in the cluster can host the connection to a virtual server. The user or client application doesn't know which node is actually hosting the virtual server.

Note   Any nonclustered service or application can run on a cluster node without being managed as a virtual server.

Multiple virtual servers representing multiple applications can be hosted in a cluster, as shown in Figure 4.2.

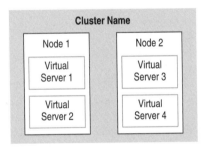

Figure 4.2   Physical view of virtual servers under the Cluster service

Figure 4.2 illustrates a two-node cluster with four virtual servers; two virtual servers exist on each node. The Cluster service manages the virtual server as a resource group, with each virtual server resource group containing two resources: an IP address and a network name that's mapped to the IP address.

Application client connections to a virtual server are made by a client session that knows only the IP address that the Cluster service publishes as the virtual server's address. The client view is simply a view of individual network names and IP addresses. Using the example of a two-node cluster supporting four virtual servers, the client view of the cluster nodes and four virtual servers is illustrated in Figure 4.3.

As shown in Figure 4.3, the client is aware of only the IP addresses and names and doesn't need to detect information about the physical location of any of the virtual servers. This allows the Cluster service to provide highly available support for the applications running as virtual servers.

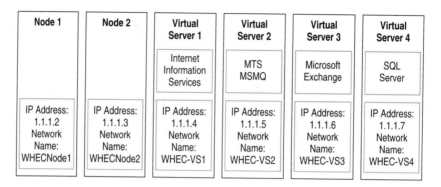

Figure 4.3   Client view of the Cluster service virtual servers

In the event of an application or server failure, the Cluster service moves the virtual server resource group to another node in the cluster. When such a failure occurs, the client detects a failure in its session with the application and attempts to reconnect in exactly the same manner as the original connection. The client is able to establish a new connection because the Cluster service maps the published IP address of the virtual server to a surviving node in the cluster during recovery operations. The client doesn't need to know that the application is now physically hosted on a different node in the cluster.

Note that while this provides high availability of the application or service, session state information related to the failed client session is lost unless the application is designed or configured to store client session data on disk for retrieval during application recovery. The Cluster service enables high availability but doesn't provide application fault tolerance unless the application itself supports fault-tolerant transaction behavior. For example, the Microsoft Dynamic Host Configuration Protocol (DHCP) service stores client data and can recover from failed client sessions. DHCP client IP address reservations are saved in the DHCP database. If the DHCP server resource fails, you can move the DHCP database to an available node in the cluster and restart the DHCP service and use restored client data from the DHCP database.

Failover

The Cluster service implements failover automatically when hardware or application failure occurs. You can also trigger failover manually. The algorithm for both situations is identical, except that in a manually initiated failover, resources are gracefully shut down. In the case of failure, they're forcefully shut down.

When an entire node in the cluster fails, its resource groups are moved to one or more available servers in the cluster. Automatic failover is similar to planned administrative reassignment of resource ownership, except that automatic failover is more complicated because the normal shutdown phase isn't gracefully performed on the failed node.

When automatic failover occurs, the Cluster service determines which resource groups were running on the failed node and which nodes should take ownership of the various groups. All nodes in the cluster that are capable of hosting the resource groups negotiate among themselves for ownership. This negotiation is based on node capabilities, current load, application feedback, or the node preference list. The node preference list is part of the resource group properties and is used to assign a resource group to a node. Once negotiation of the resource group is complete, all nodes in the cluster update their databases and keep track of which node owns the resource group.

For each resource group, you can specify (in a node preference list) a preferred server and one or more prioritized alternatives for each resource. This prioritizing enables *cascading failover*, in which a resource group can survive multiple server failures, each time cascading, or failing over, to the next server on its node preference list. Cluster administrators can set up different node preference lists for each resource group on a server so that, in the event of a server failure, the groups are distributed among the cluster's surviving servers.

An alternative to cascading failover is *N+1 failover*. In N+1, the node preference lists of all cluster groups identify the standby cluster nodes to which resources should be moved during first failover. The standby nodes are servers in the cluster that are mostly idle or whose workload can be easily preempted when a failed server's workload must be moved to the standby node.

When choosing between cascading failover and N+1 failover, a key issue for cluster administrators is the location of the cluster's excess capacity for accommodating the loss of a server. With cascading failover, the assumption is that every other server in the cluster has some excess capacity to absorb a portion of any other failed server's workload. With N+1 failover, it's assumed that the "+1" standby server is the primary location of excess capacity.

Failback

When a node comes back online, the Failover Manager (which manages resources and groups and initiates failover operations) can decide to move some resource groups back to the recovered node. This process is referred to as *failback*. A resource group's properties must have a preferred owner defined in order to failback to a recovered or restarted node. Resource groups for which the recovered or restarted node is the preferred owner will be moved from the current owner to the recovered or restarted node. The Cluster service provides protection against failback of resource groups at peak processing times or for nodes that haven't been correctly recovered or restarted. A resource group's failback properties may include the hours of the day during which failback is allowed, plus a limit on the number of times failback is attempted.

Resources

A *resource* is any physical or logical component that has the following characteristics:

- Can be brought online and taken offline
- Can be managed in a server cluster
- Can be hosted (owned) by only one node at a time

To manage resources, the Cluster service communicates to a resource DLL through a Resource Monitor. When the Cluster service makes a request of a resource, the Resource Monitor calls the appropriate entry-point function in the resource DLL in order to check and control the resource's state.

Dependent Resources

A *dependent resource* is one that requires another resource, known as a *dependency,* to operate. For example, a network name must be associated with an IP address. Because of this requirement, a Network Name resource is dependent on an IP Address resource. Dependent resources are taken offline before their dependencies; likewise, they are brought online after their dependencies. A resource can specify one or more resources on which it's dependent.

A resource can also specify a list of nodes, known as *preferred nodes,* on which it's able to run. When you organize resources into groups, it's important to consider preferred nodes and dependencies.

A *dependency tree* is a series of dependency relationships. For example, the SQL Server resource depends on the SQL Server Network Name resource, and the Network Name resource depends on the IP Address resource. A dependent resource and all of its dependencies must be in the same resource group.

Cluster Service Architecture

The Cluster service is designed as a separate, isolated set of components that work together with the Windows 2000 Advanced Server and Windows 2000 Datacenter Server operating systems. This design avoids introducing complex processing system schedule dependencies between the Cluster service and the operating system. However, some changes in the base operating system are required to enable cluster features. These changes include the following:

- Support for dynamic creation and deletion of network names and addresses
- Modification of the file system to enable closing open files during disk drive dismounts
- Modifying the input/output (I/O) subsystem to enable sharing disks and volume sets among multiple nodes

Apart from these changes and other minor modifications, cluster capabilities are built on top of the Windows 2000 foundation.

The Cluster service is based on a *shared-nothing* model of cluster architecture. This model refers to how servers in a cluster manage and use local and common cluster devices and resources. In the shared-nothing cluster, each server owns and manages its local devices. Devices common to the cluster, such as a common disk array and connection media, are selectively owned and managed by a single server at any given time.

The shared-nothing model makes it easier to manage disk devices and standard applications. This model doesn't require any special cabling or applications and enables the Cluster service to support standard Windows 2000–based and Windows NT–based applications and disk resources.

The Cluster service uses standard Windows 2000 Server drivers for local storage devices and media connections. In addition, the Cluster service supports several connection media for the external common devices that need to be accessible by all servers in the cluster. External storage devices that are common to the cluster require SCSI devices that support standard Peripheral Component Interconnect (PCI)–based SCSI connections as well as SCSI over Fibre Channel and SCSI bus with multiple initiators.

Fiber connections are SCSI devices hosted on a Fibre Channel bus instead of a SCSI bus. Conceptually, Fibre Channel technology encapsulates SCSI commands within the Fibre Channel and makes it possible to use the SCSI commands that the Cluster service is designed to support. Fibre Channel is a technology for 1-Gbps data transfer that maps common transport protocols such as SCSI and IP, merging networking and high-speed I/O in a single connectivity technology. Fibre Channel technology gives you a way to address the distance and the address-space limitations of conventional channel technologies.

Figure 4.4 illustrates components of a two-node server cluster that may be composed of servers running Windows 2000 Advanced Server, Windows 2000 Datacenter Server, or Windows NT Server 4, Enterprise Edition, with shared storage device connections that use SCSI or SCSI over Fibre Channel.

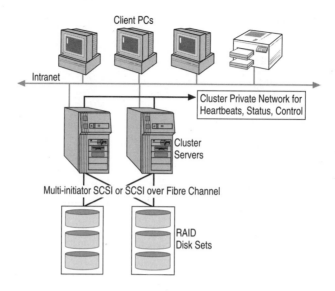

Figure 4.4   Two-node server cluster running Windows 2000 Advanced Server, Windows 2000 Datacenter Server, or Windows NT Server 4, Enterprise Edition

Windows 2000 Datacenter Server supports four-node clusters and requires device connections that use a Fibre Channel connection, as shown in Figure 4.5.

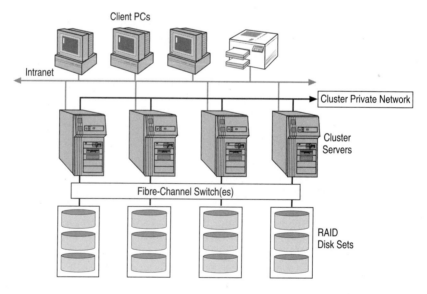

Figure 4.5   Four-node server cluster running Windows 2000 Datacenter Server

Quorum Disks

One of the most important components of the cluster storage system is the *quorum disk,* which is a single disk in the system designated as the *quorum resource*. The quorum disk provides persistent physical storage across system failures. The cluster configuration is kept on the disk, and all nodes in the cluster must be able to communicate with the node that owns it. The configuration data, in the form of recovery logs, contains details of all of the changes that have been applied to the cluster database. This process provides node-independent storage for cluster configuration and state data.

Quorum Resource and the Cluster Database

The cluster database is an integral part of the formation of a server cluster. When a node joins or forms a cluster, the Cluster service must update the node's private copy of the cluster database. When a node joins a cluster, the Cluster service can retrieve the data from the other active nodes. However, when a node forms a cluster, no other node is available. The Cluster service uses the quorum resource's recovery logs to update the node's cluster database. To ensure cluster unity, Windows 2000 uses the quorum resource to ensure that only one set of active, communicating nodes is allowed to operate as a cluster. A node can form a cluster only if it can gain control of the quorum resource. A node can join a cluster or remain in an existing cluster only if it can communicate with the node that controls the quorum resource.

Lesson Summary

A server cluster is a group of independent computer systems working together as a single system to ensure that mission-critical applications and resources remain available to clients. The Cluster service refers to the collection of components on each node that perform cluster-specific activity, and resource refers to the hardware and software components within the cluster that are managed by the Cluster service. A server cluster runs several pieces of software that fall into two categories: the software that makes the cluster run (clustering software) and the software that you use to administer the cluster (administrative software). Windows 2000 Advanced Server and Windows 2000 Datacenter Server use the server cluster components to create server clusters. These components include the Cluster service, Resource Monitor, resource DLL, Cluster Administrator, Cluster Automation Server, the cluster database, and network and disk drivers. Cluster objects are the physical and logical units that the Cluster service manages. Objects include server cluster networks, network interfaces, nodes, resource groups, and resources. The Cluster service is based on a shared-nothing model of cluster architecture. One of the most important components of the cluster storage system is the quorum disk, which is a single disk in the system designated as the quorum resource. The cluster database is an integral part of the formation of a server cluster.

Lesson 2: Planning Server Cluster Configurations

The Cluster service in Windows 2000 Advanced Server and Windows 2000 Datacenter Server provides a foundation for server clusters. When one server in a cluster fails or is taken offline, another server in the cluster takes over the operations of the failed server. Clients using server resources experience little or no interruption of their work because support for resources is moved from one server to the other. When implementing Windows clustering into a network design, you must consider many factors and prepare the environment that supports the clusters. For example, you must select which applications to run on a server cluster, and you must determine failover policies for resource groups. This lesson focuses on those aspects of planning a server cluster that you should consider when designing your network.

After this lesson, you will be able to

- Plan a server cluster and identify the possible failures that can interrupt access to resources
- Choose applications to run on the cluster
- Determine failover policies for resource groups, choose a domain model, and plan resource groups

Estimated lesson time: 25 minutes

Planning a Server Cluster

You should consider a number of steps when planning a server cluster, including identifying network risks, choosing applications to run on the cluster, choosing a domain model, choosing a cluster model, planning resource groups, determining failover policies, planning fault-tolerant storage, and determining capacity requirements. This section discusses each of these steps.

Identifying Network Risks

With Windows 2000, you can use server clusters to provide increased availability. However, server clusters aren't designed to protect all components of your workflow in all circumstances. For example, clusters aren't an alternative to backing up data; they protect the availability of data only, not the data itself.

When you configure a cluster, you should identify any possible single points of failure in your network environment. In general, you should try to minimize those points of failure and provide mechanisms that will maintain service when a failure occurs.

Windows 2000 Advanced Server and Windows 2000 Datacenter Server include built-in features (in addition to the Cluster service) that protect certain computer and network processes during failure. These features include two redundant array of independent disks (RAID) implementations: mirroring (RAID-1) and striping with parity (RAID-5). You should note, however, that software implementations of RAID are used to protect a computer's internal drives, not the external storage used by the cluster.

To further increase the availability of network resources and prevent the loss of data, do the following:

- Consider having replacement disks and controllers available at your site. Always make sure that any spare parts you keep on hand exactly match the original parts, including network and SCSI components. The cost of two spare SCSI controllers can be a small fraction of the cost of having hundreds of clients unable to use data.

- Consider providing uninterruptible power supply (UPS) protection for individual computers and the network itself, including hubs, bridges, and routers. Computers running Windows Server support UPS. Many UPS solutions provide power for 5 to 20 minutes, which is long enough for the operating system to do an orderly shutdown when power fails.

Choosing Applications to Run on the Cluster

You can adapt many, but not all, applications to run on a server cluster. Of those that can, you don't need to set them all up as cluster resources. The following criteria determine whether an application can adapt to server clustering failover mechanisms:

- The application must use Transmission Control Protocol/Internet Protocol (TCP/IP) or Distributed Component Object Model (DCOM), Named Pipes, or remote procedure call (RPC) over TCP/IP for its network communications in order to run on a server cluster. Applications that use only NetBIOS Enhanced User Interface (NetBEUI) or Internetwork Packet Exchange (IPX) protocols can't take advantage of cluster failover.

- The application must be able to store its data in a configurable location—that is, on the disks attached to shared buses. Some applications that can't store their data in a configurable location can still be configured to failover. However, in such cases access to the application data is lost at failover because the data is available only on the disk of the failed node.

- The application must support NTLM authentication. Clients can't use Kerberos to authenticate a connection to a virtual server.

In addition to these specifications, client applications that connect to the server application must be able to retry and recover from temporary network failures. During failover, client applications experience a temporary loss of network connectivity. If the client application is configured to recover from temporary network connection problems, it's able to continue operating after a server failover.

Cluster-Aware and Cluster-Unaware Applications

Applications that can be failed over can be divided into two groups: those that support the Cluster API and those that don't. Applications that support the Cluster API are defined as *cluster-aware*. These applications can register with the Cluster service to receive status and notification information, and they can use the Cluster API to administer clusters. Applications that don't support the Cluster API are defined as *cluster-unaware*. If cluster-unaware applications meet the TCP/IP and remote-storage criteria, you can still use them in a cluster and often configure them to failover.

In either case, applications that keep significant state information in memory aren't the best applications for clustering because information that's not stored on disk is lost at failover.

Choosing a Domain Model

Nodes in a server cluster must belong to the same domain. The cluster nodes, which must be configured with Windows 2000 Advanced Server or Windows 2000 Datacenter Server, can be either member servers or domain controllers. If you configure your cluster nodes as domain controllers, you must account for the additional overhead that's incurred by the domain controller services. If you configure the cluster nodes as member servers, the cluster's availability depends on the availability of the domain controller, which must be high.

In large networks running on Windows 2000, domain controllers can require substantial resources to replicate the directory and authenticate clients. For this reason, many applications, such as Microsoft SQL Server and Message Queuing, should not be installed on domain controllers in order to maximize performance. However, if you have a very small network in which account information rarely changes and in which users don't log on and off frequently, you can use domain controllers as cluster nodes.

Choosing a Server Cluster Model

Server clusters can be categorized into different configuration models. You should choose a cluster model that best matches your organization's needs. Cluster models are discussed in more detail in Lesson 3, "Choosing a Server Cluster Model."

Planning the Resource Groups

You can take six steps to organize your applications and other resources into groups. This section reviews each of these steps.

Listing All Server-Based Applications

Make a list of all applications that will run on the cluster nodes, regardless of whether or not you plan to use them with the Cluster service. You can determine your capacity needs by adding up the resources necessary for each resource group and the resources necessary for those applications and services that will run independently of the Cluster service.

Sorting the List of Applications

Determine which applications on your list can use failover and which applications will reside on cluster nodes but won't use failover (because it's inconvenient, unnecessary, or impossible to configure). Although you don't set failover policies for these applications or arrange them in groups, they still use a portion of the server capacity.

Note   Before clustering an application, review the application license or check with the application vendor. Each application vendor sets its own licensing policies for applications running on clusters.

Listing All Other Resources

Determine which hardware, connections, and operating system software a server cluster can protect in your network environment. For example, the Cluster service can failover print spoolers to protect client access to printing services and failover file-server resources to maintain client access to files. In both cases, capacity is affected, such as the random access memory (RAM) required to service the clients.

Listing All Dependencies for Each Resource

Once you have a complete list of all the resources, determine which ones are your core resources, and then determine which ones support the core resources. For example, a SQL Server resource would be your core resource, and Network Name, IP Address, and Disk resources would support the SQL Server resource. All these resources must be in the same group to ensure that the Cluster service keeps interdependent resources together at all times.

Making Preliminary Grouping Decisions

Once you've listed all your resources and their dependencies, you're ready to make a preliminary decision about how to group these resources. In many cases resource groupings are very apparent because dependencies restrict how you can group some resources.

When grouping together resources, you should adhere to these guidelines:

- A resource and its dependencies must be together in a single group.
- A resource can't span groups.

For example, if several applications depend on a particular resource, you must include all of those applications with that resource in a single group. Suppose, for example, a Web-server application provides access to Web pages and that those Web pages provide result sets that clients access by querying an

SQL-database application through the use of Hypertext Markup Language (HTML) forms. If you put the Web server and the SQL database in the same group, the data for both core applications can reside on a specific disk volume. Because both applications exist within the same group, you can also create an IP address and network name specifically for this resource group.

When not restricted by resource dependencies, you can organize groups by administrative convenience. For example, you might put file-sharing and print-spooling resources (along with their dependencies) into one group because viewing those particular applications as a single entity makes it easier to administer the network. You can give this group a unique name for the part of your organization it serves, such as Accounting File and Print. Whenever you need to intervene with that department's file- and print-sharing activities, you'd look for this group in Cluster Administrator.

Making Final Grouping Assignments

After you list the resources that you want to group together, assign a different name to each group and create a dependency tree. A dependency tree is useful for visualizing the dependency relationships between resources.

To create a dependency tree, first write down all the resources in a particular group. Then draw arrows from each resource to each resource on which the resource directly depends.

A *direct dependency* between resource A and resource B means that no intermediary resources are between the two resources. An *indirect dependency* occurs when a transitive relationship exists between resources. For example, if resource A depends on resource B and resource B depends on resource C, there's an indirect dependency between resource A and resource C, rather than a direct one.

Figure 4.6 shows the resources in a final grouping assignment in a dependency tree.

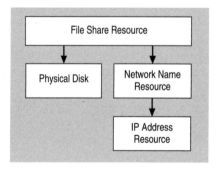

Figure 4.6   A simple dependency tree

In Figure 4.6 the File Share resource depends on the Network Name resource, which in turn depends on the IP Address resource. However, the File Share resource doesn't directly depend on the IP Address resource.

Determining Failover Policies for Groups

You must assign failover policies for each group of resources in your cluster. These policies determine exactly how a group behaves when failover occurs. You can choose which policies are most appropriate for each resource group you set up.

Failover policies for groups include three settings:

- **Failover timing**   You can set a group for immediate failover when a resource fails, or you can instruct the Cluster service to try to restart the group a designated number of times before failover occurs. If it's possible to overcome the resource failure by restarting all resources within the group, then set the Cluster service to restart the group.

- **Preferred node**   You can set a group so that it always runs on a designated node whenever that node is available. This is useful if one of the nodes is better equipped to host the group.

- **Failback timing**   You can set a group to fail back to its preferred node as soon as the Cluster service detects that the failed node has been restored, or you can instruct the Cluster service to wait until a specified hour of the day, such as after peak business hours.

Planning Fault-Tolerant Storage

Many groups include disk resources for disks on shared buses. In some cases, these are simple physical disks, but in other cases they're complex disk subsystems containing multiple disks. Almost all resource groups depend on the disks on the shared buses. An unrecoverable failure of a disk resource results in certain failure of all groups that depend on that resource.

For these reasons, you might decide to use special methods to protect your disks and disk subsystems from failures. One common solution is the use of a hardware-based RAID solution. RAID support ensures the high availability of data contained on disk sets in your clusters. Some of these hardware-based solutions are considered fault tolerant, which means that data isn't lost if a member of the disk set fails. You might also use a storage area network (SAN), which can be located on- or off-site.

Important   You can't use software fault-tolerant disk sets for cluster storage.

Hardware RAID

The Microsoft Windows Hardware Compatibility List contains many different hardware RAID configurations for clusters. Because many hardware RAID solutions provide power, bus, and cable redundancy within a single cabinet and track the state of each component in the hardware RAID firmware, they provide data availability with multiple redundancy, protecting against multiple points of failure. Hardware RAID solutions can also use an onboard processor and cache. Windows 2000 can use these disks as standard disk resources.

Note When implementing hardware RAID, you should use redundant RAID controllers to make sure that the controller won't be a single point of failure.

Storage Area Networks

A SAN is a high-speed, special-purpose network (or subnetwork) that interconnects different kinds of data storage devices with an associated data server on behalf of a larger network of users. Typically, a SAN is often part of the overall network of computing resources and it's usually clustered in close proximity to other computing resources. However, a SAN can extend to remote locations for backup and archival storage, using WAN carrier technologies such as Asynchronous Transfer Mode (ATM) or Synchronous Optical Network (SONET).

SANs support disk mirroring, backup and restore, the archival and retrieval of archived data, data migration from one storage device to another, and the sharing of data among different servers in a network. SANs can incorporate subnetworks with network-attached storage systems.

Determining Capacity Requirements

After you assess your clustering needs, you're ready to determine how many servers you need and with what specifications, such as memory and hard disk storage. Capacity planning for clusters is discussed in Chapter 7, "Capacity Planning."

Making a Decision

The process of planning your server configuration has several steps. In each of these steps you must decide which configuration is best suited to your organization. Table 4.3 describes the decisions that you must make for each of these steps.

Table 4.3   Planning Your Server Cluster

Step	Description
Identifying network risks	When implementing clusters and the environment in which they're located, you should minimize the number of single points of failure and provide mechanisms that maintian service when a failure occurs or that minimize the amount of unscheduled downtime.
Choosing applications to run on the cluster	The server applications must use TCP/IP and be able to specify where application data is stored. Client applications that connect to the server applications must be able to retry the connection and recover from temporary network failures. Server applications that keep significant state information in memory aren't good candidates for clustering.

Table 4.3   *(continued)*

Step	Description
Choosing a domain model	You can configure nodes in a cluster as member servers or domain controllers. In either case the nodes must belong to the same domain. If you configure the nodes as member servers, the availability of the cluster depends on the availability of the domain controller.
Choosing a server cluster model	Server clusters can be categorized into different configuration models. Clustering models are discussed in more detail in Lesson 3, "Choosing a Server Cluster Model."
Planning the resource groups	You should follow six steps when organizing resource groups: listing applications, sorting applications, listing other resources, listing dependencies, making preliminary grouping decisions, and making final grouping decisions.
Determining failover policies for groups	You can assign failover policies to each group of resources in a cluster. Failover policies include three settings: Failover Timing, Preferred Node, and Failback Timing.
Planning fault-tolerant storage	You should protect the clustering shared storage from failures; however, you can't use software fault-tolerant disks in that storage. Hardware-based RAID and SAN, along with redundant controllers, offer a highly available solution for cluster data.
Determining capacity requirements	After you assess your clustering needs, you should determine your capacity requirements. This process is discussed in Chapter 7, "Capacity Planning."

Recommendations

When planning a Windows 2000 Advanced Server or Windows 2000 Datacenter Server cluster, you should adhere to the following guidelines:

- Eliminate single points of failure in hardware, software, and external dependencies. Use redundant services, components, and network connections, and keep replacement components on hand.

- Choose server applications that use TCP/IP, that allow you to specify where application data is stored, and that don't keep significant amounts of state data in memory.

- Configure failover policies to meet your organization's specific needs. Configure the Failover Timing setting to restart applications if all resources within the group can be restarted to overcome failure. If one host is better equipped to host a group, configure the Preferred Node setting so that a group always runs on a designated node if that node is available. In this case you should also configure the Failback Timing setting to failback to the preferred node as soon as it has been restored.

- When configuring nodes as member servers, ensure that domain controller services for those nodes are highly available.

- When planning resource groups, be sure to group together a resource and its dependencies into one group and don't allow a resource to span groups. If several applications depend on a single resource, all those applications and the additional resource must be in one group. Group planning should also take into consideration administrative efficiency, such as combining file-sharing resources and print-spooling resources into a single group.

- Implement hardware-based RAID or a SAN and redundant controllers to make the cluster storage fault tolerant.

Example: A Server Cluster for Northwind Traders

Northwind Traders imports gift items from Southeast Asia into the United States. The company sells these items to wholesale outlets in the United States and Europe. The company is setting up a Web-based system that will allow whole-sale customers to place orders online. The site's goal is to be available all day, every day to accommodate various time zones and work schedules. The network includes a database that contains customer, product, and order information. Northwind Traders plans to use the Clustering service in Windows 2000 Advanced Server to provide highly available data.

Before implementing the cluster, Northwind Traders will use the planning process outlined in this lesson to determine how to set up the cluster. The first step is to ensure that any single point of failure in the network is eliminated. The Web site and its network infrastructure will use redundancy throughout the network to achieve high availability. For example, redundant LANs and power sources will be used to prevent failure.

Northwind Traders is using SQL Server 2000 to manage the database because SQL Server uses TCP/IP and the application is able to specify where application data is stored. A resource group will be created that contains SQL Server and any dependent resources. The failover policies for the group will be configured as follows: the Failover Timing setting will be configured to first try restarting resources before failover occurs. A preferred node, however, won't be designated. The servers are configured as member servers, so the domain controller services for that domain are designed to be highly available. Each cluster node will utilize redundant Fibre Channel host bus adapters (HBAs) to connect to a SAN. Each Fibre Channel HBA will be cross-connected to separate switches for redundancy. Each switch will also be connected to redundant Fibre Channel controllers on the external Fibre Channel storage array. The storage array itself should already have redundant internal components and built-in fault tolerance. This configuration eliminates any single point of failure throughout the entire SAN.

Figure 4.7 shows how the two servers are connected to the corporate network and the SAN. Notice that dual NICs are used for network connectivity: one for client communication and one for the private cluster communication.

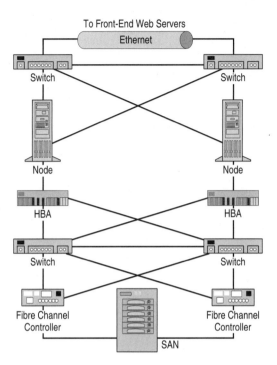

Figure 4.7   Cluster configuration with SAN

Lesson Summary

When implementing Windows clustering into a network design, you must plan the configuration of specific components within the Cluster service and prepare the environment that supports the clusters. You should minimize the number of single points of failure in your environment and provide mechanisms that maintain service when a failure occurs. Clustering applications must use TCP/IP and be able to specify where the application data is stored. You should assign the failover policies for each group of resources in your cluster to determine how a group behaves. Nodes in a server cluster can be either member servers or domain controllers, and server clusters can be categorized into different configuration models. You should follow six steps when organizing resource groups: listing applications, sorting applications, listing other resources, listing dependencies, making preliminary grouping decisions, and making final grouping decisions. You can use hardware-based RAID and redundant controllers to make cluster storage fault tolerant. After you assess your clustering needs, you're ready to determine how many servers you need and with what specifications, such as memory and hard disk storage.

Activity 4.1: Planning Resource Groups

In this activity, you'll plan the resource groups for a new cluster that you'll be implementing in your network. The cluster will be used to support a file share for your network. Because the cluster is supporting a file share, you'll have to configure it with at least one network name and IP address to allow network clients to access the services. The cluster must also identify the physical disk in the cluster storage that will be used for storage.

For each of the following steps, identify how your file server resource group will be configured:

1. List all the server-based applications.

2. Sort the list of applications. Determine which applications can use failover.

3. List all other resources.

4. List all dependencies for each resource.

5. Make preliminary grouping decisions.

6. Make final grouping assignments and create any necessary dependency trees.

Lesson 3: Choosing a Server Cluster Model

In Lesson 2, "Planning Server Cluster Configurations," you learned what steps to take in order to plan your cluster configuration. One of these steps was to choose a server cluster model. Server clusters can be categorized in three configuration models in order of increasing complexity. This lesson describes each model and provides examples of the types of applications that are suited to each one. These models range from a single-node cluster to a cluster in which all servers are actively providing services.

After this lesson, you will be able to

- Describe the three configuration models of server clusters
- Choose cluster models that are suited to specific types of applications

Estimated lesson time: 25 minutes

Server Cluster Models

Clusters can be categorized in three configuration models: single-node, active/passive, and active/active. This section describes each model and gives examples of the types of applications that are suited to each one.

Model 1: Single-Node Configuration

In Model 1, applications are configured on a single node. Although the model can use virtual servers, it can't use failover. This model has the following advantages:

- You can organize resources on a server for administrative convenience and for the convenience of your clients.
- Administrators and clients can readily see descriptively named virtual servers on the network rather than having to navigate a list of actual servers to find the shares they need.
- The Cluster service automatically restarts the various application and dependent resources after a computer has been restored following a resource failure. This is useful for applications that benefit from an automatic restart function but don't have their own mechanisms for accomplishing it.
- You can cluster the single node with a second node at a future time and the resource groups are already in place. After you configure failover policies for the groups, the virtual servers are ready to operate.

Figure 4.8 represents an example of a single-node cluster. Notice that failover can't be supported.

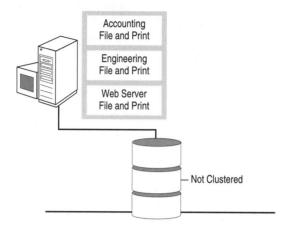

Figure 4.8   Single-node server cluster configuration

An example of using the single-node configuration would be to locate all the file
and print resources in your organization on a single computer, establishing separate groups for each department. When clients from one department need to connect to the appropriate file or print share, they can find the share as easily as they
can find an actual computer.

Note   Some applications, such as SQL Server versions 6.5 and 7, can't be
installed on a single-node cluster.

Model 2: Active/Passive Configuration

Model 2 provides maximum availability and performance for your resources but
requires an investment in hardware that's not in use most of the time.

In this model, one node, referred to as the *primary node,* supports all clients
while its companion node is idle. The companion node is a dedicated *secondary
node* that's ready to be used whenever a failover occurs on the primary node. If
the primary node fails, the secondary node immediately picks up all operations
and continues to service clients at a rate of performance that's close to or equal to
that of the primary node. The exact performance depends on the capacity of the secondary node. This approach is often referred to as an *active/passive* configuration.
Figure 4.9 represents an example of the dedicated secondary node approach.

The active/passive configuration is best suited for the most important applications
and resources in your organization. For example, suppose your organization
maintains an e-commerce site that relies heavily on a SQL Server database. If the
database is unavailable, the site is essentially useless to your customers. As a
result, the expense of doubling your hardware in this area is justified by the ability to protect client access to your organization. If one of your SQL Server computers fails, another server is fully configured to take over its operations.

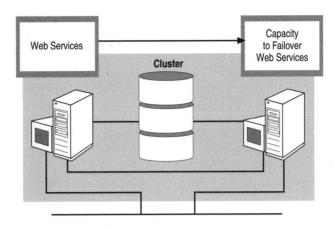

Figure 4.9   Active/passive configuration

If your budget allows for a secondary server with identical capacity to its primary node, then you don't need to set a preferred server for any of the groups. If one node has greater capacity than the other, setting the group failover policies to prefer the larger server keeps performance as high as possible.

If the secondary node has identical capacity to the primary node, set the policy to prevent failback for all groups. If the secondary node has less capacity than the primary node, set the policy for immediate failback or for failback at a specified off-peak hour.

Example of Active/Passive Configuration

An active/passive configuration represents one example of a dedicated secondary node. With an active/passive configuration, nodes in a server cluster aren't limited to providing applications that use clustering. Nodes that provide clustered resources can also support applications that aren't cluster-aware and that will fail if the server stops functioning. Figure 4.10 represents an example of an active/ passive configuration that includes cluster-aware applications and applications that are not cluster-aware.

The applications in groups 2 and 3 serve clients on one of the servers, but because they aren't cluster-aware, you don't establish failover policies for them. For example, you might use a node to run a mail server that hasn't been designed to use failover or for an accounting application that you use so infrequently that availability isn't important.

When node failure occurs, the applications that you didn't configure with failover policies are unavailable unless they have built-in failover mechanisms of their own. They remain unavailable until the node on which they run is restored; you must either restart them manually or set Windows 2000 Advanced Server or Windows 2000 Datacenter Server to start them automatically when the system software starts. The applications that you configured with failover policies failover as usual according to those policies.

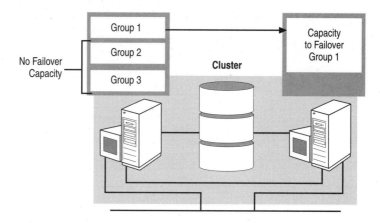

Figure 4.10   Active/passive configuration with both cluster-aware and non-cluster-aware applications

Model 3: Active/Active Configuration

Model 3 allows you to make the maximum use of your hardware resources. This configuration provides high availability and performance when both nodes are online and provides reliability and acceptable performance when only one node is online.

In this model, each node makes its own set of resources available to the network in the form of virtual servers, which clients can detect and access. In a server cluster, a *virtual server* is a set of resources, including a Network Name resource and an IP Address resource, that are contained by a resource group. A node must have enough capacity to run at optimum performance when the cluster is fully operational and enough capacity to run at acceptable performance if failover occurs. Depending on resource and server capacity specifications, all client services remain available during and after failover, but performance can decrease. Figure 4.11 represents an example of the active/active configuration.

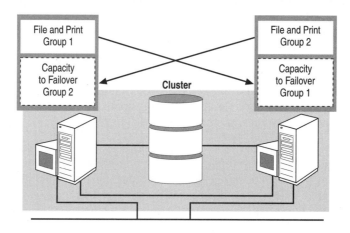

Figure 4.11   Active/active configuration

An example of using an active/active configuration would be to set up the cluster for file-sharing and print-spooling services. Multiple file and print shares are established as separate groups, one on each node. If one node fails, the other nodes temporarily take on the file-sharing and print-spooling services for all nodes. The failover policy for the group that's temporarily relocated is set to prefer its original node. When the failed node is restored, the relocated group returns to the control of its preferred node and operations resume at normal performance. Services are available to clients throughout the process with only minor interruption.

The following examples represent several types of active/active configurations.

Example 1: Clustering a Single Application Type

Your corporate intranet relies on a server that runs two large database applications. Both databases are critical to hundreds of users who repeatedly connect to this server throughout the day. During peak connect times the server can't keep up with demand, and performance often declines.

To alleviate the problem, you can attach a second server to the overloaded server, forming a cluster and balancing the load. You now have multiple servers, each running one of the database applications. If one server fails, you might experience degraded performance, but only temporarily. When the failed server is restored, the application it was running fails back and operations resume. Figure 4.12 shows two database applications running on a cluster.

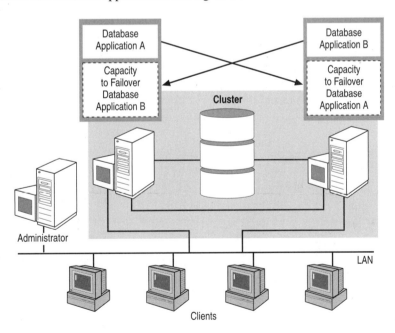

Figure 4.12   Attaching a second server to form a cluster

Example 2: Clustering Multiple Applications

Your retail business relies on two servers—one that provides file and print services and another that provides a database application for inventory and ordering information. Without the file and print services, employees can't conduct business. Without access to the database, customers can't place orders and employees can't access inventory or shipping information. Figure 4.13 shows a typical configuration used when mission-critical applications and services rely on separate servers, thus putting the applications and services at risk.

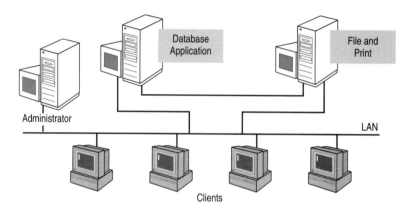

Figure 4.13 Relying on separate servers for mission-critical application and services

To ensure the availability of all services, you should join the computers into a cluster and create two groups, one on each node. One group contains all the resources needed to run the file and print services, and the other group contains all the resources for the database application, including the database. Figure 4.14 represents a solution that ensures the availability of applications in this case.

In the failover policies of each group, specify that both groups can run on either node, thereby assuring their availability if one node fails.

In Windows 2000 Advanced Server and Windows 2000 Datacenter Server, the Cluster service can detect loss of connectivity between the servers and client systems. If the Cluster service software can isolate the problem to a specific server, the Cluster service fails resource groups over to an operating server (by means of the functioning networks).

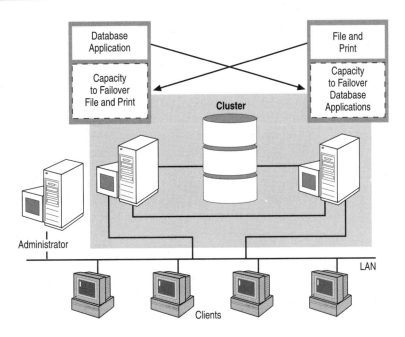

Figure 4.14   Clustering multiple applications

Example 3: Complex Hybrid Configuration

The complex hybrid configuration builds on the active/active model. This configuration allows you to incorporate the advantages of previous models and combine them into one cluster. As long as you've provided sufficient capacity, many types of failover scenarios can coexist on all the nodes. All failover activity occurs as normal according to the policies you set up. Figure 4.15 represents an example of a complex hybrid configuration in which two databases are configured to failover.

For administrative convenience, the file-and-print shares in the cluster (which don't require failover ability) are grouped logically by department and configured as virtual servers. In addition, an application that can't failover resides in the cluster and operates without any failover protection.

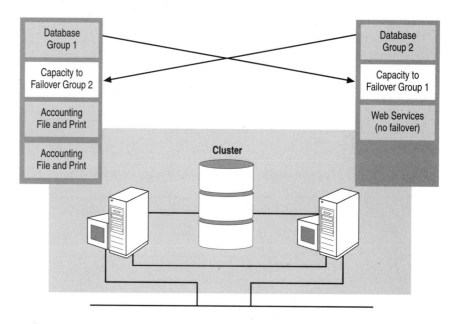

Figure 4.15   The complex hybrid configuration

Making a Decision

When choosing a server cluster model, you can select from three basic types: single-mode, active/passive, and active/active. Table 4.4 describes many of the factors to consider when deciding which configuration strategy to implement.

Table 4.4   Server Cluster Models

Strategy	Description
Model 1, single-node	With Model 1, you can organize resources for administrative convenience, use virtual servers, restart applications automatically, and more easily create a cluster later. However, this model can't make use of failover. If an application can't be restarted, it becomes unavailable.
Model 2, active/passive	Model 2 provides the maximum amount of availability for your resources. However, this model also requires an investment in hardware that's not used most of the time. If the primary node fails, the secondary node immediately picks up all operations. This model is best suited for applications and resources that must maintain the highest availability.
Model 3, active/active	Model 3 provides high availability and performance when both nodes are online and provides reliable and acceptable performance when only one node is online. Services remain available during and after failover, but performance can decrease, which can sometimes affect availability.

Recommendations

Whenever possible, you should try to use the active/passive configuration model (Model 2). This model provides the maximum availability and performance for your resources. However, as is often the case, budget constraints might limit your investment in hardware. If you can't implement the active/passive configuration, you should use the active/active model (Model 3), which requires a smaller investment in hardware but which could result in a degradation of performance should failover occur.

Example: A Highly Available Cluster for Woodgrove Bank

Woodgrove Bank plans to add online banking services. They believe that online banking will provide convenience to their customers and reduce the amount of phone support that they currently provide. Woodgrove Bank has instituted an aggressive marketing campaign to promote their Web services, so it's crucial for their online services to be highly available so customers experience the minimum number of problems when online.

A critical component of the Web services is the database that stores customer account information. The database must be continually available and perfor-mance must never be compromised, especially during peak hours. Consequently, Woodgrove Bank plans to implement an active/passive cluster model to provide the maximum availability and performance of the database resources.

Figure 4.16 shows how the active/passive mode will be used to support the data-base services.

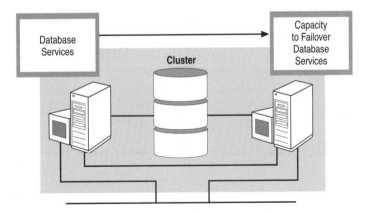

Figure 4.16   An active/passive cluster

Woodgrove Bank plans to use two identical Windows 2000 Advanced Server computers configured with SQL Server 2000. A resource group will be created for the database service and its dependent services. The failover policies will be configured so that no preferred server and no failback are set for the group. Hardware-based RAID will be used for the cluster storage.

Lesson Summary

Server clusters can be categorized in three configuration models: single-node, active/passive, and active/active. The single-node model uses only one computer and doesn't make use of failover. This model allows you to organize resources for administrative convenience, use virtual servers, restart applications, and more easily implement a cluster later. The active/passive model uses two computers: one as the primary node and the other as the secondary node. Services run on the primary node unless failover occurs. This model provides maximum availability and performance. The active/active model also uses two computers. In this configuration, each node makes its own set of resources available to the network. This model provides reliability and acceptable performance when only one node is online and high availability and performance when both nodes are online. This configuration also allows maximum use of your hardware resources.

Lab 4.1: Planning a Server Cluster

Lab Objectives

After completing this lab, you'll be able to

- Plan a server cluster
- Design resource groups and failover policies for the groups within that cluster

About This Lab

In this lab you'll plan a server cluster for Wingtip Toys. You'll be performing several of the steps described in Lesson 2 and Lesson 3: choosing a server cluster model, planning the resource groups for the cluster, and determining failover policies for the resource groups. For this lab, you can assume that some of the steps that are normally part of the cluster planning process have already been completed, as described in the scenario.

Before You Begin

Before you begin this lab, you must be able to

- Administer Windows 2000 Advanced Server
- Implement and administer the Cluster service in Windows 2000 Advanced Server

Scenario: Server Clusters for Wingtip Toys

Wingtip Toys is an online retail outlet that sells specialty toys over the Internet. The company, which markets toys to customers around the world, is a Web-based operation; they have no retail outlets or printed catalogs. As Wingtip Toys expanded into the international market, the company has seen a need to improve its Web site availability. The company has taken many steps to identify and reduce network risks by attempting to eliminate single points of failure. For example, the network now includes redundant components and network paths, multiple ISP connections, and UPS protection. Domain controller services have also been made highly available.

Wingtip Toys now wants to implement Windows clustering to support mail and database services. Exchange 2000 Server will be used for the mail services, and SQL Server 2000 will be used for the database services. The cluster will be made up of two Windows 2000 Advanced Server computers configured as member servers, and the cluster storage system will be made up of Fibre Channel connections and an offsite SAN to ensure data fault tolerance. In addition, the company wants to ensure that the services are highly available, but it wants to maximize the use of its hardware resources. The company isn't overly concerned about performance degradation should failover occur because each server can adequately support all the services.

Exercise 1: Choosing a Server Cluster Model

In this exercise you must decide which model to use for your cluster. You can choose from a single-node configuration, active/passive configuration, or active/active configuration.

1. What are the differences between the three configuration models?

2. Which configuration best suits the needs of Wingtip Toys?

Exercise 2: Planning the Resource Groups

You should follow six steps to determine how to set up the resource groups for your cluster. In many cases the decisions to make in each step are very apparent because the scenario has clearly provided the information.

Listing the Server-Based Applications

In this step you should list the applications that will be running on the cluster.

1. What are those applications?

Sorting the List of Applications

Next, you should determine which applications can and will use failover.

1. Which applications will use failover?

Listing Other Resources

After you identify which applications will use failover, you should determine what other resources will be running on this cluster.

1. Which resources should you include?

Listing Dependencies

By now you should have a list of all of the resources that will be included in the resource groups. You must determine what dependencies exist among these resources.

1. How are these resources dependent on each other?

Making Preliminary Grouping Decisions

You should now group together the resources. At this point it should be clear how the resources will be grouped together.

1. How will resources be grouped together?

2. What are the advantages of this grouping strategy?

Making Final Grouping Assignments

After you've listed the resources that you want grouped together, you can assign a name to each group and create a dependency tree for each group.

1. How would you create a dependency tree for each group?

Exercise 3: Determining Failover Policies

Once you've planned your resource groups, you can decide how to configure the failover policies for each group. These policies will determine how the group behaves if failover occurs. You must configure three settings: Failover Timing, Preferred Node, and Failback Timing.

1. How should you configure the Failover Timing setting?

2. How should you configure the Preferred Node setting?

3. How should you configure the Failback Timing setting?

Review

Answering the following questions will reinforce key information presented in this chapter. If you are unable to answer a question, review the appropriate lesson and then try the question again. Answers to the questions can be found in the appendix.

1. What objects does the Cluster service manage?

2. What are the differences between a resource group and a resource?

3. You're planning the resource groups for a cluster on your network. You've determined which applications will run on the servers and, of those, which can use failover. You've also determined the other types of resources that will be included in your list of resources, such as network names and IP addresses. What step should you take next?

4. You're planning a cluster for your organization's network. The cluster will include two Windows 2000 Advanced server computers that will run a database application and file and print services. You want the cluster configuration to support the maximum use of your cluster hardware. Which cluster configuration model should you use?

C H A P T E R   5

Network Load Balancing (NLB)

About This Chapter

Internet server programs supporting mission-critical applications—such as financial transactions, database access, corporate intranets, and other key functions—must run 24 hours a day, 7 days a week. And networks need the ability to scale performance to handle large volumes of client requests without creating delays. The Microsoft Windows 2000 Advanced Server and Datacenter Server operating systems include two clustering technologies—the Cluster service and Network Load Balancing (NLB)—that enable you to manage a group of independent servers as a single system for higher availability, easier manageability, and greater scalability. The Cluster service is intended primarily to provide failover support for critical line-of-business applications such as databases, messaging systems, and file/print services, and NLB balances incoming Internet Protocol (IP) traffic among multinode clusters. In this chapter, you'll learn how to use NLB to improve availability and scalability in your Web environment. The Cluster service is discussed in Chapter 4, "Microsoft Windows 2000 Cluster Service."

Before You Begin

To complete the lessons in this chapter, you must have

- Experience administering Windows 2000 Advanced Server and designing Windows 2000 networks
- The ability to implement the NLB service in a Windows 2000 Web environment

Lesson 1: Introduction to NLB

NLB enhances the scalability and availability of mission-critical services based on Transmission Control Protocol/Internet Protocol (TCP/IP), such as Web, Microsoft Terminal Services, virtual private networking (VPN), and streaming media servers. This service runs within cluster hosts as part of the Windows 2000 Advanced Server and Datacenter Server operating systems and requires no dedicated hardware support. To scale performance, NLB distributes IP traffic across multiple cluster hosts. It also ensures high availability by detecting host failures and automatically redistributing traffic to the surviving hosts. NLB provides remote controllability and supports rolling upgrades from the Windows NT 4 operating system. NLB's unique and fully distributed architecture enables it to deliver very high performance and failover protection, especially in comparison with dispatcher-based load balancers. This lesson provides an overview of NLB, describes how the service works, and discusses the NLB architecture.

After this lesson, you will be able to

- Describe NLB and how it works within a Windows 2000 Web environment

- Provide an overview of the NLB architecture

- Describe how you can use NLB to scale applications that manage application state data

Estimated lesson time: 30 minutes

Using Multiple Servers

An organization's Web applications typically perform such mission-critical tasks as e-commerce and financial transactions. Businesses can lose millions of dollars when mission-critical applications aren't available, so it's important that these applications are available at all times. They must be highly available and reliable. An easy and effective way to achieve availability and reliability is to use redundant servers. If you have more than one server implemented within your site and one of the servers fails, the processing requests can be redirected to another server, which provides a highly available Web site.

Adding just a few servers can increase your availability tremendously. If you have one server with only 90 percent availability, adding just one server increases your availability for the cluster to 99 percent, or only 14.4 unavailable minutes each day. That's because the probability of both failing at once is 0.1 squared, or 0.01. With seven available servers, you have 99.99999 percent availability—at least for the Web farm. The availability will be far better with better hardware, of course.

Adding Web servers also helps your site handle larger loads in an elegant manner: adding Web servers provides linear scalability (provided there aren't other bottlenecks in your system). For example, if you need to handle 10 times the number of Hypertext Transfer Protocol (HTTP) client requests, you should use 10 times as many servers, assuming that other factors, such as network bandwidth, don't create bottlenecks or limit availability.

Figure 5.1 shows the performance of servers in a Windows 2000 Web environment.

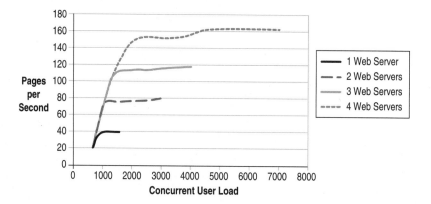

Figure 5.1   Scalability increasing as more Web servers are added to the Web farm

When you implement a site on a Web farm, you must distribute the processing load across the hosts. The processing requests received by the cluster are directed to the different hosts in the cluster so that response time is low and the application throughput is high. Each host in the cluster runs a separate copy of the server programs required by the application. For example, if the purpose of the cluster were to support File Transfer Protocol (FTP) services, each host in the cluster would be configured as an FTP server. Load balancing distributes the incoming client requests across the cluster hosts.

Load Balancing Solutions

As discussed in Chapter 1, "Introduction to Designing Highly Available Web Solutions," there are a number of ways to implement load balancing:

- Round-robin Domain Name System (DNS)
- Load-balancing switches
- Windows 2000 Advanced Server or Windows 2000 Datacenter Server NLB
- Microsoft Application Center 2000

Round-robin DNS involves setting up your site's DNS server to return the set of all the IP addresses of the servers in the cluster in a different order on each successive request. The client typically forwards the request to the first IP address in the list of IP addresses returned. Consequently, the request is directed to a different server in the cluster, and the traffic is distributed across the servers.

Load-balancing switches, such as Cisco LocalDirector, redirect TCP requests to servers in a server farm. These switches provide a highly scalable, interoperable solution that's also very reliable. To implement load balancing, the LocalDirector presents a common virtual IP address to the requesting clients and then forwards the requests to an available server.

Windows 2000 Advanced Server and Windows 2000 Datacenter Server NLB distributes the IP traffic across multiple Web servers that provide TCP/IP services. NLB presents a common virtual IP address for the entire cluster and transparently partitions client requests across the multiple servers in the cluster. NLB provides high availability and high scalability to the Internet applications.

Application Center 2000 also supports NLB. Although Application Center doesn't actually install NLB on Windows 2000 Advanced Server or Windows 2000 Datacenter Server, it provides a enhanced management interface that's integrated into the NLB service that's already included in both operating systems. However, if Application Center 2000 is installed on Windows 2000 Server (which doesn't provide NLB), Application Center 2000 will install NLB automatically.

Windows 2000 NLB

NLB provides scalability and high availability to enterprise-wide TCP/IP services, such as Web, Terminal Services, proxy, VPN, and streaming media services. NLB brings special value to enterprises deploying TCP/IP services, such as e-commerce applications, that link clients with transaction applications and back-end databases.

NLB servers (also called hosts) in a cluster communicate among themselves to provide the following benefits:

- **Scalability**   NLB scales the performance of a server-based program, such as Internet Information Services (IIS), by distributing its client requests across multiple servers within the cluster. As traffic increases, you can add additional servers to the cluster, with up to 32 servers possible in any one cluster.

- **High availability**   NLB provides high availability by automatically detecting a server's failure and repartitioning client traffic among the remaining servers within 10 seconds while providing users with continuous service.

NLB distributes IP traffic to multiple copies (or instances) of a TCP/IP service, such as a Web server. Each service runs on a host within the cluster. NLB transparently partitions the client requests among the hosts and lets the clients access the cluster using one or more virtual IP addresses. From the client's point of view, the cluster appears to be a single server that answers these client requests. As enterprise traffic increases, network administrators can simply plug another server into the cluster.

For example, the clustered hosts in Figure 5.2 work together to service network traffic from the Internet. Each server runs a copy of an IP-based service, such as Internet Information Services (IIS) 5.0, and NLB distributes the networking workload among them. This speeds up normal processing so that Internet clients see faster turnaround on their requests. For added system availability, the back-end application (a database, for example) can operate on a two-node cluster running the Cluster service.

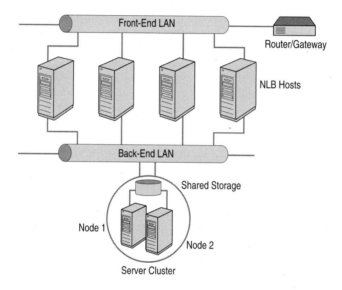

Figure 5.2   A four-host NLB cluster working as a single virtual server to handle network traffic

Each host runs its own copy of the server with NLB distributing the work among the four hosts.

How NLB Works

NLB scales the performance of a server-based program, such as a Web server, by distributing its client requests among multiple servers within the cluster. With NLB, each host receives each incoming IP packet, but only the intended recipient accepts it. The cluster hosts concurrently respond to different client requests or to multiple requests from the same client. For example, a Web browser may obtain the various images within a single Web page from different hosts in a load-balanced cluster. This speeds up processing and shortens the response time to clients.

By default, NLB distributes the load equally among all the hosts in the cluster. However, you can specify the load percentage that each host handles. Using these percentages, each NLB server selects and handles a portion of the workload.

Clients are statistically distributed among cluster hosts so that each server receives its percentage of incoming requests. This load balance dynamically changes when hosts enter or leave the cluster. However, the load balance doesn't change in response to varying server loads (such as CPU or memory usage). For applications such as Web servers, which have numerous clients and relatively short-lived client requests, NLB's ability to distribute workload through statistical mapping efficiently balances loads and provides fast response to cluster changes.

NLB cluster servers emit a heartbeat message to other hosts in the cluster and listen for the heartbeat of other hosts. If a server in a cluster fails, the remaining hosts adjust and redistribute the workload while maintaining continuous service to their clients. Although existing connections to an offline host are lost, the Internet services still remain continuously available. In most cases (for example, with Web servers), client software automatically retries the failed connections and the clients experience a delay of only a few seconds in receiving a response.

Figure 5.3 provides a high-level picture of how NLB works. In short, traffic is sent to all the hosts, but only one host decides to pick it up.

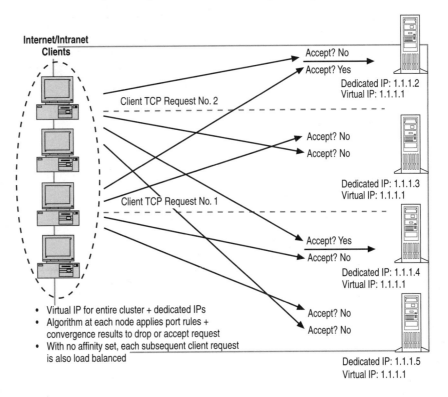

Figure 5.3   How NLB processes client requests

The statistical mapping of client IP addresses and IP ports to hosts results in a very even load balance; a good figure is to have all your load-balanced servers running the same load, ±5 percent. In addition to an even load, you need a very fast, very efficient load-balancing algorithm so that you can maintain high throughput. NLB meets these requirements by precisely sending a particular client to a particular host.

Load Balancing Algorithm

NLB employs a fully distributed filtering algorithm to map incoming clients to the cluster hosts. This algorithm was chosen to enable cluster hosts to make a load-balancing decision independently and quickly for each incoming packet. It was optimized to deliver statistically even loads for a large client population making numerous, relatively small requests, such as those typically made to Web servers. When the client population is small or the client connections produce widely varying loads on the server, the load-balancing algorithm is less effective. However, its algorithm's simplicity and speed allow it to deliver very high performance, including both high throughput and low response time, in a wide range of useful client/server applications.

Network Load Balancing load balances incoming client requests by directing a selected percentage of new requests to each cluster host; you can set the load percentage in the NLB Properties dialog box for each port range to be load-balanced. The algorithm doesn't respond to changes in the load on each cluster host (such as the CPU load or memory usage). However, the mapping is modified when the cluster membership changes, and load percentages are renormalized accordingly.

When inspecting an arriving packet, all hosts simultaneously perform a statistical mapping to quickly determine which host should handle the packet. The mapping uses a randomization function that calculates a host priority based on the client's IP address, port, and other state information maintained to optimize load balance. The corresponding host forwards the packet up the network stack to TCP/IP, and the other cluster hosts discard it. The mapping doesn't vary unless the membership of cluster hosts changes, ensuring that a given client's IP address and port will always map to the same cluster host. However, the particular cluster host to which the client's IP address and port map can't be predetermined because the randomization function takes into account the current and past cluster's membership to minimize the process of remapping.

The load-balancing algorithm assumes that client IP addresses and port numbers (when client affinity isn't enabled) are statistically independent. (Client affinity is discussed later in this lesson.) This assumption can break down if a server-side firewall is used that proxies client addresses with one IP address and, at the same time, client affinity is enabled. In this case, all client requests will be handled by one cluster host and load balancing is defeated. However, if client affinity isn't enabled, the distribution of client ports within the firewall usually provides good load balance.

Convergence

NLB hosts periodically exchange multicast or broadcast heartbeat messages within the cluster. This allows them to monitor the cluster's status. When the cluster's state changes (such as when hosts fail, leave, or join the cluster), NLB invokes a process known as *convergence,* in which the hosts exchange heartbeat messages to determine a new, consistent state of the cluster and to elect the host with the highest priority as the new default host. When all cluster hosts have reached consensus on the cluster's correct new state, they record the change in cluster membership upon completion of convergence in the Windows 2000 event log. Figure 5.4 illustrates the NLB convergence process.

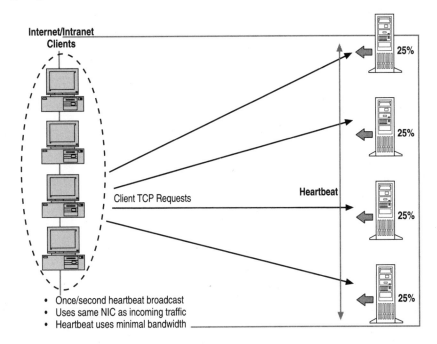

Figure 5.4 NLB failure recovery/convergence

During convergence, the hosts continue to handle incoming network traffic as usual, except that traffic for a failed host doesn't receive service. Client requests to surviving hosts are unaffected. Convergence terminates when all cluster hosts report a consistent view of the cluster membership for several heartbeat periods. If a host attempts to join the cluster with inconsistent port rules or an overlapping host priority, completion of convergence is inhibited. This prevents an improperly configured host from handling cluster traffic.

At the completion of convergence, client traffic for a failed host is redistributed to the remaining hosts, as shown in Figure 5.5. If a host is added to the cluster, convergence allows this host to receive its share of load-balanced traffic.

Expansion of the cluster doesn't affect ongoing cluster operations and is achieved in a manner transparent to both Internet clients and to server programs. However, it might affect client sessions because clients may be remapped to different cluster hosts between connections.

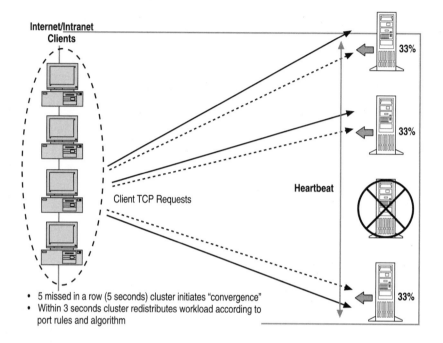

Figure 5.5   An NLB cluster with one failed host

Once per second, every host broadcasts a heartbeat message conveying its state, its logic's state, and its port rule policy. The other hosts examine these messages to verify a consistent membership of the cluster.

The local area network (LAN) resources that the heartbeats occupy is very small—in fact, measured in the tens of kilobytes—because the broadcast is only one packet per second per host. It's an *n*-fold algorithm, not an *n* algorithm.

If, over a 5-second period, any host recognizes that another host has dropped out or a new member has been added, that host will enter the convergence process. In that process, the host will double the rate of heartbeat messages. During the convergence process, the other hosts continue to respond to client requests.

However, the clients that would have been targeted to the failed host don't see any response. Their existing connections die, and any new connections they produce that map to that failed host aren't serviced. Instead, within a 10-second period, these clients are remapped to the other hosts and a failover is achieved or the cluster recognizes a newly added host.

It's important to understand that the cluster doesn't stop servicing traffic during the convergence process. For example, say you add a new Windows 2000–based host to an existing Windows NT–based cluster. Because you forgot to change the default port rules, that new port will be inconsistent with the Windows NT–based cluster. In this case, convergence will just continue until you pull that inconsistent host out of the cluster and fix its port rules. And while this may seem odd, it's the only way to ensure consistent load balancing across the hosts.

Client Affinity

NLB session support uses a process called *client affinity,* which allows a client to be mapped to the same host during a session. After the initial client request, which is distributed like any other request, NLB looks at only the source IP address and not the source port information. Therefore, a client with a given IP address will always map to a particular cluster host, and any session state that's maintained in that cluster host will persist across those connections. The client won't suddenly be mapped to another host at connection boundaries.

Figure 5.6 illustrates how client affinity works after a client makes an initial request.

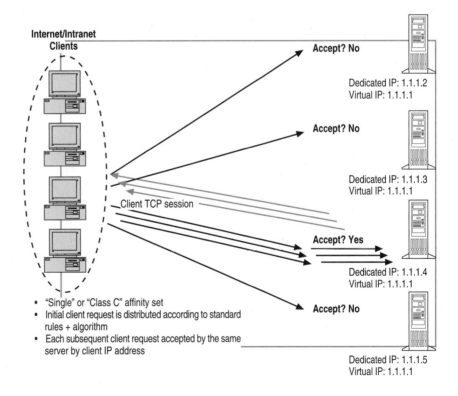

Figure 5.6 An NLB cluster with one failed host

You can establish two types of client affinity: Single or Class C. These two types help maintain client sessions. With Single affinity, NLB pins that client to a particular host without setting a timeout limit; this mapping is in effect until the cluster set changes. The trouble with Single affinity is that in a large site with multiple proxy servers, a client can appear to come from different IP addresses. To address this, NLB also includes Class C affinity, which specifies that all clients within a given Class C address space will map to a given cluster host. However, Class C affinity doesn't address situations in which proxy servers are placed across Class C address spaces. Currently the only solution is to handle it at the Active Server Pages (ASP) level.

NLB Architecture

To maximize throughput and availability, NLB uses a fully distributed software architecture. An identical copy of the NLB driver runs in parallel on each cluster host. The drivers arrange for all cluster hosts on a single subnet to concurrently detect incoming network traffic for the cluster's primary IP address (and for additional IP addresses on multihomed hosts). On each cluster host, the driver acts as a filter between the network adapter's driver and the TCP/IP stack, allowing the host to receive a portion of the incoming network traffic. In this way, incoming client requests are partitioned and load balanced among the cluster hosts.

NLB runs as a network driver logically situated beneath higher-level application protocols, such as HTTP and FTP. Figure 5.7 shows the implementation of NLB as an intermediate driver in the Windows 2000 network stack.

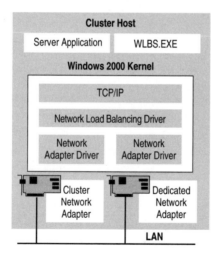

Figure 5.7   NLB running as an intermediate driver between the TCP/IP protocol and network adapter drivers within the Windows 2000 protocol stack

This architecture maximizes throughput by using the broadcast subnet to deliver incoming network traffic to all cluster hosts and by eliminating the need to route incoming packets to individual cluster hosts. Since filtering unwanted packets is faster than routing packets (which involves receiving, examining, rewriting, and resending), NLB delivers higher network throughput than dispatcher-based solutions. As network and server speeds grow, NLB's throughput also grows proportionally, thus eliminating any dependency on a particular hardware routing implementation. For example, NLB has demonstrated 250 megabits per second (Mbps) throughput on gigabit networks.

NLB's architecture takes advantage of the subnet's hub architecture, switch architecture, or both, to deliver incoming network traffic simultaneously to all cluster hosts. However, this approach increases the burden on switches by occupying additional port bandwidth. This is usually not a concern in most intended applications, such as Web services and streaming media, since the percentage of incoming traffic is a small fraction of total network traffic. However, if the client-side network connections to the switch are significantly faster than the server-side connections, incoming traffic can occupy a prohibitively large portion of the server-side port bandwidth. The same problem arises if multiple clusters are hosted on the same switch and you haven't set up virtual LANs for individual clusters.

During packet reception, the fully pipelined implementation of NLB overlaps the delivery of incoming packets to TCP/IP and the reception of other packets by the network adapter driver. This speeds up overall processing and reduces latency because TCP/IP can process a packet while the Network Driver Interface Specification (NDIS) driver receives a subsequent packet. It also reduces the overhead required for TCP/IP and the NDIS driver to coordinate their actions, and in many cases it eliminates an extra copy of packet data in memory. During packet sending, NLB also enhances throughput and reduces latency and overhead by increasing the number of packets that TCP/IP can send with one NDIS call. To achieve these performance enhancements, NLB allocates and manages a pool of packet buffers and descriptors that it uses to overlap the actions of TCP/IP and the NDIS driver.

Application State Data

Application state refers to data maintained by a server application on behalf of its clients. If a server application (such as a Web server) maintains state information about a client session—that is, when it maintains a client's *session state*—that spans multiple TCP connections, it's usually important that all TCP connections for this client be directed to the same cluster host. Shopping cart contents at an e-commerce site and Secure Sockets Layer (SSL) authentication data are examples of a client's session state.

You can use NLB to scale applications that manage session state spanning multiple connections. When its client affinity parameter setting is enabled, NLB directs all TCP connections from one client IP address to the same cluster host. This allows session state to be maintained in host memory. However, should a server or network failure occur during a client session, a new logon may be required to reauthenticate the client and reestablish session state. Also, adding a new cluster host redirects some client traffic to the new host, which can affect sessions, although ongoing TCP connections aren't disturbed. Client/server applications that manage client state so that it can be retrieved from any cluster host (for example, by embedding state within cookies or pushing it to a back-end database) don't need to use client affinity.

To further assist in managing session state, NLB provides an optional client affinity setting that directs all client requests from a TCP/IP class C address range to a single cluster host. With this feature, clients that use multiple proxy servers can have their TCP connections directed to the same cluster host. The use of multiple proxy servers at the client's site causes requests from a single client to appear to originate from different systems. Assuming that all of the client's proxy servers are located within the same 254-host class C address range, NLB ensures that the same host handles client sessions with minimum impact on load distribution among the cluster hosts. Some very large client sites may use multiple proxy servers that span class C address spaces.

In addition to session state, server applications often maintain persistent, server-based state information that's updated by client transactions, such as merchandise inventory at an e-commerce site. You should not use NLB to directly scale applications such as Microsoft SQL Server (other than for read-only database access) that independently update interclient state because updates made on one cluster host won't be visible to other cluster hosts. To benefit from NLB, applications must be designed to permit multiple instances to simultaneously access a shared database server that synchronizes updates. For example, Web servers with ASP should have their client updates pushed to a shared back-end database server.

Using NLB

When you install Windows 2000 Advanced Server or Windows 2000 Datacenter Server, NLB is automatically installed. It operates as an optional service for LAN connections, and you can enable it for one LAN connection in the system; this LAN connection is known as the *cluster adapter*. No hardware changes are required to install and run NLB. Since it's compatible with almost all Ethernet and Fiber Distributed Data Interface (FDDI) network adapters, it has no specific hardware compatibility list.

IP Addresses

The cluster is assigned a primary IP address, which represents a virtual IP address to which all cluster hosts respond. The remote control program provided as a part of NLB uses this IP address to identify a target cluster. Each cluster host also can be assigned a dedicated IP address for network traffic unique to that particular host within the cluster. NLB never load balances traffic for the dedicated IP address. Instead, it load balances incoming traffic from all IP addresses other than the dedicated IP address.

When configuring NLB, it's important to enter the dedicated IP address, primary IP address, and other optional virtual IP addresses into the TCP/IP Properties dialog box in order to enable the host's TCP/IP stack to respond to these IP addresses. You always enter the dedicated IP address first so that outgoing connections from the cluster host are sourced with this IP address instead of a virtual IP address. Otherwise, replies to the cluster host could be inadvertently load balanced by NLB and delivered to another cluster host. Some services, such as the Point-to-Point Tunneling Protocol (PPTP) server, don't allow outgoing connections to be sourced from a different IP address, and thus you can't use a dedicated IP address with them.

Host Priorities

Each cluster host is assigned a unique host priority in the range of 1 to 32, with lower numbers denoting higher priorities. The host with the highest host priority (lowest numeric value) is called the *default host*. It handles all client traffic for the virtual IP addresses that's not specifically intended to be load-balanced. This ensures that server applications not configured for load balancing receive only client traffic on a single host. If the default host fails, the host with the next highest priority takes over as default host.

Port Rules

NLB uses port rules to customize load balancing for a consecutive numeric range of server ports. Port rules can select either multiple-host or single-host load balancing policies. With multiple-host load balancing, incoming client requests are distributed among all cluster hosts, and you can specify a load percentage for each host. Load percentages allow hosts with higher capacity to receive a larger fraction of the total client load. Single-host load balancing directs all client requests to the host with highest handling priority. The handling priority essentially overrides the host priority for the port range and allows different hosts to individually handle all client traffic for specific server applications. You can also use port rules to block undesired network access to certain IP ports.

By default, NLB is configured with a single port rule that covers all ports (0–65,535) with multiple-host load balancing and single-client affinity. You can use this rule for most applications. It's important that this rule not be modified for VPN applications and whenever IP fragmentation is expected. This ensures that fragments are efficiently handled by the cluster hosts.

Lesson Summary

An easy and effective way to achieve availability and reliability is to use redundant servers. NLB provides scalability and high availability to enterprise-wide TCP/IP services by distributing its client requests among multiple servers within the cluster. NLB employs a fully distributed filtering algorithm to map incoming clients to the cluster hosts. Cluster hosts periodically exchange multicast or broadcast heartbeat messages within the cluster, allowing the hosts to monitor the cluster's status. When the cluster's state changes (such as when hosts fail, leave, or join the cluster), NLB invokes a process known as convergence. Client affinity allows a client to always map to a particular cluster host so that the session state data can persist. Application state refers to data maintained by a server application on behalf of its clients. To maximize throughput and availability, NLB uses a fully distributed software architecture. The cluster is assigned a primary IP address, which represents a virtual IP address to which all cluster hosts respond. Each cluster host is assigned a unique host priority in the range of 1 to 32, with lower numbers denoting higher priorities. NLB uses port rules to customize load balancing for a consecutive numeric range of server ports.

Lesson 2: Planning NLB Clusters

NLB allows you to scale IP services across as many as 32 hosts in a cluster. Because NLB is a fully distributed software solution, it can run on every host in parallel, so if one host fails, the cluster continues to run. NLB leverages the ability of switches and hubs to deliver traffic in parallel to all the clustered hosts, allowing it to deliver much higher throughput than a centralized solution. At the same time, NLB allows you to assign a virtual IP address to the cluster, which presents a single system image of the cluster to the clients. When implementing NLB, you must consider a number of factors as you plan how to set up the clusters in your organization. For example, you must determine how many hosts should be included in a cluster. This lesson describes each step that you should follow when planning NLB clusters in your organization.

After this lesson, you will be able to

- Plan an NLB cluster and identify the possible failures that can interrupt access to resources
- Choose applications to run on an NLB cluster
- Determine the size of the NLB cluster
- Optimize NLB clusters

Estimated lesson time: 25 minutes

Planning for NLB

You should consider a number of steps when planning an NLB cluster, including identifying network risks, determining which applications to use, choosing an NLB model, sizing NLB clusters, determining capacity requirements, and planning for fault tolerance. This section discusses each of these steps.

Identifying Network Risks

When you identify network risks, you identify the possible failures that can interrupt access to network resources. Single points of failure can include hardware, software, or external dependencies, such as power supplied by a utility company or dedicated wide area network (WAN) lines.

In general, you provide maximum availability when you minimize the number of single points of failure in your environment and provide mechanisms that maintain service when a failure occurs.

In the case of NLB, you also provide maximum availability when you do the following:

- Load balance only the applications that are appropriate to NLB.
- Make sure that application servers are properly configured for the applications they're running.

A principal goal of NLB is to provide increased availability. A cluster of two or more computers ensures that if one computer fails, another computer is available to continue processing client requests. However, NLB isn't designed to protect all aspects of your workflow in all circumstances. For example, NLB isn't an alternative to backing up data. NLB protects only access to the data, not the data itself. Also, it doesn't protect against a power outage that would disable the entire cluster.

Windows 2000 Advanced Server has built-in features that protect certain computer and network processes during failure. These features include RAID-1 (disk mirroring) and RAID-5 (disk-striping with parity). When planning your NLB environment, look for areas where these features can help you in ways that NLB can't.

Determining Which Applications to Use

In general, NLB can scale any application or service that uses TCP/IP as its network protocol and is associated with a specific TCP or User Datagram Protocol (UDP) port.

An application can run on an NLB cluster under the following conditions:

- The connection with clients is configured to use IP.
- The application to be load balanced uses TCP or UDP ports.
- Multiple identical instances of an application can run simultaneously on separate servers. If multiple instances of an application share data, there has to be a way to synchronize the updates.

NLB uses *port rules* that describe which traffic to load balance and which traffic to ignore. By default, NLB configures all ports for load balancing. However, you can modify the configuration that determines how incoming network traffic is load balanced on a per port basis. To modify the default behavior, you create port rules that cover specific port ranges.

The following list includes examples of services and their associated ports:

- HTTP, used by applications such as IIS: port 80
- HTTP Secure (HTTPS), used with Secure Sockets Layer (SSL) for encrypting Web traffic: port 443

- FTP, used for downloading files: port 21, port 20, and ports 1024–65535
- Trivial File Transfer Protocol (TFTP) servers, used by applications such as Bootstrap Protocol (BOOTP): port 69
- Simple Mail Transport Protocol (SMTP), used by applications such as Microsoft Exchange: port 25
- Terminal Services: port 3389

To be load balanced successfully, an application or service must be designed to allow multiple instances (multiple copies of a program) to run simultaneously, one on each cluster host. For example, an application must not make updates to a file that will in turn be synchronized with updates made by other instances unless it explicitly provides a means to do so. To avoid this problem, set up a back-end database server to handle synchronized updates to shared-state information.

In addition, you commonly use NLB with the following servers:

- **VPN servers**   An extension of a private network that encompasses links across shared or public networks such as the Internet
- **Streaming media servers**   Software (such as Microsoft Media Technologies) that provides multimedia support, allowing you to deliver content through the use of Advanced Streaming Format over an intranet or the Internet

After you've determined that your organization would benefit from load balancing PPTP or streaming traffic, NLB is a good choice for VPN servers and streaming media servers.

Note   Before load balancing an application in an NLB cluster, review the application license or check with the application vendor. Each application vendor sets its own licensing policies for applications running on clusters.

Choosing an NLB Model

You can configure NLB by using one of four models. Each model has specific advantages and disadvantages. Lesson 3, "Choosing an NLB Model," discusses each of these models.

Sizing NLB Clusters

Cluster size, defined as the number of hosts participating in the cluster (which can be up to 32 in an NLB cluster), is based on the number of computers required to meet the anticipated client load for a given application.

For example, if you determine that you need six computers running IIS in order to meet the anticipated client demand for Web services, then NLB will run on all six computers and your cluster will consist of six cluster hosts.

As a general rule, add servers until the cluster can easily handle the client load without becoming overloaded. The maximum cluster size you need is determined by network capacity on a given subnet. The exact number depends on the nature of the application.

Note   Always be sure that there's enough extra server capacity so that if one server fails, the remaining servers can accommodate the increased load.

When the cluster subnet approaches saturation of the network, add an additional cluster on a different subnet. Use round-robin DNS to direct clients to the clusters. You can continue to add clusters in this manner as the network demand grows. Since round-robin DNS contains only cluster IP addresses, clients are always directed to clusters instead of to individual servers and therefore never experience an outage due to a failed server. In some deployments requiring high bandwidth, you could use round-robin DNS to split incoming traffic among multiple, identical NLB clusters.

In Figure 5.8, the IP request discovers DNS (www.proseware.com), which resolves to the virtual IP address of NLB Cluster 1 (10.1.0.1) and passes the request to that NLB cluster. Subsequent requests are then sent to Cluster 2 (10.2.0.1) and Cluster 3 (10.3.0.1) and then continue in a round-robin fashion.

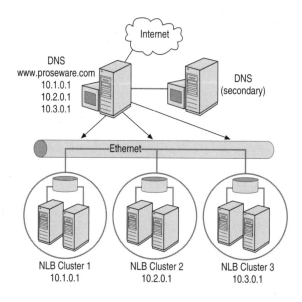

Figure 5.8   Round-robin DNS among identical NLB clusters

You can use a switch to separate incoming traffic in cases where you have more than one cluster. If you use network switches and you deploy two or more clusters, consider placing the clusters on individual switches so that incoming cluster traffic is handled separately. A switch is used to connect cluster hosts to a router or other source of incoming network connections.

Determining Capacity Requirements

After you determine your cluster size, you're ready to configure individual cluster hosts. In general, you should base this determination on the types of applications you plan to load balance and the client demand you anticipate on these applications. Some server applications, such as file and print servers, are extremely disk-intensive and require very large disk capacities and fast input/output (I/O). Cluster capacity requirements are discussed in more detail in Chapter 7, "Capacity Planning."

Planning for Fault-Tolerant Disks

Disk failure can result in the irrecoverable loss of data and will cause NLB to stop functioning, along with the server and all its other applications. For this reason, you might want to consider using special methods to protect your disks from failure. Two common solutions are software-based or hardware-based RAID. The use of a fault-tolerant RAID solution ensures that data isn't lost if a member of a disk set fails.

In a hardware solution, the controller interface handles the creation and regeneration of redundant information, and data is stored across an array of disks. In Windows, the software handles the creation and regeneration functions, and data is stored across an array of disks or across a set of virtual drives.

Disk arrays consist of multiple disk drives coordinated by a controller. Individual data files are typically written to more than one disk in a manner that, depending on the RAID level used, can improve performance or reliability.

Note that if a fault occurs, there's no fault tolerance until it is repaired. Few RAID implementations can withstand two simultaneous failures. When you replace the failed disk, you can regenerate the data by using the redundant information. Data regeneration occurs without bringing in backup tapes or performing manual update operations to cover transactions that took place since the last backup. When data regeneration is complete, all data is current and again protected against disk failure. The ability to provide cost-effective high data availability is the key advantage of disk arrays.

Software RAID

Windows 2000 Advanced Server supports three software RAID solutions: RAID-0, RAID-1, and RAID-5. Only RAID-1 and RAID-5 provide for fault tolerance. The purpose of RAID-1 and RAID-5 is to guard against the loss of data in the event of a catastrophic hard disk failure. Any server on which NLB is running can benefit from this. If a disk fails, the server will continue to operate as if no disk failure had occurred, as will NLB itself and the load-balanced applications.

The major differences between RAID-1 volumes and RAID-5 volumes are hardware requirements, performance, and cost. Choosing between mirrored and RAID-5 volumes depends on your computing environment. RAID-5 volumes are a good solution for data redundancy when most activity consists of reading data. For example, if your network has a server on which you maintain all copies of the programs used by the people at that site, this might be a good case for using a RAID-5 volume. It enables you to protect the programs against the loss of a single disk in the striped volume. In addition, the read performance improves because of the concurrency of the reads across the disks that make up the RAID-5 volume.

In an environment in which the information is frequently updated, using mirrored volumes is usually better. However, you can use a RAID-5 volume if you want redundancy and if the mirror's storage overhead cost is prohibitive.

Hardware RAID

The computers on which NLB is installed can use a variety of hardware RAID configurations. Because many hardware RAID solutions provide power, bus, and cable redundancy within a single cabinet and track the state of each component in the hardware RAID firmware, they provide data availability with multiple redundancies, protecting against multiple points of failure.

Hardware RAID solutions also use an onboard processor and cache to provide outstanding performance. Windows 2000 and NLB can use these devices as standard disk resources. Though much more expensive than software RAID, hardware RAID is generally considered the superior solution.

Making a Decision

The process for planning an NLB cluster includes a number of steps. In each step you must make decisions about hardware and software configurations. Table 5.1 describes many of the considerations that you should take into account for each step.

Table 5.1   Planning an NLB Cluster

Step	Description
Identifying network risks	When implementing NLB clusters and the environment in which they're located, you should minimize the number of single points of failure and provide mechanisms that maintain service as a failure occurs. You should also load balance only applications that are appropriate to NLB and make sure application servers are configured for the applications they're running.
Determining which applications to use	The applications must use IP to connect with clients and must use TCP or UDP ports. Multiple instances of the application must be able to run simultaneously on separate servers. If multiple instances share data, there must be a way to synchronize updates.

Table 5.1   *(continued)*

Step	Description
Choosing an NLB model	You can configure NLB by using one of four models. NLB models are discussed in Lesson 3, "Choosing an NLB Model."
Sizing NLB clusters	Cluster size is based on the number of computers required to meet the anticipated client load. You should add servers until the cluster can easily handle the client load without becoming overloaded. The maximum size of the cluster is determined by network capacity. You can use round-robin DNS for clusters on different subnets.
Determining capacity requirements	You should base the size of the cluster hosts on the types of applications and the client demands. Determining capacity requirements is discussed in Chapter 7, "Capacity Planning."
Planning for fault-tolerant disks	You can use RAID to implement disk fault tolerance. RAID can be implemented as a hardware solution or a software solution. Windows 2000 supports two fault-tolerant software solutions: RAID-1 and RAID-5.

Recommendations

When planning an NLB cluster, you should adhere to the following guidelines:

- Eliminate single points of failure in hardware, software, and external dependencies. Use redundant services, components, and network connections, and keep replacement components on hand. Configure servers for the applications that they're running and use only applications appropriate to NLB.

- Choose applications that use TCP/IP as their network protocol and are associated with specific TCP or UDP ports.

- Add enough servers to the cluster until the cluster can easily handle the client load. Be sure that there's enough capacity so that if one server fails, the remaining servers can accommodate the increased load. Use round-robin DNS for clusters on different subnets.

- Use hardware RAID solutions for disk fault tolerance.

Example: An NLB Cluster for Northwind Traders

Northwind Traders imports gift items from Southeast Asia and sells these items to wholesale outlets in the United States and Europe. The company is setting up a Web-based system that will allow wholesale customers to place orders online. The goal of the site is to be available all day, every day, to accommodate various time zones and work schedules. To support this goal, Northwind Traders plans to use NLB to provide highly available Web servers.

Before implementing the cluster, Northwind Trading will use the planning process outlined in this lesson to determine how to set up the cluster. The first step is to ensure that any single points of failure in the network are eliminated. The Web site and its network infrastructure will use redundancy throughout the network to achieve high availability—for example, redundant switches and Internet Service Provider (ISP) connections will be used.

Northwind Trading is using IIS to provide Web services because IIS uses TCP/IP as its network protocol and is associated with port 80. In addition, multiple instances of IIS can run simultaneously on separate servers. Initially, the cluster will include six hosts. Northwind Trading projects that this many hosts can handle client load even if a server fails. The subnet in which the cluster is located will easily handle the cluster traffic and its projected growth. Multiple clusters aren't necessary at this time.

To provide fault tolerance for each host, hardware RAID solutions—along with redundant controllers—will be used. Northwind Traders believes that hardware RAID's initial expense is worth the improved performance, as compared to a software RAID solution.

Figure 5.9 shows how the NLB cluster will be configured for the Northwind Traders Web site. Notice that redundant switches and ISP connections are included in the design.

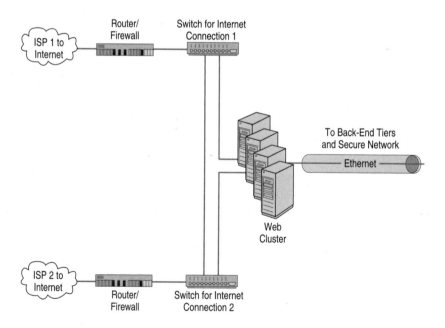

Figure 5.9   NLB cluster for the Northwind Traders Web site

Lesson Summary

Before implementing an NLB cluster in your Windows 2000 network, you should follow specific steps as you plan the configuration of that cluster. First, you should identify network risks and eliminate any single points of failure. Your main goal in implementing NLB clusters and the network in which they reside is to provide increased availability. You must also determine which applications to run in your NLB clusters. Applications must use TCP/IP for network connections and must use TCP or UDP ports. Before implementing an NLB cluster, you should plan which NLB model you'll use, how many hosts will be in the cluster, and what each host's capacity requirements are. As a general rule, you should add servers until the cluster can easily handle the client load. Finally, you must plan for disk fault tolerance. You can make disks fault tolerant by using hardware RAID or software RAID. Windows 2000 Server supports three types of software RAID solutions: RAID-0, RAID-1, and RAID-5; but only RAID-1 and RAID-5 provide fault tolerance. Although it's much more expensive than software RAID, hardware RAID is generally considered the superior solution.

Activity 5.1: Using Round-Robin DNS for Multiple Clusters

You're a network administrator for Blue Yonder Airlines, a worldwide airline with service to 27 countries. You recently implemented online reservations and ticketing services. Customers can now access the airline's Web site, view information about services and schedules, and book their trips, purchase tickets, and request seat assignments. To ensure high availability, you're using IIS on multiple servers that are configured as an NLB cluster. The Web site has been highly successful, and you now find that the cluster subnet is approaching saturation.

You decide to implement a second cluster on a different subnet. You plan to use round-robin DNS to resolve the DNS name (www.blueyonderairlines.com) to each cluster's virtual IP address. The original cluster's IP address is 10.1.0.1, and the new cluster's IP address will be 10.2.0.1.

You decide to create a high-level sketch of the round-robin DNS and NLB cluster components in your network.

1. How should this configuration look?

2. What option other than round-robin DNS can you consider to balance the load between clusters?

Lesson 3: Choosing an NLB Model

In Lesson 2, "Planning NLB Clusters," you learned what steps you needed to take in order to plan your NLB cluster. One of the steps is to choose an NLB model. NLB clusters can be categorized into four configuration models, which address single and multiple network adapters as well as unicast and multicast modes of operation. In this lesson, you'll learn how NLB uses unicast and multicast modes to distribute network traffic. The lesson also discusses the four configuration models you can use when planning an NLB cluster.

After this lesson, you will be able to

- Describe the unicast and multicast modes of operation in NLB
- Describe the advantages and disadvantages of each NLB model
- Choose which NLB model to implement in your organization

Estimated lesson time: 30 minutes

NLB Cluster Models

NLB can operate in two modes: unicast and multicast. For each mode, you can configure the cluster hosts with one network adapter or with multiple network adapters. As a result, you can choose from four NLB models when planning your NLB clusters. These models are based on the combination of operational modes and the number of network adapters. This section describes the issues related to the unicast and multicast operational modes and each of the four models.

Distribution of Cluster Traffic

NLB uses Layer-2 broadcast or multicast to distribute incoming network traffic simultaneously to all cluster hosts. In its default unicast mode of operation, NLB reassigns the Media Access Control (MAC) address of the network adapter for which it's enabled (called the *cluster adapter*), and all cluster hosts are assigned the same MAC address. Incoming packets are thereby received by all cluster hosts and passed up to the NLB driver for filtering. To ensure uniqueness, the MAC address is derived from the cluster's primary IP address entered in the NLB Properties dialog box. For example, if a primary IP address is 1.2.3.4, the unicast MAC address is set to 02-BF-1-2-3-4. NLB automatically modifies the cluster adapter's MAC address by setting a registry entry and then reloading the adapter's driver; the operating system doesn't have to be restarted.

If the cluster hosts are attached to a switch instead of a hub, the use of a common MAC address would create a conflict because Layer-2 switches expect to see unique source MAC addresses on all switch ports. To avoid this problem, NLB uniquely modifies the source MAC address for outgoing packets; a cluster MAC address of 02-BF-1-2-3-4 is set to 02-*h*-1-2-3-4, where *h* is the host's priority within the cluster. This technique prevents the switch from learning the cluster's actual MAC address, and as a result, incoming packets for the cluster are delivered to all switch ports. If the cluster hosts are connected directly to a hub instead of to a switch, you can disable NLB's masking of the source MAC address in unicast mode in order to avoid flooding upstream switches. You do this by setting the NLB registry parameter MaskSourceMAC to 0.

NLB's unicast mode has the side effect of disabling communication between cluster hosts using the cluster adapters. Because outgoing packets for another cluster host are sent to the same MAC address as the sender, the network stack loops these packets back within the sender, and they never reach the wire. You can avoid this limitation by adding a second network adapter card to each cluster host. In this configuration, NLB is bound to the network adapter on the subnet that receives incoming client requests, and the other adapter is typically placed on a separate, local subnet for communication between cluster hosts and with back-end file and database servers. NLB uses only the cluster adapter for its heartbeat and remote control traffic.

Note that communication between cluster hosts and hosts outside the cluster is never affected by NLB's unicast mode. Network traffic for a host's dedicated IP address (on the cluster adapter) is received by all cluster hosts because they all use the same MAC address. Because NLB never load balances traffic for the dedicated IP address, NLB immediately delivers this traffic to TCP/IP on the intended host. On other cluster hosts, NLB treats this traffic as load-balanced traffic (since the target IP address doesn't match another host's dedicated IP address), and it might deliver it to TCP/IP, which would discard it. Note that excessive incoming network traffic for dedicated IP addresses can impose a performance penalty when NLB operates in unicast mode due to the need for TCP/IP to discard unwanted packets.

NLB provides a second mode called multicast mode for distributing incoming network traffic to all cluster hosts. This mode assigns a Layer-2 multicast address to the cluster adapter instead of changing the adapter's station address. For example, the multicast MAC address is set to 03-BF-1-2-3-4 for a cluster's primary IP address of 1.2.3.4. Because each cluster host retains a unique station address, this mode alleviates the need for a second network adapter for communication between cluster hosts, and it also removes any performance penalty from the use of dedicated IP addresses.

NLB's unicast mode induces switch flooding in order to deliver incoming network traffic to all cluster hosts simultaneously. When NLB uses multicast mode, switches often flood all ports by default to deliver multicast traffic. However, NLB's multicast mode gives the system administrator the opportunity to limit switch flooding by configuring a virtual LAN within the switch for the ports corresponding to the cluster hosts. You can accomplish this by manually programming the switch or by using Internet Group Management Protocol (IGMP) or Generic Attribute Registration Protocol (GARP) Multicast Registration Protocol

(GMRP). The current version of NLB doesn't provide automatic support for IGMP or GMRP.

NLB implements the Address Resolution Protocol (ARP) functionality needed to ensure that the cluster's primary IP address and other virtual IP addresses resolve to the cluster's multicast MAC address. (The dedicated IP address continues to resolve to the cluster adapter's station address.) Some routers currently don't accept an ARP response from the cluster that resolves unicast IP addresses to multicast MAC addresses. You can overcome this problem by adding a static ARP entry to the router for each virtual IP address. You can obtain the cluster's multicast MAC address from the Network Load Balancing Properties dialog box or from the WLBS.EXE remote-control program. The default unicast mode avoids this problem because the cluster's MAC address is a unicast MAC address.

NLB doesn't manage any incoming IP traffic other than TCP traffic, UDP traffic, and Generic Routing Encapsulation (GRE) traffic (as part of PPTP traffic) for specified ports. It doesn't filter IGMP, ARP (except as described above), the Internet Control Message Protocol (ICMP), or other IP protocols. All such traffic is passed unchanged to the TCP/IP protocol software on all of the hosts within the cluster. As a result, the cluster can generate duplicate responses from certain point-to-point TCP/IP programs (such as ping) when the cluster IP address is used. Because of TCP/IP's robustness and ability to deal with replicated datagrams, other protocols behave correctly in the clustered environment. These programs can use the dedicated IP address for each host to avoid this behavior.

Unicast support is enabled by default. If multicast support is enabled, a single network adapter can handle both client-to-cluster traffic and dedicated traffic without difficulty. However, the use of a second network adapter may improve performance by handling dedicated traffic concurrently with the original network adapter.

NLB handles the resolution of the cluster's primary IP address to its associated multicast cluster MAC address within the ARP on your router. In some cases the ARP implementation on a given router might not support the use of a multicast MAC address. If this problem arises, the cluster won't be accessible from outside the local subnet. To correct this problem, you must create a static ARP entry within the router.

Should you disable multicast support (causing the host to revert to unicast mode), NLB automatically instructs the driver belonging to the cluster adapter to override the adapter's unique, built-in network address and to change its MAC address to the cluster's MAC address. This is the address used on all cluster hosts. You don't need to configure the network adapter manually to recognize this address.

Note   Some network adapters don't support changing their MAC addresses. If you experience this problem, you must install a network adapter that does.

NLB with Network Hardware Switches

NLB hosts in a single cluster must all be on the same broadcast subnet and connected to each other through either a hub or a switch. Network hardware switches mediate between a network and computers or other switches, routing packets from the network to the correct computer.

If you connect NLB hosts with a switch, the switch must be Level-2 rather than Level-3 or higher, because all the hosts share the same IP address (the cluster IP address) and Level-3 switches direct network packets (incoming client requests) according to the destination computer's IP address.

In unicast mode, each host's unique MAC address is replaced with the same cluster MAC address. Identifying all the hosts with one MAC address makes it possible to distribute incoming client requests (network packets) to all the hosts.

However, most Level-2 switches require that each port be associated with a unique source MAC address. NLB addresses this requirement in unicast mode by enabling the MaskSourceMAC feature by default.

When MaskSourceMAC is enabled, NLB masks the source MAC address for outgoing packets so that for each port the switch continues to see a unique source MAC address. This satisfies the switch's requirement that each port be associated with a unique MAC address. Figure 5.10 shows a representative configuration of an NLB cluster in unicast mode with MaskSourceMAC enabled and attached to a Level-2 switch.

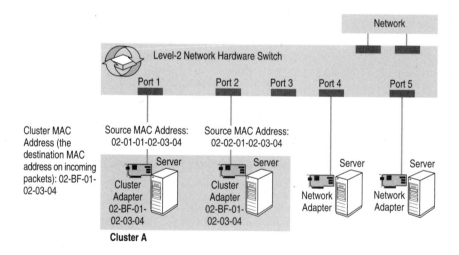

Figure 5.10   NLB cluster running in unicast mode with MaskSourceMAC enabled

Masking the cluster MAC address on outgoing packets prevents the switch from associating the cluster MAC address with a single port. When a client request (which contains the cluster MAC address) enters the switch, the switch doesn't recognize the MAC address in the packet and so sends the packet to all ports. This process is referred to as *switch flooding.*

In unicast mode, NLB induces switch flooding by design, so that packets sent to the cluster's virtual IP address go to all the cluster hosts. Switch flooding is part of the NLB strategy of obtaining the best throughput for any specific load of client requests.

If, however, the cluster shares the switch with other (nonclustered) computers or other clusters, switch flooding can add to the other computers' network overhead by including them in the flooding.

You can avoid flooding nonclustered computers by putting a network hub between the switch and the NLB cluster hosts and then disabling the MaskSourceMAC feature. The hub delivers each packet to every host, and the switch associates the cluster MAC address with a single port, satisfying the switch's requirement that each port be associated with a unique MAC address.

Caution   Using a network hub to solve the problem of switch flooding has one major flaw. It introduces one massive single point of failure for the cluster—that is, if the hub fails, the entire cluster goes down. Unfortunately, there is no other way to prevent switch flooding.

Placing the NLB hosts downstream (toward the cluster) from a hub doesn't reduce the bandwidth for downstream packets. However, all upstream (from the cluster) traffic must flow through the hub. To optimize use of the hub, you can also connect each host's second network adapter back to another port in the switch for outbound packets, as shown in Figure 5.11.

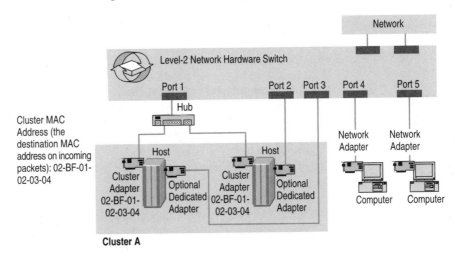

Figure 5.11   NLB cluster running in unicast mode, with MaskSourceMAC disabled

This configuration shown in Figure 5.11 has the following benefits:

- Routing outbound packets through network adapters that aren't attached to the hub improves use of the hub's capacity.

- Use of the capacity for multiple upstream pipes from the switch to the network is improved, because multiple cluster hosts can send traffic to different upstream pipes simultaneously.

- Using two network adapters to separate each cluster host's inbound and outbound network traffic improves the cluster hosts' handling of network traffic.

Finally, if you choose not to use a hub as described here (for example, if the NLB cluster doesn't share the Level-2 switch with any other computers), you can put a Level-3 switch upstream from the Level-2 switch to prevent switch flooding of other interconnected Level-2 switches.

NLB Configuration Models

NLB can operate in two modes: unicast and multicast. In unicast mode, the cluster's MAC address is assigned to the computer's network adapter and the network adapter's built-in MAC address isn't used. In multicast mode, the cluster's MAC address is assigned to the computer's network adapter, but the network adapter's built-in address is retained so that both addresses are used—the first for client-to-cluster traffic and the second for network traffic specific to the computer.

You can choose from four configuration models when planning an NLB cluster: single network adapter in unicast mode, multiple network adapters in unicast mode, single network adapter in multicast mode, and multiple network adapters in multicast mode.

NLB doesn't support a mixed unicast/multicast environment. All cluster hosts must be either multicast or unicast; otherwise, the cluster won't function properly. However, there's no restriction on the number of network adapters; different hosts can have a different number of adapters.

Single Network Adapter in Unicast Mode

This model is suitable for a cluster in which ordinary network communication among cluster hosts isn't required and in which there's limited dedicated traffic from outside the cluster subnet to specific cluster hosts.

The model has the following advantages:

- Only one network adapter is required.

- This model is the most straightforward configuration (because unicast mode is the default).

- Unicast mode works with all routers.

It also has the following disadvantages:

- Ordinary network communication among cluster hosts is impossible.

- Because there's only one network adapter, overall network performance might suffer.

Note that in this model the computer can also handle traffic from inside the subnet if the IP datagram doesn't carry the same MAC address as on the cluster adapter.

When using unicast mode with a single network adapter, the adapter's own unique MAC address is disabled. The cluster MAC address (which NLB automatically generates) replaces this address. The adapter becomes, in effect, the cluster adapter. Both the dedicated IP address and the cluster IP address resolve to the cluster MAC address.

Because all cluster hosts share the same MAC address, and because the original MAC address isn't used, ordinary network communication among hosts isn't possible. However, the computer can still handle traffic originating from outside the subnet in which the cluster is located and from inside the subnet if the IP datagram doesn't carry the same MAC address as on the cluster adapter.

Multiple Network Adapters in Unicast Mode

This model is suitable for a cluster in which ordinary network communication among cluster hosts is necessary or desirable, and in which there's comparatively heavy dedicated traffic from outside the cluster subnet to specific cluster hosts.

The model has the following advantages:

- This model is the preferred configuration that's used by most sites because a second network adapter may enhance overall network performance.

- This configuration permits ordinary network communication among cluster hosts.

- Unicast mode works with all routers.

It has the following disadvantage:

- The configuration requires a second network adapter.

When multiple adapters are installed in unicast mode, the first network adapter is the cluster adapter. The cluster IP address resolves to this adapter's cluster MAC address (which NLB automatically generates). If the cluster adapter's dedicated IP address is used, this IP address also resolves to the cluster MAC address.

The cluster adapter handles client-to-cluster traffic. If the dedicated IP address is used, the computer can also handle traffic originating from outside the subnet in which the cluster is located and from inside the subnet if the IP datagram doesn't carry the same MAC address as on the cluster adapter.

The second network adapter is the dedicated adapter. This adapter's IP address resolves to the adapter's built-in MAC address. The dedicated adapter handles network traffic specific to the computer, including traffic from both inside and outside the subnet in which the computer is located.

Single Network Adapter in Multicast Mode

This model is suitable for a cluster in which ordinary network communication among cluster hosts is necessary or desirable but in which there's limited dedicated traffic from outside the cluster subnet to specific cluster hosts.

The model has the following advantages:

- Only one network adapter is required.
- It permits ordinary network communication among cluster hosts.

It has the following disadvantages:

- Because there's only one adapter, overall network performance might suffer.
- Some routers might not support the use of a multicast MAC address.

Note that in this model the computer can also handle traffic from inside the subnet if the IP datagram doesn't carry the same MAC address as on the cluster adapter.

When using multicast mode with a single network adapter, NLB automatically generates a cluster MAC address for the network adapter. The adapter's own unique MAC address is retained. The cluster IP address resolves to the cluster MAC address. The dedicated IP address resolves to the original MAC address. Because both MAC addresses are used, there are no constraints on network traffic, except for the load placed on the network adapter.

Multiple Network Adapters in Multicast Mode

This model is suitable for a cluster in which ordinary network communication among cluster hosts is necessary and in which there's heavy dedicated traffic from outside the cluster subnet to specific cluster hosts.

The model has the following advantages:

- Because there are at least two network adapters, overall network performance might be enhanced.
- This configuration permits ordinary network communication among cluster hosts.

It has the following disadvantages:

- It requires a second network adapter.
- Some routers might not support the use of a multicast MAC address.

If multiple adapters are used in multicast mode, the first network adapter is the cluster adapter. The cluster IP address resolves to this adapter's cluster MAC address (which NLB automatically generates). If the cluster adapter's dedicated IP address is used, this IP address resolves to the adapter's original built-in MAC address. The cluster adapter, therefore, can handle both client-to-cluster traffic and traffic specific to the computer, including all traffic from both inside and outside the subnet in which the computer is located.

The second network adapter is the dedicated adapter. This adapter's IP address resolves to the adapter's built-in MAC address. The dedicated adapter handles network traffic specific to the computer, including traffic from both inside and outside the subnet in which the computer is located.

Making a Decision

When planning your NLB cluster, you should use one of the four configuration models. Table 5.2 describes each of these models.

Table 5.2   Choosing a Configuration Model

Strategy	Description
Single network adapter in unicast mode	Unicast mode is the default configuration for NLB and works with all routers. However, ordinary network communication among hosts isn't possible, and network performance might be compromised.
Multiple network adapters in unicast mode	Unicast mode is the default configuration for NLB and works with all routers. In addition, ordinary network communication among hosts is possible, and network performance might be enhanced. However, at least two network adapters are required.
Single network adapter in multicast mode	Only one network adapter is required, and ordinary network communication among hosts is possible. However, this isn't the default configuration, network performance might suffer, and some routers might not support the use of a multicast MAC address.
Multiple network adapters in multicast mode	Performance might be enhanced, and ordinary network communication among hosts is possible. However, this isn't the default configuration, at least two network adapters are required, and some routers might not support the use of a multicast MAC address.

Recommendations

Multicast mode has many advantages; but because multicast mode is incompatible with some routers, unicast mode is often a better solution when implementing NLB. Unicast mode, with multiple network adapters, is the preferred configuration used by most sites. This model is easier to configure because it's the default mode, permits ordinary network communication among hosts, and works with all routers. The fact that at least two network adapters are required is usually not a problem because most organizations supporting a Web infrastructure have a front-end Internet network and a back-end corporate network—a configuration that requires each host in an NLB cluster to have at least two network adapters.

Example: An NLB Configuration for the Baldwin Museum of Science

The Baldwin Museum of Science is implementing a load-balancing solution that uses a Layer-2 switch and an NLB cluster that contains four hosts, as shown in Figure 5.12. The cluster is configured for the unicast mode of operation, and each host contains multiple network adapters. The Layer-2 switch provides dedicated collision-free communication between network devices and enables multiple simultaneous data transmission between two ports, increasing network capacity. When a Layer-2 switch starts, it builds a table of each network adapter card's MAC addresses with the port number to which the adapter is connected.

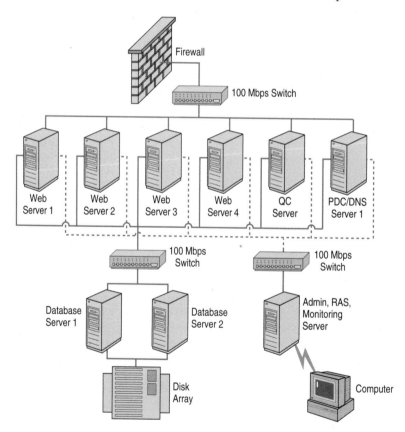

Figure 5.12   Baldwin Museum of Science hardware configuration

In NLB, the MAC address is replaced with the cluster network adapter's MAC address, which is used by all the cluster hosts. For an incoming request, the switch forwards the request to all the ports associated with the cluster MAC address. Based on a hashing algorithm, one of the hosts will accept the packet and the other hosts will ignore it. After processing, the data packet is sent back to the port from which the packet was originally received.

Figure 5.12 shows the use of a Layer-2 switch and an NLB cluster. The switch can handle multiple conversations at the same time at the full bandwidth. Therefore, if one cluster host is processing one request, and the cluster receives another request, another host can pick up the data packet and begin processing. This ensures the system's high performance.

Lesson Summary

NLB can operate in two modes: unicast and multicast. For each mode you can configure the cluster hosts with one network adapter or with multiple network adapters. In its default unicast mode of operation, NLB reassigns the MAC address of the network adapter for which it's enabled and all cluster hosts are assigned the same MAC address. In multicast mode, NLB assigns a Layer-2 multicast address to the cluster adapter instead of changing the adapter's station address. If you connect NLB hosts with a switch, the switch must be Level-2 rather than Level-3 or higher. You can choose from four configuration models when planning an NLB cluster: single network adapter in unicast mode, multiple network adapters in unicast mode, single network adapter in multicast mode, and multiple network adapters in multicast mode. Unicast mode, with multiple network adapters, is the preferred configuration used by most sites. This model is easier to configure because it's the default mode, it permits ordinary network communication among hosts, and it works with all routers.

Lab 5.1: Planning an NLB Cluster

After completing this lab, you'll be able to

- Determine which applications to run in the cluster
- Choose an NLB configuration model

About This Lab

In this lab, you'll plan an NLB cluster for Litware, Inc. You'll be performing two of the steps described in Lessons 2 and 3: determining which applications to run in the cluster and choosing a configuration model. For this lab you can assume that some of the steps that are normally part of the cluster-planning process have already been completed, as described in the scenario.

Before You Begin

Before you begin this lab, you must be able to

- Administer Windows 2000 Advanced Server
- Implement and administer NLB in Windows 2000 Advanced Server

Scenario: NLB Cluster for Litware, Inc.

Litware, Inc., develops and markets software products for publishers, printers, and other related industries. The company wants to provide Web-based services to its customers. The site will also be used to market the company's products to potential customers. Company administrators have begun to plan the network infrastructure, which will use an *n*-tier structure to deliver services. The administrators have attempted to eliminate any single points of failure in the design. For example, the network will include redundant components and network paths, multiple ISP connections, and uninterruptible power supply (UPS) protection. The network will also include redundant Cisco routers to manage incoming Internet requests. These routers don't accept ARP responses from a cluster that resolves unicast IP addresses to multicast MAC addresses.

The administrators also want to implement Windows clustering to support their Web, database, and mail services. IIS will be used for the Web services, SQL Server will be used for the database services, and Exchange Server will be used for the mail services. The first cluster that will be implemented is an NLB cluster at the front-end tier. Each host in the cluster will be configured with a hardware-based RAID storage solution. The cluster will include six hosts, which should handle incoming traffic adequately even if a failure occurs.

Exercise 1: Determining Which Applications to Run in the Cluster

In this exercise, you must decide which application or applications to run in the NLB cluster. You're mainly concerned with IIS, SQL Server, and Exchange Server.

1. What type of applications can you run on an NLB cluster?

2. Which application or applications will you run in the NLB cluster and why would you choose those applications?

3. Is there any application that shouldn't be run on the NLB cluster, and if so, why not?

Exercise 2: Choosing an NLB Model

In this exercise, you must choose which configuration model to use for your NLB cluster. You can choose from four configuration models when planning an NLB cluster: single network adapter in unicast mode, multiple network adapters in unicast mode, single network adapter in multicast mode, and multiple network adapters in multicast mode.

1. What are the advantages and disadvantages of each of these configuration models?

2. Which configuration model should you use?

Review

Answering the following questions will reinforce key information presented in this chapter. If you're unable to answer a question, review the appropriate lesson and then try the question again. Answers to the questions can be found in the appendix.

1. How does NLB work?

2. What are the differences between Single affinity and Class C affinity?

3. How does NLB manage session state that spans multiple connections?

4. You're a network administrator at Trey Research. You're responsible for administering the company's Web site and its infrastructure. You want to implement an NLB cluster to run IIS. You've identified network risks and eliminated any single points of failure. The cluster will include four hosts, and each host will be configured to use RAID-5 for fault-tolerant storage. You'll determine the host's capacity requirements after you've planned the rest of the cluster. What other decision must you make?

5. You're planning a small NLB cluster for your organization's network. The cluster will contain only two computers. Each computer will be configured with only one network adapter. You want the configuration to support ordinary network traffic between the computers. Which NLB configuration model should you use?

C H A P T E R   6

Microsoft Application Center 2000

About This Chapter

Microsoft Application Center is a strategic server product in Microsoft's .NET Enterprise Servers tier. Application Center was developed to provide a competitively priced, yet robust tool for scaling and managing a broad range of Web-based business applications. Its feature set, which includes load-balancing and server synchronization, can support COM+ applications. Application Center is integrated with core Microsoft Windows 2000 Server services, such as Network Load Balancing (NLB), and because of its level of integration, it extends the core operating system services by providing tools such as application publishing. It's positioned in the .NET Enterprise Servers tier so that it's able to integrate fully with other middle-tier servers and services, as well as the development tools layer. In this chapter you'll learn about the functionality supported by Application Center and learn what factors you must consider when planning an Application Center cluster. Lesson 3 deals specifically with Component Load Balancing (CLB), an Application Center feature that provides dynamic load balancing for COM+ applications.

Before You Begin

To complete the lessons in this chapter, you must have

- Experience administering Windows 2000 Server and designing Windows 2000 networks
- The ability to implement the NLB service in a Windows 2000 Web environment
- The ability to implement NLB and CLB in Application Center 2000

Lesson 1: Introduction to Application Center

Application Center 2000 maintains a high level of availability by allowing Web site administrators to group Windows 2000 Server computers into clusters and manage Web site content and applications easily. Administrators can manage content and configuration settings on a single server, reducing the time required to update a Web site. Application Center 2000 divides Web site content and code into *applications* that can be updated independently. These applications can consist of any combination of Hypertext Markup Language (HTML) and Active Server Pages (ASP) files, COM+ components, Windows registry settings, and Internet Information Services (IIS) settings. Each server in the cluster hosts a copy of the application, which Application Center keeps synchronized. Application Center NLB and CLB technologies support clusters made of Windows 2000 Server computers. Web browsers, such as Microsoft Internet Explorer, see each cluster as a very large and very reliable Web server. This lesson gives you an overview of Application Center and the features that allow you to create NLB and CLB clusters.

After this lesson, you will be able to

- Describe Application Center and how it's used
- Identify and describe the features that are supported by Application Center
- Provide an overview of the Application Center architecture

Estimated lesson time: 25 minutes

Platform Components of a Web Site

The key tenet of distributed Web-based applications is the logical partitioning of an application into three tiers:

- Presentation
- Business logic
- Data access and storage

By using component-based programming techniques to partition applications along these lines and by using the services provided by the Windows operating system, developers can build highly scalable and flexible applications.

A simple application model consists of a client that communicates with the middle tier, which itself consists of the application server and an application containing the business logic. The application, in turn, communicates with a back-end database that's used to supply and store data.

Presentation Services

The Presentation layer consists of either a rich or thin client interface to an application. The rich client, which uses the Microsoft Win32 application programming interface (API), provides a full programming interface to the operating system's capabilities and uses components extensively. Arguably not as robust or as capable of offering the performance levels of a rich client, the thin client (Web browser) is rapidly becoming the interface of choice for many developers. A developer is able to take advantage of several simple-yet-robust scripting languages to build business logic that can be executed on any of the three application tiers. With full support for HTML, dynamic HTML (DHTML), and Extensible Markup Language (XML) object models, the thin client is able to provide a visually rich, flexible, and interactive user interface to applications. Thin clients have the added advantage of providing a greater degree of portability across platforms.

Business Logic/Application Services

This layer is divided into application servers (IIS, Site Server, Commerce Server 2000, and Systems Network Architecture [SNA] Server) and services, which are available to support clients. Web application logic, typically consisting of ASP written in Virtual Basic Scripting Edition (VBScript), is processed in the IIS server space. You can write ASP-based or Component Object Model (COM)–based applications to take advantage of Microsoft Transaction Server (MTS), Microsoft Message Queue Server (MSMQ), directory services, and security services. Application services, in turn, can interact with several data services on the back end.

Data Access and Storage

The following data services support data access and storage:

- Microsoft ActiveX Data Objects (ADO), which provides simplified programmatic access to data by using either scripting or programming languages
- Object linking and embedding (OLE) database, which is an established universal data provider developed by Microsoft
- XML, which is a markup standard for specifying data structures

XML is a recent standard put forward by the Internet community. Whereas HTML focuses on how information is rendered by the browser and displayed on the screen, XML's goal is to handle a data structure and its representation.

Overview of Application Center

Application Center is a tool for creating, deploying, and managing Web- and component-based applications, which are typically line-of-business applications that require a high level of availability and need to provide acceptable response time. The servers hosting these applications are expected to handle traffic that's characterized by high volumes, exponential growth curves, and load fluctuations.

Application Center is designed to provide the capital cost advantages of the scale-out model, while at the same time reducing operations costs—one of the main advantages espoused by proponents of the scale-up model. In addition to these cost advantages, Application Center provides the following benefits:

- **Manageability** You can manage Application Center through a centralized management console that's minimal and familiar. You use this console to organize and manage replication, load balancing, and the monitoring of Web and COM+ applications.

- **Scalability** Application Center is both linear and flexible. You can add servers to a cluster as needed to accommodate seasonal peaks and remove them (and reallocate them within the organization) as the load decreases.

- **Reliability** Application Center eliminates the single point of failure associated with scaling up or hardware-based load balancing. It also transparently removes a server from operation in the event of a hardware or software failure.

Good performance, of course, is desirable in any product. In addition to offering optimal load balancing algorithms for different types of applications, Application Center provides tools for monitoring system performance and allows the system administrator to adjust load on a server-by-server basis. This approach recognizes the realities of heterogeneous server farms and provides far greater flexibility than the one-size-fits-all approach.

Application Center Features

The features summarized in Table 6.1 provide the essential tools needed to allow you to create and manage load-balanced clusters. Different elements of the product feature set are accessible through its Microsoft Management Console (MMC) snap-in or through the Web browser.

Table 6.1 Application Center Features

Feature	Description
Cluster services	Common tasks for administering the cluster configuration (for example, creating a cluster or adding a member) are easy to execute by using wizards or the graphical user interface.
Load balancing	Application Center supports integrated NLB and CLB.
Synchronization and deployment	System settings, content, and applications are replicated across the cluster, either automatically or on demand. Content can be deployed within a cluster or to another cluster.

(continued)

Table 6.1   *(continued)*

Feature	Description
Monitoring	Real-time event, performance, and health monitoring are supported, and historical data is accessible.
Programmatic support	Scripting support is available for performing common Application Center management tasks and accessing the event and monitoring data. You can complete selected administrative tasks with a set of command-line tools.
Local and remote administration	You can administer a cluster locally or through a secure remote connection.
High availability	Requests and transactions are automatically rerouted to another member if a server failure occurs.

Load Balancing

Application Center provides several options for implementing load balancing on a cluster, including integrated NLB, CLB, or no load balancing.

Integrated NLB

With this option, load balancing is actually carried out by the NLB that's part of Windows 2000 Advanced Server or Datacenter Server. Application Center provides an interface that's integrated with NLB.

Note   Although it isn't included with Windows 2000 Server, NLB is automatically installed on a system running Windows 2000 Server when Application Center is installed on that system.

The Application Center user interface makes configuring an NLB cluster easier by removing much of the configuration detail and, through the use of a wizard, by reducing the number of decisions that a user must make. The wizard also conducts hardware and software diagnostics to ensure that a minimal workable platform is available to support load balancing. For example, it checks for the correct number of network adapters and Internet Protocol (IP) addresses.

When configuring NLB for your cluster, you must select an appropriate load-balancing algorithm for the cluster. This algorithm, or affinity, is based on the source of the bulk of the incoming client requests. Integrated NLB uses three types of affinity settings, as described in Table 6.2, to identify the algorithm that's used.

After you've created a cluster, you can use the MMC console to change the affinity setting for a cluster that's using integrated NLB.

Table 6.2   NLB Affinity Settings

Affinity	Description
None	Multiple requests from the same client can access any cluster member. The IP address and port number identify the client.
Single	Multiple requests from the same client must access the same cluster member. This is the default setting for intranet clients. The IP address identifies the client.
Class C	Multiple requests from the same Transmission Control Protocol/Internet Protocol (TCP/IP) Class C address range must access the same cluster member. This is the default setting for Internet clients because it provides optimum support for *sticky sessions*, in which a client request establishes a server-side state that's used in subsequent requests during the same session.

Another load balancing configuration option that Application Center provides is the ability to adjust individual server weights in response to performance data or to accommodate different classes of members.

CLB

CLB is an Application Center service. The decision to use CLB should be based on a thorough analysis of your application requirements before hosting components on back-end servers. An inherent system overhead is associated with client requests that traverse the network and with selecting a server to satisfy the client request. You should consider CLB in these situations:

- Security is a major concern and you want to segregate COM objects behind an additional firewall.

- COM objects are relatively large and you want to run them on the fastest servers available.

- Applications are partitioned into *n*-tiers, either for development or design reasons. If you're using NLB for your front-end servers and want to route component requests to a back-end COM+ server, the Application Center user interface easily lets you specify a target.

- Scaling is important. A single cluster can use multiple COM+ clusters to service component requests.

Note   For applications that are relatively small or that use a limited number of components, instantiating COM objects locally on a front-end Web server may provide the best performance.

No Load Balancing

There may be situations in which you don't need or want to have load balancing enabled; for example, it's not necessary for application testing and staging or for controller redundancy. You might want to use the no load balancing option in the following situations:

- **Application testing and staging**   You can create a cluster for testing and staging that consists of a single server or a small number of members. In this scenario, load balancing isn't really necessary.

- **Controller redundancy**   In environments where a cluster is very small, such as two or three servers, you may want to have a completely redundant member on standby to serve as a backup controller. You'd keep its content synchronized to the active controller, but you wouldn't have it responding to client requests.

Synchronization and Deployment

Every aspect of a cluster's composition and configuration needs to be synchronized to the cluster controller. Application Center deals with both aspects of the synchronization issue by replicating both controller settings and application settings. You achieve partial or full synchronization of a cluster by replicating configuration and application settings. A replication engine that uses custom drivers makes the links to the various configuration stores and copies their settings to the target servers.

This holistic approach has an added benefit: in the event of a controller failure, you can make any member the new cluster controller. You can do this on demand with minor configuration changes to the member.

You can replicate a single application to cluster members or replicate all the applications that are currently hosted on the controller. Site information contained in the AllSites category, or in custom definitions, may include any of the following information, which is replicated when you synchronize a cluster:

- Web Content and ASP applications
- COM+ applications
- Virtual sites (and their associated Internet Server Application Programming Interface [ISAPI] filters) and content
- Global ISAPI filters
- File system directories and files

- Metabase configuration settings
- Exportable CryptoAPI (CAPI) server certificates
- Registry keys
- System data source names (DSNs)
- Windows Management Instrumentation (WMI) settings used by Application Center

By default, the cluster is synchronized whenever new content is added (only the new content is replicated) or fully synchronized every 60 minutes. You can disable this feature completely or change the time frequency for the synchronization schedule.

Note   You can exclude specific members from being part of cluster synchronization.

As with application deployment, you can explicitly replicate a single application or all of the applications on the controller. This gives you flexibility in staging and deploying new applications, which you may want to test on part of a cluster before deploying the application to all of the members.

Note   In Application Center, an application is defined as a collection of all the required software resources for a Web site or COM+ application. For example, an application can consist of Web site content, COM+ applications, certificates, and registry keys. This approach allows the administrator to think of sites as logical groupings. An application may contain more than one Web site, or no Web sites at all, and still be replicated across a cluster.

Monitoring

In order to maintain a production environment successfully, you must be able to monitor the behavior and performance of its key components: the network servers, and applications. A robust monitoring environment—one that provides real time and historical data—enables you to keep an eye on the overall health and performance of any given system. (Historical performance data is particularly useful when it comes to capacity planning.)

Application Center provides a central viewing point for obtaining this kind of information, which is encapsulated by the monitoring and logging of event, performance, and health data, as described in Table 6.3.

Table 6.3   Monitoring and Logging Data

Monitored Objects	Description
Events	Numerous objects and applications running on a server or cluster generate events (actions that take place on your server or cluster). All Windows 2000 events and some Application Center events are logged in the Windows event log.
Performance	Performance is indicated by a collection of performance counters that indicate the amount of resource consumption. The counters may indicate, for example, that 70 percent of the total hard disk space is in use or that there have been 1,897 requests per second for the Web service. Application Center uses a set of default counters to give you an overview of both server and cluster performance. These counters cover a broad range of system-related information, from the amount of available memory to the number of ASP page requests serviced per second.
Health	Application Center creates several default data collectors—with predefined thresholds—for use in monitoring server and cluster health. Some of the default collectors are toggled as active, while others are inactive and can be activated at any time. Note that data collectors are used to collect, receive, and retain specific WMI data.

Application Center Architecture

Through its implementation of the shared nothing model, Application Center provides a high level of availability for all cluster members, including the controller. Every member is, in essence, a mirror image of the cluster controller.

With integrated NLB installed, each member "hears" incoming client requests, so if one member fails, the other members can continue servicing these requests. Because a failed member is taken offline in the background and load balancing is automatically reconfigured to distribute client requests, Application Center provides an effective environment for providing computing availability. In addition, its transparent isolation mechanism shields users from the effects of server failure.

If a controller fails, cluster administrative activities such as synchronization can't take place until a new controller is designated; however, load-balanced request handling continues to function.

When coupled with its automated e-mail notification and flexible administration features, the shared nothing implementation provided by Application Center ensures a highly available environment for clusters.

Note   Although Application Center clusters provide high levels of server availability, fault tolerance (as it's defined) and the fault-tolerant state aren't supported. If a member crashes or is intentionally taken out of the cluster, all clients that rely on the state stored on that particular member will lose their state.

Architectural Layers

The architecture for Application Center, illustrated in Figure 6.1, consists of three major layers:

- User Interface
- Feature Set
- Operating System

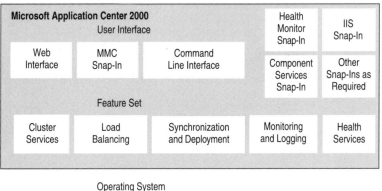

Figure 6.1   The Application Center architecture

User Interface

The Application Center user interface provides access to the product feature set through an MMC snap-in, the Web browser, and the Microsoft Windows command prompt. The MMC provides full access to the product feature set, but access to cluster administration and monitoring tasks is also possible—although to a lesser extent—by using Internet Explorer or the Application Center command-line tool at the Windows command prompt.

Feature Set

This layer is divided into the following broad categories:

- Cluster services
- Load balancing
- Synchronization and deployment
- Monitoring and logging
- Health services

Operating System

The main elements of the operating system that the user interface and feature set layers interact with are the MMC (IIS version 5.0), the metabase, COM+, NLB, and WMI. The Microsoft SQL Server engine is outside this layer, but it's integrated with the operating system and used solely for handling cluster-related data storage and retrieval.

Clustering Scenarios

Application Center 2000 supports three primary clustering scenarios:

- Single-node clusters
- Standard Web clusters
- COM+ application clusters

Single-Node Cluster

It can be useful to operate Application Center on a single server without the context of a multimember cluster. Application Center treats a single-node cluster, or stand-alone server, as a cluster of one member. Typically, the most common single-node cluster is a stager. A *stager* is a server on which content is placed prior to being placed on a production server. On this stager, you can experiment with and fully test the quality and functionality of content from development and test environments before deploying the content to production environments.

In addition to stagers, other single-node clusters can benefit from Application Center without operating in a clustered environment. These servers can use Application Center for the following tasks:

- Deploying applications to or from other members or clusters
- Viewing health and status alongside other clusters
- Viewing performance data and event logs alongside other clusters

Standard Web Cluster

The most typical Application Center clustering scenario is a Web cluster serving Web sites and local COM+ components. You can distinguish such clusters by their load balancing implementation, whether they use NLB or other load-balancing devices. Clustering multiple servers together has the following advantages:

- **Failover protection**   Each member is essentially a backup of the cluster controller.

- **Increased application availability**   With multiple members serving sites and applications, clients can experience uninterrupted service even through failures or problems on individual members.

- **Increased scalability**   You can add and remove members without affecting client availability.

- **Increased performance**   Client workload is distributed throughout the cluster, so that each individual member receives less load, which enhances performance.

NLB Web Clusters

With NLB, Application Center provides seamless integration so that NLB cluster creation and member addition is simplified and you can handle common administrative tasks, such as setting members online and offline, through the Application Center user interface. NLB dynamically distributes client workload as members are set online and offline. Figure 6.2 shows a typical one-tier Web cluster that's running NLB.

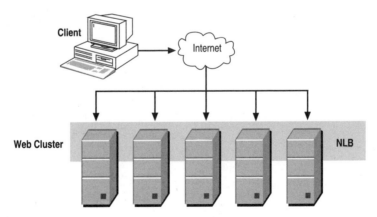

Figure 6.2   NLB Web cluster

Non-NLB Web Clusters

For typical non-NLB clusters, an external load-balancing device is used to distribute incoming client requests. Figure 6.3 shows a typical one-tier, non-NLB Web cluster.

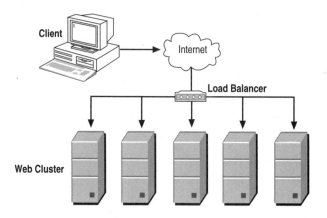

Figure 6.3   Non-NLB Web cluster

COM+ Application Cluster

A COM+ application cluster processes COM+ application requests for clients. These clients can include Windows-based clients and Web clusters. A COM+ application cluster relieves Web clusters and Windows-based clients from processing COM+ components. To support Windows-based clients, the cluster can use NLB or other load balancers to distribute incoming client requests. Figure 6.4 shows a COM+ application cluster that's running NLB.

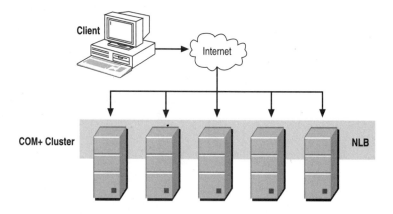

Figure 6.4   COM+ application cluster that uses NLB

You can create Web clusters that use CLB to load balance the activation requests for COM+ components and forward these requests from the Web cluster to the

COM+ application cluster for processing. In a two-tier Application Center clustering environment, one tier handles requests for Web sites and the second tier handles requests for COM+ components. The performance in this environment might not match the performance of a single Web cluster because data must be transmitted between the Web cluster and the COM+ application cluster.

Although you get the best performance by activating COM+ applications locally, creating a separate cluster to process COM+ components has the following advantages:

- Security is increased because you can place firewalls between Web clusters and COM+ application clusters so that clients accessing the Web cluster are restricted from accessing the COM+ application cluster.

- If the COM+ applications consume extensive processing resources, Web servers might become unresponsive. You can create a separate COM+ application cluster to relieve the Web cluster of processing these COM+ applications. Since the Web cluster doesn't process the COM+ applications, it can achieve better performance in serving Web sites.

- Manageability of server applications is increased because COM+ applications are isolated on a separate cluster from Web clusters. The two separate clusters allow you to have different developers and administrators maintaining each cluster independently.

- Clients of mixed environments can be supported. COM+ application clusters can accept requests from both clients accessing the Web cluster and clients running Windows-based applications.

COM+ applications clusters are discussed in more detail in Lesson 3, "Designing CLB Clusters."

Lesson Summary

Application Center is a tool for creating, deploying, and managing Web- and component-based applications. Application Center allows administrators to group Windows 2000 Server computers into clusters and easily manage Web site content and applications. The key tenet of distributed Web-based applications is the logical partitioning of an application into three tiers: presentation, business logic, and data access and storage. Application Center includes the following features: cluster services, load balancing, synchronization and deployment, monitoring, programmatic support, local and remote administration, and high availability. Application Center provides several alternatives for implementing load balancing on a cluster. Application Center supports three load balancing options: Integrated NLB, CLB, or no load balancing. Application Center synchronizes every aspect of a cluster's composition and configuration and provides a central viewing point for obtaining monitoring-related information. The architecture for Application Center consists of three major layers: User Interface, Feature Set, and Operating System. Application Center 2000 supports three primary clustering scenarios: single-node clusters, standard Web clusters, and COM+ application clusters.

Lesson 2: Planning Application Center Clusters

Application Center allows you to build multitiered clusters that can use various load balancing techniques to provide high availability, scalability, and robustness. Application Center supports NLB and CLB. A typical Application Center cluster topology is based on an *n*-tier solution that includes a Web-tier cluster for serving content to the client. It's the Web-tier cluster that uses IIS and NLB to satisfy incoming IP requests. The topology might also include an additional tier to support a COM+ application cluster, which would rely on CLB to respond to COM+ requests. When implementing an Application Center cluster, you must consider a number of factors as you plan how to set up the clusters in your organization. For example, you must select a cluster type and determine how session state will be managed. This lesson describes each step that you should follow when planning Application Center clusters in your organization.

After this lesson, you will be able to

- Plan server configurations and determine IP addresses
- Select a cluster type and, where appropriate, a load balancing configuration
- Determine how session state will be maintained

Estimated lesson time: 25 minutes

Planning for Application Center 2000

You should consider a number of steps when planning an Application Center cluster. This section discusses many of those steps.

Planning Server Configurations

Before attempting to set up a cluster controller and create a cluster, you have to assess the processing capabilities of the servers that you plan to use in your cluster. The servers must have enough resources to comfortably run Windows 2000 Server, Advanced Server, or Datacenter Server; Application Center; Application Center Event and Performance Logging (optional); IIS 5.0; and the applications running on the cluster—whether they're Web-based or COM+ applications.

Memory

The official minimum memory for running Application Center on Windows 2000 Advanced Server is 256 MB of RAM on a 400 MHz system. However, you must consider several factors when determining a server's memory requirements. For example, Windows 2000 Server and IIS require at least 256 MB of RAM, although between 512 MB and 1 GB is recommended. You should consider the high end of the range if the site is hosting an e-commerce application, contains a large amount of content, uses dynamic pages extensively, uses COM+ applications, or has a high volume of traffic. Remember that the IIS cache size defaults to half the available amount of real memory.

Fixed Disk

The disk partition must contain adequate space for all the installed programs, paging file space, and site content. You also have to factor in the space required for content replication. Because the replication engine copies all the content to a temporary directory on the destination server and then moves these files to the appropriate folders during synchronization, the required disk space is approximately double the volume of the content to be replicated.

Note The Synchronization Service uses a two-phase commit process to ensure data integrity, which is why the replication engine uses a temporary directory on a target.

Finally, you should allow enough free space to support disk defragmentation. A minimum of 15 percent of the disk should be free to support effective defragmentation. (A higher percentage of free disk space will improve disk defragmentation.)

Network Adapters

Each system should have at least two network adapters if it's part of a load-balanced cluster and *must* have at least two if you're going to use NLB. The front-end adapter (also called the *load-balanced adapter*) is used for front-end traffic such as NLB heartbeats, convergence, and load balancing. The back-end adapter, also called the *management-traffic adapter*, is used for back-end traffic generated by different cluster activities, notably content replication and synchronization.

You need two network adapters for two reasons. First, this enables NLB to bypass a loopback condition that occurs when using unicast mode. Second, the replication engine that Application Center provides uses COM calls extensively, and replication will fail if a connection gets dropped or reset. IP address changes or deletions can cause connection drops or resets, which is why using the front-end network adapter for the high-volume data transfers that typify content replication is risky. This issue isn't exclusive to replication but includes other Application Center features, such as cluster services and monitoring.

Hardware

Although Application Center will run on any server that meets the minimum requirements, homogenous hardware is recommended. This is the best way to ensure balanced and consistent performance across a cluster and to make it easier for you to tune your servers for optimum performance.

If you're using NLB or one of the compatible third-party load balancers, you can adjust load-balancing weights to compensate to some extent for performance differences between servers. However, remember that each cluster member is synchronized to the controller. As a result, there's little leeway in customizing individual configurations, especially IIS.

Note   You can use multiple disk partitions, but the idea of homogeneity extends to the file system structure on a disk partition. Identical file system structures are required (System Root, Program Files path, Application Center path), and it's strongly recommended that you use Microsoft NT file system (NTFS) rather than file allocation table (FAT) 32.

The main factors in selecting homogenous systems for a cluster are the number of CPUs, CPU speed, disk partitioning/formatting, and memory on each server.

Determining IP Addresses

Application Center supports several IP address binding scenarios for the front-end and back-end adapters. In most cases a single Dynamic Host Configuration Protocol (DHCP)–assigned address is bound to the back-end adapter. For the front-end adapters, IP addressing is a little more complicated.

Note   After installing Application Center you should verify that NetBIOS over TCP/IP is enabled for each IP address.

For the Controller
If your cluster uses NLB, the controller requires a minimum of one static IP address bound to the front-end adapter. This single IP address serves as the cluster IP address for the adapter and there's no dedicated IP address, which is restrictive from a network management perspective. For example, you can't ping the front-end adapter on a specific server by using the IP address because the address is common to all the cluster members in a load-balanced cluster.

For a Member
In an NLB cluster, the front-end adapter requires a minimum of one IP address, which can be either static or assigned by DHCP. When the member is added to the cluster, Application Center binds the cluster IP address to the adapter. Once again, network management considerations should determine whether you want to use one or two IP addresses on the front-end adapter.

Figure 6.5 illustrates a server configuration for an Application Center cluster member that's using NLB. In this example there are two static IP addresses bound to the front-end network adapter. The first is a dedicated IP address that enables you to communicate directly with the front-end adapter. The second is the cluster IP address that carries the load-balanced cluster traffic.

Subnets
In the configuration shown in Figure 6.5, the front-end and back-end adapters are on separate subnets. There are two reasons for this. First, using separate subnets

provides a more secure implementation by isolating the back-end (internal) traffic from the front-end (external) traffic. (Another technique for isolating network traffic is to use network segments.) Second, using separate subnets improves traffic distribution over the network adapters when you're using NLB. This has to do with the way Application Center configures adapter interface metrics and the way NLB routes traffic. If you create a cluster that uses NLB, Application Center sets the interface metric for the load-balanced adapter to be one higher than the interface metric for other cards on the same computer.

For example, assume that you have a server configured with two adapters, both of which are on the same subnet. If the interface metric for the back-end adapter is 1, Application Center sets the interface metric for the load-balanced adapter (the front end) at 2. When a response is sent to the client, NLB routes it to the adapter on the same subnet that has the lowest interface metric. In this scenario, outgoing traffic is routed to the back-end adapter, which is where Application Center transmits all cluster management and synchronization traffic. Depending on the amount of traffic on the back end, this could have an adverse impact on services, such as the Synchronization Service.

Separate subnets aren't mandatory; however, they're supported if you decide to use them for your clusters.

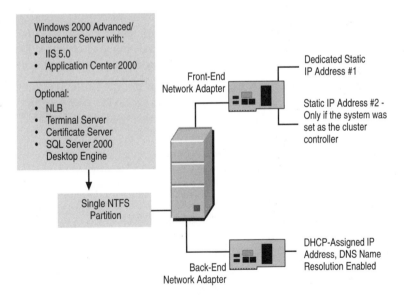

Figure 6.5   Cluster member configuration

Selecting the Cluster Type

Cluster type refers to the primary role of your cluster. The type is determined, for the most part, by the type of content and applications that are hosted. The following three options are available when setting up a cluster:

- **General/Web cluster**   This cluster hosts Web sites and local COM+ applications or is used for general-purpose activities, such as server management or staging applications. (A fairly common server configuration is one that has COM+ components running on the same computer but out-of-process in their own COM+ processes.)

  If NLB is detected during the Application Center configuration analysis, the only available option is General/Web cluster. In order to use the other options, unbind NLB and restart the cluster setup process.

- **COM+ application cluster**   This cluster hosts only COM+ applications that can be referenced by other servers in a General/Web cluster or COM+ routing cluster or by Windows-based applications.

  If you choose the COM+ Application cluster option, you must identify one of two sources for client calls. The first option is applications running on other servers, such as Web servers running ASP and CLB. The second option is desktop COM client applications, which are typically written in a Win32 development environment such as Microsoft Visual Basic. In the case of Win32-based applications, two network adapters are required on each cluster member because NLB is used as the load-balancing technology. In scenarios where the clients are Web or routing clusters, you can use CLB.

- **COM+ routing cluster**   This cluster's primary role is routing requests to a COM+ application cluster, although it can also function as a Web server cluster.

  A COM+ routing cluster uses CLB to route activation requests for COM+ components from clients to a COM+ application cluster. A COM+ routing cluster is essentially a load balancer for COM+ components that are on a COM+ application cluster. COM+ routing clusters are useful when requests for COM+ applications come from a combination of Web-based and Windows-based applications. For most cases you don't need to create a separate COM+ routing cluster; you can create Web clusters that perform CLB.

Selecting a Load Balancing Configuration

If you plan to choose either a General/Web cluster or a COM+ routing cluster as the cluster type, you must also decide which load balancing configuration you'll use in your cluster. Application Center supports three load balancing options:

- NLB
- Non-NLB solutions
- No load balancing

NLB is selected by default unless the server analysis indicates that only one network adapter is present or that DHCP is enabled on both network adapters. If either of these conditions exists, NLB is disabled and the only available options are third-party load balancing or no load balancing.

Network Load Balancing

Application Center allows you to set up and configure NLB quickly without any manual configuration tasks. If the default settings applied by the wizard aren't sufficient, you can modify the settings by using the Application Center user interface or by using the Properties dialog box for the appropriate network adapter. Application Center also provides seamless integration with NLB so that you can use the Application Center user interface to complete common administrative tasks, such as setting members online and offline.

If you configured NLB prior to creating a cluster in Application Center, you can reconfigure those settings or use the existing setting and replicate them to members. If you want to modify any settings, you should do so before adding any members. By doing so, the members that you add acquire the proper settings. If you modify settings after adding members, you might disrupt the cluster.

Non-NLB Solutions

To distribute incoming client requests, Application Center provides integration with NLB and also supports other load balancers. You can monitor and manage these third-party load balancing devices through Application Center to provide a complete cluster administration solution. With third-party load balancing integration, Application Center monitors cluster member status, sets members online and offline, and synchronizes content and configuration for all Web sites, including IP addresses bound to Web sites. To integrate these devices with Application Center, you must configure communication between the device and Application Center.

Because all members are synchronized with the cluster controller, you should ensure that all content and configuration exist on the controller before adding any members. Unpredictable behavior might result if content or configuration on members is different from the controller.

The Microsoft Application Center 2000 Resource Kit provides tools for third-party load balancing integration, including a WMI provider that you can use to monitor your device. This provider allows your device to indicate member status, such as online and offline status or if a member encounters errors. With this provider you can view member status from the Application Center user interface rather than from the device. This capability allows you to view all aspects of the cluster from within Application Center; you don't need to view some aspects (such as synchronization status) from Application Center and other aspects (such as member status) from your load-balancing device.

No Load Balancing

You might decide that you don't need or want to use load balancing. For example, load balancing isn't necessary for application testing and staging.

Maintaining Session State

In load-balanced environments, all client requests are subject to load balancing. Clients who have established session state must also have their requests processed by particular members. Otherwise, clients can experience disruption in their sessions if their requests are load balanced to a member on which the session information doesn't exist.

To forward Hypertext Transfer Protocol (HTTP) requests to particular members in load-balanced environments, Application Center provides the request forwarder. The request forwarder ensures that the following types of requests are forwarded to the controller:

- IIS administration requests
- Microsoft FrontPage publishing
- Web Distributed Authoring and Versioning (WebDAV) publishing
- Web-based administration requests

Maintaining Session State

The request forwarder provides generic support for maintaining session state by using cookies to associate clients with particular members. Subsequent requests containing the cookie are forwarded to the appropriate member.

For example, if a client creates a session on member A, subsequent requests might be load balanced to member B. Because member B might not have the appropriate session information (thus disrupting the session), the request forwarder sends subsequent requests to member A by using information supplied in a cookie.

By default, request forwarding is enabled only for sites that use ASP session state. These sites have session state enabled as an option under Application Configuration in IIS. The alternative is to enable request forwarding for all Web sites.

Request forwarding might affect performance because the request forwarder processes requests after they've been load balanced; it doesn't eliminate load balancing for any requests.

Generally, you achieve the best performance by preventing the Web cluster from having any involvement with session state. For example, you can keep session information in a SQL Server database while state is maintained in a client's cookie. Because the Web cluster doesn't manage session state, you can disable or remove the request forwarder.

Optimizing Performance

Request forwarding imposes minimal overhead as it forwards requests. To minimize performance degradation, you can disable request forwarding for certain file types. You may also want to disable or remove the request forwarder to optimize Web clusters that don't use ASP session state.

Making a Decision

The process for planning an Application Center cluster includes a number of steps. In each one you must make decisions about hardware and software configurations. Table 6.4 describes many of the issues that you should consider for each step.

Table 6.4   Planning an Application Center Cluster

Step	Description
Planning server configurations	When planning server configuration, you must ensure that each computer has enough resources to run all the necessary applications. You must take into account the amount of memory and disk space and the number of network adapters on each server. You must also consider whether you'll use homogenous hardware when setting up your servers.
Determining IP addresses	For each server in the cluster, at least one IP address must be bound to the back-end adapter and one to the front-end adapter. The IP address bound to the front-end adapter serves as the cluster IP address. In addition, front-end and back-end adapters can be on separate subnets.
Determining cluster type	When you set up an Application Center cluster, you can choose one of three cluster types: General/Web cluster, COM+ application cluster, or COM+ routing cluster.
Selecting a load balancing configuration	For General/Web clusters and COM+ routing clusters, you must select which load balancing configuration you'll use for the cluster. You can select Network Load Balancing, other load balancing, or no load balancing.
Maintaining session state	When setting up a cluster, you must determine whether the cluster will maintain session state or whether you want to use another method for managing session state.

Recommendations

When planning an Application Center cluster, you should adhere to the following guidelines:

- Use enough memory in each system to adequately support all applications that will run on that system, including Application Center, the Windows 2000 operating system, IIS, and any other services running on the cluster.

- The disk partition must contain adequate space for all installed programs, paging files, site content, replication, and defragmentation.
- You should configure each server in the cluster with at least two network adapters.
- You should use homogenous hardware to ensure balanced and consistent performance across the cluster.
- You should configure the back-end network adapter with one IP address, preferably a DHCP-assigned address. You should configure the front-end adapter with two static IP addresses, one that's common to all cluster members and one that's unique to the individual server. The front-end and back-end adapters should be on separate subnets.
- You should select the cluster type appropriate to the cluster being configured. The General/Web cluster is the type used for your basic Web cluster. You use the COM+ application type only when implementing a separate tier to support COM+ applications.
- When planning a General/Web cluster or COM+ routing cluster, it's recommended that you use NLB rather than another type of load balancing. NLB is inexpensive to implement and requires less administration.
- You should generally try to avoid having your Web cluster involved with session state.

Example: An Application Center Cluster

An example of an Application Center cluster deployment infrastructure is illustrated in Figure 6.6. In this example there are two Application Center clusters, each running in its own Windows domain. As an additional management and security measure, you can establish organizational units within each domain. By positioning these clusters between the two firewalls that demarcate the perimeter network, you can create a highly secure cluster environment. Notice that each uses a different type of load-balancing configuration. The left cluster uses a third-party load-balancing device, and the right cluster uses NLB.

The infrastructure illustrated in Figure 6.6 is meant only to serve as a starting point for designing and implementing a robust and secure cluster topology. Your business needs will dictate the requirements for back-end database servers or clusters, component servers or clusters, and multilevel testing/staging configurations.

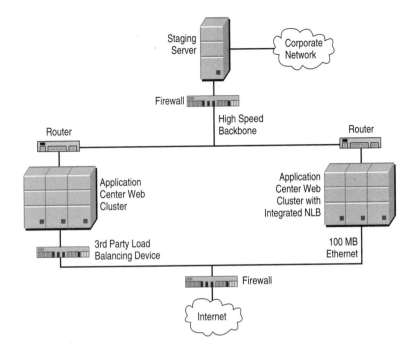

Figure 6.6 Application Center deployment infrastructure

Lesson Summary

You should consider a number of steps when planning an Application Center
cluster. The first step is to plan the server configuration. You must take into account
the amount of memory and disk space. In addition, each cluster member should have
at least two network adapters. It's also recommended that you use homogenous
hardware. You should configure the front-end network adapters with at least
one IP address, which is the cluster IP address. In most cases a single DHCP-
assigned address is bound to the back-end adapter. When setting up a cluster, you
can choose from one of three cluster types: General/Web cluster, COM+ application cluster, and COM+ routing cluster. If you select the General/Web cluster
option or the COM+ routing cluster option, you must also select one of the three
load-balancing configurations supported by Application Center: NLB, non-NLB
solutions, or no load balancing. Clients who have established session state must
also have their requests processed by particular members. To forward HTTP
requests to particular members in load-balanced environments, Application Center
provides the request forwarder. Generally, you'll achieve the best performance by
preventing the Web cluster from having any involvement with session state.

Activity 6.1: Identifying Components of Application Center Clusters

You're a network administrator at Contoso Pharmaceuticals. The company, which provides services to physicians around the country, is implementing a Web site to provide online services to the clients. Because physicians must be able to access pharmaceutical information at any time, the Web site must be available 24 hours a day, 7 days a week. You plan to achieve this availability by implementing Application Center clusters into your network. For security and maintenance reasons, you decide to implement COM+ application cluster on a tier separate from the Web cluster.

You create a diagram similar to the one shown in Figure 6.7 to map out the network topology.

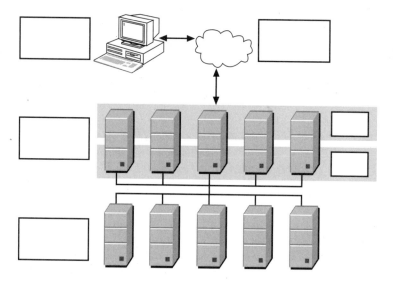

Figure 6.7   Application Center Web cluster and COM+ application cluster

1. In the diagram above, label the following components: client, Internet, Web-tier cluster, COM+ cluster, NLB, and CLB.

2. What are the different cluster types supported by Application Center?

3. Which cluster type would you use to host Web sites and to support NLB and CLB?

Lesson 3: Designing CLB Clusters

CLB allows COM+ components to be load balanced. COM+ components are compiled software objects that are usable from a variety of different languages including VBScript (VBS), ASP, Visual Basic, and C++. They provide a useful way of bundling software into convenient and reusable entities. In CLB, the COM+ components are located on servers in a separate COM+ application cluster. Calls to activate COM+ components are load balanced to different servers within the COM+ cluster. The decision-making elements of the CLB software run on the Web tier, although some information-gathering CLB software does run on the COM+ cluster. In this lesson you'll learn how CLB works and how you can implement it in your network environment.

After this lesson, you will be able to

- Describe CLB and how it's integrated into Application Center clusters
- Design multitiered clusters that allow you to load balance your COM+ applications

Estimated lesson time: 30 minutes

CLB

CLB is an Application Center feature that provides dynamic load balancing for COM+ application components. In order to enable CLB, an Application Center COM+ application cluster must activate components when requests are received from either a General/Web cluster, COM+ routing cluster, or clients running the Win32 API. Functionally, an Application Center Web cluster and COM+ routing cluster are the same; both support CLB and can route requests to a COM+ application cluster.

Note   Only COM+ object activation is load balanced by CLB. Queued components can't be load balanced.

COM

At the root of CLB is the component architecture that comprises the Component Object Model (COM). When object-based software is written to this standard, it provides a generic mechanism by which software services can be made available. It allows software to be written in varying languages and operating systems. Key to this flexibility is the COM interface.

A COM component exposes functionality through one or more interfaces. To use a COM component, client software has to be written in a language that can communicate with the interface. Languages such as Visual Basic, ASP, VBS, JavaScript, and Visual C++ can all do this. The interface itself is simply a table of numbers that hold the address of the methods supported by the interface, as shown in Figure 6.8.

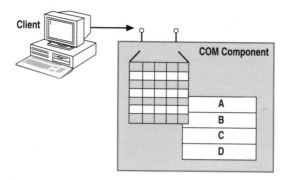

Figure 6.8   Interfaces on a COM component

COM components are typically housed within dynamic-link libraries (DLLs) or executable (.exe) files. They can be installed on the client or located on a remote computer. When used remotely, the call is made through a mechanism called Distributed COM (DCOM) that's based upon Remote Procedure Calls (RPCs).

COM+ Services

COM+ Services is supplied as part of the Windows 2000 operating system and provides a suite of services based on COM and MTS. COM+ Services provides enterprise functionality such as transaction support, object lifetime services, security services, events, and queued components.

COM+ Components

COM+ components are COM components that can take advantage of COM+ Services. One of the requirements for a COM+ component is that it carry configuration information, which is a set of attributes that allows the underlying COM architecture to discover whether a particular COM+ Service is supported—for example, transaction support or load balancing.

COM+ components are grouped together into packages known as *applications*, which aren't the same as Application Center applications. A COM+ application is a grouping of COM+ components, whereas an Application Center application is a list of resources that are used in a business solution.

How CLB Works

CLB has two major parts:

- **CLB software**   Used to load balance a COM+ cluster
- **COM+ application cluster**   An Application Center cluster that activates and runs COM+ components

CLB Software

The CLB software is responsible for determining the order in which COM+ cluster members are used for activating COM+ components.

The business logic that creates the COM+ component runs on the Web-tier cluster. This will typically be a Visual Basic ASP script that calls CreateObject when a COM+ component is required. (Internally this translates to a call to CoCreateInstance.) With CLB, instead of creating the component on the local server, a routing list and server response timetable is used to help pass the COM+ component activation request through to a load-balanced COM+ cluster. A COM+ cluster member then creates the component and returns an interface to the client. CLB has no further active involvement with the component once it's been created.

Routing List

The routing list exists on each member of the Web-tier cluster and contains a list of the COM+ cluster members to be load balanced, as shown in Figure 6.9. The routing list can also exist on the COM+ routing cluster, which is used solely for routing purposes and has no Web-tier functionality.

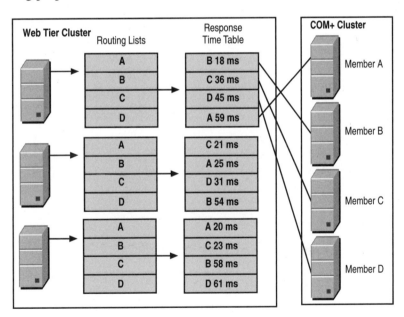

Figure 6.9   Routing lists and response times

The routing list is initially created by the administrator on the Web-tier cluster controller and then automatically synchronized to each cluster member. It's therefore impossible to have cluster members with routing lists containing different COM+ cluster members. One big advantage of having the routing list on each Web-tier cluster member is that there's no single point of failure. If a given Web-tier cluster member stops—by design or not—other members will continue to load balance the COM+ cluster through their own routing lists.

Response Timetable

Every 200 milliseconds, the CLB software running on each host in the Web-tier cluster polls each member on its routing list. From the polling responses, it builds an in-memory table listing the COM+ cluster members ranked by response time. The faster the member's response, the higher its position in the table. The Web-tier member uses the response timetable in a round-robin manner to pass incoming activation requests to the COM+ cluster members. As activation requests are received, the fastest, least busy COM+ cluster member is used first, followed by the next (slower) member for subsequent requests. Once the table has been exhausted, the next request is routed through the first table entry. Further activations proceed through the table as before. This continues until the next scheduled response time update occurs, and activation is reset to the beginning of the freshly load-balanced table.

Each Web-tier cluster member maintains a COM+ cluster member response timetable. No attempt is made to synchronize these values across the Web-tier cluster as the list wouldn't be replicated fast enough to keep up with changing COM+ cluster load.

COM+ Application Cluster

As with the Web-tier cluster, the administrator creates the COM+ cluster with the New Cluster Wizard in Application Center. Each member of the cluster has to have the same copy of the COM+ component installed. A deployment wizard is available for installing the components. Once it's created, the component needs to be aware of its existence within a CLB cluster.

Cluster-Aware COM+ Components

To use CLB, COM+ components must be written to be cluster-aware. In COM+, components shouldn't retain per-component state information because this adversely affects scalability and transaction management. Components can't be recycled unless they're stateless; per-component state information can't cross transaction boundaries. Component state needs to be stored either in persistent state, such as a database management system, where it can be accessed from any cluster member, or it should be stored with the client, such as cookie information stored on an Internet client's computer.

When to Use CLB

Although CLB is a very effective tool for building distributed solutions, sometimes it might not be the best solution. The key issues are performance, manageability, and security. Understanding these issues will help you build better cluster topologies.

Performance

However attractive or functional a Web site is, it won't succeed if users don't get satisfactory performance from it. Two issues are important to an effective Web site:

- **Throughput**   The work done by Web site
- **Response time**   The time taken to give feedback to a user

CLB can have an impact on both throughput and response time.

Throughput   Throughput performance declines when an application or service makes a call across a network. Using CLB will obviously affect throughput performance, which you need to account for in making cluster architecture decisions. Table 6.5 shows the number of calls per second on a single threaded Visual Basic COM component that returns "Hello, world" as string property. The client is early bound and doesn't release references between calls to retrieve the property.

Table 6.5   COM Component Throughput

Scenario	Calls per Second	Relative Speed
COM+ server application, run over a 10Base-T network	625	1.0x
COM+ server application, Out Proc, same box	1,923	3.08x
COM+ library application, In Proc, same box	3,333	5.33x

It's clear that calls over the network yield slower throughput than calls to software installed on the same computer. This is true in all software communication, whether it's through Microsoft software or something else. For this reason, CLB isn't an effective solution where throughput is absolutely critical. In this case it's better to install the COM+ components locally on the Web-tier cluster members (as shown in Figure 6.10), thus avoiding cross-network calls. CLB support is lost, but load balancing is still available through NLB.

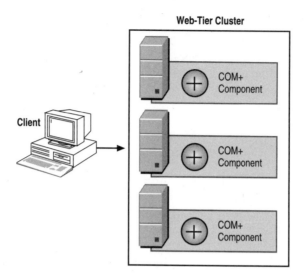

Figure 6.10   COM+ components on the Web tier

Response Time   Ensuring that users have a fast response to Web site visits is obviously very important, and Web site architecture greatly affects this. COM+ components running on the Web-tier cluster may perform work that perceptively degrades the Web site's response. If response time for non-COM+ component work is more important than component throughput, one solution is to move the COM+ components to a COM+ cluster tier, as shown in Figure 6.11.

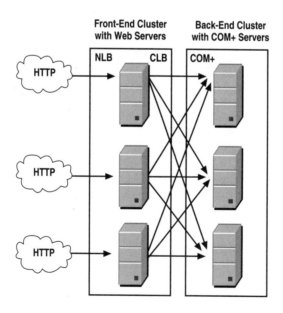

Figure 6.11   Two-tier cluster model with NLB and COM+ application clusters

Having a separate tier for COM+ applications lightens the workload for the Web-tier cluster because service time for clients not using COM+ components is improved—for example, clients accessing static Web pages. Obviously, when COM+ component work is required, you won't see response time improvement. In fact, performance will probably degrade since cross-network calls will be taking place.

Another option for implementing CLB is to move the routing lists onto a separate COM+ routing cluster, as shown in Figure 6.12. This configuration makes the workload for the Web-tier even lighter because no CLB-specific work takes place on it.

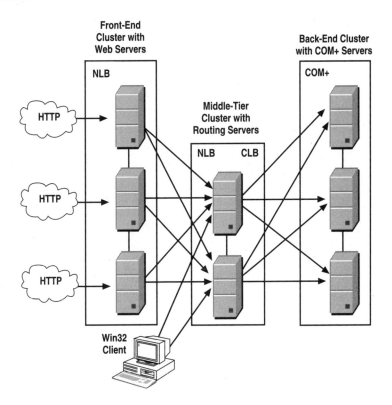

Figure 6.12   A three-tier cluster with load balancing across all tiers

This configuration is good for non-COM+ component work on the Web tier, but it introduces even more performance degradation for COM+ components as a result of cross-network calls. However, one advantage of having a third tier is that the middle routing cluster can handle Win32 client requests as well as front-end Web requests.

Manageability

Using a separate COM+ cluster helps improve manageability. It allows the differing needs of a Web site's COM+ components and IP requests to be easily and separately managed. For example, many organizations house their COM+ components on servers in different physical locations. Using a separate COM+ cluster allows independent management of the cluster. It's also possible to have a COM+ cluster that's shared across multiple Web-tier clusters or vice versa.

Security

A common use for CLB is to enhance Web site security. When used as the means to access data, COM+ components can use their role-based, or programmatic, security mechanisms to safeguard data. This potentially could be compromised if the components are placed on the Web-tier cluster. Calls received by the Web-tier cluster may come from an untrustworthy client looking to take illegal advantage of the COM+ components installed on the cluster member. CLB allows you to avoid this problem by moving the COM+ components off the Web-tier cluster onto a COM+ cluster. The COM+ cluster is often protected by a firewall (Firewall B in Figure 6.13), and it allows components to be created only from calls that have originated within the Web-tier cluster and not from the client. Figure 6.13 also shows a perimeter network protecting the Web tier through two encompassing firewalls.

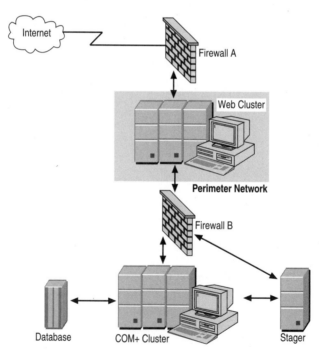

Figure 6.13   COM+ cluster behind a firewall

Making a Decision

When deciding whether to implement a COM+ application cluster, you should take into account performance, manageability, and security. Table 6.6 lists the factors that you should consider when making a decision.

Table 6.6 Implementing a COM+ Application Cluster

Consideration	Factors
Performance	You should consider throughput and response time when determining whether to use CLB. Throughput can decline when calls must be made over a network, although response time can sometimes be improved.
Manageability	Using a separate tier for a COM+ application cluster provides for independent management of COM+ applications. You can manage components and IP requests easily and separately.
Security	You can enhance security through the use of a separate tier for a COM+ application cluster. Security can sometimes be compromised when COM+ components are placed on the Web-tier cluster.

Recommendations

Although Application Center supports multi-tier scenarios, you shouldn't implement these scenarios simply as de facto models for distributing application components. There are good reasons for distributing applications across tiers as well as for keeping everything on a single tier. You have to analyze your technical and business requirements fully before making this decision. This question has no single correct answer.

The main reasons for setting up separate Web and COM+ application server tiers include the following:

- **Security**   You can place an additional layer of firewalls between one tier and the other.

- **Administrative partitioning**   Different groups of developers and administrators are responsible for the HTML/ASP and COM+ applications. Putting the two groups on different tiers prevents problems between the groups.

- **Cluster sharing**   Sharing a single COM+ application cluster among multiple Web clusters can better utilize resources.

- **Increasing response time**   In some scenarios (for example, a low-throughput environment where each request is very expensive), sending multiple costly COM+ requests from a single Web request to a COM+ application cluster will increase response time—but not throughput.

Note   In a high-throughput environment, this benefit is muted, because load will be balanced evenly around the cluster whether or not it's multitiered.

The main reasons for choosing not to set up separate Web and COM+ application server tiers include the following:

- **Performance**   Remote access is more expensive than running locally, and overall performance degrades if you split a single front-end cluster into two clusters without adding more hardware.

- **Administrative complexity**   Managing two clusters is more complex than managing one.

- **Difficulty making full use of the hardware**   You must carefully balance hardware between the Web cluster and COM+ application cluster. Adding capacity becomes more complex, and it's likely that one tier or the other will end up with less capacity. This causes a bottleneck that requires more hardware to maintain optimal headroom; in addition, more monitoring is necessary to balance hardware utilization.

- **Dependency maintenance**   Whenever you add a member to the COM+ application cluster, you must update the cluster on the front end with the new membership list of the back-end component members.

Note   You also can use a COM+ routing cluster, but this has its own set of problems and you have an additional tier to manage, with its inherent monitoring and throughput problems.

It's clear that high performance and CLB don't necessarily go hand-in-hand and that it's critical that Web site designers be aware of these limitations. CLB is a great tool for building distributed solutions; however, you must be careful using it. Although using it will adversely affect throughput performance, other advantages, such as security, manageability, ease of setup, and load balancing, make it a valuable tool.

Example: A CLB Cluster for Consolidated Messenger

The Consolidated Messenger company is implementing a multitiered network to support their Web site. The Web portion of the network will include three tiers. The front-end tier will contain an NLB cluster. Each computer in the cluster will support Web services. The middle tier will contain a COM+ application cluster. The Web cluster and COM+ application cluster each will include three Windows 2000 Advanced Server computers. CLB will run on the Web cluster to support the COM+ application cluster. The network will also include a back-end tier that will contain a data cluster. The data cluster will contain two Windows 2000 Advanced Server computers, and the Microsoft Windows Cluster service will be used to provide highly available data services.

Figure 6.14 shows the topology of the Web portion (perimeter network) of Consolidated Messenger's network. Notice how COM+ applications are separated out from the Web tier.

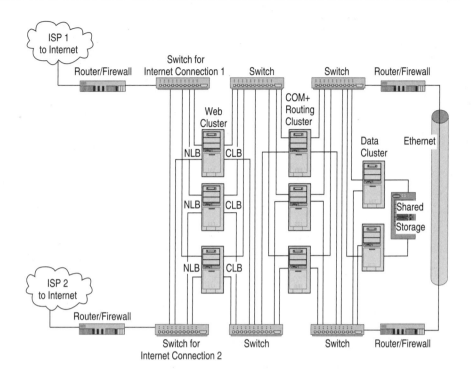

Figure 6.14 A multitiered network environment that uses NLB, CLB, and the Cluster service

Lesson Summary

CLB provides dynamic load balancing for COM+ application components. At the root of CLB is the component architecture that comprises the Component Object Model. CLB has two major parts: CLB software, which is used to load balance a COM+ cluster, and the COM+ cluster, an Application Center cluster that activates and runs COM+ components. A routing list exists on each member of the Web-tier cluster and contains a list of the COM+ cluster members to be load balanced. Each Web-tier cluster member maintains a COM+ cluster member response timetable. As with the Web-tier cluster, the administrator creates the COM+ cluster with the New Cluster Wizard in Application Center. When deciding whether to use CLB, you must take into consideration performance, manageability, and security. High performance and CLB don't necessarily go hand-in-hand. Although using CLB will adversely affect throughput performance, other advantages, such as security, manageability, and ease of setup, might offset the effects on throughput.

Lab 6.1: Designing Application Center Clusters

After completing this lab, you'll be able to

- Design a General/Web cluster
- Design a COM+ routing cluster
- Design a COM+ application cluster

About This Lab

In this lab you'll design three clusters that will support NLB and CLB. The designs will focus on the network topology to support these three clusters. The clusters will be implemented in a multitiered environment that takes full advantage of Application Center's load-balancing capabilities.

Before You Begin

Before you begin this lab, you must be able to

- Administer Windows 2000 Advanced Server and Application Center 2000
- Implement and administer NLB in Windows 2000 Advanced Server and Application Center 2000
- Implement and administer CLB in Application Center 2000

Scenario: Clusters for Trey Research

The Trey Research company provides research and information services for customers around the world. The company plans to implement online services for their customers and wants those services to be available 24 hours a day, 7 days a week. The portion of the network that will support their Web site must incorporate redundant services, components, and network paths in order to eliminate any single points of failure. Initially, the company will maintain only one Web site instead of multiple sites in different geographical locations. Data will be stored in a back-end cluster that uses the Cluster service in Windows 2000 Advanced Server. Additional clusters will be supported through the use of Windows 2000 Advanced Server Application Center. Because the Web site is a low throughput environment (a lot of static Web pages), response time for non-COM+ component work is more important than component throughput. In addition, Win32 clients must be able to access the COM+ applications. As the administrator of this network, you decide to implement a multitiered environment that supports a Web cluster, a COM+ routing cluster, and a COM+ application cluster.

Exercise 1: Designing a General/Web Cluster

In this exercise, you must design the General/Web cluster that supports the Web services. Your design should include the basic network infrastructure that supports the company's Web site. The topology should include redundant Internet Service Provider (ISP) connections, switches, and network paths. In addition, you should define the perimeter network and the route to the corporate (secure) network. At this point, your network design should also include the General/Web cluster and the data cluster.

1. How should you draw your network design?

2. How would client requests be distributed to the hosts in General/Web cluster once those requests have passed through the firewall?

3. Based on the current network configuration, where would COM+ applications reside?

Exercise 2: Designing a COM+ Routing Cluster

In this exercise, you'll modify the network topology that you designed in Exercise 1. Your network design should now incorporate the COM+ routing cluster. Although you wouldn't normally add a routing cluster to a network without also adding a COM+ application cluster, for the purposes of this exercise add only the routing cluster to indicate where it would be placed in relation to the other network components. Also be certain to add the necessary components to avoid any single points of failure in your network design.

1. How should you draw the network design?

2. On which cluster or clusters would you now run NLB?

3. What's the primary role of the COM+ routing cluster?

Exercise 3: Designing a COM+ Application Cluster

In this exercise you'll add the COM+ application cluster to your network topology. Be sure to add the necessary switches and paths to prevent any single points of failure. At this point in the design process you should also add a Win32 client and indicate where it connects to the network.

1. How should you draw the network design?

2. On which tiers should you run CLB and NLB?

3. How is network performance affected by running COM+ applications on a cluster separate from the General/Web cluster?

Review

Answering the following questions will reinforce key information presented in this chapter. If you're unable to answer a question, review the appropriate lesson and then try the question again. Answers to the questions can be found in the appendix.

1. How is NLB in Application Center integrated with NLB in Windows 2000 Advanced Server?

2. In what scenarios should you consider using CLB?

3. What are the three primary clustering scenarios?

4. You're the network administrator at Graphic Design Institute, and you want to improve the availability of your company's Web site. You decide to implement an Application Center cluster to support the Web services. In planning the cluster, you decide to include three hosts, each of which is configured with enough resources to run Windows 2000 Advanced Server, Application Center, Event and Performance Logging, and IIS 5.0. You also plan to configure the cluster network adapters on a subnet separate from the back-end network adapters. Which cluster type and load balancing configuration should you use?

5. Your company is implementing a Web site and is evaluating how to structure clusters and load balancing on your network. Throughput performance is critical to the operation and should be maintained at the highest possible level. In addition, management wants to keep network administration as uncomplicated as possible and to make full use of the hardware that they have available. Which type or types of Application Center clusters (General/Web, COM+ routing, or COM+ application) should you implement in this site?

CHAPTER 7

Capacity Planning

About This Chapter

When planning to implement a Web site, you must ensure that the network and its components can handle the number of users who will access it. *Capacity planning*—the process of measuring a Web site's ability to deliver content to its visitors at an acceptable speed—is essential to making sure that your system will perform adequately when a peak number of users are accessing the applications and services in your network. Slow performance and unavailable service can encourage your customers to try other Web sites—and perhaps never return to yours. As a result, you must try to plan, to the best of your ability, for the greatest number of users who will try to use your site at the same time, and from that determination, you must ensure that your network's hardware and software have sufficient capacity to meet anticipated demand. In this chapter you'll be introduced to a number of issues related to capacity planning. You'll also learn how to estimate user costs, such as CPU and memory usage, and how to plan your network's capacity requirements.

Before You Begin

To complete the lessons in this chapter, you must have

- Experience administering Microsoft Windows 2000 Server and designing Windows 2000 networks
- Experience planning network capacity

Lesson 1: Introduction to Capacity Planning

The goal of any Web site is to present users with a high-quality experience. When users face slow response times, timeouts and errors, and broken links, they become frustrated and often turn to other sites to find what they're looking for. To prevent this, you must provide an infrastructure that can handle not only average levels of demand but also peak levels and beyond. Capacity planning makes it possible to calculate how much hardware is necessary to meet users' demands. These calculations allow you to identify bottlenecks in the network design that can cause performance degradation and lead to poor user experiences. You can then modify the design or implement the changes needed to eliminate these bottlenecks. However, before you can plan your network's capacity requirements, you must be familiar with several basic concepts that are important to your understanding of the issues involved in capacity planning. This lesson introduces you to these concepts by describing how network traffic, performance, availability, and scalability are all factors in the capacity planning process.

After this lesson, you will be able to

- Identify and describe issues that are relevant to capacity planning

Estimated lesson time: 25 minutes

Traffic

When a browser requests information from a Web server, it first establishes a Transmission Control Protocol (TCP) connection with the server. The browser then sends the request through the connection, and the server sends out pages in response to the requests. This interchange of incoming requests and outgoing responses is referred to as *traffic*.

Traffic is only partly predictable. It tends to occur in bursts and clumps. For example, many sites might experience activity peaks at the beginning and end of the workday but have lower levels of activity in the middle of the day. In addition, the size of these peaks might vary from day to day. Not surprisingly, a direct relationship exists between the amount of traffic and the network bandwidth necessary to support that traffic. The more visitors to your site and the larger the pages provided by the server, the more network bandwidth that's required.

Suppose your Web site is connected to the Internet through a DS1/T1 line, which can transmit data at 1.536 megabits per second (Mbps). The Web server displays static Hypertext Markup Language (HTML), text-only pages that average 5 kilobytes (KB) per page. Each transmission carries with it a packet overhead that contains header information. For a 5-KB file, the overhead might average 30 percent of the file's size. For larger files, the overhead accounts for a smaller percentage of network traffic.

Figure 7.1 illustrates how a load is distributed over a T1 line for a 5-KB page request.

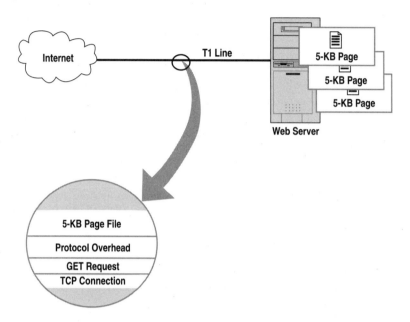

Figure 7.1   Transmitting a 5-KB page over a T1 line

Table 7.1 shows the traffic generated by a typical request for a 5-KB page. Many of the figures are only estimates. The exact number of bytes sent varies for each request.

Table 7.1   Traffic Generated by 5-KB Page

Traffic Type	Bytes Sent
TCP connection	180 (approximately)
GET request	256 (approximately)
5-KB file	5,120
Protocol overhead	1,364 (approximately)
TOTAL	6,920 (55,360 bits)

The standard transmission rate for a T1 line is 1.544 Mbps. Under normal conditions, the available bandwidth is 1.536 Mbps, or 1,536,000 bits per second. (The available bandwidth is reduced because 8,000 bits is required for framing the bit stream.) To determine the maximum rate of pages per second that your network can support, you should divide the bits per second of the T1 line by the bits generated for a 5-KB page request. In this case you'd divide 1,536,000 by 55,360, which comes to a maximum transmission rate of 27.7 pages per second.

Of course, if you add graphics to your files, the results will be considerably different. In addition, if each page has several images, if the images are relatively large, or if the pages contain other multimedia content, download time will be much longer.

Given a page of moderate size and complexity, there are several ways to serve more pages per second:

- Remove some images from the page.
- Use smaller pictures if you currently send large ones or compress the existing pictures. (If they're already compressed, compress them further.)
- Offer reduced-size images with links to larger ones and let the user choose.
- Use images of a file type that's inherently compact, such as a .gif or a .jpg file, to replace inherently large file types, such as a .tif file.
- Connect to the network by using a faster interface or by using multiple interfaces. Note that this option resolves the issue at the server but not necessarily at the client.

A site that serves primarily static HTML pages, especially those with simple structure, is likely to run out of network bandwidth before it runs out of processing power. On the other hand, a site that performs a lot of dynamic page generation or that acts as a transaction or database server uses more processor cycles and can create bottlenecks in its processor, memory, disk, or network.

Client-Side Network Capacity

Server-side network capacity isn't the only factor to consider when determining bandwidth limitations. The client computer is limited by its connection to the Internet. It can take a considerable amount of time, relative to a server's output, for a browser to download a page.

Suppose you want to download a page that, including overhead, totals about 90 KB (about 720 kilobits). Ignoring latencies, which typically add a few seconds before any of the data arrives, it takes roughly 25 seconds to download 720 kilobits through a 28.8 kilobits-per-second (Kbps) connection if everything is working perfectly. Figure 7.2 illustrates the process of downloading the 90-KB page.

If any blocking or bottlenecking is going on at the server, if the network is overloaded and slow, or if the user's connection is slower than 28.8 Kbps, the download will take longer. For example, a poor phone line connection can affect the download rate.

If the client computer has a higher-bandwidth connection on an intranet, the download time should be much shorter. If your Web site is on the Internet, however, you can't count on a majority of users having faster connections until the next wave of connection technology becomes well established. Although many users now use

56 Kbps modems, many (if not most) telephone lines are too noisy to allow full-speed connections with 56 Kbps modems. In some areas cable modem and Digital Subscriber Line (DSL) technologies are being used extensively. For this reason, it's impossible to tell which connection mode users will use to connect to your site.

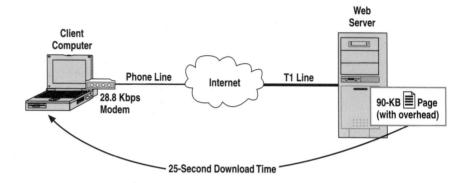

Figure 7.2   Downloading a 90-KB page (including overhead) through a 28.8 Kbps modem

Table 7.2 lists the relative speeds of several network interface types, based on a 5-KB text-only page. Numbers of pages transmitted at speeds faster than the standard Ethernet rate of 10 Mbps are rounded.

Table 7.2   Network Interface Speeds

Connection Type	Connection Speed	5-KB Pages Sent per Second
Dedicated Point-to-Point Protocol/ Serial Line Internet Protocol (PPP/SLIP) using a modem	28.8 Kbps	Roughly half of 1 page
Frame Relay or fast modem	56 Kbps	Almost 1 page
Integrated Services Digital Network (ISDN)	128 Kbps	Just over 2 pages
Typical digital subscriber line (DSL)	640 Kbps	Almost 11 pages
Digital signal level 1 (DS1)/T1	1.536 Mbps	26 pages
10-Mb Ethernet	8 Mbps (best case)	(Up to) 136 pages
Digital signal level 3 (DS3)/T3	44.736 Mbps	760 pages
Optical carrier 1 (OC1)	51.844 Mbps	880 pages
100-Mb Ethernet	80 Mbps (best case)	(Up to) 1,360 pages
Optical carrier 3 (OC3)	155.532 Mbps	2,650 pages
Optical carrier 12 (OC12)	622.128 Mbps	10,580 pages
1-gigabit-per-second (Gbps) Ethernet	800 Mbps (best case)	(Up to) 13,600 pages

Server-Side Network Capacity

It takes about 52 connections at 28.8 Kbps to saturate a DS1/T1 line. If no more than 52 clients simultaneously request a 90-KB page (including overhead) and if the server can keep up with the requests, the clients will all receive the page in 25 seconds (ignoring the typical delays).

If 100 clients simultaneously request that same page, however, the total number of bits to be transferred will be 100 times 720,000 (720 kilobits). It takes between 47 and 48 seconds for that many bits to travel down a DS1/T1 line. At that point the server's network connection, not the client's, is the limiting factor.

Figure 7.3 shows the relationship between concurrent connections and saturation for DS1/T1 and DS3/T3 lines, assuming all clients are using a modem transmission speed of 28.8 Kbps and are always connected. A DS3/T3 line carries nearly 45 Mbps, about 30 times as much capacity as a DS1/T1 line, and it takes more than 1,500 clients at 28.8 Kbps to saturate its bandwidth. Moreover, the increase in download time for each new client is much smaller on a DS3/T3 line. When there are 2,000 simultaneous 28.8 Kbps connections, for example, it still takes less than 33 seconds for a client to download the page.

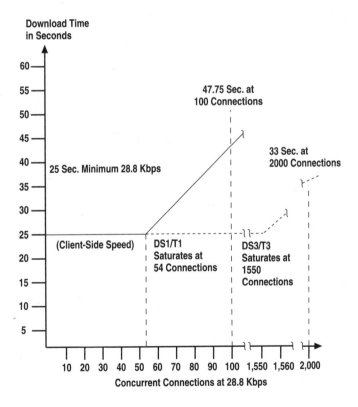

Figure 7.3 Download time versus server network bandwidth

The data shown in Figure 7.3 assumes that the server is capable of performing the relevant processing and handling of 2,000 simultaneous connections. That's not the same as handling 2,000 simultaneous users: users occasionally stop to read or think and typically spend only a modest percentage of their time downloading, except while receiving streaming multimedia content. Because of this difference between users and connections, the number of users that Internet Information Server (IIS) 5.0 can support is larger than the figures would seem to indicate. A Web server on a DS1/T1 line can typically handle several hundred users connecting at 28.8 Kbps, and with a DS3/T3 line the number typically climbs to 5,000 or more. While these numbers are derived from actual servers, you can expect performance to vary with differing content types and user needs and with the number and type of services being performed by a particular computer.

Essentially, the network performance differences shown here scale linearly, and the scaling continues at larger data-transfer rates. If you have two DS3/T3 lines, for example, you can serve approximately twice as many clients as you can with one, provided that you have enough processor power to keep up with user demand and that no bottlenecks prevent your servers from maximizing their processing power.

Performance

The performance of Web applications is critical in determining the site's capacity. Testing is the only way to find out a Web application's capacity and performance. The Web Capacity Analysis Tool (WCAT) and Web Application Stress Tool (WAST) utilities (included on the Windows 2000 Server Resource Kit companion CD) are useful testing tools. Before writing an application, however, it's useful to have a sense of the performance capabilities of different Web application types. In IIS 5.0, Internet Server Application Programming Interface (ISAPI) applications running as in-process dynamic-link libraries (DLLs) generally offer the best performance. After that, the next best solution is Active Server Pages (ASP) applications, followed by Common Gateway Interface (CGI) applications.

For most applications, the recommendation is to use scripting in ASP pages to call server-side components. This strategy offers performance comparable to ISAPI performance, with the advantage of more rapid development time and easier maintenance.

Table 7.3 shows the results of performance tests run on a beta version of IIS 5.0. The application ran on uniprocessor and multiprocessor kernels for Secure Sockets Layer (SSL) connections and non-SSL connections. The hardware and software used for the tests are described on the next page.

Table 7.3   Performance Testing of IIS 5.0

Test	Non-SSL 1 CPU	Non-SSL 2 CPUs	Non-SSL 4 CPUs	SSL 1 CPU	SSL 2 CPUs	SSL 4 CPUs
ISAPI in-process	517	723	953	50	79	113
ISAPI out-of-process	224	244	283	48	76	95
CGI	46	59	75	29	33	42
Static file (FILE8K.TXT)	1,109	1,748	2,242	48	80	108
ASP in-process	60	107	153	38	59	83
ASP out-of-process	50	82	109	28	43	56

The figures given in Table 7.3 are the actual numbers of pages per second that were served during testing. Each test repeatedly fetched the same 8-KB file. Note that different computer types will provide different performance for the same test. In addition, the performance of different application types depends greatly on the application's task. For these tests the task was a relatively light load, so the differences among the various methods are maximized. Heavier tasks result in performance differences that are smaller than those reflected in the table.

The following hardware and software were used for the test:

- The servers were Compaq Proliant 6500 (4 × Pentium Pro 200 MHz) with 512 MB of 60 nanoseconds (ns) RAM.
- The clients were Gateway Pentium II machines, 350 MHz with 64 MB RAM.
- The network was configured as follows:
  - Clients used one Intel Pro100+ 10/100 MB network adapter card.
  - The server used four Intel Pro100+ 10/100 MB network adapter cards.
  - Four separate networks were created to distribute the workload evenly for the server, with four clients per network. Two Cisco Catalyst 2900 switches were used, each having two Virtual LANs (VLANs) programmed.
- The following software was used:
  - The server was configured with Windows 2000 Advanced Server and IIS 5.
  - The clients were configured with Windows 2000 Professional.
  - WAST was used to test the site.

Note   These tests were conducted with out-of-the-box computers and programs. No additional registry changes or performance enhancements were administered.

Availability

Some sites can afford to fail or go offline; others can't. Many financial institutions, for example, require 99.999 percent availability or better. Site availability takes two forms: the site needing to remain online if one of its servers crashes and the site needing to remain online while information is being updated or backed up. As discussed in earlier chapters, you can achieve site availability through the use of redundant services, components, and network connections. For example, services can be made redundant through the use of Network Load Balancing (NLB) and the Cluster service.

Availability is an important consideration when planning your network's capacity requirements. You must first determine what type of availability you're trying to achieve. How many 9s are you trying to adhere to? Although 99.999 percent might be ideal, it might not be realistic—or necessary—for your organization. In other words, how much can your organization afford to spend to ensure that your network can always meet your peak capacity requirements?

You must determine whether the problems caused by your site's unavailability offset the expense of trying to keep it online. If you require 99.999 percent availability or better, then you must ensure that users won't be prevented from accessing your resources because your site has reached its capacity. If, on the other hand, you need to achieve only 99 percent availability or less, you might be less concerned with your site occasionally being unavailable to users because your site has reached its capacity limits, particularly if peak capacity is rare.

Scalability

The scalability of your site is a primary consideration when you're ready to upgrade it to improve availability, increase the number of concurrent users, or decrease its latency for faster response times. A site's scalability goes hand in hand with its availability. Upgrading your site shouldn't lead to unplanned or unnecessary downtime. You should take two types of scaling into consideration when upgrading your site: scaling up and scaling out. Scalability is discussed in more detail in Lesson 3: "Planning Network Capacity."

Lesson Summary

Four factors are important to capacity planning: network traffic, performance, availability, and scalability. Traffic is the interchange of incoming requests and outgoing responses between two computers. Traffic is often unpredictable and occurs in bursts and clumps. To determine the maximum rate of pages per second that your network can support, you should divide the bits per second of the network connection (such as a T1 line) by the bits generated for the page request. A server's capacity isn't the only factor to consider when determining bandwidth limitations. The client computer is limited by its connection to the Internet. The performance of Web applications is critical in determining the site's capacity.

Testing is the only way to find out the capacity and performance of a Web application. You can use the WCAT and WAST utilities to test an application. Different computer types will provide different performance for the same test, and the performance of different application types depends greatly on the application's task. Availability is an important consideration when planning your network's capacity requirements. You must determine whether the problems caused by your site's unavailability offset the expense of trying to keep it online. The scalability of your site is a primary consideration when you're ready to upgrade it in order to improve availability, increase the number of concurrent users, or decrease its latency for faster response times.

Lesson 2: Calculating User Costs

You can determine the appropriate capacity level for your Web site by measuring the number of visitors the site receives and the demand each user places on the server and then calculating the computing resources (CPU, RAM, disk space, and network bandwidth) that are necessary to support current and future usage levels. Site capacity is determined by the number of users, server capacity, configuration of hardware and software, and site content. As the site attracts more users, capacity must increase or users will experience performance degradation. By upgrading the computing infrastructure, you can increase the site's capacity, thereby allowing more users, more complex content, or a combination of the two. However, before you can plan your network's capacity requirements or determine an upgrade strategy, you must be able to calculate the costs imposed on the system by each user. This lesson explains how you can calculate those costs so that you can plan your network's capacity.

After this lesson, you will be able to

- Calculate costs of CPU, memory, and disk usage
- Calculate network bandwidth

Estimated lesson time: 30 minutes

Overview of Calculating Costs

At its most basic level, capacity planning can be expressed as a simple equation:

Number of supported users = hardware capacity ÷ load on hardware per user

In this equation, *number of supported users* refers to concurrent users and *hardware capacity* refers to both server and network capacity.

Generally, capacity planning is based on two concepts:

- You can decrease the load that each user puts on the hardware, or you can increase the number of supported users. This is done through planning, programming, and configuring the site content to make more efficient use of computing resources.
- You can configure the site infrastructure to increase hardware capacity, or you can increase the number of supported users. Options include scaling the hardware out (adding more servers) or up (upgrading the existing servers).

If you want to increase the complexity of the site's content, thereby increasing the load on hardware per user, and still maintain the number of supported users, then you must increase the site's hardware capacity. This supports either the scaling up or scaling out decision. However, if you want to be able to support more users, you must either simplify the site content or increase hardware capacity. This supports the decision to decrease the load on hardware per user.

Operational Parameters

The primary benchmark to use when determining whether a Web site is operating at an acceptable level is *latency*, or how long a user has to wait for a page to load once a request has been made. Note that although some servers may be capable of handing every request they receive, the load on the servers might create unacceptable wait times, requiring a better performing solution if the site is to operate efficiently and at a level of service users are willing to accept.

In general, static content such as normal HTML pages and graphics don't contribute to server latency nearly as much as dynamic content such as ASP pages or other content that requires database lookups. Even when a Web server is able to deliver a large number of ASP pages per second, the turnaround time per ASP page can be unacceptable. The chart shown in Figure 7.4 illustrates the latency experienced by users of a four-processor Web server as the number of users and ASP requests increases.

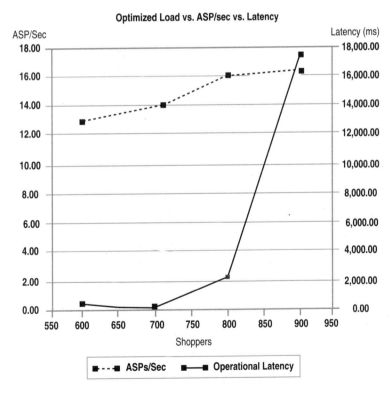

Figure 7.4   ASP pages per second versus latency

This site's capacity is between 700 and 800 concurrent shoppers per second. Note that the wait time rises dramatically as the number of users exceeds 800. This is unacceptable. This server's performance peaks at just over 16 ASP requests per second. At this point the users are waiting roughly 16 seconds for their pages, due to extensive context switching.

Calculating Cost Per User

You should take five steps to determine your cost per user: analyzing the typical user, calculating CPU cost, calculating memory cost, calculating disk cost, and calculating network cost. In order to illustrate each of these steps, a fictitious company—Northwind Traders—is used to demonstrate how user costs are calculated. Sample test results, used to simulate capacity testing through such means as the WAST test utility, are provided as needed, along with any additional data necessary to calculate cost per user.

Note Calculating user costs is an involved and detailed process. The purpose of this lesson is merely to give you an overview of that process and try to illustrate, through the use of examples, how the basic calculations are made. It's strongly recommended that you study additional sources so that you have a complete understanding of the process of calculating costs.

Analyzing the Typical User

The first step you need to take in calculating user costs is to determine how the typical user will use your site. By determining the operations that users perform and how often they perform them, you can estimate how much demand a user places on the system. For the purpose of this lesson, the term *operation* refers to all files that are included in the processing of the primary page. This can include graphic files, ASP include files, or other supporting files. To the user it seems like a single operation or page.

To do this, you must compile a user profile by analyzing the site's usage log files. The more accurate the user profile, the more accurate capacity planning will be. For this reason, it's better to use logs gathered over a long period of time (at least a week) to obtain accurate averages.

You should gather the following types of data:

- The number of visitors the site receives
- The number of hits each page receives
- The rate at which transactions take place

You can use the number of visits to each page to profile typical operations for the site. Table 7.4 provides a profile report for a typical user of the Northwind Traders Web site. The table contains the simulated results gathered from test data.

Table 7.4   Typical User Profile for Northwind Traders Web Site

Operation	Operations per Session	Operations per Second (Frequency)	Percent of Total
Add Item	0.24	0.00033	2.00%
Add+Checkout	0.02	0.00003	0.17%
Add+Clearitems	0.04	0.00006	0.33%
Basket	0.75	0.00104	6.25%
Default	1.00	0.00139	8.33%
Listing	2.50	0.00347	20.83%
Lookup	0.75	0.00104	6.25%
New	0.25	0.00035	2.08%
Product	4.20	0.00583	35.00%
Search	1.25	0.00174	10.42%
Welcome	1.00	0.00139	8.33%
TOTAL	12.0	0.01667	99.99%

This table shows the 11 operations that account for nearly 100 percent of the hits received by the entire site. On big sites, the load might be distributed over a larger set of operations. As a rule, you should generate a report that lists the pages or operations responsible for at least 90 percent of the site's total hit count.

Calculating CPU Cost

In a typical environment, the Web servers place more demand on the CPU than the data servers do. As a result, this example focuses on measuring the CPU capacity on the Web servers. However, you should perform these calculations on all types of servers in the site where CPU power might become a bottleneck.

Page requests per second and CPU use grow with the number of users. However, when CPU use reaches the maximum, it results in lower page requests per second. Therefore, the number of page requests processed per second at the point at which CPU use reaches 100 percent is the maximum.

Before you can calculate an operation's CPU cost, you need to know the following information:

- Page throughput (requests per second)
- CPU utilization (percentage of available CPU at optimum page throughput)
- Number of times a page is used per operation (request per operation)
- Upper bound of your CPU

You can calculate an operation's cost by multiplying the number of pages by the cost per page. This calculation is based on megacycles (MC). The MC is a unit of processor work; 1 MC is equal to 1 million CPU cycles. As a unit of measure, the MC is useful for comparing performance between processors because it's hardware independent. For example, a dual-processor 400 MHz Pentium II has a total capacity of 800 MC.

The first step in calculating the CPU cost per user is to calculate the CPU cost per operation (in MC). You can use the following formula to calculate the cost:

CPU usage ÷ Requests per second × Requests per operation = Cost per operation

To calculate the CPU usage, use the following formula:

CPU utilization × Number of CPUs × Speed of the CPUs (in MHz) = CPU usage

For example, suppose your computer is a dual-processor 400 MHz Pentium II. A browse operation results in 11.5 requests per second with CPU utilization of 84.10 percent. There are two page requests per operation. You'd first determine the CPU usage, as follows:

$0.8410 \times 2 \times 400 = 672.8$

You can then determine the CPU usage per operation, as follows:

$672.8 \div 11.5 \times 2 = 117.01$ MC

Table 7.5 provides the CPU cost for each of the main operations of the Northwind Traders Web site. The figures are based on a dual-processor 400 MHz Pentium II.

Table 7.5   CPU Costs per Operation

Operation	CPU Utilization	Requests/Sec	Requests per Operation	CPU Cost per Operation (MC)
Add Item	96.98%	23.31	2	66.57
Add+Checkout	94.31%	18.48	7	285.79
Add+Clearitems	95.86%	22.29	4	137.62
Basket	91.73%	16.81	1	43.65
Default	98.01%	102.22	1	7.67
Listing	91.87%	21.49	1	34.20
Lookup	99.52%	75.40	2	21.19
New	96.61%	65.78	2	23.50
Product	94.81%	18.23	1	41.61
Search	95.11%	37.95	2	40.10
Welcome	96.97%	148.93	1	5.21

Once you've determined each operation's CPU cost, you can calculate the CPU cost per user by using the following formula:

Cost per operation × Operations per second = Cost per user

For example, the cost of an Add Item operation is 66.57 MC. Based on the profile of the typical user, you know that the number of operations per second is 0.00033. So you'd use the following calculation to determine the cost per typical user:

$$66.57 \times 0.00033 = 0.0222 \text{ MC}$$

Table 7.6 shows the CPU usage for the typical user for each operation.

Table 7.6   CPU Costs per User

Operation	CPU Cost per Operation (MC)	Operations per Second (frequency)	CPU Usage per User (MC)
Add Item	66.57	0.00033	0.0220
Add+Checkout	285.79	0.00006	0.0171
Add+Clearitems	137.62	0.00104	0.1431
Basket	43.65	0.00003	0.0013
Default	7.67	0.00139	0.0107
Listing	34.20	0.00347	0.1187
Lookup	21.19	0.00104	0.0220
New	23.50	0.00035	0.0082
Product	41.61	0.00583	0.2426
Search	40.10	0.00174	0.0698
Welcome	5.21	0.00139	0.0072
TOTAL			0.6627

The total indicates that the cost of the total user profile is 0.6627 MC per user. This number reflects the cost of an average user performing the operations described by the user profile. You can use this number to estimate the site's capacity, based on the assumed user profile.

For example, suppose the upper bound for your dual-processor 400 MHz Pentium II is 526 MHz. The cost of 100 concurrent users is 100 × 0.6627 = 66.27 MC. The cost for 790 users is 523.53 MC. Both numbers of users are within the limits of the upper bound. However, more than 790 concurrent users would exceed your CPU capacity.

If you can't upgrade or add processors to increase your CPU capacity, you can take two main steps to improve CPU efficiency:

- Add network adapters. If you're administering a multiprocessor system that doesn't distribute interrupts symmetrically, you can improve the distribution of the processor workload by adding network adapters so that there's one adapter for every processor. Generally, you add adapters only when you need to improve your system's throughput.

- Limit connections. Consider reducing the maximum number of connections that each IIS 5.0 service accepts. Although limiting connections can result in connections that are blocked or rejected, it helps ensure that accepted connections are processed promptly.

Calculating Memory Cost

Some Web services, such as IIS 5.0, run in a pageable user-mode process. The process in IIS 5.0 is called Inetinfo (INETINFO.EXE). When a process is pageable, the system can remove part or all of it from RAM and write it to disk if there isn't enough free memory.

If part of the process is paged to disk, the service's performance suffers, as shown in Figure 7.5.

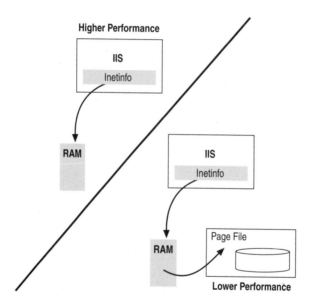

Figure 7.5   Paging a process to disk

It's very important to make sure that your server or servers have enough RAM to keep the entire process in memory at all times. The Web, File Transfer Protocol (FTP), and Simple Mail Transfer Protocol (SMTP) services in IIS run in the Inetinfo process. Each of the current connections is also given about 10 KB of memory in the Inetinfo working set (assuming that the application is running in-process).

The working set of the Inetinfo process should be large enough to contain the IIS object cache, data buffers for IIS 5.0 logging, and the data structures that the Web service uses to track its active connections.

You can use System Monitor to monitor the working set of INETINFO.EXE. Because ISAPI DLLs run in the out-of-process pool by default, you'll need to monitor them separately from INETINFO.EXE. unless you've changed that setting, and you'll also need to be aware that out-of-process counter information is added together. This makes it difficult to single out any one process or application. (If your site uses custom ISAPI DLLs, those DLLs should incorporate their own counters so that you can monitor them individually.)

You should log this data for several days. You can use performance logs and alerts in System Monitor to identify times of unusually high and low server activity.

If the system has sufficient memory, it can maintain enough space in the Inetinfo working set so that IIS 5.0 rarely needs to perform disk operations. One indicator of memory sufficiency is how much the size of the Inetinfo process working set varies in response to general memory availability on the server. Make sure to examine data collected over time, because these counters display the last value observed rather than an average.

IIS 5.0 relies on the operating system to store and retrieve frequently used Web pages and other files from the File System Cache. The File System Cache is particularly useful for servers of static Web pages, because Web pages tend to be used in repeated, predictable patterns.

If cache performance is poor when the cache is small, use the data you've collected to deduce the reason that the system reduced the cache size. Note the available memory on the server and the processes and services running on the server, including the number of simultaneous connections supported.

When you add physical memory to your server, the system allocates more space to the file system cache. A larger cache is almost always more efficient, but typically it's a case of diminishing returns—each additional megabyte of memory adds less efficiency than the previous one. You must decide where the trade-off point is: the point at which adding more memory gets you so little improvement in performance that it ceases to be worthwhile.

Servers running IIS 5.0, like other high-performance file servers, benefit from ample physical memory. Generally, the more memory you add, the more the servers use and the better they perform. IIS 5.0 requires a minimum of 64 MB of memory, but at least 128 MB is recommended. If you're running memory-intensive applications, your server could require a much larger amount of memory to run optimally. For example, most of the servers that service the MSNBC Web site have at least 1 GB of memory.

Because memory usage doesn't directly relate to the number of concurrent users but rather to the content of the site (caching, out-of-process DLLs, etc.), a cost per user can't be calculated aside from the 10 KB per connection. In this instance you should monitor

- The amount of Inetinfo that's paged out to disk
- Memory usage during site operation
- The efficiency of the cache utilization, or the cache-hit ratio
- The number of times the cache is flushed
- The number of page faults that occur

Calculating Disk Cost

Web services such as IIS 5.0 write their logs to disk, so there's usually some disk activity, even when clients are hitting the cache 100 percent of the time. Under ordinary circumstances, disk activity, other than that generated by logging, serves as an indicator of issues in other areas. For example, if your server needs more RAM, you'll see a lot of disk activity because there are many hard page faults. But there will also be a lot of disk activity if your server houses a database or your users request many different pages.

Since IIS caches most pages in memory, the disk system is rarely a bottleneck as long as the Web servers have sufficient installed memory. However, the Microsoft SQL Server computer does read and write to the disk on a frequent basis. SQL Server also caches data but uses the disk a lot more than IIS. For that reason, the capacity testing for Northwind Traders focuses on the SQL Server computer. However, you should calculate capacity on all servers where disk activity could become a bottleneck. You can use a tool such as System Monitor to record a site's disk activity while a WAST script is running for each operation.

Note   This section is concerned with disk utilization and the effects of read and write operations. Determining whether you have adequate disk storage is a process separate from this one. Storage requirements are discussed in Lesson 3, "Planning Network Capacity."

For the SQL Server computer used by Northwind Traders, the percentage of disk utilization is based on a calibration of a maximum of 280 random seeks per second. For example, when the Pentium II server generates 2.168 Add Item operations, the SQL Server computer performs 9.530 disk seeks (for a disk utilization of 3.404 percent). You should calculate disk cost by dividing disk seeks per second by operations per second (which you'll have determined as part of the user profile). In this case the Add Item operation generates 4.395 disk seeks per shopper operation.

You can use the following equations to determine disk costs:

Disk reads per second ÷ Operations per second = Disk read cost per operation

Disk writes per second ÷ Operations per second = Disk write cost per operation

Table 7.7 illustrates the results from calculating disk reads on the Northwind Traders site.

Table 7.7   Disk Read Measurements for Northwind Traders

Operation	Disk Reads per Second	Operations per Second	Percentage of Disk	Disk Cost
Add Item	9.530	2.168	3.404%	4.396
Basket	7.050	8.728	2.518%	0.808
Checkout	19.688	0.903	7.031%	21.803
Clearitems	8.956	9.384	3.199%	0.954
Default	0.248	28.330	0.089%	0.009
Delitem	4.628	3.633	1.653%	1.274
Listing	0.148	5.533	0.053%	0.027
Lookup	0.063	12.781	0.023%	0.005
Lookup_new	9.275	12.196	3.313%	0.760
Main	0.120	8.839	0.043%	0.014
Browse	0.103	6.033	0.037%	0.017
Search	0.100	8.205	0.036%	0.012
Welcome	0.080	31.878	0.029%	0.003

Once you've calculated the disk cost per read operation, you must calculate the disk costs of write operations.

You can then use your calculations for your read and write operations to calculate your disk costs per user per second. As in your CPU cost calculations, you should multiply your cost per operation by operations per second. For example, if your disk cost for a Default read operation is 0.0009 and your usage for that operation is 0.003804 operations per second, your disk cost per user for that operation is 0.0000034 kilobytes per second (KBps).

Once you've calculated the cost per operation, you can add those costs together to arrive at the total disk load per user per second. You can then use that number to determine your disk system's capacity, which will be based on the load supported by your particular disk configuration.

Calculating Network Cost

Network bandwidth is another important resource that can become a bottleneck. You can calculate total network cost from the sum of the costs of the individual operations. However, two network costs are associated with each shopper operation: the connection between the Web client and the Web server and the connection between the SQL Server computer and the Web server. Sites that are more complex can have more types of connections, depending on the number of servers and the site's architecture.

Note   On a switched Ethernet LAN, traffic is isolated so network costs aren't added together. On an unswitched Ethernet LAN, network traffic is cumulative so network costs are added together.

When a user performs an operation, the action generates network traffic between the Web server and the Web client, as well as between the Web server and the data server (if a database needs to be accessed).

For example, suppose the Add Item operation for Northwind Traders shows that optimal throughput is 0.000293 operations per second. The network cost of Add Item is 5.627 KBps per operation between the Web client and the Web server and 129.601 KBps between the Web server and the SQL Server computer, as shown in Figure 7.6. Most of the traffic generated by the Add Item operation is between the Web server and the SQL Server database.

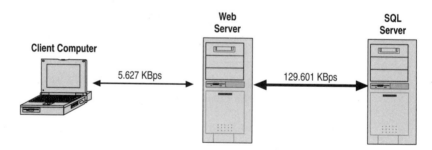

Figure 7.6   Network costs of an Add Item operation

You can figure out the network cost per user per operation by using the following formula:

(Operations/sec. × Web network cost) + (Operations/sec. × Data network cost) = Cost per user per second

For example, you'd use the following calculation to determine the cost per user per second for the Add Item operation:

$(0.000293 \times 5.627) + (0.000293 \times 129.601) = 0.039622$

Table 7.8 shows the total bytes transmitted per operation (total network cost per user per second) on an unswitched Ethernet LAN. *Web network cost* represents the bytes transmitted per operation between the Web client and the Web server. *Data network cost* represents the bytes transmitted per operation between the SQL Server computer and the Web server.

Table 7.8   Network Costs for Northwind Traders

Operation	Usage Profile Operations per Second	Web Network Cost	Data Network Cost	Cost per User per Second (Web Server)	Cost per User per Second (SQL Server)	Total Cost per User per Second
Add Item	0.000293	5.627	129.601	0.001649	0.037973	0.039622
Add Item + Checkout	0.000183	24.489	55.215	0.004481	0.010104	0.014586
Default (home page)	0.003804	1.941	0	0.007384	0	0.007384
Listing	0.000421	25.664	23.134	0.010805	0.009739	0.020544
Login	0.000288	17.881	1.380	0.00515	0.000397	0.005547
Product	0.006102	21.548	21.051	0.131486	0.128453	0.259939
Register	0.000176	5.627	129.601	0.00099	0.02281	0.0238
Search (Bad)	0.000170	20.719	10.725	0.003522	0.001823	0.005345
Search (Good)	0.002391	20.719	10.725	0.049539	0.025643	0.075183
TOTAL						0.45195

The network cost per user is 0.45195 KBps. You can use this figure to calculate the total network traffic. For example, if 100 concurrent users are accessing your site, the total network traffic is 45.195 KBps. For 10,000 users, the total traffic is 4,519.5, and for 20,000 users, the total traffic is 9,039 KBps.

If the network is a Carrier Sense Multiple Access with Collision Detection (CSMA/CD) Ethernet network running at 100 Mbps, or 12.5 megabytes per second (MBps), collisions will cause network congestion. For this reason, you shouldn't push network utilization above 36 percent, which means no more than 4.5 MBps on the network. The Northwind Traders network reached the 4.5 MBps threshold at about 10,000 users, which is the site's capacity. At 20,000 users, the network will become congested due to excessive collisions and a bottleneck will result.

Note   Remember to measure network traffic for the entire site and not just for individual servers.

As your site grows, network capacity can become a bottleneck, especially on sites where the ASP content is relatively simple (low CPU load) and the content (like static HTML or pictures) is relatively large. A few servers can easily serve the content to thousands of users, but the network might not be equipped to handle it. In some cases most of the traffic on the network flows between the Web server and the SQL Server computer.

Lesson Summary

You should take five steps to determine your cost per user: analyzing the typical user, calculating CPU cost, calculating memory cost, calculating disk cost, and calculating network cost. You must analyze the typical user so that you can estimate how much demand a user places on the system. You can estimate this demand by determining the operations that users perform and how often they perform them. Once you've created a typical user profile, you can calculate CPU usage. You can calculate the cost per user per operation by first calculating the CPU cost of an operation. You can then determine the CPU usage per operation and then add those calculations together to arrive at a cost per user. In addition to CPUs, you should make sure that your server or servers have enough RAM to keep the entire process in memory at all times. If you're running memory-intensive applications, your server could require a much larger amount of memory to run optimally. Because memory usage doesn't relate directly to the number of concurrent users, but rather to the site's content, a cost per user can't be calculated aside from the 10 KB per connection. To determine disk usage, you must calculate read operations as well as write operations. You can then use your calculations for your read and write operations to calculate your disk costs per user per second. You should multiply your cost per operation by operations per second. Once you've calculated the cost per operation, you can add those costs together to arrive at the total disk load per user per second. Network bandwidth is another important resource that can become a bottleneck. You can calculate total network cost from the sum of the costs of the individual operations.

Activity 7.1: Calculating CPU Usage

You're the network administrator for Blue Yonder Airlines. A new search functionality has been added to your company's Web site, and you want to calculate the CPU usage for the Search operation. You're testing the operation on a server that's configured with three 400 MHz Pentium II processors.

Table 7.9 provides the parameters you should use when calculating Web usage.

Table 7.9   CPU Usage Information for Search Operation

Type of Information	Details
CPU utilization (percentage of available CPU at optimum page throughput)	92.47%
Page throughput (pages per second)	18.21
Number of times a page is used per operation (requests per operations)	2
User profile operations per second (frequency)	0.00139
Upper bound of CPU	786 MHz

1. Your first step is to determine the CPU cost per operation. In order to calculate this cost, you must first determine the CPU usage. How do you calculate the CPU usage for the Search operation?

2. Now that you've calculated the CPU usage, you can use that calculation to determine the cost of the operation. How do you calculate the CPU cost for the Search operation?

3. You can now use the cost per operation to figure out the cost per user. How do you calculate the CPU cost per operation per use?

Activity 7.2: Calculating Network Bandwidth

The Wingtip Toys company has hired you to administer its Web site, which is located on an unswitched Ethernet LAN. In the past users have often had trouble accessing the company's Web site. You want to determine the network cost per user. You plan to do this by first determining the cost per operation. You decide to start with the Add Item operation.

Table 7.10 provides the parameters you should use when calculating Web usage.

Table 7.10   Network Usage Information for Add Item Operation

Type of Information	Details
Usage profile operations per second	0.003804
Web network cost	4.297
Data network cost	119.36

1. Your first step is to determine the cost per user for the Web server. How do you calculate that cost?

2. Next you must determine the cost per user for the data server. How do you calculate that cost?

3. How do you calculate the total cost per user per second?

Lesson 3: Planning Network Capacity

When planning the capacity requirements for your Web site, you must determine the installation's current and future needs and then choose the hardware and software that meets those needs. The planning process includes many steps, such as determining the site's purpose, identifying the user base, and finding potential bottlenecks. This lesson describes each of the steps that make up the capacity planning process.

After this lesson, you will be able to

- Identify and describe the steps necessary to plan your Web site's capacity
- Plan the capacity requirements for your Web site

Estimated lesson time: 30 minutes

The Planning Process

Planning for your network's capacity requirements involves a number of steps. This section describes each of them.

Determining the Purpose and Type of Site

When you begin to plan the capacity requirements for your site, you must identify the site's purpose and what type of site you'll create. For example, you might be creating a transaction site that allows users to retrieve and store information, typically in a database. A transactional site involves both reliability and security requirements that don't apply to other types of sites.

In addition to determining the type of site, you must determine whether the site will support some form of dynamic content. Dynamic content takes many forms and can be provided by a wide variety of Internet and database technologies, such as SQL, ASP, ISAPI, or CGI.

At its simplest, dynamic content involves the Web server contacting a database, retrieving data, formatting it, and then sending it to a user's browser as a Web page. For example, if a user wants to see information on a specific product, the server might contact a SQL Server database to retrieve the product's description, a photo, price information, and whether or not the product is in stock. The resulting page would display in the user's browser using conventional HTML as if it were a static Web page, but it would be created on the fly by the server when the user requests it. A site that makes use of dynamic content requires much more processing capability than a static site.

Identifying the User Base

The next step in calculating your Web site's capacity is to determine how many people typically use the site concurrently. This data usually comes from two main sources: market analysis and systems analysis.

If a site has yet to be built or launched, the site's owners and operators probably will have commissioned a market analysis report that seeks to predict how much traffic the site can expect to receive at the time of the launch and afterward. Keep in mind that, as with any forecast, these numbers can be inaccurate.

If the site is already up and running, you should analyze your Web server log files to get a picture of how many hits the site receives at any given time as well as any usage trends that would indicate whether parts of the site have become more or less popular over time. When calculating how many users a site currently supports, remember to base your calculations on peak usage, rather than on typical or average usage.

Figure 7.7 shows an example of site usage. The chart illustrates average usage figures for a Web site that receives a great number of hits in the morning, fewer in the afternoon, and fewer still in the evenings. When planning capacity, this site's operators should use data from the mornings as a baseline.

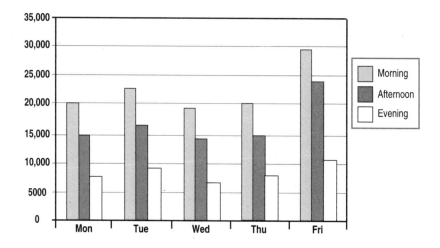

Figure 7.7   Web site usage numbers

The site draws about 29,000 hits over six hours on Friday mornings, averaging 1.34 users per second. Taking the total number of weekly hits and averaging them over all seven days yields a much lower figure, 0.54 users per second. Using this lower figure as a baseline for capacity planning can lead to capacity shortfalls during busy periods.

You can determine the number of concurrent users by dividing the number of users by sessions totals. For example, if the site receives 500,000 users per day at an average session time of 11 minutes, you would use the following calculation to find the number of concurrent users:

500,000 ÷ (24 hours × 60 minutes ÷ 11 minutes per session) = 3,819 users

Of course, this doesn't mean you can expect to see 3,819 users at any random time. Sometimes the traffic will peak at a much higher figure; therefore, one of the most important principles of capacity planning is to use peak activity, rather than average activity, as a baseline. As a rule of thumb, account for usage spikes and peaks by multiplying the average number of concurrent users by 2 (although this multiplier may differ depending on the nature of the site). In this case, doing this yields a figure of 7,600 concurrent users. If your site experiences peak traffic that's more than twice the average traffic, consider this fact when determining where to set the baseline.

Determining Hardware Needs

You can determine your site's hardware requirements by taking the number of anticipated or measured visitors that a site will have during a period of time and comparing it with the hardware's capacity.

CPU Requirements

Web applications tend to be processor-bound. Contention issues, caused by more than one thread trying to execute the same critical section or access the same resource, can cause frequent expensive context switches and keep the CPU busy even though the throughput is low. It's also possible to have low CPU utilization with low throughput if most threads are blocked, such as when waiting for the database.

There are two basic ways to get the processing power you need: you can add additional processors to each server, or you can add servers.

Adding processors to an existing server is often less expensive (and less trouble-some) than adding servers. But for most applications there comes a point when adding processors doesn't help. In addition, there is a limit to the number of processors that the operating system can support.

Adding servers allows you to scale linearly to as large a Web farm as you need. (Linear scaling means that two servers handle twice the load of one, three servers handle three times the load, nine servers handle nine times the load, and so on.)

Suppose you're using a dual-processor 400 Pentium II computer that is running Windows Server 2000, and you determine that the CPU capacity is 1,350 users. Your site should support 7,600 concurrent users. To determine how many servers you'll need to handle peak traffic, you must divide 7,600 by 1,350, as follows:

7,600 concurrent users ÷ 1,350 users per server = 6 servers

At times of normal usage, the load on the six servers will be lower, as shown here:

3,800 concurrent users ÷ 6 servers = 634 users per server

This means that the site is operating at 50 percent of site capacity when serving the anticipated amount of users. This is very important to sites that might experience usage spikes from time to time.

Memory Requirements

RAM access (at about 10 ns) is about a million times faster than disk access (about 10 ms), so every time you have to swap a page into memory, you're slowing down the application. Adding sufficient RAM is the best and least expensive way to get good performance from any system.

You can make sure your application has enough memory by checking the paging counters (paging should be rare once the application is running) and by checking the working set size, which should be significantly smaller than available RAM in Windows 2000.

Storage Requirements

Network storage solutions are rapidly becoming available as the number and size of enterprise networks increase. Every organization has different priorities for selecting media and methods for data storage. Some are constrained by costs, and others place performance before all other considerations.

As you assess your storage needs, you need to compare the possible loss of data, productivity, and business to the cost of a storage system that provides high performance and availability. Consider the following needs before you develop your storage management strategy:

- Technologies that are the most cost-effective for your organization
- Adequate storage capacity that can easily grow with your network
- The need for rapid, 24-hour access to critical data
- A secure environment for data storage

When looking for the most cost-effective solution, you need to balance the costs of purchasing and maintaining hardware and software with the consequences of a disastrous loss of data. Costs can include the following expenses:

- Initial investment in hardware, such as tape and disk drives, power supplies, and controllers
- Associated media such as magnetic tapes and compact discs
- Software, such as storage management tools and a backup tool
- Ongoing hardware and software maintenance costs
- Staffing
- Training in how to use new technologies
- Off-site storage facilities

Compare these costs to the following expenses:

- Replacement costs for file servers, mail servers, or print servers
- Replacement costs for servers running applications such as SQL Server or Systems Management Server (SMS)
- Replacement costs for gateway servers running Routing and Remote Access Service (RRAS), SNA Server, Proxy Server, or Novell NetWare
- Workstation replacement costs for personnel in various departments
- Replacement costs for individual computer components, such as a hard disk or a network card

Another important factor to consider when you select a storage system is speed of data recovery. If you lose the data on a server, how fast can you reinstate that data? How long can you afford to have a server (or an entire network) down before it begins to have a serious impact on your business?

Storage technology changes rapidly, so it's best to research the relative merits of each type before you make a purchasing decision. The storage system you use needs to have more than enough capacity to back up your most critical data. It should also provide error detection and correction during backup and restore operations.

Database Server and Disk Requirements

The database is a potential bottleneck that can be very difficult to fix. For read/write real-time data you have to have exactly one copy of the data, so increasing database capacity is much trickier. Sometimes the bottlenecks will be in the database server, sometimes they'll be in the disk array.

If database server capacity becomes an issue, you have a number of options. If CPU capacity is the issue, add additional CPUs. Database applications such as SQL Server make good use of additional processors. If the disk is the bottleneck, use a faster disk array. More RAM can help as well if the database application uses advanced caching techniques.

Another option is to split the database across multiple servers. The first step is to put the catalog database on a server or set of servers. Because the catalog is usually read-only, it's safe to replicate the data. You can also split off read-mostly data, such as customer information. But if you need multiple copies, replicating the information properly is more difficult.

However, it's possible that your site could get so busy that the read/write data has to be segmented. This is relatively simple for most applications; you can segment based on postal code, name, or customer ID. But for some database applications, it takes application programming in the database access layer to make this work. The layer has to know the server to go to for each record. However, applications such as SQL Server support splitting a table across multiple computers, with no application programming.

Determining Network Bandwidth

Once you determine how many users you want to serve during a given time, you have the lower limit for your network connection bandwidth. You need to accommodate both normal load and usage spikes.

Of course, the type of site you operate has a large effect on this issue. For example, if you're largely or entirely subscriber-based, or if your site is only on an intranet or an intranet/extranet combination, you probably already have a good idea of the maximum spike size. If, on the other hand, you issue software revisions to an audience of unknown size on the Web, there may not be a good way to predict the size of resulting spikes. You might, in fact, have to measure one or more actual occurrences to decide whether your bandwidth is sufficient.

A number of potential bottlenecks can occur in your networking hardware. First, your connection to the Internet might not be fast enough for all the bits you're sending. If your application becomes very popular, you might need to obtain a higher-speed connection or redundant connections. Redundant connections also increase your reliability and availability. You can reduce your bandwidth requirements to prevent bottlenecks by reducing the amount of data you send, especially graphics, sound, and video. Your firewall can also become a bottleneck if it's not fast enough to handle the traffic you're asking it to handle.

Note that you can't run an Ethernet network at anywhere near its theoretical capacity because you'll create many collisions (two senders trying to transmit at the same time). When a collision happens, both senders must wait a random amount of time before resending. Some collisions are inevitable, but they increase rapidly as your network becomes saturated, leaving you with almost no effective bandwidth.

You can reduce collisions a great deal by using switches rather than hubs to interconnect your network. A switch connects two ports directly rather than broadcasting the traffic to all ports so that multiple pairs of ports can communicate without collisions. Given that the prices of switches have significantly decreased in the last few years, it's usually a good idea to use a switch rather than a hub.

Defining the Site Topology

Each site has unique capacity requirements that can be affected by various considerations, such as available hardware and budget, available physical space for servers, and the amount of time the site is allowed to be offline. These requirements can have a direct effect on the design and construction of the site's physical infrastructure.

Figure 7.8 provides a sample of a site topology. Note that the diagram represents only one possible strategy for designing the network topology. Each organization has its own needs and consequently necessitates its own network design.

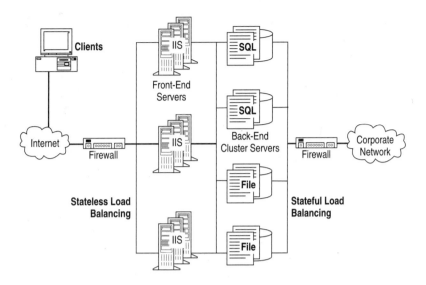

Figure 7.8   Sample site topology

When addressing site topology, consider the following questions:

- What other server operations (such as backups and content replication) can influence site capacity? Because capacity measurements don't include these extraneous operations, you should measure the resources that these operations use and add them to the server in addition to the capacity required to handle Web traffic.

  For example, some calculations are based on the fact that ASP pages are cached and objects are in memory. When content replication takes place, IIS flushes most of its cache or Windows swaps a lot of the cache to disk, which causes paging and degrades system performance. You should determine how much memory content replication takes and then add it to the amount of memory your calculations predict are necessary to achieve the desired capacity.

  A server rarely does only one thing at a time but rather performs a "symphony" of different operations at once. A carefully tuned server environment is like a well-conducted symphony. You can't let only one operation run and then measure it and expect that measurement to be accurate. Often servers and entire sites have scheduled operations, such as content replication or content precaching, that takes place at regular intervals.

- How often do you expect usage spikes to occur? The general rule is to plan enough capacity for twice the average number of concurrent users. If you anticipate significant usage spikes that exceed this baseline, plan for surplus CPU, disk, memory, and network capacity. Remember to take growth into consideration, as well as possibly more complex content in the future.

- How important is it to be operational 100 percent of the time? How often will servers be offline for maintenance? If 100 percent site availability is critical, plan for system redundancy. Duplicate critical resources and eliminate single points of failure.

    One way to do this is to use cluster technologies. You can use NLB to cluster Web servers, and the Cluster service to cluster SQL Server computers. With these technologies in place, you can take some servers offline for upgrades or repairs while the remaining servers continue to run the site.

- When will you undertake capacity planning again? What growth do you expect? How will content complexity change? Over time, the average number of concurrent users on a site rises or falls, the content and content complexity change, and the typical user profile changes. These changes can have a big impact on a site's capacity. Take change and growth into account when doing capacity planning and undertake it regularly or whenever these factors change sufficiently to affect site capacity.

Finding Potential Bottlenecks

Find out what's likely to break first. Unless your site is extremely small, you'll need a test lab to discover the bottlenecks. The following steps provide a guideline for determining potential bottlenecks:

1. Draw a block diagram showing all paths into the site. Include, for example, links to FTP download sites as well as other Uniform Resource Locators (URLs).

2. Determine what machine hosts each functional component (database, mail, FTP, and so on).

3. Draw a network model of the site and the connections to its environment. Define the topography throughout. Identify slow links.

4. For each page, create a user profile that answers the following questions:

    - How long does the user stay on the page?

    - What data gets passed to (or by) the page?

    - How much database activity (or other activity) does the page generate?

    - What objects live on each page? How system-friendly are they? (That is, how heavily do they load the system's resources? If they fail, do they do so without crashing other objects or applications?)

    - What is the threading model of each object? (The *agile* model, in which objects are specified as both-threaded, is typically preferable and is the only appropriate choice for application scope.)

5. Define which objects are server-side and which are client-side.

6. Build a lab. You'll need at least two computers, because if you run all the pieces of WCAT on one computer, your results will be skewed by the tool's own use of system resources. Monitor the performance counters at 1-second

intervals. When ASP service fails, it does so abruptly, and an interval of 10 or 15 seconds is likely to be too long—you'll miss the crucial action. Relevant counters include CPU utilization, pool nonpaged bytes, connections/sec, and so on.

7. Throw traffic at each object, or at a simple page that calls the object, until the object or the server fails. Look for the following:

   ▪ Memory leaks (steady decrease in pool nonpaged bytes and pool paged bytes)

   ▪ Stop errors and Dr. Watsons

   ▪ Inetinfo failures and failures recorded in the Event Log

8. Increase the loading until you observe a failure; document both the failure itself and the maximum number of connections per second you achieve before the system tips over and fails.

9. Go back to the logical block diagram, and under each block fill in the amount of time and resources each object uses. This tells you which object is most likely to limit your site, presuming you know how heavily each one will actually be used by clients. Change the limiting object to make it more efficient if you can, unless it's seldom used and well off the main path.

10. Use the Traceroute utility among all points on the network. Clearly, you can't trace the route throughout the entire Internet; but you can certainly examine a reasonable number of paths between your clients and your servers. If you're operating only on an intranet, trace the route from your desk to the server. This gives you a ballpark estimate of the routing latencies, which add to the resolution time of each page. Based on this information, you can set your ASP queue and database connection timeouts.

Upgrading Your Web Site

Once you've determined how many users per server your site can support, you can consider scaling the site to support more users or to better serve the users you already have.

You can use three basic strategies to upgrade your site:

▪ Increase the number of users per server

▪ Increase the total number of concurrent users the site can support

▪ Decrease the latency of the site for faster response times

To implement these strategies, you can use one or more of the following options:

▪ **Optimizing content**   Redesign your dynamic content to impose less of a burden on the site architecture. You can do this by writing *smarter* ASP or by changing the site so the average user (as defined by the user profile) calls *heavy* ASPs less often.

- **Improving server performance (scaling up)**   Add more and faster CPUs and more memory; upgrade to faster software, such as upgrading from Windows NT 4 to Windows 2000; and tune the server by optimizing software configuration.
- **Adding servers (scaling out)**   Add more servers to your Web clusters.

Measure the effect of these changes by analyzing your site before and afterward and then comparing the results. This can also help you predict the effects of future changes.

Scalability

Scalability refers to how well a computer system's performance responds to changes in configuration variables, such as memory size or numbers of processors. This, however, is often difficult to gauge because of the interaction of multiple variables, such as system components of the underlying hardware, characteristics of the network, application design, and the operating system's architecture and capabilities. Organizations need to have the flexibility to scale server-based systems up or out without compromising the multipurpose and price performance advantages of the operating system platform.

Scaling up is achieved by adding more resources, such as memory, processors, and disk drives, to a system. Hardware scalability relies on one large extensible machine to perform work.

Scaling out is achieved by adding more servers. Scaling out delivers high performance when an application's throughput requirements exceed an individual system's capabilities. By distributing resources across multiple systems, you can reduce contention for these resources and improve availability. Clustering and system services, such as reliable transaction message queuing, allow applications to scale out in this manner. Software scalability depends on a cluster of multiple moderately performing machines working in tandem. NLB, in conjunction with the use of clustering, is part of the scaling out approach to upgrading. The greater the number of machines involved in the load balancing scenario, the higher the throughput of the overall server farm.

Scaling out allows you to add capacity by adding more Web servers to an existing cluster or by adding more clusters. Although more expensive than upgrading a server, adding a server often gives a bigger performance increase and confers operational flexibility.

Making a Decision

The process for planning your network's capacity requirements includes a number of steps. In each step you must make decisions about your site's operations. Table 7.11 describes many of the considerations you should take into account for each step.

Table 7.11   Capacity Planning

Step	Description
Determining the purpose and type of site	You must decide on the type of site, such as transactional, e-commerce, or information. You must also decide whether the site will have dynamic (as opposed to static) content, and if so, how that content will be delivered. For example, will you be using ASP or ISAPI?
Identifying the user base	You must determine how many people will be using the site concurrently.
Determining hardware needs	You must base your hardware requirements on the number of anticipated concurrent users at peak usage times. To get the processor power you need, you can add additional processors to each server or add more servers. You should also ensure that you have plenty of RAM to avoid having to swap pages into memory. Decisions about disk storage strategies must balance the cost of equipment against the consequences of a loss of data.
Determining network bandwidth	You must base your bandwidth requirements on the number of anticipated concurrent users at peak usage times.
Defining the site topology	When defining the site topology, you must decide what server operations can influence site capacity, how often you expect usage spikes, how important is it to be operational 100 percent of the time, and what kind of growth you expect.
Finding potential bottlenecks	You should test your site to try to find any potential bottlenecks.
Upgrading your Web site	When necessary, you should either scale out or scale up your site. You can also streamline content to improve performance.

Recommendations

When planning your Web site's capacity requirements, you should adhere to the following guidelines:

- Identify your number of concurrent users by performing a market analysis (if the site hasn't been launched yet) or by analyzing your Web server logs (if the site is already running).

- Use peak traffic figures to determine the maximum number of concurrent users.

- Base hardware and network bandwidth needs on the peak number of concurrent users. Processor power and RAM must be sufficient to avoid performance degradation at times of peak usage. Storage should be adequate enough to ensure the performance and availability required for your Web site.

- The site topology must take into consideration server operations such as backup and replication, performance during expected usage spikes, availability requirements, and expected future growth.

- Test for potential bottlenecks before implementing your site.

- Upgrade your site by scaling out or scaling up. Scaling out generally provides a larger increase in performance and greater operational flexibility.

Example: Capacity Planning for Coho Vineyard

Coho Vineyard is implementing a Web site to help market its organization. Before implementing the site, the company tested for potential bottlenecks to try to determine where problems might arise. Figure 7.9 shows the network topology for the Web site.

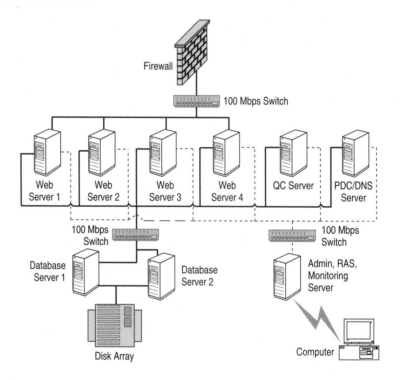

Figure 7.9   Coho Vineyard site topology

The Coho Vineyard site includes four identical Web servers that are configured as an NLB cluster. In addition to the network connecting the Web servers to the Internet, the Web servers are also connected through a private local area network (LAN) to the database tier and other specialized servers. These include the queued components server (for credit card authorizations and fulfillment), the box that runs the primary domain controller (PDC), and the Domain Name

System (DNS) service. For data services, the site uses a failover cluster of two servers connected to a common RAID disk array. An administrative and monitoring network is connected to all of the computers. This means that the Web servers are connected to three networks; each of these servers is configured with three network adapters.

Each of the Web servers is configured with two 400 MHz processors. When the Coho Vineyard administrators load-tested the site, they discovered processing degradation at peak loads. When a third processor was added to each computer, performance increased by about 30 percent, which was enough to handle anticipated peak usage.

Each Web server is configured with 256 MB of memory. Throughout the testing and analysis process, memory never appeared to be an issue. Paging was rare, so no configuration changes were made to memory.

During the test phase, the administrators discovered that the database wasn't working very hard and that the Web servers were sometimes very busy and then sometimes very slow. The problem resulted from using a 100 Mbps hub to connect the Web servers with the database servers. Because all the traffic was going through the hub, it had become swamped, thereby blocking the system from processing transactions quickly. When the administrators replaced the hub with a switch, the bottleneck was removed.

Database server capacity hasn't been an issue for Coho Vineyard's site. Only about 25 percent of the data servers' capacity is being used, even when all four Web servers are running at 100 percent CPU utilization. Disk and memory capacity have also proven to be more than adequate.

Lesson Summary

Planning your network's capacity requirements involves several steps. The first step is to determine the site's purpose and type. You must know what the site will be used for and what kind of content it will support. You must also identify how many people will be using the site concurrently. Your estimate should take into account peak usage as well as average per user usage. Once you've determined your estimated number of concurrent users, you can then plan your hardware and network bandwidth needs. Both these needs should take into account the site's peak usage number of concurrent users. Your system should have enough processing power and memory to meet the demands of peak usage. When assessing your storage requirements, you must weigh the expense of a system that provides high performance and availability against possible loss of data, productivity, and business. Overall, your site topology should take into consideration server operations, expected peak usage, availability requirements, and growth. You should also look for potential bottlenecks in your site to find out what's likely to break first. When you upgrade your site, you can improve performance and availability by optimizing content, improving server performance, or adding servers.

Lab 7.1: Planning CPU and Bandwidth Capacity

After completing this lab, you'll be able to

- Calculate the CPU usage and bandwidth usage per user
- Determine the number of Web servers and CPUs necessary to support your users
- Determine the capacity of your network bandwidth

About This Lab

In this lab you'll determine the capacity requirements for your network. You'll be focused specifically on CPU capacity (and the number of Web servers) and the capacity supported by your network bandwidth.

Before You Begin

Before you begin this lab, you must be able to

- Administer Windows 2000 Advanced Server
- Understand basic network and computer concepts related to user capacity

Scenario: Capacity Planning for Adventure Works

Adventure Works is a nationwide tour company that provides vacation packages to clients traveling around the world. The company is upgrading its Web services so that clients will be able to log on to the site so that they can receive information about packages customized to their specific needs. Until now users were simply able to access the site to view information about the various packages. To deliver the new services, administrators will be implementing a SQL Server back end. ASP will be used to access and display data from the database. The Adventure Works network is a 100-Mbps Ethernet network. Figure 7.10 provides an overview of the company's network topology.

Normally, the site services about 1,000 to 3,000 concurrent users, although at peak times that number can increase to up to 6,000 users. The company doesn't anticipate that the number of users will increase too greatly when the new services are implemented. The Web servers are each configured with three 400 MHz processors. The upper bound per computer is 755 MHz. As the administrator, you must determine the number of processors necessary to support the current usage and you must assess how much capacity the network supports.

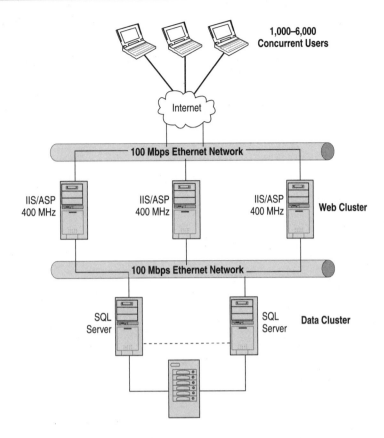

1,000–6,000
Concurrent Users

Internet

100 Mbps Ethernet Network

IIS/ASP
400 MHz

IIS/ASP
400 MHz

IIS/ASP
400 MHz

Web Cluster

100 Mbps Ethernet Network

SQL
Server

SQL
Server

Data Cluster

Figure 7.10   The network topology of Adventure Works

Exercise 1: Identifying the User Base

In this exercise you must identify the number of concurrent users on which to base your capacity calculations. From there you must calculate the CPU and network costs per operation.

1. How many concurrent users should your network support?

Once you've determined the number of users, you can then calculate the CPU usage per users. The first step in performing these calculations is to identify the applicable operations and the data about each of those operations. Based on your analysis, you've identified the operations and necessary information about each operation (shown in Table 7.12).

Table 7.12   Operations in the Adventure Works Network

Operation	CPU Utilization	Requests per Second	Request per Operation	Operations per Second
Default	96.15%	96.98	1	0.00128
Add Item	92.08%	26.21	3	0.00102
Listing	93.42%	29.29	2	0.00329
Lookup	98.99%	82.08	2	0.00121

2. What's the first step you must take to calculate the CPU usage per user?

3. What's the next step that you should take to calculate the CPU usage per user?

4. What's the CPU cost for each operation?

5. Once you've determined the cost per operation, you can determine the cost per user per operation, and from there, determine the cost per user. What's the cost per user for each operation?

6. What's the total cost per user for CPU usage?

Now that you've determined the CPU usage per user, you can determine the network usage per user. Based on your analysis, you've identified the necessary information about each operation (shown in Table 7.13).

Table 7.13   Network Costs of Operations

Operation	Operations per Second	Web Network Costs	Data Network Costs
Default	0.003682	1.845	0
Add Item	0.000254	4.978	127.756
Listing	0.000523	26.765	24.123
Lookup	0.001134	25.678	25.564

7. Your first step is to calculate the network costs per operation. What's the network cost for the Default operation?

8. What are the network costs of the remaining three operations?

9. What are the total network costs per user?

Exercise 2: Determining CPU Requirements

In this exercise you'll determine how many Web servers you need in order to support the current number of users. You'll base your calculations on the costs per user that you determined in Exercise 1. At this point you should have all the base information that you need to calculate your CPU requirements.

1. How much processing power does each server have and how much of that can be used?

2. What is the total cost per user for CPU usage?

3. How many concurrent users can the CPUs in each Web server support?

4. Once you've determined how many concurrent users each machine will support, you should round down that amount to a whole number and use that figure to calculate the number of servers that you need. How many Web servers should your cluster contain?

Exercise 3: Determining Bandwidth Capacity

In this exercise you'll calculate whether your current network can support the number of concurrent users. You'll base your calculations on the costs per user that you determined in Exercise 1. At this point you should have all the information you need to make these calculations.

1. What's the network bandwidth and how much of that bandwidth should you utilize when planning your capacity requirements?

2. How many concurrent users will your network support?

Review

Answering the following questions will reinforce key information presented in this chapter. If you are unable to answer a question, review the appropriate lesson and then try the question again. Answers to the questions can be found in the appendix.

1. You're a network administrator at Contoso Pharmaceuticals. Your network is connected to the Internet by a T1 line. You want to know the maximum transmission rate for a 5-KB page. With overhead, a page transmission runs about 55,360 bits. What's the maximum transmission rate over the T1 line?

2. You're implementing new tools on your company's Web site. You want to find out how long it will take users to download a 90 KB page (including overhead) over a 28.8 Kbps modem and a 56 Kbps modem. How many seconds will it take each type of user to download the page?

3. Your company is implementing new services on their Web site. The new services include data access to a back-end SQL Server database. In testing and analysis, you discovered that the Add Item operation responds more slowly than you expected. You determine that the disk cost for the operation is 4.395 and the usage for that operation is 0.012345 operations per second. What's the disk cost per user per second for the Add Item operation?

4. You're planning your network's capacity requirements. The site will be a transaction site that will allow users to store and retrieve information. Content will be dynamic: ASP hitting a SQL Server database. You anticipate 5,000 concurrent users at peak usage. What other steps should you take?

C H A P T E R   8

Directory Services

About This Chapter

A *directory service* is a network service that identifies all resources on a network and makes them accessible to users and applications. The directory service is the central authority that manages the identities of distributed resources and brokers the relationships between those resources, allowing them to work together in a cohesive framework accessible to administrators and users. In Microsoft Windows 2000 Server, directory services are implemented through the Active Directory service. Active Directory organizes resources on your network and simplifies access to those resources. This chapter introduces you to Active Directory and provides an overview of how Active Directory is structured and how directory information is replicated throughout your network. The chapter also explains how to plan the Active Directory physical structure in your network through site and replication planning.

Before You Begin

To complete the lessons in this chapter, you must have

- Experience administering Windows 2000 Server and designing Windows 2000 networks

- Experience administering Active Directory and the Windows 2000 Domain Name System (DNS) service

Lesson 1: Introduction to Active Directory

Active Directory includes the directory. The directory stores information about network resources and the services that make the information available and useful. The directory stores such objects as users, printers, servers, databases, groups, services, computers, and security policies. Active Directory is integrated with Windows 2000 Server and provides simplified administration, scalability, open standards support, and support for standard name formats. In this lesson you'll be introduced to how Active Directory is integrated into Windows 2000 Server and you'll learn about the Active Directory structures. This lesson also describes the Active Directory replication process.

After this lesson, you will be able to

- Provide an overview of Active Directory and describe how the service is structured
- Explain how Active Directory replication works

Estimated lesson time: 25 minutes

Overview of Active Directory

Active Directory organizes resources hierarchically into *domains*, which are logical groupings of servers and other network resources. The domain is the basic unit of replication and security in a Windows 2000 network. Each domain contains one or more domain controllers. When a change is made to a domain controller, that change is replicated to all other domain controllers in the domain.

Active Directory stores information by organizing its directory into sections that permit storage for a large number of objects. The directory can expand as an organization grows, allowing administrators to scale their installations to meet the demands of their growing organization.

Active Directory Integration with DNS

Active Directory can exist within the scope of the Domain Name System (DNS) used for the Internet namespace. The Active Directory namespace is made up of one or more hierarchical domains beneath a root domain registered as a DNS namespace. Because Active Directory uses DNS as its domain naming and location service, Windows 2000 domain names are also DNS names.

By integrating with DNS, Active Directory can store and replicate DNS zone databases. Normally, zones are stored as text files on name servers. These files are then synchronized among DNS name servers. This system requires a replication process separate from that of Active Directory and the domain controllers. However, when DNS is integrated with Active Directory you can configure a domain controller as a DNS name server so that zone data is stored as an Active Directory object and is replicated as part of the domain replication process.

Note The Windows 2000 DNS service must run on the domain controllers to be integrated with Active Directory.

Lightweight Directory Access Protocol

Active Directory uses Lightweight Directory Access Protocol (LDAP) as its core protocol. It's the only wire protocol supported by Active Directory. LDAP, which is an open Internet standard that runs directly over Transmission Control Protocol/Internet Protocol (TCP/IP), is a communication protocol designed for use on TCP/IP networks. LDAP can also run over User Datagram Protocol (UDP) connectionless transports.

LDAP defines how a directory client can access a directory server and how the client can perform directory operations and share directory data. It allows users and applications to query, create, update, and delete information stored in Active Directory. In addition, LDAP allows Active Directory to operate with other vendor directory services.

Active Directory Objects

Active Directory objects represent the physical entities that make up a network. For example, users, printers, and computers are Active Directory objects. Every object is an instance of a particular class. A class defines the attributes available to an instance of that class. An attribute can be present in an object only when the object's class permits that attribute.

When you create an object in Active Directory, you must provide values for the object's attributes. You can add only values that are in accordance with the rules stored in the directory schema. For example, when you create a user object, you must provide values for the Full Name attribute and the User Login Name attribute. Without these values, you can't create a user object because values are required by the directory schema.

In Active Directory objects can be either leaf objects or container objects. A leaf object doesn't store other objects, but a container object can. An object class is a container if at least one other class specifies it as a possible superior. As a result, any object class defined in the schema can become a container.

Active Directory Schema

The Active Directory schema defines the types of objects and the types of information about those objects that can be stored in the directory. Two types of definitions are in the schema: attributes and classes.

Attributes are defined only once and can be used in multiple classes. For example, the Description attribute is used in many classes, but it's defined only once.

Classes, also referred to as object classes, describe the possible Active Directory objects that can be created. Each class is a collection of attributes. For example, the User class includes attributes such as First Name, Last Name, and Display Name. Every object in Active Directory is an instance of an object class.

Active Directory Structure

Active Directory can be separated into those components that make up the logical structure and those that make up the physical structure. The two structures are completely separate from each other.

Logical Structure

The logical structure is made up of domains, trees, forests, and organizational units (OUs), as shown in Figure 8.1.

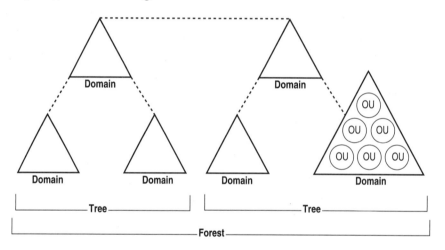

Figure 8.1   Active Directory logical structure

This structure mirrors your organization's structure by grouping resources logically by name rather than by physical location. In Active Directory a network's physical structure is transparent to the user.

Domains

The domain is the core unit of the logical Active Directory structure. In a domain, network objects, such as users and computers, are grouped together to form an administrative and security boundary. Security policies and settings are confined to one domain and don't cross from one to another.

Active Directory allows you to organize objects logically so that account and resource management at the domain level is easier and more efficient. You can also publish resources and information about domain objects. When working with multiple domains, you can scale Active Directory to accommodate your administrative and publishing needs by partitioning the directory so that each domain can better serve the particular needs of its user group.

A domain stores information about all network objects within that domain. However, Active Directory can be made up of more than one domain, and a domain can span more than one physical location. In theory, a domain can contain up to 10 million objects, although 1 million objects per domain is more practical.

Above all, a domain is a security boundary. You can use access control lists (ACLs) to control access to domain objects. For example, you can use ACLs to control which users can access specific objects and what type of access those users have to the objects. In Active Directory, objects can include computers, contacts, groups, printers, users, shared folders, and other objects defined in the schema.

Trees

A *tree* is a hierarchical grouping of Active Directory domains. You can create a tree by adding one or more child domains to a parent domain. For example, suppose the parent domain is wingtiptoys.com. You can create two child domains, us.wingtiptoys.com and eu.wingtiptoys.com, and one other domain, sea.us.wingtiptoys.com, that's a child of us.wingtiptoys.com, as shown in Figure 8.2.

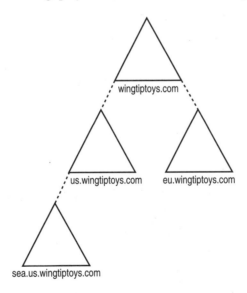

Figure 8.2   Domain tree for the Wingtip Toys company

Notice that the domains in the tree share a contiguous namespace and hierarchical naming structure. Trees must follow DNS standards. The domain name for a child domain is appended to the parent domain. In addition, all domains within a tree share a common schema and global catalog, which is a central repository of information about objects in a tree. Trust relationships are automatically created between parent and child domains.

Forests

A *forest* groups together one or more domain trees. Although the trees have different naming structures, they share a common schema. In addition, all domains in a forest share a common global catalog. Figure 8.3 shows two domain trees, wingtiptoys.com and tailspintoys.com, which have been grouped together to create a forest.

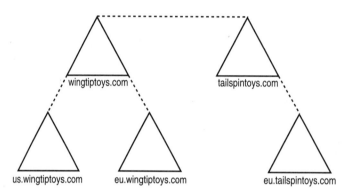

Figure 8.3   Domain forest for the Wingtip Toys company and the Tailspin Toys company

The forest enables communication across the entire organization even though the domains operate independently. An implicit two-way transitive trust exists between the domains and domain trees.

Organizational Units

Within each domain you can organize objects into logical administrative groups that mirror your organization's structure. An *organizational unit (OU)* is an Active Directory container that can contain such objects as users, groups, and computers. An OU can also contain other OUs. The OU hierarchy within one domain is independent from other domains; each domain can implement its own OU hierarchy.

An OU is the smallest unit in a domain to which you can delegate administrative authority. As a result, you can group together resources in a way that reflects your organization's administrative model. You can apply administrative settings to objects within the OU and grant administrative permissions to specific users for objects within a specific OU without compromising the entire domain's security.

Physical Structure

Active Directory's physical structure, which is independent of the logical structure, consists of sites and domain controllers.

Sites

In Active Directory, a *site* is made up of one or more IP subnets that are connected by highly reliable and fast links. A site often shares the same boundaries as the local area network (LAN). Computers in a site should be well connected, as you'd expect with computers in the same subnet. You should develop multiple sites for wide area networks (WANs) because servicing requests or replicating directory information across WANs can be highly inefficient. Network connections within a site should be at least 512 kilobits per second (Kbps), with an available bandwidth of 128 Kbps or higher.

Sites aren't part of the namespace. They map your network's physical structure, and there's no necessary correlation between your network's physical structure and its domain structure. A site can contain multiple domains, and a domain can contain multiple sites, as shown in Figure 8.4.

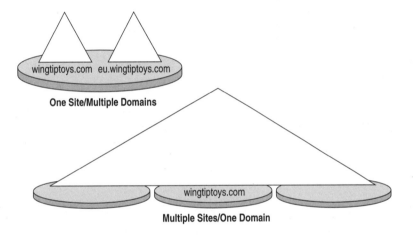

Figure 8.4   One site for multiple domains and multiple sites for one domain

Sites facilitate authentication. When a client logs on to a domain, the logon mechanism first searches for domain controllers that are located in the same site as the client, increasing the efficiency of the authentication process. Selecting a domain controller that's well connected to the client makes handling the request more efficient. If a client has to look outside the local site for a domain controller, the authentication process can put strain on the network.

Sites also facilitate replication, which is discussed later in this lesson.

Domain Controllers

A *domain controller* is a computer running one of the Windows 2000 Server operating systems and Active Directory. Each domain can contain one or more domain controllers. A domain controller stores a complete copy of all Active Directory information for that domain, manages changes to that information, and replicates those changes to other domain controllers in that domain. Multiple domain controllers in a domain provide fault tolerance.

When the first domain controller is created in a forest, the global catalog is also created. The *global catalog* is a central repository of information about objects in a tree or a forest. It stores a full replica of all objects in the directory for its host domain and a partial replica of all objects contained in the directory of every other domain in the forest. The global catalog enables logon to a native-mode domain by providing universal group membership information to a domain controller when a logon process is initiated. It also enables finding directory information regardless of which domain in the forest actually contains the data.

When a user logs on to a native-mode domain, the global catalog provides universal group membership information for the account that's sending the logon request to the domain controller. If the domain has only one domain controller, the domain controller and the global catalog are the same server. If the network has multiple domain controllers, the global catalog is hosted on the domain controller that is configured as such. If a global catalog isn't available when a user initiates a network logon process, the user is able to log on only to the local computer.

You can achieve the best network performance by locating a global catalog in every site, since a global catalog is necessary to complete the logon authentication process.

Active Directory Replication

Active Directory allows users and services to access directory information at any time from any computer in the domain tree or forest. Each time an object is added, modified, or deleted, the updated directory data must be relayed to other domain controllers. However, the need for directory data to be distributed must be balanced against the need to optimize network performance. If directory updates are constantly distributed to all other domain controllers in the domain, they'll consume your network resources.

The replication process is based on three directory partitions:

- **Schema**   Defines the classes and attributes used to define the objects in the forest. Each forest contains one schema partition.
- **Configuration**   Defines the logical structure of the Active Directory deployment. Each forest contains one configuration partition.
- **Domain**   Describes the objects in a domain. Each domain contains one domain partition.

Schema and configuration information is replicated to all domain controllers in the forest. The domain data for a particular domain is replicated to every domain controller within it. However, the objects in every domain, and a subset of the properties of all objects in the forest, are replicated to the global catalog.

Multimaster Operations

Active Directory uses multimaster replication to synchronize directory information. Multimaster replication allows any domain controller to accept and replicate directory changes to any other domain controller. All domain controllers within a domain are equivalent; there's no master domain controller. If one domain controller is unavailable, other domain controllers can continue to update the directory. Domain controllers can be distributed across the network and be located in multiple physical sites.

Domain controllers keep track of how many changes they've made to their copy of the directory, as well as how many changes they've received from domain controllers that are their replication partners. This process makes updating a domain controller that's been disconnected from the network easy, because it's clear which directory information has changed and therefore needs to be replicated. Because changes are tracked by a numerical sequence, not by time, the need for synchronized clocks is eliminated in all but the most unusual cases, such as when resolving conflicting changes.

Single-Master Operations

Some changes are impractical to perform in multimaster fashion. As a result, certain domain controllers are assigned roles in order to perform single-master operations. In any Active Directory forest, five operations master roles are assigned to one or more domain controllers: schema master, domain naming master, relative ID master, infrastructure master, and PDC emulator.

Each forest must contain only one schema master and only one domain naming master. The *schema master* controls all updates and modifications to the schema, and the *domain naming master* controls the addition or removal of domains in the forest.

Each domain must contain only one relative ID master, infrastructure master, and PDC emulator. The *relative ID master* allocates sequences of relative IDs to each of the various domain controllers in its domain, and the *infrastructure master* updates the group-to-user references whenever the members of groups are renamed or changed.

If the domain contains computers operating without Windows 2000 client software or if it contains Microsoft Windows NT backup domain controllers, the *PDC emulator* acts as a Windows NT Primary Domain Controller (PDC). It processes password changes from clients and replicates updates to the backup domain controllers.

Bridgehead Servers

A *bridgehead server* is the point at which directory information is exchanged with another site. You can specify a preferred bridgehead server if you want to designate a specific computer to transmit and receive information. If a high level of directory information is typically exchanged, a computer with more bandwidth can ensure that these exchanges are handled promptly.

If you specify multiple preferred bridgehead servers, only one will be the active preferred bridgehead server at any time. If the active preferred bridgehead server fails, Active Directory will select another preferred bridgehead server to take its place. If no active preferred bridgehead server is available and no other preferred bridgehead servers are available either, Active Directory will select another domain controller in the site to be the preferred bridgehead server. This can be problematic if the domain controller that Active Directory selects doesn't have the bandwidth to efficiently handle the increased requirements imposed on a preferred bridgehead server.

You must specify a preferred bridgehead server if your deployment uses a firewall to protect a site. Establish your firewall proxy server as the preferred bridgehead server, making it the contact point for exchanging information with servers outside the firewall. If you don't do this, directory information may not be exchanged.

A preferred bridgehead server is the preeminent server for the exchange of Active Directory information in and out of the site. Other domain controllers can still exchange directory information if the need arises, but under normal conditions the bridgehead server is the first choice to receive and send all directory traffic.

Lesson Summary

Active Directory organizes resources hierarchically into domains and is integrated with DNS. Active Directory can exist within the scope of DNS Internet namespace and can store and replicate DNS zone databases. Active Directory uses LDAP as its core protocol. Active Directory objects represent the physical entities that make up a network, and the schema defines the types of objects and the types of information about those objects that can be stored in the directory. The logical structure in Active Directory is made up of domains, trees, forests, and OUs, and the physical structure is made up of sites and domain controllers. The two structures are completely separate from each other. A domain is the core unit of the logical Active Directory structure. In a domain, network objects, such as users and computers, are grouped together to form an administrative and security boundary. A site is made up of one or more IP subnets that are connected together by highly reliable and fast links. Sites aren't part of the namespace. They map the physical structure of your network. Active Directory allows users and services to access directory information at any time from any computer in the domain tree or forest. Active Directory uses multimaster replication to synchronize directory information. However, some domain controllers are assigned roles in order to perform single-master operations. Five operations master roles are assigned to one or more domain controllers: schema master, domain naming master, relative ID master, PDC emulator, and infrastructure master. A bridgehead server is the point at which directory information is exchanged with another site.

Lesson 2: Planning the Active Directory Physical Structure

To a large degree, the availability of Active Directory services in your network is determined by how you've designed Active Directory's physical structure. Your design of the physical structure must take into account site design, replication, optimizing network traffic, confining authentication to a specific segment of your network, and the placement of domain controllers, global catalog servers, and operations masters. This lesson describes the steps that you should take when planning the Active Directory physical structure.

After this lesson, you will be able to
- Define a site structure and determine where to place domain controllers, global catalog servers, and operations masters
- Define a replication strategy

Estimated lesson time: 30 minutes

Planning Process

When planning the physical structure of Active Directory services in your network, you must define a site structure in order to determine where domain controllers should be placed, define an intersite replication strategy, and determine where global catalog servers and operations masters should be placed. This lesson describes each of these steps.

Defining a Site Structure

In Lesson 1 you learned that a site is made up of one or more subnets connected by highly reliable and fast links. Sites have two main roles: to facilitate client authentication and streamline directory replication traffic.

When a client attempts to log on to a domain, it sends its request to a domain controller that's within the same site, if one is available. If one isn't available, the client attempts to communicate with domain controllers in any other site. The authentication process is much more efficient if a client can be authenticated by a domain controller that's well connected, usually within the same site. You should also take site structure into account when you use firewalls to connect network segments. In most cases you'd want to control the authentication (and replication) traffic that crosses the firewall.

In addition to affecting the authentication process, the site structure affects directory replication. Active Directory handles intrasite replication differently from intersite replication. As a result, bandwidth is important when you plan your site structure. You must take into consideration your subnet structure, your network's LAN and WAN connectivity, the placement of perimeter networks and firewalls, and your organization's network traffic patterns. Any time two network segments are connected by links that are heavily used during some parts of the day and idle at others, you should create separate sites to prevent replication traffic from competing with other traffic during high usage hours.

Designing a Site Structure

When setting up Active Directory sites, you must take into account how your organization is set up in terms of geographic locations and connectivity. You need to know how the network is subnetted and how those subnets are connected. You must also determine the speed of the connections and the average available bandwidth during normal business hours.

Generally, you should create a site for each of the following:

- A LAN or set of LANs that are connected by a high-speed link

- A perimeter network that's separated from another network segment by a firewall

- A location that's reachable only by Simple Mail Transfer Protocol (SMTP) mail (and doesn't have direct connectivity to the rest of the network)

When you're designing your Active Directory site structure, you're basically taking your network's physical topology and creating a more general topology that's based on available bandwidth, network reliability, and network segmentation, as is the case for a perimeter network. If you want particular clients to log on to a specific set of domain controllers, you should define your site structure so that only those domain controllers are in the same site as the clients.

Placing Domain Controllers

Once you've determined how you'll set up your Active Directory sites, you can decide how you'll place domain controllers in those sites. The availability of domain controllers determines Active Directory availability and the ability of users to be authenticated. Each domain requires at least one domain controller, although each domain should include at least two domain controllers to avoid any single points of failure. However, the number of domain controllers that you place in a particular domain should be determined by your fault tolerance and your organization's load distribution requirements.

When deciding how many domain controllers to place in your domain and where to put them, you must determine the level of fault tolerance that you want to ensure in that site. You must also take into account the connections between sites and whether you want to confine client authentication to specific domain controllers. You should put a domain controller into a site under the following conditions:

- A large number of clients connect to the site.

- You want clients to be authenticated at a specific set of domain controllers.

- The connection to other sites is slow, near capacity, or sometimes unavailable.
- The connection to other sites is through a firewall.
- The site is accessible only by using SMTP mail.

To ensure optimum network response time and application availability, you should place at least one domain controller in each site and two domain controllers in a domain. However, you should place additional domain controllers in a site in the following situations:

- A large number of clients use the site. If there's not enough processing power to service requests, performance will lag and clients might experience slow logon times and slow authentication when attempting to access resources.
- Intersite connections are relatively slow, unreliable, or near capacity. If a single domain controller fails, clients must connect to domain controllers in other sites. If the site links are unreliable, users might not be able to log on to their computers.
- You want clients to be authenticated at a specific set of domain controllers. In these cases you might want to prevent users from going to another site to request authentication if a domain controller fails. For example, you might want to ensure that client requests generated within a perimeter network are always authenticated on that side of the firewall.

In some situations you might not want to place a domain controller in a site, such as a site with a small number of users or a small site that has client computers but no servers. However, to ensure high performance and availability, most sites should contain at least one domain controller and some sites should have multiple domain controllers.

Defining an Intersite Replication Strategy

After you've defined your site structure and determined the placement of domain controllers, you can plan your intersite replication strategy. Planning for intersite replication consists primarily of determining how site links will be configured. Site links, which are logical, transitive connections between sites, allow you to customize how Active Directory replicates information between sites.

Once you create site links, the Knowledge Consistency Checker (KCC) automatically creates the appropriate connection objects that connect domain controllers. The KCC uses the site links to determine replication paths between two sites. Unlike connection objects, you must create the site links manually.

By default, all site links are transitive. However, if you disable this transitivity for a transport, all site links for that transport are affected and none of them are transitive. In that case you must create site link bridges to provide transitive replication. A site link bridge connects two or more site links in a transport to create a link between two sites that don't have an explicit site link. However, because site links are transitive by default, it's seldom necessary to create site link bridges.

For each intersite transport, the KCC automatically designates a domain controller in each site as a bridgehead server and creates connection objects between the bridgehead servers. You can also specify a preferred bridgehead server in situations where you want to control which server is the replication point for that site.

For each site link that you create, you must provide the following information:

- **Replication schedule**   The scheduled times and days on which replication polling occurs over a seven-day interval. The default daily schedule allows polling to occur all day, every day.
- **Replication interval**   The scheduled intervals in which replication polling occurs. The default polling interval is three hours.
- **Replication transport**   The type of transport used by the site link. You can choose IP or SMTP.
- **Link cost**   The relative bandwidth of the connection, as compared to other site links. You can choose between 1 and 32,767. Lower values should indicate better connectivity and higher usage priority. The default link cost is 100.

You should configure your site links according to available bandwidth, network usage patters, and type of transport. To create more reliable, fault-tolerant replication, configure additional site links to provide redundant replication paths.

Your site link configurations must be optimized for your specific network environment. For example, suppose your organization's network is divided into four sites. Figure 8.5 shows the site topology for these sites. The solid lines connecting the sites represent an IP transport type. The dotted line represents an SMTP transport type.

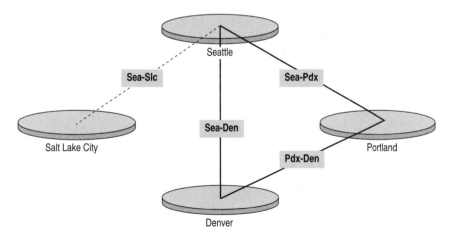

Figure 8.5   Active Directory site topology

In addition to the four sites, the figure shows four site links. Table 8.1 shows a possible configuration strategy for your organization. The strategy would take into account your network structure and capacity.

Table 8.1   Site Link Parameters

Site Link	Replication Schedule	Replication Interval	Transport Type	Link Cost
Sea-Pdx	Always	1 hour	IP	25
Sea-Den	1800 to 0600, daily	30 minutes	IP	100
Pdx-Den	1800 to 0600, daily	15 minutes	IP	50
Sea-Slc	1800 to 0600, daily	15 minutes	SMTP	100

Three out of the four site links are scheduled for replication at off-peak hours only. The Sea-Pdx site link allows replication to occur every hour, all day, every day. This would be a good strategy to use if the connection between the Seattle and Portland sites is reliable and has plenty of bandwidth. Notice, however, that a longer polling interval has been configured. On the other hand, the Sea-Slc site link replicates every 15 minutes, but only during off-peak hours.

Placing Global Catalog Servers and Operations Masters

The final step in planning your Active Directory physical structure is to determine where you'll place the global catalog servers and the operation masters.

Placing Global Catalog Servers

A global catalog server holds a copy of the global catalog. The global catalog's availability is crucial to the operation of Active Directory. For example, the logon process requires that the global catalog be available to determine group memberships when a user logs on to a native-mode domain. If the global catalog isn't available, the domain controller refuses the logon request.

To achieve optimum network response time and application availability, you should locate at least one global catalog server in each site to provide clients with a local computer to service query requests. If you want to increase availability for a site, you should add more global catalog servers. Place additional global catalog servers in a site in the following situations:

- A large number of clients use the site.
- Intersite connections are relatively slow, unreliable, or near capacity.

Placing Operations Masters

Active Directory supports five operations masters: schema master, domain naming master, relative ID master, PDC emulator, and infrastructure master. A forest must contain exactly one schema master and one domain at any one time. Each domain in the forest must contain exactly one relative ID master, one PDC emulator, and one infrastructure master at any one time. When you create the first domain in a new forest, all operations master roles are assigned to the first domain controller. As you add child domains and create trees in the forest, Active Directory automatically assigns operations master roles according to the structure of the forest.

In a domain containing only one domain controller, all five operations master roles are assigned to that domain controller. In a domain that contains more than one domain controller, you can assign the roles to different domain controllers. When assigning operations master roles, you should adhere to the following guidelines:

- Make one domain controller the operations master and make another domain controller a standby operations master.

- In large domains, place the relative identifier master and PDC emulator on separate domain controllers. Both servers should be direct replication partners with a standby operations master.

- Don't assign the infrastructure master role to a domain controller that's hosting the global catalog, although you should assign this role to a domain controller that's well connected to a global catalog in the same site. Note that if all domain controllers in the domain are hosting the global catalog, it doesn't matter which domain controller is the infrastructure master.

Making a Decision

The process of planning the Active Directory physical structure includes defining a site structure, defining a replication strategy, and determining where to locate domain controllers, global catalog servers, and operations masters. Table 8.2 lists the specific steps that you should follow when planning the physical structure and describes what factors you should take into consideration for each step.

Table 8.2 Planning the Active Directory Physical Structure

Step	Description
Defining a site structure	Each site should be made up of one or more subnets connected by highly reliable and fast links.
Placing domain controllers	Each domain must include at least one domain controller and at least two domain controllers to provide fault tolerance. To determine how many additional domain controllers to place in your domain, you must take into account your fault tolerance and distribution requirements.
Defining an intersite replication strategy	For each site link you must configure a replication schedule, replication interval, replication transport, and link cost.

(continued)

Table 8.2   *(continued)*

Step	Description
Placing global catalog servers and operations masters	A copy of the global catalog must be available to every domain controller in your network. In addition, a forest must contain exactly one schema master and one domain naming master at any one time. Each domain in the forest must contain exactly one relative ID master, one PDC emulator, and one infrastructure master at any one time.

Recommendations

When planning the Active Directory physical structure, you should adhere to the following guidelines:

- Create a site for each LAN or set of LANs connected by high-speed links, any perimeter networks separated from other network segments by firewalls, and any location reachable only by SMTP.

- Place at least one domain controller in each site and two domain controllers in each domain. Place additional domain controllers in a site when a large number of clients access the site; intersite connections are relatively slow, unreliable, or near capacity; or clients should be authenticated at a specific set of domain controllers.

- Configure your site links according to available bandwidth, network usage patterns, and type of transport. If appropriate, configure additional site links to provide redundant replication paths.

- Locate at least one global catalog in each site. Place additional global catalog servers in a site when a large number of clients access the site or intersite connections are relatively slow, unreliable, or near capacity.

- Provide a standby operations master. In large domains, place the relative identifier master and PDC emulator on separate domain controllers. Don't assign the infrastructure master role to a domain controller that's hosting the global catalog unless all domain controllers in the domain are global catalog servers.

Example: Active Directory Physical Structure for Woodgrove Bank

Woodgrove Bank has implemented a Windows 2000 native-mode network that includes only one domain. The network includes a perimeter network to support the bank's Web operations. In setting up Active Directory, administrators created a site in the perimeter network and another site inside the corporate network. The sites are separated because the two network segments are connected by a firewall, and administrators wanted Web clients to be authenticated from within the perimeter network and not the corporate network.

To ensure high performance and availability, two domain controllers are included in the perimeter network site. Each of these domain controllers is configured with the global catalog. Additional domain controllers are located in the corporate network. To facilitate fault tolerance in the corporate network and to minimize traffic across the firewall, redundant domain controllers have been configured to act as backups for the global catalog server and the operations master.

Figure 8.6 illustrates how Active Directory is integrated into the network to provide fault tolerance, maximum network performance, and separate operations on either side of the firewall to support the bank's Web operations.

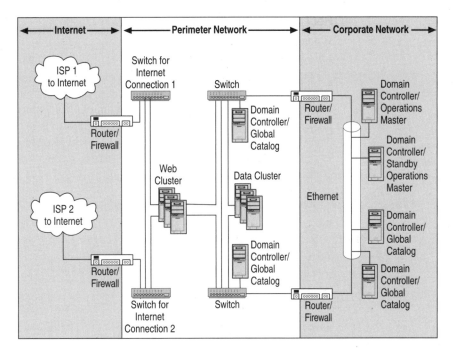

Figure 8.6 Active Directory integrated into the perimeter network

Lesson Summary

When planning the physical structure of Active Directory, you must define a site structure, determine where domain controllers should be placed, define an intersite replication strategy, and determine where global catalog servers and operations masters should be placed. Site structures facilitate client authentication and streamline replication traffic. You should create a site for each LAN or set of LANs that are connected by a high-speed link, a perimeter network that's separated from another network segment by a firewall, or a location that's reachable only by SMTP mail. Each domain requires at least one domain controller, although it should include at least two to avoid creating any single points of failure. You should place a domain controller in a site when a large number of clients connect to the site; when you want clients to be authenticated at a specific set of domain controllers; when the connection to other sites is slow, near capacity, or sometimes unavailable; or when the connection to other sites is through a firewall. You should place additional domain controllers in a site when a large number of clients use the site; when intersite connections are relatively slow, unreliable, or near capacity; or when you want clients to be authenticated at a specific set of domain controllers. Planning for intersite replication consists primarily of determining how site links will be configured. For each site link, you must configure the replication schedule, replication interval, replication transport, and link cost. To achieve optimum network response time and application availability, you should locate at least one global catalog server in each site to provide clients with a local computer to service query requests. Place additional global catalog servers in a site when a large number of clients use the site or when intersite connections are relatively slow, unreliable, or near capacity. When assigning operations master roles, you should make one domain controller the operations master and make another domain controller a standby operations master. In large domains, place the relative identifier master and PDC emulator on separate domain controllers. Don't assign the infrastructure master role to a domain controller that's hosting the global catalog.

Lab 8.1: Planning the Physical Structure

After completing this lab, you will be able to

- Plan an Active Directory site structure and replication strategy
- Determine the placement of domain controllers, global catalog servers, and operations masters

About This Lab

In this lab you'll plan the Active Directory physical structure for Northwind Traders. You'll be concerned mainly with Active Directory's implementation as it relates the company's Web site and perimeter network. The exercises in this lab coincide with the steps described in Lesson 2, which include defining a site structure, defining an intersite replication strategy, and determining the placement of domain controllers, global catalog servers, and operations masters.

Before You Begin

Before you begin this lab, you must be able to

- Administer Windows 2000 Advanced Server
- Administer Active Directory and the DNS service

Scenario: Network Structure for Northwind Traders

Northwind Traders is implementing a Windows 2000 network that will host a Web site that will be available to external clients through the Internet. Admin-istrators have designed a network topology that includes a perimeter network to support the Web services. The network uses one namespace (northwindtraders.com) for internal and external users. The network is confined to one physical location that's a well-connected LAN set up as a single domain. All connections are fast and reliable.

The perimeter network contains a front-end tier that supports a Web cluster and a back-end tier that supports a Data cluster. The perimeter network is separated from the private corporate network by a firewall. Figure 8.7 shows the network topology of the perimeter network.

As one of the administrators, you're responsible for planning the Active Directory physical structure for your network. You must design a site structure, prepare a replication strategy, and decide on the placement of domain controllers, global catalogs, and operations masters.

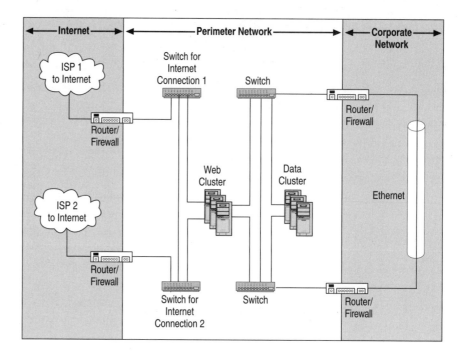

Figure 8.7   Network topology for Northwind Traders

Exercise 1: Defining a Site Structure

In this exercise you must determine how you should set up Active Directory sites for the Northwind Traders network. Remember that in defining a site structure you're working with your network's physical topology and creating a more general topology that's based on available bandwidth, network reliability, and network segmentation. As you plan site structure, refer to Figure 8.7.

1. What criteria should you use when deciding how to structure your sites?

2. How many sites should you create for this site and where should they be located?

3. Why have you chosen this site structure?

4. Assume that the private corporate network is spread across several physical locations connected by WAN links. How would that affect your site structure?

Exercise 2: Placing Domain Controllers

In this exercise you must determine where you'll locate the domain controllers. You should base your decisions on the site structure that you created in Exercise 1. One of your goals in determining where to place domain controllers is to ensure that client requests for authentication within the perimeter network don't pass through the firewall into the corporate private network, even in the event of domain controller failure. In addition, client requests generated within the corporate network shouldn't have to pass through the firewall into the perimeter network for authentication, even in the event of domain controller failure.

1. What guidelines should you follow when determining where to place domain controllers?

2. In which sites would you include a domain controller?

3. How many domain controllers should you include in your network?

Exercise 3: Defining an Intersite Replication Strategy

In this exercise you'll determine how to set up Active Directory intersite replication for the Northwind Traders network. Remember that planning for intersite replication consists primarily of deciding how site links will be configured. Of course, replication is facilitated by your site structure, which you determined in Exercise 1. You'll now take that structure and plan how you'll configure the necessary site links.

1. What guidelines should you follow when determining how to configure site links?

2. What site links do you need to configure for the Northwind Traders network?

3. What configuration information must you provide for each site link?

4. You decide that replication between the perimeter network and the private network should occur throughout the day at regular intervals. You want domain controllers on both sides of the firewall to remain relatively current, but you don't want to overwhelm the network. You plan to restrict directory replication to 12 times a day at regular intervals, every day of the week. How should you configure the site link?

Exercise 4: Placing Global Catalog Servers and Operations Masters

In this exercise you'll determine where you should place global catalog servers and operations masters. You'll base your decision on the site structure and domain placement that you determined in the previous exercises. You believe that, given the size of your network, four domain controllers are enough to handle the network load and provide fault tolerance. You'd prefer not to add any equipment at this time.

1. What guidelines should you follow when determining where to place global catalog servers?

2. Where should you locate global catalog servers in the Northwind Traders network?

3. What guidelines should you follow when determining where to place operations masters?

4. Where should you place the operations masters?

Review

Answering the following questions will reinforce key information presented in this chapter. If you're unable to answer a question, review the appropriate lesson and then try the question again. Answers to the questions can be found in the appendix.

1. What are Active Directory objects and what's the purpose of the Active Directory schema?

2. What are the components of the Active Directory logical structure and the physical structure?

3. What are the five operations master roles assigned to one or more domain controllers?

4. You're planning the Active Directory physical structure for your organization. Your network is made up of three domains. Each domain is in a separate geographical location connected by a WAN link, and each location is a fast, reliable LAN with ample bandwidth. One of the LANs includes a Web site that's set up in a perimeter network, which is connected to the private network through a firewall. What's the minimum number of Active Directory sites that you should create for this network?

5. Your network is made up of two Active Directory sites. You're configuring a site link between the two sites. You configure replication to occur during non-business hours at intervals of 15 minutes. How often will the directory be replicated during business hours?

C H A P T E R   9

Application Integration

About This Chapter

The Internet's ever-increasing popularity has changed the architecture of distributed computing and how we think of application design. In many organizations the client/server topology, which consists of two tiers, is being replaced by multi-tiered environments in which computing tasks are spread across multiple layers, each of which provides specific functionality. As a result, applications no longer simply sit on a client or server and respond to client requests. For many applications, particularly ones that are Web-related, application components are distributed across multiple layers that are each assigned a particular computing task. In this model, an application might respond to a client request that's initiated through a thin client, such as Microsoft Internet Explorer. The application, which is hosted on an Internet Information Services (IIS) server or another Web server, might require access to resources such as Component Object Model (COM) objects or data stores in order to respond to the client request. These resources might be on separate layers, or tiers, depending on the network configuration. In this chapter you'll learn how to design a content and application topology that supports a distributed environment. You'll also learn how to design a database and a messaging integration strategy.

Before You Begin

To complete the lessons in this chapter, you must have

- A basic understanding of multitier Web application design and middle-tier (business logic layer) technologies

- An understanding of how Network Load Balancing (NLB) and Component Load Balancing (CLB) are implemented in a multitiered environment

Lesson 1: Defining a Web Application Strategy

As a result of the Internet, its related technologies, and the adoption of Internet standards, many organizations, particularly larger ones, have a growing need for data access that's faster and more reliable than the client/server application model provides. Consequently, these organizations have moved toward a distributed application design that divides computing tasks along application tiers, which usually include a presentation layer, a business logic layer, and a data layer. Although this strategy requires more analysis and design at the start, in the end it greatly reduces maintenance costs and increases functional flexibility. In this lesson you'll be introduced to the distributed application model. From this information you'll learn how to determine where to place Web components to work within this distributed topology and how to develop an application deployment and synchronization strategy.

After this lesson, you will be able to

- Determine where to place Web components
- Develop an application deployment and synchronization strategy

Estimated lesson time: 30 minutes

Application Integration

In the past, the two-tier model's ease and flexibility drove the development and deployment of business applications, and it still does for many smaller companies. However, with the advent of the Internet, many organizations have adopted a multitiered architecture for their applications. This distributed design must take into account two considerations: determining where to place the components that support distributed applications and determining how to deploy and synchronize these applications.

Placing Components That Support Distributed Applications

A distributed application divides computer tasks along logical layers so that major pieces of functionality are isolated. In most systems the multitier model is divided into three layers, which are described in Table 9.1.

Table 9.1   Distributed Application Model

Layer	Description
Tier 1 (presentation layer)	The client tier represents the entire user experience. At this layer, the user can input data, view the result of requests, and interact with the underlying system. In a Web environment, a browser acts as the user interface to carry out these functions. In a non-Web environment, a stand-alone, front-end application acts as the user interface.

(continued)

Table 9.1   *(continued)*

Layer	Description
Tier 2 (business logic layer)	The middle tier encapsulates an organization's business logic. This layer connects the user at one end and the data at the other end through the use of processing rules that closely mimic everyday business tasks. In a Web application the middle tier might include Active Server Pages (ASP) files and COM objects.
Tier 3 (data layer)	The data tier provides the data store for the application and, subsequently, the client using the application to access that data. The third tier might contain a structured data store such as Microsoft SQL Server, an unstructured data store such as Microsoft Exchange, or a transaction-processing mechanism such as Message Queuing.

Note that application tiers don't always correspond to the network structure. For example, IIS and ASP might run on a front-end cluster to handle incoming requests, while the COM objects might run on a separate cluster on a separate network. Or they all might run on the same front-end cluster (but still be considered separate application layers).

Figure 9.1 illustrates how application services can be provided through a distributed design.

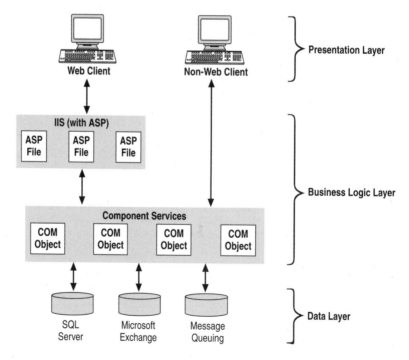

Figure 9.1   Three-tier application architecture

Unlike client/server applications, the distributed application is flexible and not limited to one or two computing tiers. A multitiered network structure allows you to scale out your applications through the use of additional tiers, additional computers, additional clusters, or even additional geographic locations. In addition to increasing scalability, the distributed model can increase availability and reliability through the use of redundant services and components.

Application-Specific Technologies

The distributed model relies on application-specific technologies to provide services to the client. Some of these technologies exist on the client tier. For example, client-side scripts run within the browser, using the processing power of the user's computer. Another example of a technology that runs in the client tier is ActiveX controls, which you can use to customize the user interface or use as plug-in applications (such as the RealNetworks streaming audio/video player).

In addition to client-side technologies, the distributed application also uses middle-tier technologies, which include Common Gateway Interface (CGI) applications, Internet Server Application Programming Interface (ISAPI) extensions and filters, and ASP. Table 9.2 provides a brief description of each of these technologies.

Table 9.2   Middle-Tier Technologies

Technology	Description
CGI applications	A CGI application is an executable program that runs on the Web server. Remote users can launch a CGI application by requesting a Uniform Resource Locator (URL) that contains the name of the CGI application. CGI applications scale poorly on the Microsoft Windows operating system.
ISAPI extensions and filters	An ISAPI extension is a run-time dynamic-link library (DLL). An ISAPI extension performs better than a CGI application, although ISAPI presents some maintenance problems. An ISAPI filter allows you to intercept specific server events before the server itself handles them. As a result, you can create filters to provide such services as customer authentication or automatic redirection. ISAPI filters can cause performance degradation.
ASP	ASP is a scripting environment that allows you to create dynamic content and Web-based applications. Scripts in ASP pages are easier to write and modify than CGI or ISAPI, and you can use ASP to perform the same kinds of tasks. However, when ASP pages are first compiled, they can be much slower than plain Hypertext Markup Language (HTML) and ISAPI, but after the compiled version is cached, subsequent requests are significantly faster.

IIS and Distributed Web Applications

IIS plays a pivotal role in making distributed applications available to the Web client. IIS provides the following core functionality:

- Establishing and maintaining Hypertext Transfer Protocol (HTTP) connections
- Reading HTTP requests and writing HTTP responses
- Modifying HTTP headers
- Obtaining client certificate information
- Managing asynchronous connections
- Mapping URLs to physical paths
- Managing and running applications
- Transmitting files

At the heart of many distributed applications is ASP. ASP extends the basic functionality of IIS by providing a link to the COM architecture. IIS and Component Services work together to provide the following functionality:

- Isolating applications into distinct processes
- Managing communication between COM objects
- Coordinating transaction processing for transaction ASP applications

In IIS, Web application resource files are grouped together into a logical namespace, which allows you to share data throughout the namespace and run the application in an isolated process. When an ASP file is requested, IIS processes the request by using the ASP DLL, which is an ISAPI DLL.

Figure 9.2 illustrates how an ASP request is processed in IIS. The numbered steps shown in the illustration are described below.

When a browser from a client computer requests an ASP page, the following events occur:

1. The client browser sends an HTTP request for the ASP page to the Web server.
2. When IIS sees the .ASP extension on the requested page, the service recognizes the page as a script-mapped file and sends it to the ASP.DLL ISAPI extension for processing.
3. The ASP.DLL extension compiles and caches the ASP file. The extension processes any include directives before compiling any server-side script.
4. IIS creates the resulting HTML page, which is then sent back to the client.
5. When the client receives the page, it loads any client-side objects, executes client-side script, and displays the Web page according to HTML specification.

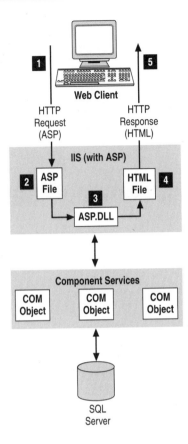

Figure 9.2   An ASP request from IIS

IIS and ASP work together to support the distributed application. IIS essentially coordinates the efforts of the application so that COM objects, and subsequently data from the data store, can be accessed in order to generate a response to the initial request.

Deploying and Synchronizing Application Content

Application deployment refers to the process of moving a set of code from one distributed environment to another. In the case of Web applications, this set of code includes all files, COM objects, scripts, configuration settings, and any other required components that support the application.

Ideally, your deployment process should move through three distributed environments—development, testing/staging, and production, as shown in Figure 9.3. You create content in the development environment and administer it in the production environment. Once in the production environment, you should be able to synchronize changes throughout a cluster to maintain the consistency of the content within that cluster.

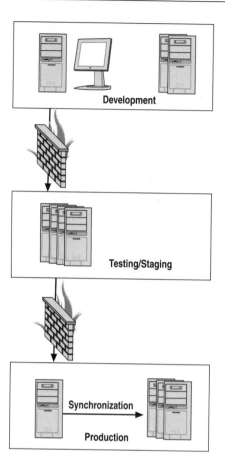

Figure 9.3   The application deployment process

Many tools have been developed to support the deployment of application content. For example, Microsoft Application Center 2000 includes the New Deployment Wizard, which allows you to deploy applications from a source server to a specified target. Tools like the New Deployment Wizard help system administrators maintain a secure, yet usable, buffer between their testing and production environments.

When deploying your applications into a clustered environment, you should consider several factors:

- Whether you want to avoid any downtime
- Whether you use scheduled downtimes for maintenance
- Whether there are times when a live update will have minimal impact on your users

Ideally, if you schedule downtime for maintenance, you should deploy your applications at that time. However, this isn't realistic for organizations that strive for high availability. If this is the case, you must choose a time that will affect the fewest users.

You should also take into account the type of application that you're deploying. An application that contains COM+ components requires a different strategy from an application that contains only static content. This section provides an overview of deploying applications with static content and deploying COM+ applications.

Deploying Applications with Static Content

When you deploy an application that consists solely of static Web pages and graphics, you don't have to reset the Web services because there are no ISAPI filters or COM+ components that require resets. This provides far more flexibility in your deployment strategy than if ISAPI filters or COM+ components are included.

In most cases you can deploy applications that contain only static content by first performing a single deployment from the stager to the Web cluster controller. From there, you can replicate the content to the other members of the cluster. With some administrative applications, such as Application Center 2000, replication occurs automatically as cluster members are synchronized. However, you can disable automatic synchronization on the target cluster and manually synchronize the new application across the cluster after the deployment has finished.

In some cases you might decide that a particular cluster member shouldn't be serving content at the same time that new content is being replicated to the system because a particular computer has a lower capacity than other members. If so you can take that member out of the load-balancing loop, synchronize the cluster, and then bring that member back online.

Deploying COM+ Applications

When you deploy COM+ applications, Web services are reset on the target computers. As a result, you can't deploy COM+ applications without affecting the existing client connections, so you should plan your deployment strategy around times that will affect the fewest users.

If you're deploying your applications to a Web cluster that contains the COM+ components, your strategy should include several fundamental steps:

1. Take the cluster controller and one member of the cluster out of the load-balancing loop.

2. Deploy the applications to those two computers.

3. After the services have been reset, bring the two servers back online for load balancing.

4. Repeat the process for the remaining members.

If you're deploying your applications to a Web cluster and a separate COM+ application cluster, you should deploy your applications in two phases:

1. Deploy the COM+ objects to the COM+ application cluster.
2. Deploy the rest of the application to the Web cluster.

When you deploy your COM+ objects, you'll most likely have to deploy the controller and each member of the cluster separately. If you're using CLB on the Web cluster, you should remove the COM+ controller or member from the routing list as you're deploying the COM+ objects. Be sure to add the server back to the routing list once you've deployed the components. After you've deployed the COM+ objects, you can deploy the rest of the applications to the Web cluster by following the same steps used to deploy applications to a Web cluster that contains the COM+ components.

Making a Decision

When integrating distributed applications into your Web environment, you must take into account the placement of components that support those applications and how to deploy application content. Table 9.3 describes the factors that you must consider when planning your distributed applications.

Table 9.3   Integrating Distributed Applications

Strategy	Considerations
Determining where to place the components that support distributed applications	Web applications are distributed across multiple tiers: the presentation layer, the business logic layer, and the data layer. The presentation layer contains the client browser, which acts as a user interface to the application and data. The business logic layer includes the Web services, ASP, files, and objects that support the organization's business logic. The data layer provides the data store for the application.
Developing an application deployment and synchronization strategy	A deployment strategy should take into account whether downtimes are scheduled for maintenance or when the fewest users access the system. In addition, deployment strategies are different for applications that contain static content only and COM+ applications.

Recommendations

When determining where to place the components that support distributed applications, you should determine your application requirements and apply those requirements to a distributed environment. For example, all your Web applications will rely on the presentation layer and the business logic layer. At the very least, the client browser (in the presentation layer) will access services by connecting to an IIS computer (in the business logic layer). The business logic layer will contain HTML pages, ASP pages, or both, in addition to other static content, such as graphics. This layer will also contain any of the server-side technologies that support the application. If your application includes access to a data store, you should incorporate a data layer into your design.

When planning a strategy for deploying Web applications into your distributed environment, your first approach should be to deploy your applications during scheduled downtime. If this approach isn't possible, you should adhere to the following guidelines:

- When you deploy applications with static content, perform a single deployment from the stager to the Web cluster controller. From there, replicate the content to the other members of the cluster.

- When you deploy COM+ applications to a Web cluster that contains the COM+ components, deploy the applications to one or two members at a time, starting with the controller.

- When you deploy COM+ applications to a Web cluster and a separate COM+ application cluster, do it in two phases: deploy the COM+ objects to the COM+ application tier and then deploy the rest of the application to the Web tier.

Example: A Distributed Application for Trey Research

Trey Research is implementing Web-based services to support its customer base. It plans to develop an application that allows clients to access information from a data store. The application will be distributed across a multitiered environment, as described in Table 9.4.

Table 9.4   Trey Research Application

Tier	Description
Presentation layer	At this tier users will access the Web site through a browser. Client-side scripts will be used to validate form inputs.
Business logic layer	This tier will include IIS. ASP will be used to process client requests. ASP will call COM+ objects, which, in turn, will access the data store. The COM+ objects will be stored in the Web cluster.
Data layer	This tier will include SQL Server, which will be used to store data.

Figure 9.4 shows how the components are distributed across the environment to support client requests and application processing.

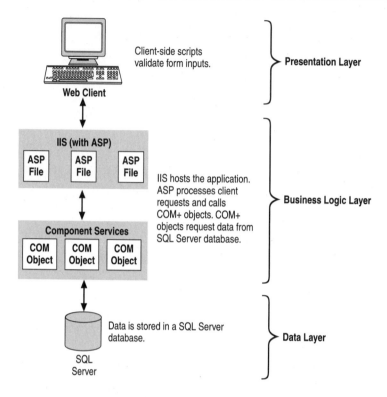

Figure 9.4   Trey Research application

Lesson Summary

When you integrate an application into a distributed environment, you must take into account where to place components that support the application and how to deploy and synchronize that application. A distributed application divides computer tasks along logical layers so that major pieces of functionality are isolated. In most systems the multitier model is divided into three layers: the presentation layer, the business logic layer, and the data layer. The distributed model relies on application-specific technologies that exist either on the presentation layer (such as ActiveX controls) or the business logic layer (such as ASP). ASP extends the basic functionality of IIS by providing a link to the COM architecture. IIS and ASP work together to support the distributed application. When deploying your applications into a clustered environment, you should consider whether you want to avoid any downtime, whether you use scheduled downtimes for maintenance, and whether there are times when a live update will have minimal impact on your users. You should also take into account the type of application that you're deploying. An application that contains COM+ components requires a different deployment strategy from an application that contains only static content.

Activity 9.1: Deploying a Web Application

Trey Research is implementing a Web-based application to market its services. The application will consist of static content only. No COM+ objects or ISAPI filters will be used. After the application was developed, it was deployed to a testing/staging server. You must define a strategy for deploying the application into the production environment. The environment includes one Web cluster that contains four members. The cluster uses NLB and Application Center 2000 to load balance the cluster. Each cluster member runs IIS as its Web service. Because the Web site supports other applications that must remain highly available, no downtime is scheduled for maintenance. You want to deploy the new application with as little disruption to service as possible.

1. What's the first step of your deployment strategy?

2. What's the second step of your deployment strategy?

3. How will Web services be affected by this deployment strategy?

Lesson 2: Designing a Database Web Integration Strategy

In Lesson 1, "Defining a Web Application Strategy," you were introduced to applications that are distributed across a multitiered environment. One of the components of this environment is the data tier, which provides the data store for applications that are responding to client requests for data. To support requests, Microsoft provides three data access technologies: Open Database Connectivity (ODBC), OLE DB, and ActiveX Data Objects (ADO). ASP and COM components can use these technologies to access data from local data sources such as SQL Server databases. This lesson describes ODBC, OLE DB, and ADO and explains how ASP and COM components can use them to communicate with a data source. The lesson also describes the steps you should follow when planning your integration strategy.

After this lesson, you will be able to

- Explain how you can use ODBC, OLE DB, and ADO to communicate with various data sources

- Describe the steps necessary to use ASP and COM components to access data from a data store

- Describe the steps necessary to integrate your database into your Web environment

Estimated lesson time: 30 minutes

Web Database Access

Many of today's Web applications rely on a relational database (such as a SQL Server database) or another type of data store to provide accurate information to users. Because of the demands of user interactivity and application complexity, the information must be accessible in way that makes it easy to manipulate and modify. To facilitate this accessibility, Microsoft provides several technologies that enable data access, including ODBC, OLE DB, and ADO. Each of these technologies is described in Table 9.5.

Table 9.5   Data Access Technologies

Technology	Description
ODBC	ODBC is a standardized method for accessing data in relational databases. Although ODBC is fast and lightweight, it's a common method not optimized for any specific data source.
OLE DB	OLE DB, like ODBC, is an open specification. OLE DB is a set of COM interfaces that can communicate with any data source, including relational data sources, such as SQL Server databases, and nonrelational data sources, such as Microsoft Excel spreadsheets, e-mail data stores, and text files. With ADO, you can access databases, indexed sequential access method (ISAM), text, or hierarchical data sources.

Table 9.5 *(continued)*

Technology	Description
ADO	ADO is a collection of objects that exposes the attributes and methods used to communicate with an OLE DB data source. It provides a common programming model designed to work with OLE DB. ADO is ideal for server-side scripting and is the recommended technology for data access for ASP applications.

Server-side ASP and COM components can access ADO, which uses OLE DB providers to communicate with the data source. A *provider* is any component that allows technologies such as ADO to access data in a uniform way through the OLE DB interfaces. A provider manages access to the data source. Figure 9.5 illustrates how ASP and a COM component access data from a SQL Server database. The OLE DB provider used to access data from a SQL Server database is SQLOLEDB.

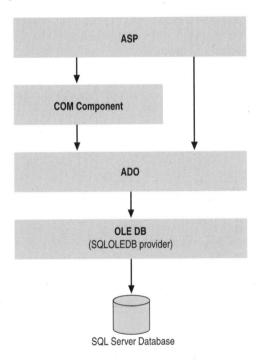

Figure 9.5 Accessing data from a SQL Server database

When designing your strategy for integrating a database into your Web application, your planning process should include a number of steps, including setting up permissions, optimizing database connections, using stored procedures to manage data, managing data files, and scaling out your database. The rest of this section describes each of these steps.

Note   This lesson focuses on server-side solutions to database access because these solutions are browser-independent, which is often preferable in mixed-browser environments like the Internet. However, Microsoft also supports technologies that facilitate client-side programming, such as Remote Data Service (RDS). For more information about these technologies, refer to the *Microsoft Windows 2000 Server Resource Kit* or to *http://www.microsoft.com/windows2000*.

Setting Up Permissions

Before an application can access data from a database, permissions must be set up properly. This is especially true when a database, such as a SQL Server database, and IIS are running on different computers, which is the most likely scenario in a distributed environment. In a Windows 2000 environment, connections to a SQL Server computer are set up by default to use named pipes. A *named pipe* is a high-level interprocess communication mechanism used by network computers. Named pipes provide connection-oriented messaging by using pipes. However, in most cases, the connection type often needs to be changed to the Transmission Control Protocol/Internet Protocol (TCP/IP) network library or another nonauthenticated protocol.

In order for a client to gain access to a named pipe, and subsequently the SQL Server database, the SQL Server computer must validate the client, which can occur in one of two ways:

- The server uses a workgroup-style validation in which identical user names and passwords are created on the client and the server.

- The server uses a domain-style method in which both the client and server are domain members.

When attempting to validate a connection, the SQL Server computer uses the identity of the user associated with the Web connection. If the connection is anonymous, you must ensure that a guest account has been created that corresponds to the IUSR_*computername* account and that permissions have been granted to that account to allow it to log on to the SQL Server computer. There are a number of methods that you can use to support an anonymous logon, including the following two:

- Add the IUSR_*computername* account to the local user account database on the SQL Server computer.

- Enable the Windows 2000 Guest user account on the SQL Server computer.

You can also set up your system to support user authentication. For example, if you configure IIS to use Integrated Windows authentication, IIS tries to connect to the SQL Server computer by using the user's security context. As with anonymous users, the connection attempts to use a named pipe to connect to the SQL

Server computer if SQL Server is located on a separate computer from IIS. When Windows 2000 detects the attempt to use a named pipe that has been opened in a different user context, it closes the pipe, according to its security rules. To avoid this situation, you can use a nonauthenticated protocol, such as the TCP/IP network library, between the IIS computer and the SQL Server computer.

Note that in a highly available environment, SQL Server 2000 will often be installed on a cluster configured with the Cluster service. Currently in Windows 2000, clients can't use Kerberos to authenticate a connection to a cluster virtual server. If Kerberos can't be used, the clients attempt to authenticate with Windows NT LAN Manager (NTLM) authentication. (SQL Server 2000 supports NTLM authentication.) You shouldn't disable NetBIOS over TCP/IP or restrict NTLM authentication on clients that will be communicating with cluster virtual servers.

Optimizing Database Connections

Managing database connections can be a significant challenge with distributed Web applications. The process of opening and maintaining connections can severely affect the database server's resources, even when no information is transmitted. As a result, connectivity performance can be affected. Table 9.6 describes several steps you can take to optimize your database connections.

Table 9.6   Optimizing Connections

Step	Description
Enhancing application performance on SQL Server	In the registry, change the threading model for the main ADO component from Apartment to Both. Don't make this change if you intend to use ADO to connect to a Microsoft Access database.
Setting the connection timeout	Limit the amount of time that your application will wait for a connection to the database. A surge in database activity can cause the database to become backlogged, resulting in increased waiting periods. Excessive delays increase the amount of time a user must wait to learn that a request can't be processed.
Closing your connections	Design your application to close connections as soon as they're no longer needed to reduce the demand on database resources and to make those resources available to other users.
Sharing active connections	Design your application to share connections whenever possible, and don't use connections that you don't need.
Increasing the size of the record cache	Request multiple records at one time in order to increase connection throughput. You can increase the number of records that the provider will retrieve at one time into local memory.

Using Stored Procedures to Manage Data

A *stored procedure* is a precompiled set of queries that's stored on the database server. You can use stored procedures to simplify development and speed up complex queries. They control which operations are performed and which database fields are accessed.

Stored procedures are a useful way of providing security to your database because you can grant users and applications execute permission on the stored procedures without providing direct access to the underlying views and tables. That way, data can't be accessed by using query tools, except for the application front-end.

Managing Data Files

When you create a database, you must specify an initial size for the data files, which includes the database files and the transaction log. One way you can tune your database's performance is by properly configuring the sizing of those files. When you first set up the database, the data files should be large enough to avoid the input/output (I/O)–intensive operation of autogrowing data files. If the size of the initial files is too small, the database management system (DBMS) will have to frequently increase the size of the data files, which can degrade performance.

In addition to the initial size, you should set a maximum size appropriate to your storage system. For example, if the server uses Small Computer System Interface (SCSI) disks, you shouldn't allow the data files to grow beyond 85 percent of the drive's capacity. Beyond that, SCSI disk performance begins to degrade.

Scaling Out Your Database

You can scale out your database to provide high availability and performance to your Web applications. Three technologies that you can use are data partitions, failover clustering, and log shipping.

Partitioning Your Data

Partitioning refers to the process of distributing data from one table into multiple, identical tables on different servers. Once the data is partitioned, you can use distributed partitioned views to access that data. In SQL Server, you first create the member tables and then you create the partitioned view, which merges all the data so that the table divisions are transparent to users and applications. From the perspective of the users and applications, it doesn't matter if the view is made up of one table or eight—it looks and acts like one entity. The partitioned view provides seamless integration of data access to all the member tables.

Figure 9.6 illustrates how a distributed partitioned view accesses data. The CustomerData view accesses the Customer1, Customer2, and Customer3 tables. Each table contains a subset of the data that's included in the CustomerData view.

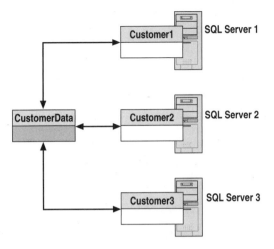

Figure 9.6   Accessing data through a distributed partitioned view

A copy of the distributed partition view resides in each partitioned database. For the partitioned view to be usable, all servers that contain a member table that participates in a view must be available. There is no built-in fault tolerance for partitioned views. If a server in the partitioned view fails, the view can't access data from any of the member tables, even if the query isn't requesting data from the table on the failed server.

You should partition only those tables whose use is appropriate for partitioning. When you're designing a partition strategy, carefully consider how the request will be routed to the member tables. Your most important goal should be to minimize the amount of processing that the server needs to perform in order to return the requested data. Partitioning is related to data usage.

For example, suppose your database contains customer and sales data and you find that requests for data usually focus on sales region. A good strategy might be to partition data based on region. In this case you'd create member tables in which each one has the horizontally partitioned data for one or more regions. The partitioned view will retrieve data from all member servers according to how that data has been queried and will submit data only to the member server containing the data for a particular region.

Another way to access partitioned data is through *data-dependent routing,* which is an application-based approach that uses code to determine where the target data is located. Connections are then routed to the appropriate server. You can use data-dependent routing instead of partitioned views or in combination with them. In data-dependent routing, the information on how to go after the data is made available to the application.

When accessing data through distributed partitioned views, data partitioning alone doesn't provide high availability. However, two high-availability solutions that you can use in conjunction with partitioning are failover clustering and log shipping.

Setting Up Failover Clustering

SQL Server 2000 failover clustering is built on top of the Cluster service in Windows 2000 Advanced Server and Windows 2000 Datacenter Server. Failover clustering in SQL Server has three main components:

- **Virtual server name**   The name that all applications and clients use to refer to the instance of SQL Server

- **Virtual server IP address**   The IP address (or addresses) that all external connections will use to reach the instance of SQL Server

- **Virtual server administrator account**   The SQL Server service account, which must be a domain administrator

In SQL Server, an *instance* is an installation of SQL Server that's completely separate from any other installations. However, instances can share underlying components that affect how SQL Server works in a clustered environment. SQL Server allows you to set up multiple instances per server.

SQL Server 2000 supports two types of failover clustering: single instance (similar to an active/passive cluster) and multiple instances (similar to an active/active cluster). These two types of failover clustering are described in Table 9.7.

Table 9.7   Types of Failover Clustering

Type of Clustering	Description
Single instance	This type of cluster contains only one active instance of SQL Server, which is owned by a single node. All other nodes in the cluster are in a wait state. The waiting node is enabled if the active node fails.
Multiple instances	This type of cluster supports up to four nodes. Although SQL Server can support up to 16 instances, having more than 4 instances isn't recommended (1 instance per node). One strategy that you can use in a multiple-instance cluster is an N+1 topology. In this configuration all nodes are active except one. The passive node remains in standby and is configured as the primary failover computer.

Implementing Log Shipping

Part of implementing a database into a distributed design is ensuring that database's availability. One method that you can use to protect your database is *log shipping,* which is a process of copying transaction logs from a primary SQL Server computer and applying them sequentially (on a scheduled basis) to another SQL Server computer. If the primary SQL Server computer fails, you can direct your application to the backup server. Depending on when the last transactions were applied, your backup server will either be up to date or only slightly out of sync. Log shipping can work in conjunction with failover clustering.

Table 9.8 describes many of the factors that you should take into consideration when planning to implement log shipping.

Table 9.8   Configuring Log Shipping

Strategy	Description
Synchronizing data	You must determine how often the log data should be synchronized by taking into account how close the secondary server should be behind the primary server. In other words, how many transactions can you afford to lose? By default, transactions logs are backed up every 15 minutes.
Placing the servers	The location of the servers is important. Log shipping allows you to disperse log data across geographical areas, which is recommended. At a minimum, the primary and secondary servers should be on separate grids, and the log-shipping pair should never exist on the same server.
Connecting the servers	The log-shipping pair must be able to communicate with each other. Ideally, the servers should communicate log-shipping information over a private local area network (LAN) rather than share the network bandwidth. You should also configure the servers with higher bandwidth network cards, if your network infrastructure can support them.
Planning secondary server capacity	The secondary server should have the same capacity as the primary server to ensure that the application will perform as expected should failover occur.
Generating database backups	In most cases you can use the secondary server to perform full database backups because the secondary server is only out of sync by a small increment of time. This strategy keeps the primary server free of the overhead and contention incurred by the backup process.

In general, failover clustering is a better high-availability solution than log shipping (although you can use the two together). For example, failover clustering is fast and automatic, while log shipping is slow and manual. In failover clustering, all transactions are rolled forward if completed or rolled back during the failover process. In log shipping, if the primary server is unavailable, the last transactions can't be retrieved. However, log shipping is generally less expensive than failover clustering and does provide a high level of protection—just not as much as failover clustering.

Making a Decision

The process of designing a database Web integration strategy includes five steps. Table 9.9 describes the considerations that you should take into account for each of these steps.

Table 9.9   Integrating a Database into Your Application

Factor	Considerations
Setting up permissions	When you set up permissions for data access in a Web environment, you must take into account whether users will access the site anonymously or whether they'll have to be authenticated in order to access the site.
Optimizing database connections	When optimizing database connections, you should take into account application performance, connection time-outs, closing your connections, sharing active connections, and the size of the record cache.
Using stored procedures to manage data	Stored procedures can simplify development, speed up complex queries, and provide a security structure for protecting data.
Managing data files	You can fine-tune the performance of your database by controlling the limits and rate at which the data files can grow.
Scaling out your database	When scaling out your database to achieve high availability and performance, you can use data partitioning, failover clustering, and log shipping.

Recommendations

You can use ASP and components to access data through ADO. This process allows you to integrate your database into your distributed Web applications. When determining how to integrate your database into your distributed application, you should adhere to the following guidelines:

- If users connect to your Web site anonymously, you must ensure that a guest account is created that corresponds to the IUSR_*computername* account and that permissions are granted to the account.

- If user logon must be authenticated, you should use a nonauthenticated protocol, such as the TCP/IP network library, between the IIS computer and the SQL Server computer.

- To optimize connections you should use the Both threading model, limit connection time-outs, close and share connections, and increase the size of the record cache.

- Use stored procedures to access data and carefully manage the sizing of your data files.

In addition to following these guidelines, you should take steps to scale out your database in order to provide highly available data to your applications. You can use partitioning to facilitate the scaling out process. Your goal in partitioning data should be to minimize the amount of processing that the server needs to perform to return the requested data.

Although partitioning alone isn't enough to ensure highly available data, you can use it in conjunction with failover clustering, log shipping, or both. If partitioning isn't appropriate for your organization, you should still implement failover clustering or log shipping. Whenever you're trying to ensure high availability, your first choice should be clustering because it provides the quickest and most automatic failover and is virtually transparent to users and applications.

Example: Database Integration for Margie's Travel

Margie's Travel is implementing a Web site that provides travel information to the company's customers. Much of the information is generated dynamically from content stored in a database. Customers on the Web can access the site at *http://www.margiestravel.com/*. From there they can search for the information they need.

The site supports this functionality by using ASP-based applications and COM+ components to access a SQL Server database. The application will use stored procedures to access the data. A multitiered topology is used to distribute the application components across the presentation tier, business logic tier, and data tier, as shown in Figure 9.7.

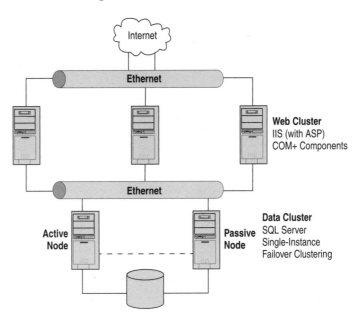

Figure 9.7   Database integration in a distributed environment

The business logic layer comprises a Web cluster that's configured with IIS and ASP. The COM+ components are located on the same Web cluster. The SQL Server database is located on the data layer, which is set up as a single-instance failover cluster. One node is configured with an active instance of SQL Server, and a second node is configured with a waiting instance of SQL Server. Both servers in the failover cluster are identical and each can easily support the anticipated number of data requests at peak times. Users will log on anonymously, so an appropriate guest account has been configured on the SQL Server computers.

Lesson Summary

Microsoft provides several technologies that enable data access, including ODBC, OLE DB, and ADO. Server-side ASP and COM components can access ADO, which uses OLE DB providers to communicate with the data source. Before an application can access data from a database, permissions must be set up properly. The method used to ensure data access depends on whether users access the site anonymously or whether they must be authenticated. You can optimize database connections by using the Both threading model, limiting the connection time-outs, closing and sharing connections, and increasing the size of the record cache. When accessing data, your application should use stored procedures when possible because they simplify development, speed up complex queries, and provide a security structure. Database integration should also take into account data files configuration. You should set an appropriate initial size and maximum size. You can use data partitions, failover clustering, and log shipping to scale out your database and provide high availability and performance. Partitioning refers to the process of distributing data from one table across multiple, identical tables on different servers. Failover clustering builds on the Windows 2000 Cluster service and provides failover and failback protection to your database services. Log shipping refers to the process of copying transaction logs from a primary SQL Server computer and applying them sequentially (on a scheduled basis) to another SQL Server computer to provide a backup server that's either up to date or nearly up to date.

Activity 9.2: Partitioning Data in a SQL Server Database

Lucerne Publishing stores a large amount of data in its SQL Server database. Because of this, performance suffers during peak hours. As the network administrator, you decide to partition the data so that the system can perform more transactions during peak usage. You plan to partition the data across three instances of SQL Server. However, you want to maintain the high availability that your site currently supports. Your budget provides for up to six identical servers. You decide to use all six computers to create three single-instance failover clusters.

1. How should you set up the failover clusters?

One of the tables in the database is named Customers. You partition this table across the three clusters based on the sales region in which the customer is located. Your company is split into six sales regions, so you partition the data so that each partition includes two regions. However, your ASP application must be able to request data from customers in all three regions.

2. What methods can your application use to access the data?

Your organization decides to implement four Windows 2000 Datacenter Server computers. However, you still want to support partitioning the data into three partitions while still providing failover protection.

3. How can you configure your failover clustering?

Lesson 3: Designing a Microsoft Exchange Web Integration Strategy

Exchange 2000 Server is tightly integrated with Web technologies. IIS, which is now coupled with Exchange, is required on all Exchange 2000 Server computers. IIS is responsible for client protocols and manages all HTTP, Post Office Protocol version 3 (POP3), Internet Message Access Protocol version 4 (IMAP4), Network News Transfer Protocol (NNTP), and Simple Mail Transfer Protocol (SMTP) client requests. All Exchange 2000 protocols are hosted within the IIS process. Exchange 2000 HTTP also supports Web Distributed Authoring and Versioning (WebDAV), which allows rich collaborative interaction with the Web Storage System in Exchange. As a result of its interaction with IIS, Exchange can support Web-based access to its e-mail services, which is implemented through the Microsoft Outlook Web Access component of Exchange. This lesson introduces you to Outlook Web Access and describes several steps that you should take when designing an Exchange integration strategy in order to provide browser-based messaging to your clients.

After this lesson, you will be able to

- Provide an overview of how Outlook Web Access delivers Web-based messaging services to your Internet clients
- Design a strategy for implementing Exchange 2000 into your Web environment

Estimated lesson time: 30 minutes

Outlook Web Access

Outlook Web Access allows users to gain access to their mailboxes from nearly any location that supports Internet connectivity. Because client access is through a browser, access isn't limited by operating system or location, and client computers don't have to be configured with a special e-mail client.

Outlook Web Access supports various Web browsers, including Netscape Navigator 4.08 and later, Internet Explorer 4.01 Service Pack 1, and Internet Explorer 5 and later. When used with Internet Explorer 5, Outlook Web Access provides clients with a user experience similar to Microsoft Outlook. Outlook Web Access supports such functionality as the preview pane, drag and drop functionality, HTML text editing, and right-click menu options.

Web browsers other than Internet Explorer 5 can also take advantage of Outlook Web Access as long as they comply with HTML 3.2 and JavaScript. However, these browsers don't support as many features as Internet Explorer 5. Yet even when using Internet Explorer 5, Outlook Web Access doesn't support all the functionality of Outlook. For example, with Outlook Web Access, you can't work offline, create Outlook rules, or access tasks and journal items.

When a user tries to access an object in Outlook Web Access, a series of events occurs. Figure 9.8 provides an overview of these events. Each step is described below.

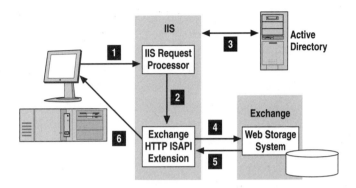

Figure 9.8   Accessing Exchange objects on the Web

When a user attempts to open a message, the following events occur:

1. A user accesses the mailbox by calling a URL and clicks a message to open it.

2. The IIS request processor calls the Exchange HTTP ISAPI extension, which parses the information in the request and determines the action to be performed.

3. The IIS server determines whether the user has rights to gain access to the item.

4. The extension parses the correct form and queries Web Storage System to bind the data.

5. The Web Storage System sends the data back to the Exchange HTTP ISAPI extension.

6. The Exchange HTTP ISAPI extension renders the data in HTML or Extensible Markup Language (XML), based upon the browser type and version, and sends it to the client.

Outlook Web Access uses IIS to receive requests and pass them to the Web Storage System. The Web Storage System stores and manages documents, e-mail messages, Web pages, multimedia streams, data elements, and other items in a semistructured, hierarchical database. Outlook Web Access doesn't use Messaging Application Programming Interface (MAPI) to communicate with the data store and doesn't use ASP for client access. Clients use HTTP and WebDAV to communicate with the Outlook Web Access service.

To implement Outlook Web Access into your Web environment, you must determine an Exchange topology, ensure system availability, and plan your Web access authentication. The following sections discuss each of these tasks.

Determining an Exchange Topology

When designing an Exchange topology, you have two options from which to choose: installing Exchange in a single-server environment or installing Exchange in a multiserver environment.

In a single-server environment, the client connects directly to the Exchange 2000 Server computer that hosts the mailbox. You must add an Exchange virtual root and a public virtual root to IIS. The virtual roots point to their corresponding directories in Exchange.

Although the single-server environment requires less equipment and administrative overhead, it limits how effectively you can implement Exchange 2000 Server in your environment and which methods you can use to ensure high availability. For example, suppose your system requires Secure Sockets Layer (SSL) connections. The steps necessary to encrypt and decrypt data are processor-intensive. If the data store is also located on the same server, processing power must be shared among the different types of operations, and it becomes more difficult to maximize performance for any one type of operation.

Achieving fault tolerance can also become more complicated in the single-server environment because you have to factor in load-balancing issues with issues surrounding the management of stored data.

On the other hand, a multiserver environment provides far more flexibility and can provide a more secure and highly available model. In a multiserver environment, the front-end server communicates directly with the client and forwards requests to the back-end server for processing. The back-end server hosts the data store. Figure 9.9 illustrates how a multiserver environment is set up.

A multiserver environment provides a number of benefits:

- The multiserver model supports a unified namespace. You can disperse groups of users across back-end databases but allow them to connect to the front-end server by using a single server name.
- You can isolate back-end servers from attacks. You can locate back-end servers behind a firewall or on a different subnet. Front-end servers can each be configured with one network interface card (NIC) that connects to the Internet and another NIC that connects to the secure, internal LAN.
- Multiple servers allow you to isolate processing tasks. Front-end tasks can be performed on computers separate from the processing of data that occurs on the back-end. For example, SSL processing can occur on the front-end servers only. From there, the front-end and back-end servers can communicate without the overhead of SSL.

The multiserver model has the added benefit of being easier to scale out and make fault-tolerant. You can use Windows 2000 NLB to set up a front-end cluster that's load balanced, and use the Windows 2000 Cluster service to set up a back-end cluster to provide failover protection to the data store.

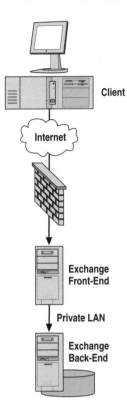

Figure 9.9   Multiserver Exchange configuration

Ensuring System Availability

As you can see in Figure 9.9, the multiserver configuration by itself provides no fault tolerance. However, by using Windows Clustering technologies (NLB and the Cluster service), you can make Outlook Web Access highly available to your Web users, as shown in Figure 9.10.

NLB balances the traffic on the front-end Exchange Server computers. If one of the servers fails, the load is distributed to the remaining servers in the cluster. Before you install Exchange 2000 Server on the front-end cluster, you should install and configure NLB. From there, you can install Exchange and configure it as the front-end server.

The Cluster service provides failover service on the back-end cluster. When failover occurs on one of the servers in that cluster, the second computer provides the services that were being provided by the failed server. When you configure the Cluster service, you must create at least one virtual server for each node. Each virtual server is responsible for one or more storage groups. A storage group is a collection of Exchange databases that share a set of transactions logs. You can configure a maximum of five databases per storage group, and each

Exchange Server computer can support up to four storage groups. As a result, you must ensure that, in the event of failover, a single node isn't supporting more than four storage groups.

For example, suppose each node in a two-node cluster is configured with two storage groups. If failover occurs, the remaining node would be supporting four storage groups. However, if each node were configured with three storage groups, the remaining node would have to support six storage groups in the event of failover, which it couldn't do.

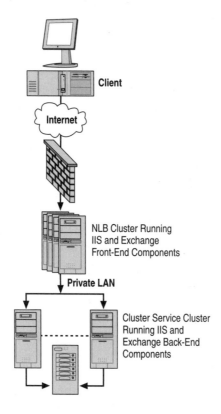

Figure 9.10   Multiserver Exchange configuration using NLB and the Cluster service

Planning Web Access Authentication

Outlook Web Access supports two forms of user authentication: Basic and Integrated Windows. Outlook Web Access also supports SSL encryption and Anonymous access.

Basic Authentication

Basic authentication is part of the HTTP specification. It's the most flexible type of authentication and is commonly used on intranets. Basic authentication is supported by most browsers and is independent of the hardware platform, but it isn't considered secure because passwords aren't encrypted when they're sent to the server. With Basic authentication, each user must enter a user name, domain, and password whenever the user logs on to be authenticated by Outlook Web Access.

Integrated Windows Authentication

Integrated Windows authentication can support Kerberos authentication or NTLM authentication. Integrated Windows authentication uses Kerberos when the client is running Windows 2000 and Internet Explorer 5. This configuration offers the best security, efficient communication, and transparency. Integrated Windows authentication uses NTLM instead of Kerberos for other client configurations. You can't use Integrated Windows authentication when Exchange is set up in a front-end/back-end configuration.

SSL Encryption

SSL encryption provides the highest level of security and operability between clients and server because the entire communication session is encrypted. By itself, SSL isn't an authentication mechanism. It provides a secure channel for other authentication mechanisms, such as Basic, and most browsers support SSL. However, SSL places an additional burden on the server, but if a front-end/back-end configuration is used, the front-end servers can usually manage SSL.

Anonymous Access

Anonymous access allows users to access specific resources without being prompted for authentication. As a result, you don't have to define accounts for these users. All browsers support anonymous access and administration is simpler.

Making a Decision

You can use Outlook Web Access to provide users with Web-based access to their e-mail accounts. To set up this service, you must determine an Exchange topology, ensure system availability, and plan your Web access authentication. Table 9.10 provides an overview of which factors you must consider when performing each of these tasks.

Table 9.10   Setting Up Outlook Web Access

Task	Considerations
Determining an Exchange topology	You can set up Exchange 2000 server in a single-server environment or a multiserver environment. In a single-server environment, the client connects directly to the Exchange 2000 Server computer that hosts the mailbox. This configuration limits how effectively you can implement Exchange 2000 Server in your environment and which methods you can use to ensure high availability. In a multiserver environment, the front-end server communicates with the client and forwards requests to the back-end server, which hosts the data store. This configuration provides more flexibility than a single-server environment and can provide a more secure and highly available model.

(continued)

Table 9.10   *(continued)*

Task	Considerations
Ensuring service availability	You can make a multiserver environment highly available by creating a front-end cluster and a back-end cluster and then implementing NLB on the front-end cluster and the Cluster service on the back-end cluster.
Planning Web access authentication	Outlook Web Access supports Basic authentication and Integrated Windows authentication. It also supports SSL encryption and Anonymous access. Integrated Windows authentication isn't supported in a front-end/back-end configuration.

Recommendations

When planning your Outlook Web Access implementation, you should use a multiserver environment. You should also create an NLB cluster on the front end of the perimeter network and a Cluster service cluster on the back end of the perimeter network. In addition, you should use SSL with Basic authentication to authenticate users.

Example: Web-Integrated Messaging for Northwind Traders

Northwind Traders provides e-mail services to its employees. Because some employees travel extensively, they can't always check their e-mail through their regular dial-up connections and e-mail clients. As a result, administrators at the company implemented the Outlook Web Access service in Exchange 2000 Server, which allows the employees to check their e-mail anywhere an Internet service is offered, such as airports, Internet cafes, or hotels.

Because employees travel to different parts of the world and may access their e-mail accounts at any time of day, any day of the week, e-mail availability had to be assured to be highly reliable. Consequently, administrators use a multi-server environment configured with Windows Clustering technologies, as shown in Figure 9.11. In addition, redundant network paths and components are used to avoid any single points of failure.

Lesson Summary

Exchange 2000 Server supports a service known as Outlook Web Access. Outlook Web Access allows users to gain access to their mailboxes through their browsers, so access isn't limited by operating system or location. To implement Outlook Web Access into your Web environment, you must determine an Exchange topology, ensure system availability, and plan your Web access authentication. When you implement Outlook Web Access, you can choose one of two Exchange topologies: a single-server environment or a multiserver environment. In a single-server environment, the client connects directly to the Exchange 2000 Server computer that hosts the mailbox. In a multiserver environment, the front-end server communicates directly with the client and forwards requests to the back-end server for processing. The back-end server hosts the data store. A multiserver environment provides far more flexibility and can provide a more secure and highly available model. If you implement a multiserver environment, you can create front-end NLB clusters and back-end Cluster service clusters to provide high availability. Outlook Web Access supports four authentication methods: Basic, Integrated Windows, SSL, and anonymous access. SSL provides the greatest security.

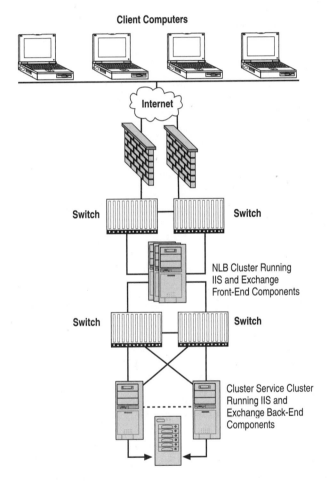

Figure 9.11   Northwind Traders Web-based e-mail service

Lab 9.1: Integrating a Web Application into a Distributed Environment

After completing this lab, you'll be able to

- Design an application topology that's distributed across multiple layers
- Incorporate Exchange 2000 Server into your Web site

About This Lab

In this lab you'll design a network topology that supports distributed applications. The applications will rely on ASP and COM+ components to access data from a SQL Server database. In addition, you'll further refine your design to provide Web-based e-mail services to your Internet users. Each exercise in this lab addresses one facet of the topology design. You'll first implement a simple Web site that supports static content. Next, you'll add database support so you can support dynamic content on your site. Finally, you'll add Web-based e-mail services to allow company employees to check e-mail when out in the field.

Before You Begin

Before you begin this lab, you must be able to

- Design a basic network topology that supports Web services
- Design NLB clusters and Cluster service clusters to support high availability in a Web environment

Scenario: Web Application and Messaging Services for Lucerne Publishing

Lucerne Publishing has operations throughout the world. The company has decided to implement a Web site that supports static content that will be used to provide general information about the company and its products. Lucerne Publishing also wants to provide specific information about the books it publishes. Because this information changes regularly, content for the site should be generated dynamically so it's easy to maintain the site and customers can easily search for specific titles. The information should be available to anyone who's interested. In addition to the customer-related services that the company wants to provide, Lucerne Publishing also wants employees working in the field to be able to access their e-mail accounts on a regular basis, regardless of where they're traveling. As the network administrator for the company, you must design a network topology that fulfills these requirements.

Exercise 1: Designing an IIS Application Structure

Lucerne Publishing is anxious to get its Web site online as quickly as possible. Initially, the company would like you to implement the Web servers so general company information can be posted as soon as possible. You plan to use Application Center 2000 to create an NLB cluster that contains three servers. You also plan to implement two Active Directory service computers within the perimeter network to support various systems as they're added to the network. Your design will include redundant component and paths to ensure high availability. In addition, you want the site to support the use of distributed applications as they're implemented into your network. COM+ components will be stored on the Web cluster.

1. How should you design the initial portion of the perimeter network?

2. Which application layers will your design initially support?

As you prepare your network design, you also want to take into consideration how the initial content will be deployed. The content consists only of static HTML pages and their supporting graphics. After the content has been developed, you'll move it to a test environment. From there, it'll be staged to the production environment.

3. How will you deploy this content?

Exercise 2: Integrating SQL Server into Your Application Structure

You've implemented the initial network design and deployed the content to the Web servers. You're now ready to set up the environment so that you can provide dynamic content to your users. Your development team has developed ASP applications that use COM+ components to access data from a SQL Server database. The applications have been tested and are ready to be staged. You plan to implement a SQL Server cluster that contains two servers. You'll use a single-instance configuration so that one server is active and the other is passive.

1. How should you modify your perimeter network's design to support the new applications?

2. You want to deploy the COM+ applications, but you don't want to take the Web services offline. How should you deploy the applications?

3. How should you set up permissions on the SQL Server computers?

4. What methods can you use to optimize connections to the database?

Exercise 3: Integrating Exchange 2000 Server into Your Web Site

Once you've integrated SQL Server into your design and deployed the COM+ applications, you're ready to integrate Exchange into your site. You plan to use a multiserver configuration for Exchange and use Windows Clustering technologies to support high availability.

1. How should you modify your perimeter network's design to support the Outlook Web Access service?

2. What benefits does a multiserver environment provide that a single-server environment can't?

3. What authentication methods does Outlook Web Access support?

4. Which authentication method would you recommend?

Review

Answering the following questions will reinforce key information presented in this chapter. If you're unable to answer a question, review the appropriate lesson and then try the question again. Answers to the questions can be found in the appendix.

1. You're the network administrator for Trey Research. You're deploying a Web application that incorporates ActiveX controls, client-side scripting, ASP, server-side scripting, COM+ components, and stored procedures. Much of the content for the site will be stored in a SQL Server database. The COM+ components will be in a COM+ application cluster separate from the Web cluster. How should you deploy the application?

2. You're managing a SQL Server database that supports several applications on your Web servers. You decide to partition several of the tables in the database to improve performance. What two methods can you use to access the partitioned data?

3. After you partition the data in your SQL Server database, you decide to implement a fault-tolerant solution to ensure the data's availability. What two high-availability solutions can you use in conjunction with partitioning?

4. You're configuring your Web site to support Outlook Web Access so that users can access their e-mail accounts through a browser. You're trying to determine how to set up the Exchange 2000 Server environment to support your users. You want the environment to support a unified namespace, and you want to isolate the data store from attacks. Which Exchange configuration model should you use?

5. You're setting up Outlook Web Access for your company's employees so that they can access their e-mail accounts through a browser. You plan to use a multiserver configuration and Windows clustering technologies to create a front-end NLB cluster and a back-end Cluster service cluster. You want to provide the highest level of security and operability between clients and servers by encrypting the entire communication session. Which protocol should you use?

CHAPTER 10

Network Security

About This Chapter

When you set up your Web site and the network infrastructure to support that
site, you must take steps to protect your network from intentional and uninten-
tional threats that might compromise your resources. The process of planning
your Web site should include a comprehensive security policy that effectively
weighs the value of the data against the costs of securing that data. However, as
you make your system more secure, you're also making that system less usable.
You shouldn't make your site so secure that your intended users can't access
your services. At the same time, you shouldn't make it so accessible that critical
resources are compromised. Planning your site's security must take into account
how users will be authenticated so that only intended users can access the site,
how users will be authorized so that they can gain access to only specific site
resources, and whether you'll use encryption to protect data as it's being transmitted across the Internet. A security strategy must also take into account

whether you'll use firewall services to further protect network resources. This chapter addresses each of these considerations in order to provide you with a comprehensive approach to planning an effective security strategy for your Web site.

Before You Begin

To complete the lessons in this chapter, you must have

- Experience administering Microsoft Windows 2000 security, including Internet Information Services (IIS) security
- Knowledge of Windows 2000 Certificate Services and client certificates
- Knowledge of firewalls and proxy services

Lesson 1: Designing an Authentication Strategy

Windows 2000 supports authenticated logon, which means that when users try to access a Windows 2000 network, they must provide credentials for authentication. These credentials usually take the form of a username and password; however, Windows 2000 can also authenticate credentials that take the form of certificates. IIS supports five authentication models: Anonymous access, Basic authentication, Integrated Windows authentication, Digest authentication, and client certificate mapping. One of these methods must be used to authenticate users before they can gain access to resources in IIS. This lesson describes each of these authentication models and provides information on how to choose an authentication model for your Web site.

After this lesson, you will be able to
- Describe the Web authentication models supported by IIS
- Determine which authentication model to use for your Web site

Estimated lesson time: 30 minutes

IIS Authentication Models

In Windows 2000, *authentication* refers to the process of verifying the identity of entities that communicate over a network. Authentication allows initial access to the operating system. For example, suppose a user is trying to log on to a computer by providing a username and password. Windows 2000 compares that username and password to an authorized list. If the credentials are valid, the user is allowed to log on to the system and can then access resources controlled by the system.

Once a user is authenticated, Windows 2000 attaches a security token to all processes (applications) that the user runs. The token identifies the user and the Windows groups to which the user belongs. If a user tries to access an object in the network, such as a file, Windows 2000 compares the user information in the token to the information in the object's access control list (ACL), which is a list of security protections that apply to the object. The ACL determines who can gain access to a resource in a Windows 2000 environment.

Before a user can access resources in IIS, that user must be authenticated. If the Web site is set up for Anonymous access, the IUSR_*computername* account is used, and users are not prompted for credentials. If the Web site is set up for nonanonymous authentication, they are prompted for credentials. The authentication process includes a number of steps:

1. The Web browser requests the page.
2. The Web server performs an authentication check. If the authentication check fails, the server sends an error message to the browser, along with information that the browser needs to resubmit the request as an authenticated request.

3. The Web browser uses the server's response to construct a new request that contains authentication information.

4. The Web server performs an authentication check. If the check is successful, the server sends the requested page back to the browser.

Each Hypertext Transfer Protocol (HTTP) request from a browser runs within the security context of the user account. The operations that are performed when the HTTP request is executed are limited by the capabilities granted to that account.

IIS supports five authentication models: Anonymous, Basic, Integrated Windows, Digest, and client certificate mapping. This rest of this section discusses each of these models.

Anonymous Access

Windows 2000 allows only valid users to log on to its system. However, the Internet, for the most part, is a very anonymous environment, and relatively few Web sites prompt visitors for a username and password. To work around this situation, IIS provides the IUSR_*computername* account so that a real Windows account can be used when you want to provide anonymous users access to your resources. The account gives anonymous users the right to log on locally. Windows 2000 uses the IUSR_*computername* account when anonymous users are authenticated with Anonymous access.

Figure 10.1 illustrates the authentication process that occurs when an anonymous user requests a page from a site that's set up with Anonymous access. From the user's perspective, the request is a straightforward process and the page is returned without the user being prompted for a username and password.

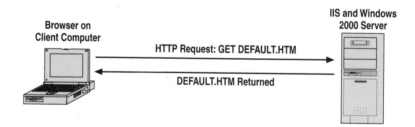

Figure 10.1   Anonymous access to the DEFAULT.HTM file

When IIS is configured for Anonymous access, a password must be created for the IUSR_*computername* account. This password must be the same in IIS and in Windows 2000. By default, the password is synchronized automatically. (The Allow IIS To Control Password check box in the Internet Services Manager tool is selected.) When this option is enabled, IIS uses a subauthenticator to inform Windows that the password is correct. Although this makes administration easier, it can present problems when a user is trying to access some network resources, such as a Microsoft Access database.

In these cases, you must disable automatic synchronization (by deselecting the check box). Authentication is then performed differently from when it is enabled. Rather than using a subauthenticator, IIS calls the LogonUser() application programming interface (API) in Windows to log the account on to the system. As a result, you must then ensure that the username and password are set up correctly in Windows 2000. If the username and password match when IIS passes them to Windows 2000, the account is successfully logged on, the security token is cached by IIS 5.0, and the account is impersonated.

Basic Authentication

Basic authentication is part of the HTTP 1.0 specification and is supported by most Web servers and most Web browsers. Unlike Anonymous access, Basic authentication requires a user to provide credentials in order to log on to the system. Users must have local logon rights to the Web server in order to be authenticated. You can use Basic authentication to track who has access to which resources, based on the user ID, so that you can restrict access to some parts of the Web server. Basic authentication uses NT file system (NTFS) security to restrict access to files on an IIS Web server.

Figure 10.2 illustrates the authentication process that occurs when a user requests a page from a site that's set up with Basic authentication. After users request the page, they're prompted for a user name and password.

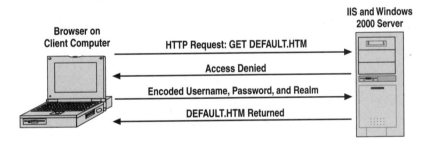

Figure 10.2   Basic access to the DEFAULT.HTM file

In Basic authentication, passwords are encoded, but not securely encrypted, so the authentication process isn't very secure. HTTP authentication headers can be intercepted and password data decoded. However, you can use Basic authentication along with Secure Sockets Layer (SSL) to establish a secure session. SSL is discussed in more detail in Lesson 3, "Designing an Encryption Strategy."

Integrated Windows Authentication

Integrated Windows authentication, which is more secure than Basic authentication, supports NT LAN Manager (NTLM) authentication and Kerberos authentication. In Integrated Windows authentication, the browser first attempts to use the current user's credentials from a domain logon. If those credentials are rejected, the user is prompted for a username and password. However, Windows 2000 doesn't send an NTLM or Kerberos challenge. Instead, it sends a Negotiate header that allows the client and server to negotiate an authentication protocol. The client then sends a response to the server.

Integrated Windows authentication is well suited to an intranet environment where all users have Windows domain accounts. However, Integrated Windows authentication has the following limitations:

- It can't be used through proxy server connections.
- It's supported only by Microsoft Internet Explorer 2 or later.
- It might not always support delegation to other servers, such as a SQL Server computer, depending on whether Kerberos or NTLM is being used, whether a nonauthenticated protocol (such as the Transmission Control Protocol/Internet Protocol [TCP/IP] network library) is used to connect to the remote server, or whether the remote server is part of a cluster.

Digest Authentication

Unlike Basic authentication, Digest authentication encrypts passwords before transmitting them from the client to the server. Authentication credentials pass through a one-way process in which the original text can't be deciphered. The server adds additional information to the credentials so that no one can intercept the transmission and use it to impersonate the true client. In addition, Digest authentication can be used though proxy server connections. However, Digest authentication is supported only for Windows 2000 domains, and only a few browsers, including Internet Explorer 5, support this authentication model.

Client Certificate Mapping

Windows 2000 supports a public key infrastructure (PKI) that provides the framework of services, technology, protocols, and standards necessary to deploy and manage a security system that's based on public key technology. Public key technology uses public keys and private keys to provide authentication, confidentiality, integrity, and nonrepudiation. Public keys and private keys must be used together to provide these services; by themselves, they can't prove that the public and private key set belong to the key set owner. The two keys are different, but they complement each other in function.

In public key technology, an intended recipient's public key is accessible by other people to use to encrypt information that will be sent to the recipient. Once encrypted, the information is sent to the recipient, who then uses the private key to decrypt that information. Figure 10.3 provides an overview of the public key process.

One of the main components of a PKI is the digital certificate. A *digital certificate* is a set of electronic credentials that are used to certify the online identities of individuals, organizations, and computers. Certificates are issued and certified by

Certification Authorities (CAs). Windows 2000 includes a CA service, which is part of Certificate Services, one of the main components of the Windows 2000 PKI.

A CA issues certificates to provide proof for verifying the identity of online entities. The certificate identifies the certificate's owner and contains the owner's public key. Certificates, which are available to anyone, are commonly distributed by means of directories, public folders, e-mail, and Web pages. A PKI provides the foundation for managing certificates and private keys throughout the certificate life cycle.

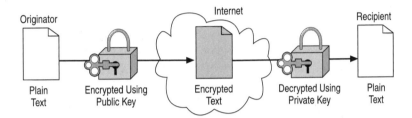

Figure 10.3   Public key technology used to encrypt information

IIS can use client certificates to authenticate users by mapping certificates to Windows 2000 user accounts. When a user presents a certificate, IIS looks at the mapping to determine which user account should be logged on, as shown in Figure 10.4. Certificate mapping is based on the client ownership of a valid authentication certificate.

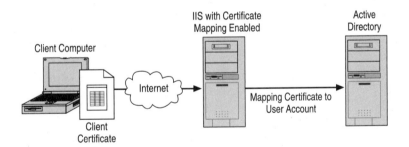

Figure 10.4   Mapping client certificate to user account

When certificate mapping is enabled in IIS, Windows 2000 authenticates users and grants rights and permissions based on the mapped user account. IIS supports two types of certificate mapping: one-to-one and one-to-many.

Note   You can use the Active Directory service to map client certificates in order to control access to network resources for domain users accounts. However, to control access to Web site resources, you should use IIS.

One-to-One Certificate Mapping

In one-to-one mapping, you map a certificate to the corresponding Windows 2000 user account for the owner of that certificate. IIS authenticates the user and grants access to resources based on user account information. To use one-to-one mapping, clients must have Windows 2000 user accounts.

Many-to-One Certificate Mapping

In many-to-one mapping, you map the certificates of many users to a single user account. The user account becomes the security context for all the users. Rights and permissions granted to the users are based on the rights and permissions granted to the user account. You can configure IIS and NTFS access rights to permit access to users with the mapped certificates or refuse access to those users. You can also use separate many-to-one certificate mappings for each group that you want to grant Web site access. In general, it's easier to administer many-to-one mappings than one-to-one mappings. One-to-one mapping is practical when you're supporting a relatively small number of clients, but when you must grant Web access to a large number of users, you should use many-to-one.

Making a Decision

IIS supports five authentication models that you can use to authenticate your Web clients. Table 10.1 provides considerations that you should take into account when choosing an authentication model.

Table 10.1   Client Authentication Models

Authentication Model	Description
Anonymous access	Anonymous access allows all Web clients to access a site and works with most browsers. IIS uses the IUSR_*computername* account to provide anonymous users with the right to log on locally. Anonymous access provides no authentication. If password synchronization is enabled, Anonymous access can't access remote resources; however, if synchronization is disabled, Anonymous access can access remote resources.
Basic authentication	Basic authentication requires that a user provide credentials in order to log on to the system. Users must have local logon rights to the Web server in order to be authenticated. Most browsers support Basic authentication. In Basic authentication, passwords are encoded, but not securely encrypted, so the authentication process isn't very secure. However, you can use Basic authentication along with SSL to establish a secure session.
Integrated Windows authentication	Integrated Windows authentication is more secure than Basic authentication, and it supports NTLM authentication and Kerberos authentication. Integrated Windows authentication can't be used through proxy server connections and has limited browser support.

Table 10.1 *(continued)*

Authentication Model	Description
Digest authentication	Digest authentication encrypts passwords before transmitting them from the client to the server, and it can be used through proxy server connections. However, Digest authentication is supported only for Windows 2000 domains, and only a few browsers, including Internet Explorer 5, support this authentication model. Digest authentication requires Active Directory.
Client certificate mapping	You can use certificate mapping in IIS to authenticate users by mapping certificates to Windows 2000 user accounts. When certificate mapping is enabled in IIS, Windows 2000 authenticates users and grants rights and permissions based on the mapped user account. IIS supports two types of certificate mapping: one-to-one and one-to-many. Certificate mapping is very scalable and secure, but not all browsers support it. In addition, certificate mapping can be cumbersome to configure.

Recommendations

You must first decide whether you even need to authenticate users who are accessing your Web site. If authentication isn't necessary, you can configure Anonymous access. If authentication is necessary, you must choose one of the other authentication models. If you can't control the type of browsers that your users are using, then you should most likely use Basic authentication. However, because Basic isn't secure, you should use it in conjunction with SSL, which is discussed in Lesson 3, "Designing an Encryption Strategy." If you can control which browsers your clients are using, you might consider one of the other authentication models, depending on how your network is configured. If you choose certificate mapping, then you must decide whether to use a one-to-one or a one-to-many mapping strategy, which will depend on the number of users you're supporting. You can use one-to-one for a small number of users, but for large numbers you should use many-to-one.

Example: Authentication Strategy for Trey Research

Trey Research maintains a Web site that provides services to its online clients. The site includes two components: one public and one private. Any Internet user can access the public component of the site; however, only a specific group of users can access the private one. Each of the users in this group must supply a username and password to access the private Web pages. Users accessing both public and private Web pages use a variety of browsers on their client computers.

The public component of the site uses Anonymous access to allow users to visit the public Web pages. The IUSR_*computername* account is configured to automatically synchronize the account's password. The private component uses Basic authentication with SSL to protect the content of this portion of the site.

Figure 10.5 provides an overview of the two authentication models used to support Trey Research clients.

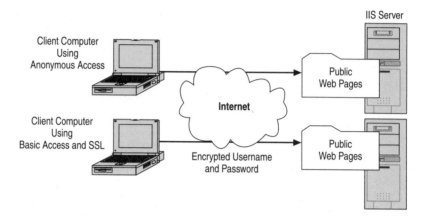

Figure 10.5   Anonymous access and Basic authentication

Lesson Summary

Before a user can access resources in IIS, that user must be authenticated. IIS supports five authentication models: Anonymous, Basic, Integrated Windows, Digest, and client certificate mapping. Anonymous access allows users to log on locally to the Web server. From the user's perspective, site access is a straightforward process, and the user isn't prompted for a username and password. Basic authentication requires that a user provide credentials in order to log on to the system. Users must have local logon rights to the Web server in order to be authenticated. Integrated Windows authentication supports NTLM authentication and Kerberos authentication. However, Integrated Windows authentication can't be used through proxy servers, has limited browser support, and doesn't always support delegation to others servers. Digest authentication encrypts passwords before transmitting them from the client to the server. However, Digest authentication is supported only for Windows 2000 domains, and only a few browsers, including Internet Explorer 5, support this authentication model. IIS can use client certificates to authenticate users by mapping certificates to Windows 2000 user accounts. IIS supports two types of certificate mapping: one-to-one and one-to-many.

Lesson 2: Designing an Authorization Strategy

Once users have been authenticated, they'll want to access resources on your site. For example, for users to be able to read HTML files, they must be authorized to access those files and the directories that contain the files. Authentication alone doesn't provide users with the rights they need to access these resources. As a result, you must a develop an authorization strategy that will provide users with these rights without compromising the security of other resources on your network. In this lesson you'll learn what factors you must consider when designing an authorization strategy. You'll also learn how to set up your NTFS and IIS security to support authorization.

After this lesson, you will be able to

- Describe how access to resources is granted to Web clients
- Determine how users will be authorized to access resources on your Web site

Estimated lesson time: 25 minutes

User Authorization

In a Windows 2000 domain, *authorization* refers to the process of allowing a user to access resources in your network. Unlike authentication, which verifies the identities of the users and allows them initial access to the operating system, authorization allows access to specific Web sites, directories, and files (by configuring IIS permissions) and specific NTFS files and folders (by configuring NTFS permissions). However, in order for a user to be authorized to access a resource, that user must first be authenticated.

Note   Configuring user authentication is a complex process, particularly when implementing distributed applications in a multitiered environment. You must take into account considerations such as delegation, application access, application topology, clustering, and a number of other factors, depending on your network configuration and security requirements. This lesson provides an overview of how to plan your authentication; however, you should review other resources as well to acquire a complete picture.

Overview of Access Process

When a user attempts to access a resource through IIS, a number of sequential events occur, as shown in Figure 10.6. The following sections describe these various events.

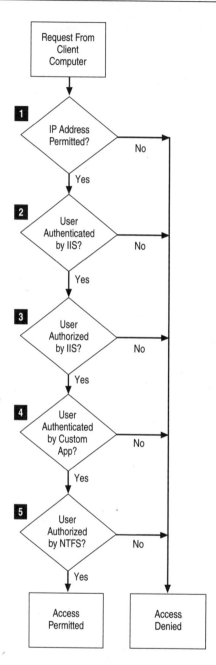

Figure 10.6   Accessing resources through IIS

1. IP Address Access Control

When a request is made for a resource, IIS determines whether the client's
Internet Protocol (IP) address should be denied access to the Web site or virtual

directory. You can configure IIS to grant or deny access to specific IP addresses, networks, or domain names. You can either grant access to all computers except those specifically listed, or you can deny access to all computers except those specifically listed. However, keep in mind that some users might try to access your site through proxy servers or firewalls—in which case the incoming connection will appear to have originated from the proxy server or firewall.

2. IIS Authentication

If IIS accepts a user's IP address, the user is authenticated by one of the following authentication methods supported by IIS: Anonymous, Basic, Integrated Windows, Digest, or client certificate mapping. A successful logon must meet the following criteria:

- Valid username and password
- No applicable Windows 2000 account restrictions (such as time of day allowed to log on)
- Account not disabled or locked out
- Account password not expired
- An applicable logon policy (such as Log On Locally)

3. IIS Authorization

Once a user is authenticated, IIS then determines what permissions have been assigned to the resource that the user is trying to access. In IIS, Web permissions apply to all users trying to access one of the site's resources. Only NTFS permissions can be configured to apply to a specific user or group of users. For example, if you configure a Web site to support the Read permission, all users who are authenticated to access that site are granted the Read permission unless NTFS permissions restrict which users can access that site. IIS and NTFS permissions are discussed in more detail later in this section.

4. Custom Application Authentication

Some organizations develop their own methods for authenticating users. For example, they might use Internet Server Application Programming Interface (ISAPI) filters or Active Server Pages (ASP) applications to support a custom authentication scheme. If custom authentication is used, users are authenticated after they've been authorized by IIS.

5. NTFS Authorization

At the base of the IIS access model is NTFS security. IIS uses the authenticated user's security context to try to gain access to a specific resource. For anonymous users, the IUSR_*computername* account is used. For authenticated users, a valid Windows account is used. If NTFS permissions don't allow specific accounts to access a resource, users associated with those accounts can't access that resource, even if they've been authenticated and authorized by IIS. NTFS permissions are discussed in more detail later in this section.

Planning IIS Permissions

As mentioned earlier, IIS permissions apply to all users who are authenticated to access a Web site. IIS permissions control access to virtual directories, whereas NTFS controls access to physical directories. You can set IIS permissions on Web sites, virtual directories, directories, and files. Table 10.2 describes the types of permissions that you can configure through IIS. Note that the Directory Browsing permission and the Index This Resource permission aren't available as file-level permissions.

Table 10.2   IIS Permissions

Permission	Description
Script Source Access	Users can access the source code for files, such as the scripts in an ASP application. This permission is available only if the Read permission or the Write permission is selected. If the Read permission is selected, the user can read source code. If the Write permission is selected, the user can write to source code.
Read	Users can view file content and properties. This permission is selected by default.
Write	Users can change file content and properties.
Directory Browsing	Users can view files lists and collections.
Log Visits	A log entry is created for each visit to the Web site, directory, or file.
Index This Resource	The Indexing Service can index this resource.

IIS permissions also allow you to set up how executable content (such as ASP pages) in a directory will operate. Table 10.3 describes the types of executable permissions that you can configure through IIS.

Table 10.3   IIS Executable Permissions

Permission	Description
None	No scripts or executables can run in this directory.
Scripts Only	Scripts can run in this directory, without having Execute permission. Use the Scripts Only permission for directories that contain ASP pages, Internet Database Connector (IDC) scripts, or other scripts.
Scripts and Executables	Executables and scripts can run in this directory, including .asp, .dll, and .exe files.

Note that if both IIS and NTFS permissions are set, the most restrictive settings take effect. For example, if you disable the IIS Read permission on a file, users won't be able to view that file, even if they're explicitly granted NTFS permissions.

Planning NTFS Permissions

NTFS permissions are based on how access to Windows 2000 objects is controlled. As you learned in Lesson 1, "Designing an Authentication Strategy," once a user is authenticated, Windows 2000 attaches a security token to all processes (applications) that the user runs. The token identifies the user and the Windows groups to which the user belongs. If the user tries to access a file, Windows 2000 compares the user information in the token to the information with the object's ACL.

Each object in Windows 2000 contains a *security descriptor,* which is the access control information associated with that object. When a user tries to access the object, Windows 2000 examines the security descriptor to determine whether the user is allowed to access the object and what action the user is allowed to take with that object. A security descriptor is a binary data structure that contains the following parts:

- **Header**   Contains a revision number and a set of control flags that describe the security descriptor's characteristics.
- **Owner**   Contains the security identifier (SID) for the object's owner.
- **Primary Group**   Contains the SID for the owner's primary group.
- **Discretionary Access Control List (DACL)**   Contains a list of access control entries (ACEs). Each ACE includes a header that specifies whether the ACE allows or denies access, a SID that identifies a particular user or group, and information about which operations are allowed or denied.
- **System Access Control List (SACL)**   Contains a list of ACEs used to audit access to an object.

The DACL controls access to the specific object. For example, if an authenticated user tries to access a directory, the security token attached to the IIS process is compared to the information in the DACL to determine whether that user has permission to access that directory. Figure 10.7 provides an overview of the authorization process that occurs when a user tries to access a directory in an NTFS partition.

You can control the information in the DACL by setting NTFS directory and file permissions, which allows you to secure individual files and directories from unauthorized access. Table 10.4 describes the types of NTFS permissions that you can configure in the DACL of a file or directory. You can either allow or deny each of these permissions. Denied permissions take precedence over allowed permissions.

When you define NTFS permissions, you must first select the specific users and groups to which you'll grant or deny access, and from there, you must specify the access permissions for each user or group. Make sure you remove all unnecessary users and groups from the DACL, as well as remove groups that are too general for your purpose. However, be careful about removing the Everyone group because removing it can cause even nonanonymous access to fail. To support nonanonymous access, you should grant the Full Control permission to the Administrator, Creator/Owner, and System accounts. In addition, you should grant the appropriate permissions to any authenticated users or groups that will be accessing the resource.

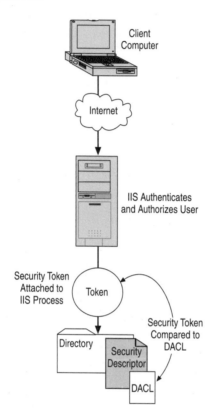

Figure 10.7   Accessing an NTFS directory through IIS

Table 10.4   NTFS Permissions

Permission	Description
Full Control	Users can modify, add, move, and delete files, their associated properties, and directories. They can change permission settings for all files and subdirectories.
Modify	Users can view and modify files and file properties, including deleting and adding files to a directory or file properties to a file.
Read & Execute	Users can run executable files, including scripts.
List Folder Contents	Users can view a list of a directory's content.
Read	Users can view files and file properties.
Write	Users can write to a file.

Making a Decision

When authorizing users to access Web resources, you must configure IIS permissions and NTFS permissions. Table 10.5 provides an overview of the considerations that you should take into account when setting up permissions.

Table 10.5   IIS and NTFS Permissions

Type of Permissions	Considerations
IIS permissions	IIS permissions apply to all users authenticated to access your Web site. You can set permissions on individual Web sites, virtual directories, directories, and files.
NTFS permissions	NTFS permissions apply to specific users and groups. You can set permissions on individual directories and files. You can either allow or deny each type of NTFS permission. Denied permissions take precedence over allowed permissions.

Recommendations

An authorization strategy is unique to the organization that's implementing the Web site. However, whatever strategy you implement, you must take into account the following characteristics of IIS and NTFS permissions:

- IIS permissions apply to all users, and NTFS permissions apply to specific users and groups. If your site supports anonymous users, you must ensure that the appropriate NTFS permissions are granted to the IUSR_*computername* account. If your site supports nonanonymous users, you must ensure that the appropriate NTFS permissions support those specific users or groups of users.

- If IIS permissions and NTFS permissions are in conflict, the most restrictive permissions are used. You must make sure that both IIS and NTFS permissions are configured in a way that prevents conflict.

- Deny permissions take precedence over allow permissions. If you deny access to an NTFS directory to a specific user, it doesn't matter what IIS permissions you grant. The user won't be able to access that directory. Also, if a user or group isn't included in the NTFS permissions, Windows 2000 interprets this as meaning that the user or group is being denied access to that directory, and directory access is denied.

You should remove all unnecessary users and groups. For example, suppose you have a Web site that supports anonymous and nonanonymous users. However, you want only the nonanonymous users to be able to access a specific directory. You grant Read permission in IIS to that directory, and you grant Read permission in NTFS to the nonanonymous users. However, you fail to remove the Everyone group in the DACL for the directory. As a result, all users will have access to that directory.

Example: Authorization Strategy for Wide World Importers

Wide World Importers implemented a Web site that supports anonymous users and a set of users who must enter a name and password in order to log on to secure areas of the site. Administrators at the company created a separate virtual root for the secure information. In addition, they created a user group (PrivateUsers) to contain all the users who had to be authenticated. As a result, the administrators had to develop two authorization strategies: one for the anonymous users and one for the nonanonymous users. The site supports static content only.

The administrators assigned the following IIS permissions to both the public site and the private site:

- Read
- Log Visits
- Index The Resource

However, they assigned different NTFS permissions to each site. Table 10.6 shows the permissions that were assigned to each user and group in the Public site.

Table 10.6   NTFS Permissions for the Public Site

User or Group	Type of Permission
Administrators	Full Control
System	Full Control
Creator/Owner	Full Control
IUSR_*computername*	Read

Table 10.7 shows the permissions that were assigned to each user and group in the Private site.

Table 10.7   NTFS Permissions for the Private Site

User or Group	Type of Permission
Administrators	Full Control
System	Full Control
Creator/Owner	Full Control
PrivateUsers	Read

Lesson Summary

Authorization allows access to specific Web sites, directories, and files (by configuring IIS permissions) and specific NTFS files and folders (by configuring NTFS permissions). When a user attempts to access a resource through IIS, a number of sequential events occur, including IP address access control, IIS authentication, IIS authorization, custom applications authentication, and NTFS authorization. IIS permissions apply to all users who are authenticated to access a Web site. You can set IIS permissions on Web sites, virtual directories, directories, and files. NTFS permissions are specific to users and groups. When a user tries to access the object, Windows 2000 examines the object's DACL to determine whether the user is allowed to access the object and what action the user is allowed to take with that object. You can control the information in the DACL by setting NTFS directory and file permissions, which allows you to secure individual files and directories from unauthorized access. When you define NTFS permissions, you must first select the users and groups to which you'll grant or deny access, and from there you must specify the access permissions for each user or group. If IIS permissions and NTFS permissions are in conflict, the most restrictive permissions are used.

Activity 10.1: Troubleshooting Access Permissions

You're an administrator for Lucerne Publishing. The company has recently implemented a Web site for anonymous users. The site contains only static content. You tested the Web site in a lab environment and everything seemed to work fine. However, anonymous users aren't able to access your site.

You review the access process to try to find the problem. You first check the Web site's properties in IIS and determine that the site is configured for Anonymous access and that all IP addresses, networks, and domains have been granted access. You then check IIS permissions and determine that the site is configured with the following properties:

- Log Visits
- Index The Resource

You next check the properties for the physical directory where the Web files are stored. Table 10.8 lists the properties for each group and user for that directory.

Table 10.8   NTFS Permissions for the Web Site

User or Group	Type of Permission
Administrators	Full Control
System	Full Control
Creator/Owner	Full Control
IUSR_*computername*	Read

1. Why can't users access the Web site?

2. Assume that the IIS Read permission has been enabled but that nonanonymous users would be accessing the account rather than anonymous users. How would you need to modify the permissions?

3. What steps in the access process occur when a user attempts to access a resource?

Lesson 3: Designing an Encryption Strategy

Windows 2000 Server supports several technologies that allow you to encrypt data transmitted across the Internet or stored on a hard disk. These technologies include SSL, Internet Protocol Security (IPSec), and Encrypting File System (EFS). By using encryption technologies, you can cryptographically encode information transmitted and received by your Web server, thereby securing the privacy and integrity of that data. This lesson describes each of these technologies and provides information on how to determine which technology to use and when to implement it.

After this lesson, you will be able to

- Describe SSL, IPSec, and EFS
- Determine when to use SSL, IPSec, and EFS

Estimated lesson time: 25 minutes

Data Encryption

One of the primary concerns of many Web administrators is how to prevent message flow to anyone other than the intended recipient. One way to ensure privacy is through the use of encryption. *Encryption* is the process of scrambling data (by applying a mathematical function) transmitted across an unsecured network, such as the Internet, so that an unintended recipient can't intercept the data. (You can also encrypt stored data.) At the heart of this process is a mathematical value, referred to as a key, that the function uses to scramble the information in a unique or complex way. Once a secure link has been established between a Web browser (on a client) and a Web server, the two systems use a session key to encrypt and decrypt information.

SSL

SSL uses a combination of symmetric encryption and public key encryption. *Symmetric encryption* means that the key used to encrypt data, the session key, is the same as the one used to decrypt it. *Public key encryption* means that two keys—one public key and one private key—are used to encrypt and decrypt data. Public key encryption is used to shield the session key from interception during transmission.

An SSL connection between the Web browser and IIS must use Hypertext Transfer Protocol Secure (HTTPS) as its protocol type, rather than HTTP. HTTPS instructs the server to use a different port for communication. By default, HTTP uses port 80, but HTTPS uses port 443.

Before a browser can establish an SSL connection with IIS, you must request and install a certificate for the IIS server. You can acquire a certificate from a trusted third party, such as VeriSign. You can also use IIS to request a certificate from Windows 2000 Certificate Services. (Note that a Web server can have only one certificate assigned to it.) A server certificate allows client computers to authenticate your server, check the validity of Web content, and establish a secure connection. The server certificate also contains a public key, which the browser uses to encrypt information about the session key to send to the server.

Figure 10.8 provides an overview of how SSL encryption works. The following list describes each step.

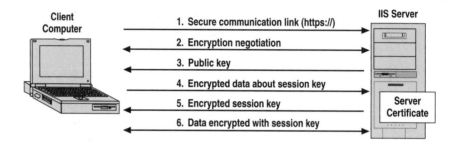

Figure 10.8   SSL encryption process

The SSL encryption process uses the following steps:

1. The Web browser establishes a secure communication link (https://) with IIS.
2. The Web browser and IIS negotiate the degree of encryption to use for secure communication.
3. IIS sends the browser its public key.
4. The Web browser uses the server's public key to encrypt data that the server will use to generate a session key. The browser sends the encrypted data to IIS.
5. IIS uses its private key to decrypt session key data. IIS then generates a session key, encrypts it with the public key, and sends it to the browser.
6. The Web browser and IIS use the session key to encrypt and decrypt transmitted data.

A session key's strength is proportional to the number of bits that make up the key. Session keys with a greater number of bits have a greater degree of security and are more difficult to forcibly decode. When a browser establishes a secure communication channel with IIS, the client and server negotiate the strongest possible level of encryption. However, the browser must be able to support the level of session key encryption that's configured in IIS. For example, if you configure IIS to support a session key strength of 40 bits or greater, the Web browser must be able to support at least a 40-bit session key.

Note   You can configure IIS to require a 128-bit minimum session key. However, because of export restrictions, the 128-bit key strength encryption feature is available only in the United States and Canada.

SSL uses a complex encryption process and requires considerable processor resources. As a result, it takes much longer to retrieve and send data from SSL directories. You should use SSL only when encrypting private data, such as authentication data or credit card numbers. You should also try to keep pages free of or limit the use of elements that consume resources but aren't necessary, such as images and sound files.

SSL works at the application layer of the TCP/IP protocol stack, which is comparable to the application, presentation, and session layers of the Open Systems Interconnection (OSI) model, as shown in Figure 10.9. (Note that IPSec is also shown in the figure. IPSec is discussed in the next section.) As a result, applications that use SSL must be SSL-aware, as are most Web browsers (such as Internet Explorer) and Web servers (such as IIS). For this reason, SSL has become an Internet standard for encrypting data and is relatively easy to implement.

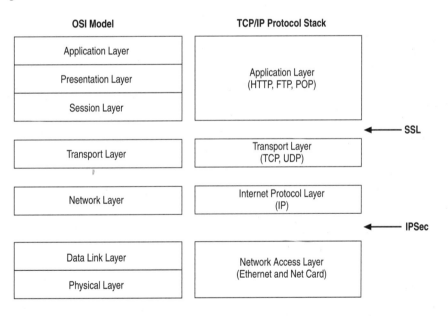

Figure 10.9   SSL and IPSec in the TCP/IP protocol stack and OSI model

Note Windows 2000 supports Transport Layer Security (TLS) as well as SSL. TLS is similar to SSL and is considered by many the likely successor to SSL. Although TLS uses a combination of public key and symmetric encryption, it supports different encryption algorithms than SSL and is an Internet Engineering Task Force (IETF) draft standard. Like SSL, applications that use TLS must be TLS-enabled.

IPSec

Like SSL, IPSec can be used to encrypt and secure data. IPSec is a suite of protocols that allow two computers to communicate over an insecure network through the use of cryptographic security services. The encryption is applied at the IP layer in the TCP/IP protocol suite (the network layer in the OSI model).

As a result, IPSec is transparent to most applications that use specific protocols for network communication, unlike SSL, which provides security only to applications that know how to use SSL. This offers a high level of protection for most applications, services, and upper layer protocols, including Transmission Control Protocol (TCP), User Datagram Protocol (UDP), and Internet Control Message Protocol (ICMP). All applications and services using IP for transport can be protected with IPSec without any modifications to those services or applications.

In IPSec communications, IP packets are encrypted by the sending computer and decrypted by the recipient computer. The packets are unreadable en route, providing end-to-end security. In addition, because of a special algorithm used to generate the same shared encryption key at both ends of the connection, the key doesn't need to be passed over the network.

Figure 10.10 provides an overview of the IPSec communication process. The following list describes the steps.

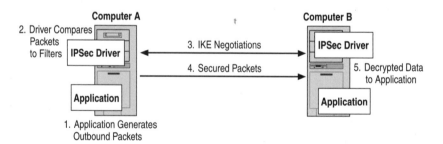

Figure 10.10 IPSec communication process

IPSec has many components and options, and IPSec communication is a detailed, complex process. However, at a high level, IPSec communication operates in the following manner:

1. An application on Computer A generates outbound packets to send to Computer B across the network.

2. The IPSec driver on Computer A compares the outbound packets against IPSec filters to determine whether the packets need to be secured.

3. If a filter indicates that a security action must be taken, Computer A begins security negotiations with Computer B, using the Internet Key Exchange (IKE) protocol. The two computers exchange identity credentials according to the authentication method specified in the security rule.

4. The IPSec driver on Computer A signs the outgoing packets for integrity, encrypts them for confidentiality, and transmits the secured packets to Computer B.

5. The IPSec driver on Computer B checks the packets for integrity, decrypts their content, and transfers them to the receiving application.

IPSec authentication methods include Kerberos authentication, public key certificates, and preshared key values. IPSec doesn't have to be configured on firewalls; however, for IPSec to work, the firewall must be configured to allow certain port and protocol IDs to pass through. In addition, the firewall can't be performing Network Address Translation (NAT) because IPSec protects the fields within the packets that NAT would normally modify.

IPSec also doesn't have to be configured on routers or servers along the network path; they simply pass along the packets in the usual manner. However, to use IPSec, the computers on both ends of the communication link must be configured with Windows 2000 and have IPSec security policies defined, so this can limit your use of IPSec for Web-based solutions unless you can restrict your client base to Windows 2000 computers. You can, however, use IPSec within your network to provide an additional layer of security. For example, you might want to use IPSec for communication between your IIS servers on a front-end tier and SQL Server computers on a back-end tier.

When implementing IPSec, you should be aware that it requires a considerable amount of processing power (even more so than SSL), so you must take into consideration system performance when implementing it.

In addition, setting up IPSec, unlike SSL, is a complex process that can involve configuring policies, rules, filters, connection types, and authentication methods. Before implementing IPSec, you should develop a security plan that defines how your security policies will be implemented in your organization.

EFS

You can use EFS to protect sensitive data that's stored on an NTFS partition. It runs as an integrated system service that's transparent to the file owner and to applications. Only the file owner can open the file and work with it.

EFS uses symmetric key encryption in conjunction with public key technology to provide confidentiality for files, while ensuring that only the file's owner can access it. EFS uses a symmetric bulk encryption key, called the *file encryption key* (FEK), to encrypt the file. The FEK is then encrypted by using the public key taken from the user's certificate, which is located in the user's profile. EFS uses the encryptor's private key to decrypt the FEK. To minimize the processor load, EFS encrypts data symmetrically with the FEK and then encrypts and decrypts the FEK asymmetrically with the public and private keys.

Although you can use EFS to encrypt or decrypt data stored on a remote computer, it doesn't encrypt the data as it's sent over the network. For that, you must use another technology, such as SSL.

Making a Decision

Windows 2000 supports several technologies that use encryption to protect data from network attacks. Three of these technologies are SSL, IPSec, and EFS. Table 10.9 discusses many of the considerations that you must take into account when deciding whether to use these technologies.

Table 10.9   Encrypting Technologies

Technology	Considerations
SSL	SSL is an Internet standard commonly used to encrypt data. Applications that use SSL must be SSL-aware, as most Web browsers and Web servers are. SSL requires considerable processor resources, compared to not encrypting and decrypting data. SSL supports authentication through the use of public key certificates.
IPSec	IPSec works at the IP layer of the TCP/IP protocol stack and is transparent to most applications. This offers a high level of protection for most applications, services, and upper layer protocols. IPSec supports authentication through Kerberos authentication, public key certificates, and preshared key values. However, to use IPSec, the computers on both ends of the communication link must be configured with Windows 2000 and have IPSec security policies defined. In addition, IPSec requires more processor power than SSL.
EFS	EFS can be used to protect sensitive data stored on a disk, but it doesn't protect data transmitted over a network.

Recommendations

In the Internet environment that exists today, you should use SSL to protect data transmitted across the Internet, unless you operate a small site and all your clients are configured with Windows 2000, in which case you might consider IPSec. If you want to add an additional layer of security to your system, you can use IPSec on the back end of your network to protect data transmitted within your private network. For highly sensitive data, you can also use EFS to encrypt that data where it's stored on a drive.

Example: Encryption Strategy for City Power & Light

City Power & Light offers an online service to its customers for reviewing their current and past charges and updating their customer profiles. Customers can access the company's public site as anonymous users; however, to view confidential information they must enter a username and password. Customers use a variety of browsers and operating systems on their computers, so access must be provided for a diverse user base. Users access the public site at *http://www.cpandl.com*. From there, they can then link to the secure site at *https://www.cpandl.com/secure*, at which time they're prompted for a username and password.

Users are authenticated through Basic authentication and their data is protected through SSL. The applications used to access confidential information are located on a virtual directory separate from the public site so that SSL is used only for those pages and for data that must be protected, which saves on processing power. Figure 10.11 provides an overview of the site structure.

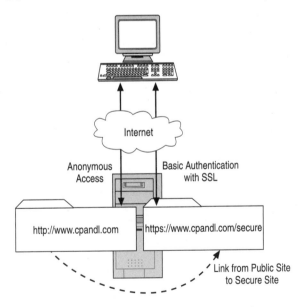

Figure 10.11   City Power & Light Web site

Lesson Summary

Encryption is the process of scrambling data (by applying a mathematical function) transmitted across an unsecured network so that data can't be intercepted by an unintended recipient. Windows 2000 Server supports several technologies that allow you to encrypt data, including SSL, IPSec, and EPS. SSL uses a combination of symmetric encryption and public key encryption. Before a browser can establish an SSL connection with IIS, you must request and install a certificate for the IIS server. Applications that use SSL must be SSL-aware, as most Web browsers and Web servers are. SSL has become an Internet standard for encrypting data and is relatively easy to implement, although it does consume more processing power than unencrypted data. IPSec is a suite of protocols that allow two computers to communicate over an insecure network through the use of cryptographic security services. IPSec is transparent to most applications that use specific protocols for network communication; however, only Windows 2000 operating systems support IPSec. IPSec uses more processing power than SSL. You can use EFS to protect sensitive data that's stored on an NTFS partition. However, EFS doesn't encrypt the data as it's sent over the network. For that, you must use another technology, such as SSL.

Lesson 4: Designing a Firewall Strategy

In Lessons 1 through 3, you learned about designing authentication, authorization, and encryption strategies in order to secure your Web site and your internal network against outside attacks. Another strategy that you can use to secure your network is to implement firewall protection. Although firewalls, by themselves, don't completely safeguard your network, they do provide an added layer of security that can help prevent access to, or the destruction of, sensitive data. This lesson provides an overview of firewalls and describes firewall strategies that you can implement in your organization.

After this lesson, you will be able to

- Describe various aspects of firewall technologies
- Design a firewall strategy to provide security to your Web site and private network

Estimated lesson time: 25 minutes

Firewall Security

A *firewall* is a combination of hardware and software that prevents unauthorized access from outside the firewall to an internal network or intranet. Firewalls restrict access to network resources by allowing traffic only through specified port numbers. They provide additional security and protection to the services that are running within the network.

Firewalls allow organizations to support Internet connectivity while minimizing the risks to sensitive data. They prevent unauthorized users from accessing your internal network resources by examining incoming and outgoing data and blocking traffic that isn't allowed. You can also use firewalls to control internal access to the Internet.

A firewall placed between your intranet and the Internet can partially protect your network from intrusion by controlling access from the Internet. However, you shouldn't place sole reliance on a firewall for Web site security. For example, viruses have been designed to breach firewalls and wreak havoc on your site. Once a firewall is breached, you must rely on other security measures to defend resources against intruders.

Data Filtering

A firewall examines and filters data as it passes through the firewall. Firewalls support various kinds of filtering. For example, Microsoft Internet Security and Acceleration (ISA) Server uses three methods of filtering data: packet filtering, circuit filtering, and application filtering.

Packet filters control the flow of IP packets to and from the firewall. Only explicitly allowed packets can pass through the firewall. Packet filtering can block packets that originate from specific Internet hosts and can reject packets associated with many common attacks. You can also use packet filtering to block packets destined to any service on your internal network. You can filter IP packets based on service type, port number, source computer name, and destination computer name.

A firewall that performs circuit filtering inspects and filters sessions rather than connections or packets. With circuit filtering, sessions, which can support multiple connections, can be established only in response to a user request. Circuit filtering supports Internet applications and services, such as Telnet, mail, news, and streaming media. The firewall allows these applications and services to perform as if they were directly connected to the Internet.

Application filters analyze a data stream for a particular application and can then inspect, screen, redirect, or modify the data as it passes through the firewall. These filters block known exploits such as unsafe Simple Mail Transfer Protocol (SMTP) commands or attacks against internal Domain Name System (DNS) servers. You can also use third-party tools in conjunction with application filters to further extend the firewall. Unlike packet filters, which examine the source, destination, and type of traffic, application filters inspect the actual content of the traffic passing through the firewall. As a result, application filters can perform application-specific tasks, such as accessing secondary connections transparently, blocking potentially harmful commands, and detecting viruses. Application filters support a number of Internet-related protocols, such as HTTP, File Transfer Protocol (FTP), and SMTP.

NAT

NAT translates private internal IP addresses to public external addresses in order to hide internally managed addresses from external networks. NAT allows you to use unregistered IP addresses internally and then use only a small number of registered IP addresses externally, which allows you to hide the internal network structure.

Some firewall services allow you to use NAT to support clients that have no special software. The firewalls provide transparent support for client computers with no special client software configured on those computers. For example, ISA Server uses SecureNAT to extend Windows 2000 NAT functionality. SecureNAT clients can be configured so that all traffic destined to the Internet is sent by way of ISA Server, either directly or indirectly, through a router. SecureNAT enables IP-based access control, content analysis by application filters, and use of the ISA Server cache through the HTTP filters. Servers that publish information to the Internet, such as mail servers, can be SecureNAT clients.

Proxy Servers

A proxy server manages traffic between programs on one network and servers on another. The proxy server responds to a request from a client program by translating the request and passing it to the Internet. When a computer on the Internet responds, the proxy server passes that response back to the client program on the computer that made the request. The proxy server computer has two network interfaces: one connected to the LAN and one connected to the Internet.

You can use Microsoft Proxy Server to regulate traffic from your LAN out to the Internet. Proxy Server acts as a gateway with firewall-class security. It allows clients and servers to access the Internet while keeping your intranet free from intruders. Proxy Server blocks inbound connections. Internal clients can initiate connections to Internet servers, but Internet clients can't initiate connections to the internal clients. Proxy Server can also restrict outbound connections.

Some firewall applications can be configured to support proxy services. For example, ISA Server can act as a proxy server for requests generated from a client browser. The browser sends the requests directly to the Web Proxy Service on the ISA Server computer to determine if Internet access is allowed.

Perimeter Networks

A perimeter network defines an area of your network—protected by firewalls—that's used to provide a secure environment in which to host your Web services and make them available to Internet clients without compromising the security of your services, applications, sensitive data, or private network. You can set up a perimeter network and its firewall configuration in several ways, depending on your organization's needs and your network's current topology; however, often the perimeter network topology falls into two categories: single firewall and back-to-back firewalls.

Single Firewall

A single firewall is the simplest way to set up your perimeter network. In this configuration, you use one firewall configured with three network interface cards (NICs). One NIC is connected to the private network, one to the Internet, and one to the perimeter network, as shown in Figure 10.12.

Using one firewall has several advantages:

- This configuration is the easiest and most inexpensive firewall solution to implement.
- The corporate network can continue to connect to the Internet should the perimeter network fail. The corporate network doesn't rely on the perimeter network for Internet connectivity.
- The perimeter network is physically separated from other networks. Even if someone were able to penetrate the perimeter network, that user couldn't go beyond the perimeter network.

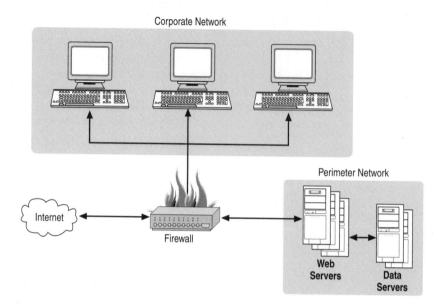

Figure 10.12   Perimeter network supported by one firewall

The main disadvantage of this configuration is that it protects the corporate network with only one layer of firewall protection. If an intruder can get past the firewall, resources in the corporate network could be in as much risk as those resources in the perimeter network. However, additional layers of firewall protection can provide more effective security.

Back-to-Back Firewalls

In a perimeter network that's configured with back-to-back firewalls, a firewall is located on either side of the perimeter network. The front end of the perimeter network is connected to the Internet through one of the firewalls, and the back end of the perimeter network is connected to the corporate network through the other firewall, as shown in Figure 10.13.

By adding an additional firewall, you're reducing the risk of compromise because an attacker would need to break into both systems to access resources in the corporate network. However, a second firewall makes configuration more complicated and expenses higher than a single firewall does. Another problem with this configuration is that the corporate network is dependent on the perimeter network to connect to the Internet. If the perimeter network experiences connectivity problems, the corporate network is also affected.

In some cases you might want to add additional firewalls between tiers in your perimeter network to minimize the number of computers accessible directly

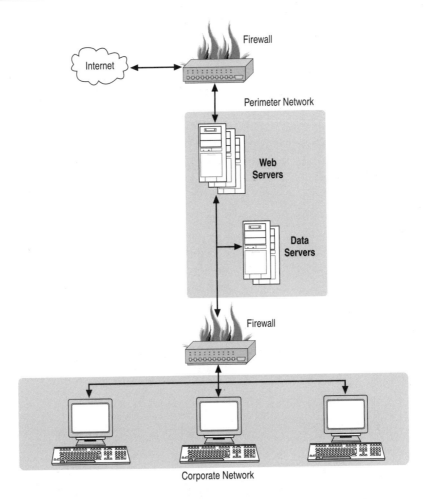

Figure 10.13   Perimeter network supported by back-to-back firewalls

through the Internet, making it more difficult to disrupt or abuse back-end servers. For example, you can place a firewall between the Web server tier and the data tier, as shown in Figure 10.14.

In this configuration the corporate network is even more difficult for a hacker to access and you can protect the back-end database servers from vulnerabilities that don't depend on the relationship between the Web servers and the database servers. You can also use the firewall to limit the IP addresses that can request data directly from the database servers. Although adding a third firewall adds even more costs and administrative overhead, it does increase security.

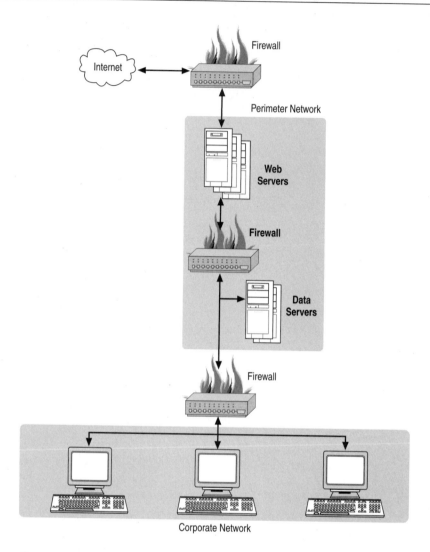

Figure 10.14   Perimeter network supported by three firewalls

Making a Decision

When you implement firewall protection in your perimeter network, you can use a single firewall or back-to-back firewalls. In addition, if you use back-to-back firewalls, you can also add firewalls between tiers in the perimeter network. Table 10.10 describes some of the considerations that you should take into account when planning your perimeter network strategy.

Recommendations

When designing a firewall strategy, you should determine how much security you need and what you can afford in terms of costs and administrative overhead.

In general, the more layers of firewall protection you can implement, the more secure your network.

Table 10.10   Perimeter Network Topology

Strategy	Considerations
Single firewall	This configuration is the easiest and most inexpensive to implement. The corporate network can continue to connect to the Internet should the perimeter network fail. The perimeter network is physically separated from other networks. However, it protects the corporate network with only one layer of firewall protection.
Back-to-back firewalls	The more layers of firewall protection you can add to your network, the more security you can provide. However, additional firewalls increase costs and administrative overhead. In addition, the corporate network is dependent on the perimeter network to connect to the Internet.

Example: A Firewall Strategy for Woodgrove Bank

Woodgrove Bank is providing Web-based services to its customers. Its perimeter network is based on a back-to-back firewall model. To provide services to its customers, they use ASP-based applications that access COM+ components from a separate physical tier. The COM+ components then access data from the databases on a third tier. In order to provide an extra level of security, administrators decided to implement a layer of firewall protection between the Web servers and the COM+ application servers, as shown in Figure 10.15. The additional firewall protects the back-end servers from vulnerabilities that don't depend on the relationship between the Web servers and the back-end servers.

Lesson Summary

A firewall prevents unauthorized access from outside the firewall to an internal network or intranet. A firewall examines and filters data as it passes through the firewall. Packet filters control the flow of IP packets to and from the firewall, circuit filters inspect and filter sessions, and application filters analyze a data stream for a particular application and can then inspect, screen, redirect, or modify the data as it passes through the firewall. NAT translates private internal IP addresses to public external addresses in order to hide internally managed addresses from external networks. A proxy server manages traffic between programs on one network and servers on another. A perimeter network defines an area of your network that's used to provide a secure environment. Two common configurations that you can use to set up your firewalls are a single firewall strategy and a back-to-back firewall strategy. A single firewall is the easiest and most inexpensive solution to implement. A back-to-back configuration with two or more firewalls provides greater security.

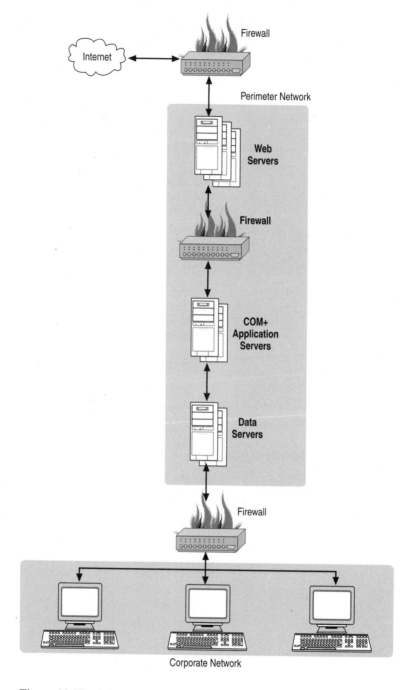

Figure 10.15 A layer of firewall protection between the Web cluster and the COM+ application cluster

Lab 10.1: Planning Your Network Security

After completing this lab, you'll be able to

- Design an authentication and encryption strategy
- Design an authorization strategy
- Design a firewall strategy

About This Lab

In this lab, you'll design a security strategy that takes into account authentication, encryption, authorization, and firewall protection. The exercises in this lab are based on a Web site that's set up for the exclusive use of a set of users who must be authenticated to access resources in the site, as described in the scenario. Note that in the first exercise authentication and encryption are grouped together (unlike the lessons in the chapter). This is because encryption goes hand-in-hand with some authentication models.

Before You Begin

Before you begin this lab, you must be able to

- Administer Windows 2000 Server and IIS
- Set up user accounts and groups in a Windows 2000 domain
- Set up IIS and NTFS permissions
- Provide an overview of how firewall protection is implemented in a Web environment

Scenario: A Security Strategy for Northwind Traders

Northwind Traders is implementing a Web site that will allow wholesale customers to access their accounts. Customers work on client computers that are configured with a broad range of operating systems and browsers. When users log on, they should be prompted for usernames and passwords in order to be authenticated into the system. Users will be authenticated through Windows accounts; no customized authentication applications or ISAPI filters will be used. Once authenticated, users should be able to read and execute ASP applications that access data from SQL Server databases. All data that's transmitted between authenticated users and the Web site should be secure in order to ensure the privacy and integrity of that data. At this time, no IP addresses, networks, or domain names will be denied access to your site.

The Web portion of the company's network will include a Web cluster and a Data cluster, as shown in Figure 10.16. All the computers in the two clusters are configured with Windows 2000 Advanced Server.

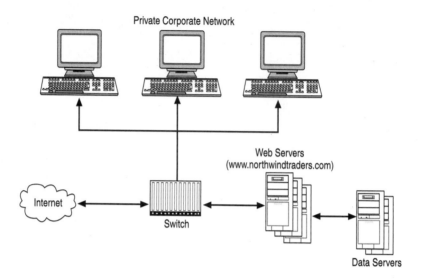

Figure 10.16 Network topology for Northwind Traders

When users access the Web site, they'll go to *http://www.northwindtraders.com.* From there, they'll be redirected to *https://www.northwindtraders.com/secure/ default.asp* and prompted for a username and password. Once authenticated, they'll view a home page that provides them with various options that allow them to find the information they need.

As the network administrator, you must design a security strategy that allows approved customers to access the resources they need on the site, prevents these users from accessing any resources beyond what they need, and prevents any unauthorized users from accessing the site. In addition, you want to use firewall protection to protect site resources, particularly the databases, and the private corporate network.

Exercise 1: Planning an Authentication and Encryption Strategy

As the network administrator, you've set up user accounts for each wholesale customer who plans to access your Web site. Because these users will all have the same level of access, you create a user group—Customers—and add each of these users to the group. You now want to set up an authentication model.

1. What authentication models does IIS support and how do these models differ?

2. Which authentication model should you use?

3. What are the limitations on the authentication model you chose?

4. In addition to authenticating users, you must ensure that all data transmitted between the users and the Web site is secure in order to ensure that data's privacy and integrity. One way to secure data is through encryption. What are several methods that you can use to encrypt data and how are those methods different?

5. How can you make data transferred between clients and the Web servers secure?

Exercise 2: Planning an Authorization Strategy

Once you've planned how users will be authenticated, you can determine how they'll be authorized to use the ASP applications. You must address two levels of authorization: IIS and NTFS. Remember, users must be able to access the ASP pages and use the tools on those pages to access the needed information. Also note that no IP addresses, networks, or domain names will be denied access to your site.

1. Before you determine how users will be authorized, you decide to review the access process so that you have a complete picture of how users will access resources. What steps will the access process follow?

2. IIS permissions apply to all users trying to access the Web site. How should you set up those permissions?

3. Unlike IIS permissions, NTFS permissions apply to specific users and groups. How should you set up those permissions?

Exercise 3: Planning a Firewall Strategy

Your firewall strategy should try to maximize the protection of your private network and your Web services, particularly the databases. You'll use your firewalls to define your perimeter network and to isolate your private network.

1. What are the two basic perimeter network topologies that you can use to set up your firewalls and how do these topologies differ?

2. You want to maximize the amount of security that you provide your network through firewalls. Which configuration should you use?

3. You also want to protect your database as much as possible through the use of firewalls. How many firewalls should you use in your network?

Review

Answering the following questions will reinforce key information presented in this chapter. If you're unable to answer a question, review the appropriate lesson and then try the question again. Answers to the questions can be found in the appendix.

1. You're the network administrator for Consolidated Messenger. Your organization is implementing an online tracking application that allows customers to determine the status of packages that are being delivered. In order to check on the status of their orders, users must supply the tracking numbers that were provided when they shipped their packages. The tracking numbers aren't tied to any user accounts or authentication data stores, and users don't have to provide any information other than the tracking numbers. Which authentication model can you use for your Web site?

2. Your company, Adventure Works, has implemented a Web site that allows users to access information about various locations around the world. The site uses ASP applications to access data from a SQL Server database. You configure the site with Anonymous access and configure IIS permissions on the Home directory with the Read permission and the Scripts Only execute permission. Next, you configure NTFS permissions on the Web directory. You add the IUSR_*computername* account to the directory and configure the account with the Read permission. When users try to access the Web site, they can read the static content on the home page but they can't execute any of the ASP applications. What is the likeliest cause of the problem?

3. You're setting up a Web site for Trey Research. Your customers must log on to the site and be authenticated in order to access resources on the site. Your customers use different types of browsers to access the site, and their computers are set up with different types of operating systems. You implement IPSec in order to protect data as it's being transmitted between the client computers and the Web servers; however, many clients are unable to establish a secure connection. What is the likeliest cause of the problem?

4. You're the network administrator for a small organization that provides online Web services to its customers. The site contains only static content, which is all located on the IIS server. IIS is configured to allow Anonymous access. You want to implement a firewall solution that's inexpensive to implement, that's easy to administer, and that separates the perimeter network from the rest of the network so that the private network isn't dependent on the perimeter network's availability in order to access the Internet. Which firewall solution should you use?

C H A P T E R   1 1

Systems Monitoring and Disaster Recovery

About This Chapter

When designing highly available Web solutions, you should take into account
two considerations that go beyond your network's actual design. The first is to
determine how you'll monitor and audit your systems in order to ensure adequate
performance, availability, and security. A comprehensive monitoring and auditing
strategy is integral to managing your Web site and to providing highly available
Web solutions in your Microsoft Windows 2000 environment. The second consideration that you should take into account is the design of a disaster recovery
strategy that protects your network from the loss of data and from machine failure. A disaster recovery strategy must encompass the possibility of failures that
can range from natural disasters to viruses. This chapter provides the information
that you need to design comprehensive plans to monitor and audit your systems
and to develop a disaster recovery strategy.

Before You Begin

To complete the lessons in this chapter, you must have

- Experience using the Performance tool and the Event Viewer tool in Windows 2000

- Experience implementing Internet Information Systems (IIS) logging

- Knowledge about the disaster recovery techniques supported by Windows 2000

Lesson 1: Designing a System Monitoring Strategy

Monitoring your site's performance and reliability is an important part of your operations. Monitoring allows you to identify potential problems before they occur so that you can prevent these problems from turning into emergencies. By monitoring a system, you can determine when to upgrade your system and whether changes made to your system are helping or hurting performance. Monitoring allows you to establish performance baselines that you can compare to monitoring data collected at a later time, allowing you to determine what changes have occurred. From this information, you can decide which actions to take. In this lesson you'll learn how to design a monitoring strategy that allows you to assess your system's performance so that you can address potential problems that might occur in your Web environment.

After this lesson, you will be able to

- Describe how to use Windows 2000 and IIS performance counters to monitor your system

- Design a strategy that monitors memory, processing, network input/output (I/O), security overhead, and Web applications.

Estimated lesson time: 35 minutes

Performance Monitoring

Windows 2000 and IIS contain objects that allow you to gather performance data from various components in your system. Performance objects typically correspond to major hardware components such as memory or processors. The objects are built into the operating system, although other programs may install their own performance objects. Each performance object contains a set of counters that provide information about specific aspects of a system or service. For example, the Processor performance object is associated with the processors on your systems. The Processor performance object contains a number of counters, such as the % Processor Time counter and the % User Time counter. Some performance objects can have multiple instances. For those objects you can track statistics for each instance.

Monitoring Tools

Microsoft provides a number of tools that allow you to monitor performance. Some of these tools are included with Windows 2000 and IIS, others are available through the Windows 2000 Server Resources Kit, and still others can be downloaded from Microsoft's Web site at *http://www.microsoft.com*. These tools use performance objects and counters to monitor systems and services. Some of the most commonly used tools are the Performance tool, Task Manager, Windows Management Instrumentation (WMI), and Event Viewer, which are described below. In addition to these four tools, Microsoft provides other tools that you can use to monitor performance. These tools are described in Table 11.1.

Table 11.1   Tools Available to Monitor Performance

Tool	Description
HTTP Monitoring Tool	Allows you to monitor Hypertext Transfer Protocol (HTTP) activity and set alerts that notify you of dramatic changes in activity
Network Monitor	Allows you to monitor network traffic
NetStat	A command-line tool that detects current network connections and lists them with information about protocol, local address, foreign address, and state
Performance Counter Check	A scriptable COM object that allows you to read performance counters from within Microsoft Windows Script Host (WSH) or from within an Active Server Pages (ASP) file
Process Explode	Allows you to view each process on the local system in detail, set thread priority, view and change security settings, and terminate processes
Process Monitor	Allows you to view each process on the local system in detail
Process Thread and Status	Allows you to view the status of all processes and threads
Process Tree	Allows you to query the process inheritance tree and stop process on local and remote computers
Process Viewer	Allows you to examine each process in detail, set process and thread priority, and stop the process if necessary
Web Application Stress Tool (WAST)	Simulates multiple browsers requesting pages from a Web site so you can gather performance and stability information about your Web applications
Web Capacity Analysis Tool (WCAT)	Simulates various workloads on client-server configurations so that you can test how your IIS 5 and network configurations will respond to different client requests for content, data, or HTML pages

Performance Tool

The Performance tool is a Microsoft Management Console (MMC) interface that contains two snap-ins: the System Monitor snap-in and the Performance Logs and Alerts snap-in. Figure 11.1 shows the Performance console and the two snap-ins. Notice that the System Monitor snap-in is active and is monitoring the

% Processor Time counter and the % User Time counter, both of which are part of the Processor object. Also notice the spikes in activity when applications are opened.

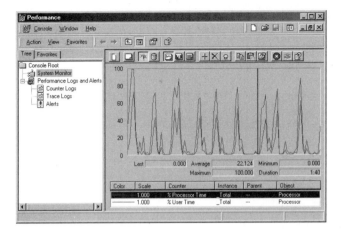

Figure 11.1   System Monitor (in the Performance console) monitoring the % Processor Time counter and the % User Time counter

The Performance console is the most effective Microsoft tool that you can use to establish a baseline of server performance. It also allows you to monitor and measure the effects of any changes you make to software or hardware. You can view performance counter readings while you're monitoring performance; graphically log counter activity, or set alerts that monitor when specified thresholds are met.

System Monitor allows you to collect and view extensive data about the usage of hardware resources and the activity of system services on computers. You can collect and view real-time performance data on a local computer or from several remote computers. You can define the data that you want to collect by type of data (objects, counters, and instances) and source of data (local computer or remote computers). To view performance data in System Monitor, you simply add specific counters to your view.

Performance Logs and Alerts allows you to collect performance data automatically from local or remote computers and save that data to logs. You can then view the logged data by using System Monitor or by exporting the data to spreadsheet programs or databases for analysis and report generation. Like System Monitor, Performance Logs and Alerts uses the performance objects, counters, and instances to provide data about hardware resources and system services. Performance Logs and Alerts supports two types of logs: counter logs and trace logs. With counter logs, data is collected at specified intervals. With trace logs, data is collected when certain activities occur, such as when a disk I/O operation or a page fault occurs.

Performance Logs and Alerts also allows you to set an alert on a counter. When you configure an alert, you must specify the alert threshold on the counter. For example, suppose you want to set an alert on the % Processor Time counter. You configure the alert so that the threshold is reached when the counter value exceeds 20 percent. You must then determine what action should be taken when the value exceeds that threshold. You can configure the alert to take any of the following actions:

- Log an entry in the Application event log
- Send a network message to a specified recipient
- Start a specified performance data log
- Run a specified program

Task Manager

Like the Performance tool, Task Manager provides performance information about your systems. Task Manager shows you a snapshot of programs and processes running on your computer. It also provides a summary of processor and memory usage, as shown in Figure 11.2.

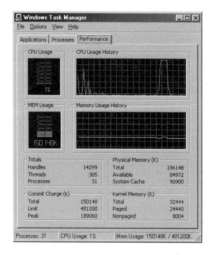

Figure 11.2   Performance tab in Task Manager

The Performance tab provides a dynamic overview of your computer's performance. It includes graphs for CPU and memory usage; the total number of handles, threads, and processes running; and the total kilobytes (KB) of physical, kernel, and commit memory. You can also configure the Performance tab to display the amount of CPU resources consumed by kernel operations.

Task Manager is useful as a quick reference to system operation and performance; however, the Performance tool provides far more capabilities. Although Task Manager uses data from some of the same performance counters used by the Performance tool, Task Manager doesn't have access to the breadth of information available from all installed counters. In addition, Task Manager doesn't support logs and alerts.

WMI

WMI is the Microsoft implementation of Web-Based Enterprise Management (WBEM), which provides uniform access to management information. WMI is integrated with the Common Information Model (CIM), an extensible object-oriented schema for managing systems, networks, application, databases, and devices. WMI allows you to monitor, track, and control system events related to software applications, hardware components, and networks.

WMI provides the infrastructure for system monitoring by exposing hardware and software diagnostics in a common application programming interface (API). You can use this infrastructure for any WMI management data.

Windows 2000 allows you to collect data about system resources, such as disks, memory, processors, and network components. By default, the operating system uses the registry to collect this data. However, you can collect this data by using the WMI interface instead of the registry. WMI consolidates data from the hardware platform, drivers, and applications and passes it on to a management information store. The data uses CIM to expose and interface with the data it holds. Together, WMI and CIM enable management applications, platforms, and consoles to perform a variety of tasks, including monitoring and logging events.

You can use WMI with the Performance tool to gather performance data. At the command prompt, type **perfmon /wmi**. The Performance tool will open as before and will include the System Monitor snap-in and the Performance Logs and Alerts snap-in. However, the data will be collected through WMI rather than through the registry.

Event Viewer

Event Viewer is another tool that allows you to monitor your system. Event Viewer maintains logs about application, security, and system events on your computer. Event Viewer allows you to view and manage event logs, gather information about hardware and software problems, and monitor Windows 2000 security.

Event Viewer supports several types of logs, including the Application log, the Security log, and the System log. Each log can contain the following types of events: Error, Warning, Information, Success Audit, and Failure Audit. Figure 11.3 shows the System log in Event Viewer. Notice that several event types are shown in the detail pane.

When you configure an alert in the Performance Logs and Alerts snap-in, you can specify that an event is logged to the Application log if the threshold is exceeded. You can then use Event Viewer to view that log to determine when and how often that alert has been triggered.

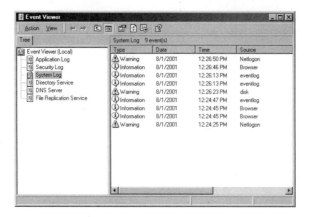

Figure 11.3   System log in Event Viewer

Event logs are used extensively in auditing your system. Auditing is discussed in Lesson 2, "Designing a Security Auditing Strategy."

Monitoring Your System

When monitoring a system that supports a Web site and its applications and data, you should start by focusing on specific areas of performance, including memory, processing, network I/O, security overhead, and Web applications. You can use the Performance tool to monitor each area. Be sure to log data for several days in order to gather a reliable cross section of activity, including unusually high and low activity.

Note   This section provides an overview of the type of performance objects and counters that you should monitor in order to evaluate your system's performance. For the names of the specific counters that you should monitor, see the *Microsoft Windows 2000 Server Resource Kit*.

Memory

Memory should be the first component in your system that you monitor. Inadequate memory can result in other parts of your system appearing as though the problems reside there. For example, what might appear on the surface as poor disk or processor performance can in fact be as a result of a memory problem. You should rule out memory performance problems before investigating other components.

In Windows 2000, the largest component of activity is the *process*. Each process contains *threads,* which are used to accomplish particular tasks. The physical RAM available to the process is called the *working set*. If the process exceeds the amount of available RAM, it can't store all of its code and frequently used data. As a result, some of this information must be stored on a disk, which results in an increase in disk activity. Figure 11.4 provides an overview of how a process and its threads use memory.

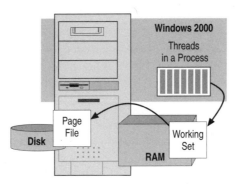

Figure 11.4   The working set of a process and its threads

When collecting data about your memory's performance, you should monitor the following components:

- **Available memory**   You should track how much physical available memory is remaining when you're running all server services. When you log availability, make certain to include peak activity.

- **Paging**   You should track the rates of disk paging to determine whether you have a memory shortage. Continuous high rates indicate a shortage. When monitoring paging, be sure to track page faults. A page fault occurs when a process requests a page in memory and the system can't find it at the requested location. If the page fault rate is high, you might need to add more memory or reduce the amount of memory dedicated to the caches.

- **File System Cache**   The File System Cache refers to the working set of the file system. The files system uses the cache to store recently used and frequently used data. By default, the system reserves about 50 percent of physical memory for the cache. A large and effective cache is vital to the efficient operation of an IIS server. However, IIS automatically trims the cache if it's running out of memory.

- **Paging file size**   The paging files back up committed physical memory. The larger the paging file, the more memory that the system commits to that file. The file should be at least twice as large as the physical memory to protect against a system crash. You can improve paging file performance by striping the file across separate physical drives.

- **Memory pool size**   The system's memory pools hold objects created and used by applications and the operating system. Only the operating system kernel can use the memory pools. There are two types of memory pools: paged and nonpaged. On IIS servers, threads that service connections are stored in the nonpaged pool along with other objects used by the service.

Your system should have enough memory to provide space for the Inetinfo working set so that Windows 2000 will not have to perform disk operations. You should check the size of the working set to determine how much its size varies in response to general memory availability on the server. Your available memory shouldn't dip below 5 percent of the amount of physical RAM on the server. You should also compare the size of the working set to the rate of page faults attributed to that process. If you can't lower the page fault rate to an acceptable level, you might have to add memory.

When reviewing performance data, you should also look at how often objects sought in the cache are found. Frequent cache misses result in increased disk I/O and decreased performance. If cache hits are low or if cache misses are high, the cache might be too small to function effectively. Cache flushes can also affect performance. Windows 2000 flushes objects from the cache if they change or if they time out before they're reused. A high rate of cache flushes associated with elevated cache misses and page faults might mean that the cache is being flushed too frequently. To measure cache flushes, you should compare the number of cache flushes to the number of cache misses and to the rate of page faults in the Inetinfo process.

As you analyze the performance data, be sure to measure cache size in relation to available memory. You want to track how small the cache gets and how often that happens. When memory is scarce, the system trims the cache, and when there is plenty of memory, the system enlarges the cache. If the cache is too small, performance can degrade. You might need to add more memory, defragment your disk, or both.

Processing

For active servers, processor bottleneck can become a problem. A bottleneck occurs when one or more processes take up nearly all the time of all the processors on a computer. If this occurs, process threads must wait in queue for processor time, and other activity stops until the queue is cleared. The processors on a Windows 2000 computer running IIS must support the operating system, IIS processes, and processes unrelated to either. You can use such tools as WCAT, WAST, and the Performance console to measure processor performance. When using any of these tools, be sure to account for the system resources used by the tool itself as you analyze performance data.

As you collect data about processor performance, be sure to include information about processor activity, IIS service connections, and IIS threads. Data about processor activity should include processor queue length and processor time percentages. Data about IIS connections should include the Web service and File Transfer Protocol (FTP) service. Data about IIS threads should include thread count, processor time, and context switches.

A long, sustained queue length indicates that a processor can't handle the load assigned to it. As a result, threads are being kept waiting. A sustained queue length of two or more threads can indicate a processor bottleneck. You can configure an alert in Performance Logs and Alerts to notify you if the processor queue length reaches an unacceptable value. You can use data about processor time percentages to determine how processor load is being distributed among processors. If all processors are being shared equally but are reaching their maximum (and causing sustained queue lengths), you might need to upgrade or add processors. If one processor is being used above all others, you might need to replace the application running in that process or move the process to another server.

Connection data allows you to identify patterns of client demand for your server. When combined with information about processor queues and lengths, connection data allows you to determine whether load levels are causing processor bottleneck. User load might be causing bottleneck if the data reveals a long, sustained processor queue, high use rates on one or more processors, or current connections reaching a plateau at a high value, indicating that some connections are being blocked out.

When analyzing data about thread count, you should determine how many threads the Inetinfo process creates and how the number of threads varies. You should also observe the processor time for each thread and the number of context switches. A large number of threads is likely to increase the number of context switches, which might interfere with performance, especially if processor utilization is more than 70 percent.

Network I/O

The main functions of IIS are to establish client connections, receive and interpret requests, and deliver files. Two factors determine how effectively IIS can perform these functions: bandwidth and capacity. Effective bandwidth relies on the link's transmission capacity, the server configuration, and the server workload. Network capacity is determined, at least in part, by the number of connections established and maintained by the server.

When collecting network I/O data, you should gather information about transmission rates and Transmission Control Protocol (TCP) connections. Transmission rate data should include bytes sent and received by the Web service, FTP service, and Simple Mail Transfer Protocol (SMTP) service. You should also collect sent and received data about TCP segments, Internet Protocol (IP) datagrams, and the network interface. TCP connection data should include information about established, failed, and reset connections.

You can use the data that you collect about transmission rates and TCP connections to determine network capacity and how often you reach that capacity. You should compare these numbers to processor and memory use to help pinpoint where any bottlenecks might be occurring. By collecting data that includes spikes in traffic over a long period of time, you can determine whether you have enough capacity to meet user demand. For example, suppose you're having problems supporting all your users at peak time. If your network interface is close to capacity at those times, but your processor and memory use are moderate, you know that you should address network capacity issues.

The number of connections that are rejected or reset might also indicate that your network connection can't support the current or increasing demand for your site. An increasing number of failures and resets or a consistently increasing rate of failures and resets can indicate a bandwidth shortage.

Security Overhead

Any layer of security that you implement in your system can affect performance. However, you can't measure security overhead simply by monitoring a separate process or threads. Many security features in Windows 2000 are integrated into the operating system and IIS. The most common way to measure security overhead is to compare performance with and without the specific security feature. When collecting data about security overhead, you should gather information about processor activity, the processor queue, physical memory used, network traffic, and latency and delays.

Analyzing data about security overhead consists primarily of comparing data collected with and without the security feature implemented. You can then use the results of these comparisons to determine whether to implement the security feature and, if so, what type of upgrading you should do in order to support that feature. For example, you might need to upgrade or add processors, add memory, or use customer hardware.

Web Applications

A poorly written Web application can result in an inefficient use of resources. For example, a script might make several references to a database instead of a single comprehensive one. If Web applications are an important part of your site, you should monitor the performance of those applications by monitoring ASP, Common Gateway Interface (CGI), and Internet Server Application Programming Interface (ISAPI) requests. You should also monitor Web service GET and POST requests.

Note   You can also configure IIS to log events in the Windows Application event log (which you can view through Event Viewer) when ASP errors occur. Events are logged when a client request for an ASP application is unsuccessful.

If your ASP requests per second are low during peak usage, your application might be causing a bottleneck. At the same time, the number of requests queued and the request wait time *should* remain low, although they will go up and down under varying loads. If the limit is reached for the number of requests that can be queued, client browsers will receive a message saying that the server is busy.

If pages are being executed quickly and don't wait for I/O, the number of requests executing is likely to be low. If pages must wait for I/O, the number of requests executing is likely to be high. If the number of requests executing is high, the number of queued requests is high, and CPU utilization is low, you may need to increase the maximum number of allowed processor threads.

If CGI and ISAPI requests drop while under increasing loads, the application itself might be causing a problem. If you're using CGI, you might want to consider converting to ASP or ISAPI.

If your data analysis reveals a problem, you might need to rewrite your application to improve performance. However, it's also possible that you need to upgrade your system to support the demand for your applications.

For many administrators, system monitoring should include the capacity to detect Web application failures automatically and then notify the appropriate individuals or services of the failure. Administrators can use Performance Logs and Alerts to create alerts based on specific counters related to applications. For example, you can configure an alert based on the Active Server Pages\Errors From Script Compilers counter so that an administrator is notified if that counter exceeds a certain limit. You can also use other tools to monitor application failures, such as Health Monitor 2.1 in Microsoft Application Center 2000.

Making a Decision

Your monitoring strategy should include collecting data about memory, processing, network I/O, security overhead, and Web applications. Table 11.2 provides an overview of the considerations that you should take into account when monitoring your system.

Table 11.2   Monitoring Your System

Component	Considerations
Memory	Memory is the most critical component to monitor because problems can appear in other areas of a system that are related to inadequate memory. When collecting data about memory, be sure to include data on available memory, paging, file system cache, paging file size, and memory pool size.
Processors	If a processor bottleneck occurs, process threads must wait in queue for processor time. When you collect processor data, include processor queue length and processor time percentages. Also monitor IIS connections and threads.
Network I/O	Two factors, bandwidth and capacity, determine how effectively IIS can establish client connections, receive and interpret requests, and deliver files. When collecting network I/O data, include information about transmission rates and TCP connections. For transmission rates, include data about bytes sent and received by the Web service, FTP service, and SMTP service and data about TCP segments, IP datagrams, and the network interface. For TCP connections, include data about established, failed, and reset connections.

(continued)

Table 11.2 *(continued)*

Component	Considerations
Security overhead	The more layers of security you implement in your system, the more performance can be affected. To determine security overhead, collect data with and without the specific security features. Include data about processor activity, the processor queue, physical memory used, network traffic, and latency and delays.
Web applications	A poorly written Web application can result in an inefficient use of resources. It's also possible that you don't have enough resources to handle the application. When collecting application data, monitor ASP, CGI, and ISAPI requests. Also monitor Web service GET and POST requests.

Recommendations

You should adhere to the following guidelines when developing your monitoring strategy:

- Log data for several days to make certain that you're gathering a reliable cross section of information.

- Monitor memory, processing, network I/O, security overhead, and Web applications.

- Monitor memory before monitoring other components. Memory data should include available memory, paging, file system cache, paging file size, and memory pool size.

- When using tools such as WCAT to run tests on a system, be sure to account for the system resources used by the tool itself.

Example: Monitoring Memory for Lucerne Publishing

Lucerne Publishing maintains a small Web site that allows users to view products online. The company is experiencing performance degradation at peak usage. Network administrators at the company first monitor memory and find that all aspects of memory appear to be operating within acceptable ranges. Next they decide to collect data about processor activity, as shown in Figure 11.5.

To monitor processor activity, administrators use the following counters:

- System\Processor Queue Length
- Processor\% Processor Time
- Processor\% Privileged Time
- Processor\% User Time
- Process\% Processor Time

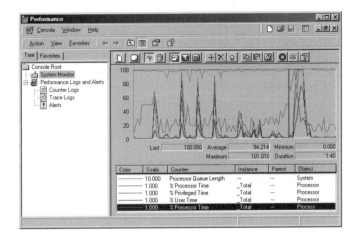

Figure 11.5   Monitoring processor activity

In reviewing the data, the administrators discover that the processor reaches peak capacity at high usage times. To address this problem, they plan to add a second processor to the system.

Lesson Summary

Windows 2000 and IIS contain performance objects that you can use to gather data about your system's performance. Each object contains a set of counters that provide performance information about specific aspects of a system or resource. Microsoft provides a number of tools that allow you to monitor performance, including the Performance tool, Task Manager, WMI, and Event Viewer. When monitoring your system, you should focus on memory, processing, network I/O, security overhead, and Web applications. Memory should be the first component in your system that you monitor. For memory, monitor available memory, paging, file system cache, paging file size, and memory pool size. For processing, monitor processor activity, IIS service connections, and IIS threads. For network I/O, monitor transmission rates and TCP connections. For security, monitor processor activity, the processor queue, physical memory used, network traffic, and latency and delays. For applications, monitor ASP, CGI, and ISAPI requests, as well as Web service GET and POST requests.

Activity 11.1: Creating a Processor Alert

You're monitoring performance on your company's Web site, and you're concerned because the system is experiencing bottlenecks during peak usage. You think that the problem is due to insufficient processing power, so you decide to monitor processor activity. You're particularly concerned about the percentage of time that the processor spends executing threads, so you use System Monitor to monitor the Processor\% Processor Time counter, as shown in Figure 11.6.

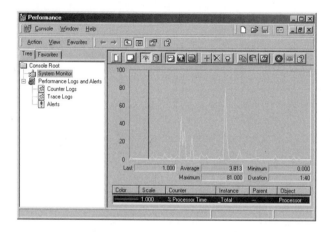

Figure 11.6   Monitoring the Processor\% Processor Time counter

Based on the information you see in System Monitor, processor usage seems well below maximum usage. However, you decide to log the event over several days to be certain that you're collecting accurate information.

1. How can you log data about processor usage and then view that data?

2. After you view the log data, you realize the processors reach maximum capacity a couple of times a day. You decide that you want to be notified whenever usage exceeds 80 percent. How can you be notified when usage exceeds the 80 percent threshold?

3. Which counters, in addition to Processor\% Processor Time, should you consider monitoring in order to collect data about processor activity?

Lesson 2: Designing a Security Auditing Strategy

Windows 2000 and IIS allow you to track the activities of users and services in order to detect possible intruders. By logging specific events, you can monitor a broad range of security-related activity. You can then view the logged activity to determine whether certain areas of your servers or sites might be subject to attacks or other security problems. Windows 2000 and IIS provide two primary methods that you use to track activity: the Windows Security log and IIS logging. You can set up Windows 2000 to record security-related events in the Security log. In addition, you can set up a Web site in IIS to log information about user activity. In this lesson you'll learn how to design an auditing strategy that uses the Security log and IIS to track activities that can affect your site's security.

After this lesson, you will be able to

- Log Windows 2000 security events in the Security log
- Log IIS activity for specific Web sites

Estimated lesson time: 25 minutes

System Auditing

Auditing refers to the process of maintaining a secure list of events on your system. For example, auditing can provide you with information about who logged into the site, when users logged in, and what files they accessed. Auditing is an essential component in any secure system. In Windows 2000 and IIS, the two primary methods that you can use to audit your system are logging Windows 2000 security events (using the Security log) and logging site activity (using IIS logging).

Logging Windows 2000 Security Events

Windows 2000 allows you to set up your system so that security-related events are recorded in the Security log. An *event* is any significant occurrence in the system or in an application that requires an entry to be added to a log. The Security log can record security events such as valid and invalid logon attempts as well as events related to resource use, such as creating, opening, or deleting files. You can specify which events are recorded in the Security log. For example, you can set up your system to log successful logon attempts. When you do, Windows 2000 records all successful logon attempts in the Security log.

Figure 11.7 provides an overview of the process that occurs when a user logs on to the system and that system is configured to audit account logons.

Once events have been recorded, you can use Event Viewer to view the contents of the Security log. Event Viewer allows you to search, filter, sort, and view details about events. You can use the log to help track changes to the security system and identify any possible breaches to security. You can also archive logs in case you need to access event information at a later date.

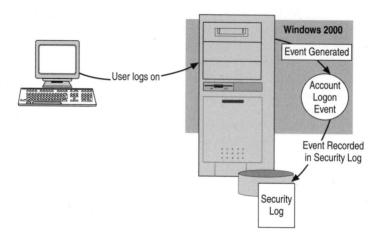

Figure 11.7   Account Logon event added to the Security log

When you view the Security log in Event Viewer, you'll see two types of log entries (assuming both types of events occurred): Success Audit and Failure Audit. A Success Audit event is an audited security access attempt that succeeded. A Failure Audit event is an audited security access attempt that failed. For example, if you configure your Group Policy settings to audit failed logon events, a Failure Audit event will be added to the Security log whenever someone attempts to log on to the system and that attempt fails.

Generating a Security log can take a large amount of disk space, so you should be careful when selecting the events to be audited. Consider the amount of disk space that you're willing to devote to the Security log. You can configure Event Viewer to overwrite log entries that are more than a specified number of days old. You can also configure the server to stop running when the Security log is full.

Setting Up Auditing

To enable auditing, you must configure your Group Policy settings in the Group Policy snap-in, as shown in Figure 11.8. For each policy, you can configure successful attempts, failed attempts, or both.

If you want to audit access to files and directories, you must first configure the Audit Object Access policy in the Group Policy snap-in. From there, you must set up auditing by configuring the properties (access control settings) of the specific directory, as shown in Figure 11.9.

Note   You can access the auditing properties by clicking the Advanced button in the Security tab of the Properties dialog box.

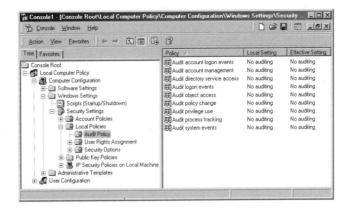

Figure 11.8   Using the Group Policy snap-in to configure audit policies

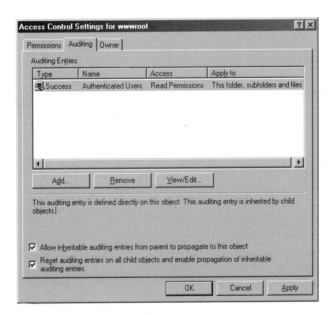

Figure 11.9   Configuring auditing in a directory's properties

Once you've set up auditing, you can review the Security log for suspicious security events in order to determine whether there have been attempts at unauthorized access to your system. You should inspect the Security log for the following types of activity:

- Invalid logon attempts
- Failed use of privileges

- Failed attempts to access and modify .bat or .cmd files
- Attempts to alter security privileges or the Security log
- Attempts to shut down the server

Logging Site Activity

In addition to configuring auditing in Windows 2000, you can configure IIS to track access to your server. IIS logging is easy to implement and can be used in conjunction with a log file analysis tool, such as WebTrends. IIS logging can help you collect data about the following types of suspicious activity:

- Multiple failed commands to the Scripts directory or another directory configured for executable files
- Attempts to upload files to the Scripts directory or another directory configured for executable files
- Attempts to access executable files (such as .bat, .exe, or .cmd files) and subvert their purpose
- Attempts to send .bat or .cmd commands to the Scripts directory or another directory configured for executable files
- Excessive requests from a single IP address attempting to overload the system or cause a denial-of-service attack

Note   A denial-of-service attack is an attack that causes system resources to be consumed so that no resources are available for other users. A denial-of-service attack can also cause a system to crash.

IIS logging allows you to record log entries about user and server activity on a Web or FTP site. You can use the logs to regulate access to content, determine content popularity, plan security requirements, and troubleshoot potential site problems.

IIS logging is more extensive than the Windows 2000 logging that you can view through Event Viewer. IIS uses modules that operate independently of other activities on the server, and you can choose the log format for each individual Web site or FTP site. In addition, you can choose not to log individual directories that are part of a site that's being logged. For example, you can enable logging for the default Web site, but you can disable logging on the IISHelp directory.

IIS logging supports four log file formats, as described in Table 11.3.

The W3C Extended format, Microsoft IIS format, and NCSA format are all American Standard Code for Information Interchange (ASCII) text formats. You can use a text editor to view these types of log files. For the ODBC Logging format, you must first create a table in the database that contains the appropriate fields for the logged data. You can then view the table as you would any other data source.

Table 11.3   Log File Formats

Format	Description
Microsoft IIS	Microsoft IIS is a fixed format that includes basic items such as the user's IP address, username, request data and time, HTTP status code, and the number of bytes received. The items are separated by commas. Microsoft IIS records more items than the NCSA Common format.
NCSA Common	The NCSA (National Center for Supercomputing Applications) Common format is a fixed format available for Web sites but not FTP sites. It records basic information about user requests such as remote host name, username, date, time, request type, HTTP status code, and the number of bytes received by the server. Items are separated by spaces.
ODBC Logging	The ODBC (open database connectivity) Logging format is a record of a fixed set of data fields in an ODBC-compliant database, such as Microsoft Access or Microsoft SQL Server. Items logged include the user's IP address, username, request date and time, HTTP status code, bytes received, action carried out, and the target.
W3C Extended	The W3C (World Wide Web Consortium) Extended format is a customizable format with a variety of different fields. You can specify which fields to include in the log. Fields are separated by spaces.

You can configure IIS logging through the properties of each Web site or FTP site. Figure 11.10 shows the Extended Properties tab of the Extended Logging Properties dialog box for the W3C Extended format. You can access this dialog box by clicking the Properties button on the Web Site tab (or FTP Site tab) of the site's Properties dialog box.

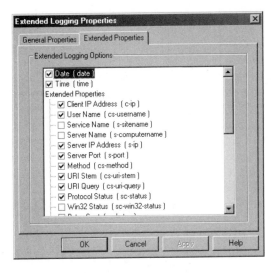

Figure 11.10   Configuring logging in IIS

Making a Decision

Windows 2000 and IIS support two main methods for auditing your system. You can log Windows 2000 security events (using the Security log) and you can log site activity (using IIS logging). Table 11.4 provides information on the considerations that you should take into account when auditing your system.

Table 11.4   Auditing Your Web Site

Type of Logging	Considerations
Windows 2000 event logging	You can configure Windows 2000 to audit security events. These events are recorded in the Security log, which you can view by using Event Viewer. To set up Windows 2000 auditing, you must configure Group Policy settings. For each policy, you can configure successful attempts, failed attempts, or both. If you want to audit access to files and directories, you must first configure the Audit Object Access policy and then set up auditing for the specific directory or file.
IIS site logging	IIS logging is easier to implement than event logging. In addition, it can be used with log file analysis tools. IIS logging can be implemented for each Web site or FTP site, and you can choose not to log individual directories that are part of a site that's being logged. In general, IIS logging is more extensive than the Windows 2000 logging.

Recommendations

Auditing is an essential part of any security plan and you should use it, but you must take into consideration the process of managing log files. You should audit only those resources that require auditing in order to conserve resources. For IIS-related auditing, you should use IIS logging. For all other auditing, you should use Windows 2000 events. You should also use Windows 2000 events when IIS logging doesn't provide you with specific types of information you might need. In general, your auditing strategy should be based on your organization's needs, your security requirements, and the availability of your resources. However, you shouldn't limit auditing because of lack of resources. It's better to supply the resources you need to maintain an efficient auditing program than not perform auditing. You must ensure that your auditing strategy includes regular review and analysis of logged data to determine potential security risks.

Example: Directory Auditing for Fourth Coffee

Fourth Coffee supports a Web site for clients to use to place orders and update customer data. Administrators at Fourth Coffee are concerned that someone might be trying to add executable files to the Scripts directory in order to introduce a virus into the system. The administrators plan to audit the directory for several days and then review the logged data for suspicious activity.

The first step that the administrators take is to configure the Audit Object Access policy in Group Policy. They set the policy to audit successful attempts and failed attempts. From there, they set up auditing on the Script directory by configuring the Create Files/Write Data access type to audit successful and failed events. Once auditing has been set up, they plan to use Event Viewer to view the Security log and review the events that have been recorded. They will review the events on a daily basis over a seven-day period to determine whether there's any suspicious activity.

Lesson Summary

Auditing refers to the process of maintaining a secure list of events on your system. In Windows 2000 and IIS, the two primary methods that you can use to audit your system are logging Windows 2000 security events (using the Security log) and logging site activity (using IIS logging). Windows 2000 allows you to set up your system so that security-related events are recorded in the Security log. Once events have been recorded, you can use Event Viewer to view the Security log's contents. When you view the Security log in Event Viewer, you see two types of log entries (assuming both types of events occurred): Success Audit and Failure Audit. To enable auditing, you must configure your Group Policy settings in the Group Policy snap-in. If you want to audit access to files and directories, you must also set up auditing in the specific directory or file. In addition to configuring auditing in Windows 2000, you can configure IIS to track access to your server. IIS logging allows you to record log entries about user and server activity on a Web or FTP site. IIS logging supports four log file formats: Microsoft IIS, NCSA Common, ODBC Logging, and W3C Extended. You can configure IIS logging through the properties of each Web site or FTP site.

Activity 11.2: Auditing a Web Site

You're a network administrator at Litware, Inc. You've implemented a Web site and you want to audit the site to ensure its security. You want to keep your logs as small as possible, so you decide to log only the date, time, client IP address, username, bytes sent, and bytes received.

1. Which method should you use to audit the Web site?

2. What tool can you use to view the logs?

You decide to audit a specific subdirectory in the Wwwroot directory. You open the properties for that subdirectory and configure auditing so that all successful and failed attempts at access generate an event. You log on to the Web site with a test user account and access the subdirectory and open several files. You then use Event Viewer to check the Security log. However, no events appear in the log.

3. Why haven't the events been recorded in the Security log?

After you configure the necessary policies, you log on to the Web site with a test user account and access the subdirectory and open several files. You then log on with another test account and try to access the directory; however, access is denied. When you view the Security log, you discover that successful events appear, but no failed attempts appear.

4. Why haven't failed events been recorded in the Security log?

Lesson 3: Designing a Disaster Recovery Strategy

Despite your best efforts to protect your systems from failure and ensure high availability to your Web clients, problems can arise and you might find yourself trying to recover from some sort of disaster, such as a destructive virus, system failure, theft or sabotage, or a natural disaster like a fire or flood. As a result, you should have a recovery plan in place in order to minimize loss of data and services. When designing a recovery strategy, you must prepare for disasters by taking steps that help to ensure a smooth recovery. For example, you should prepare Setup disks, Startup disks, and Emergency Repair Disks (ERDs) for your systems so that they're ready to use should a disaster occur. In this lesson you'll learn about the steps that you need to take in order to design a disaster recovery strategy.

After this lesson, you will be able to
- Plan a disaster recovery strategy

Estimated lesson time: 25 minutes

Disaster Recovery

A *disaster* is any situation that causes a serious disruption in your system's services. A disaster can result in data loss or machine failure, making your system unavailable to users and applications. As a result, an organization must prepare for a possible disaster by developing a disaster recovery strategy. You should take the following steps when designing a disaster recovery strategy: prepare recovery systems, collect configuration and system information, test system components, test recovery systems, and document recovery procedures.

Preparing Recovery Systems

In the event of a disaster, you must have several systems in place that allow you to perform a smooth recovery operation. To prepare for a possible disaster, you should create the Windows 2000 Setup disks, Startup disks, and ERDs. You should also back up your data on a regular basis to ensure against the loss of any critical system state data, files, or other data important to your system.

Creating Windows 2000 Setup Disks, Startup Disks, and ERDs

In some types of failure you might not be able to access certain systems in order to repair an installation or reinstall Windows 2000. For example, the computer might not support a bootable CD-ROM, or you might not be able to access directories or files. In these situations you can often use the Windows 2000 Setup disks, the Startup disks, or the ERD to access system resources or reinstall Windows 2000. In some cases, you could use these disks in conjunction with each other to repair a system. For example, you can start a repair process by using the Setup disks and then repair the problem by using the ERD.

To prepare for the possibility of a disaster, you should create all three types of disks so that they're on hand just in case. Each type of disk is described in Table 11.5.

Table 11.5   Windows 2000 Emergency Disks

Type of Disk	Description
Setup disks	The Windows 2000 Setup disks consist of four floppy disks that allow you to access your computer in case of system failure. You can use the Setup disks to start Setup, the Recovery Console, and the Emergency Repair Process. The Setup disks allow you to access your system on computers that can't be started from the CD-ROM drive. You can create the Setup disks by running the makebt32 utility on the Windows 2000 Server installation CD-ROM.
Startup disks	Each Windows 2000 Startup disk is unique to the system for which it is created. It allows you to access a drive with a faulty startup sequence. The disk can access a drive that's configured with Windows NT file system (NTFS) or the file allocation table (FAT) file system. You can use the Startup disk to help with problems that involve a corrupted boot sector, a corrupted Master Boot Record (MBR), a virus infection, a missing or corrupt NTLDR file or NTDETECT.COM file, or an incorrect NTBOOTDD.SYS file. You cannot use the Startup disk for incorrect or corrupted device drivers that have been installed into the Windows 2000 System directory or for startup problems that occur after the boat loader starts. To create a Startup disk, copy the NTLDR, NTDETECT.COM, and BOOT.INI files from your hard drive to the floppy disk. The disk should also include a copy of the correct device driver for your hard disk drive. You should create a Startup disk for each computer that you want to protect.
ERD	The ERD allows you to help repair problems with your system files (if they're accidentally erased or become corrupt), your startup environment (if you have a multiple-boot system), or the partition boot sector on the boot volume. You can create the ERD by using Windows Backup. You should create an ERD for each computer that you want to protect.

Backing Up Your Data

The only way that you can ensure that your data is protected is to back up that data on a regular schedule. If you don't back up the data, you might not be able to recover important information or settings when problems occur. Regular backups prevent data loss and damage caused by disk drive failures, power outages, virus infections, and other computer-related problems.

Window 2000 includes the Backup utility (shown in Figure 11.11), which allows you to back up programs and files, restore previously backed up data, and create an ERD.

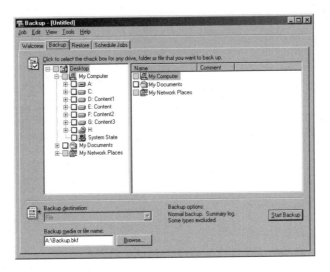

Figure 11.11   The Backup tab of the Windows 2000 Backup utility

The Backup utility is integrated with the core Windows 2000 distributed services, which means that you can use Backup to back up system state data. System state data includes the following types of information:

- Boot files and all files protected by Windows File Protection (WFP)
- Active Directory service
- Sysvol
- Certificate Services
- Cluster database
- Registry
- Performance counter configuration
- Component Services Class registration database

You can use the Backup utility to copy data to a tape drive, logical drive, removable disk, or an entire library of disks or tapes.

Collecting Configuration and System Information

In addition to preparing your recovery systems, you should maintain a record of various types of information that will help you restore your system should a disaster occur. Your documentation should be thorough and complete, and it should be stored in a safe and accessible location. Table 11.6 provides an overview of the types of information that you should maintain.

Table 11.6   Maintaining System Information

Type of Information	Description
Hardware configurations	Include information about each computer (such as type, model, serial number, basic input/output system [BIOS], complementary metal-oxide semiconductor [CMOS], and network adapters). Also include information about the disk subsystem. Record such details as type of disk, type of adapter, configured volumes, sizes, and type of disk.
Software configurations	Include information about kits, tools, and add-ons that have been installed. Record software configuration information and backups for each computer. Information should include applications and volumes on which they're installed, licensing information, installed service packs and hot fixes. Be sure to include special settings like video mode settings, if that's important to a particular machine.
Computer names and IP addresses	For each computer, record the computer name and, if applicable, the static IP address.
Domains	For each computer, record which domain that computer belongs to.
Local administrative passwords	Record in a safe location the local administrative password that was used when the backup was created.
Miscellaneous documentation	Include any other information that might be necessary when restoring a system, such as vendor documentation, internal documents, and contact information.

Testing System Components

Another important step in developing a recovery strategy is to test your components to try to predict failure situations and to practice recovery procedures. You should stress test all functionality in your system. This includes internal components such as hard disks, controllers, processors, and RAM, as well as external components, such as routers, bridges, switches, cables, and connectors.

You should try to simulate the following situations when you stress test your system:

- Heavy network loads
- Heavy disk I/O
- Heavy use of file and application servers
- Large numbers of users simultaneously logged on

Testing Recovery Systems

Once you've created your recovery systems (Windows 2000 Setup disks, Startup disks, and ERDs, as well as a data backup system), you should practice recovering from disasters that can occur. Your practice should include using the Setup disks, Startup disks, and ERDs, as well as Safe Mode and the Recovery Console. Practicing will help you determine how long a recovery process will take, whether you've backed up all the data that needs to be backed up, and whether you've collected all the configuration and system information necessary to recover from a disaster.

Your testing should help you determine which recovery procedure you should use in certain situations. For example, you might find that in some circumstances you can use Safe Mode to recover, while in other situations you must use the Setup disks along with the ERD.

Your testing should include scenarios that represent the most common causes of unexpected downtime. At a minimum, you should perform the following types of recoveries:

- Restoring data from backups
- Rebuilding redundant array of independent disks (RAID) volumes
- Promoting member servers to domain controllers to replace a failed domain controller
- Replacing components, such as hard disks, adapters, and power supplies
- Recovering MBRs and boot sectors
- Restoring Windows 2000 system files

You should test your recovery procedures before bringing a new computer or server into production.

Testing recovery procedures goes hand-in-hand with training personnel. When administrators practice recovering from a disaster, they're being trained in how to handle disasters should they occur. Properly trained personnel can reduce the likelihood of failures as well as the severity of a failure.

Documenting Recovery Procedures

Your disaster recovery strategy should include step-by-step procedures for recovering from different types of failures. You can use these procedures to test new computers before putting them into production, to train administrators and operators, and to create an operations handbook. You should update your procedures when you change your systems configuration, when you install a new operating system, or when you change the utilities that you use to maintain your system.

Making a Decision

When designing a disaster recovery strategy, you should prepare recovery systems, collect configuration and system information, test system components, test recovery systems, and document recovery procedures. Table 11.7 provides an overview of the factors that you should consider for each step that you should take when preparing for possible disasters.

Table 11.7   Disaster Recovery

Step	Considerations
Preparing recovery systems	Recovery systems include the Windows 2000 Setup disks, startup disk, and ERD. Recovery systems also include any critical system state data, files, or other data important to your system that's backed up on a regularly scheduled basis.
Collecting configuration and system information	Information necessary to restore a system should a disaster occur includes information about hardware configurations, software configurations, computer names and IP addresses, domains, local administrative passwords, and other documentation to support recovery efforts.
Testing system components	You should conduct stress tests to test all functionality in your system, including internal components as well as external ones. Tests should try to simulate heavy network loads, heavy disk I/O, heavy use of file and application servers, and large numbers of simultaneous users.
Testing recovery systems	You should use your recovery systems (Windows 2000 Setup disks, Startup disks, and ERDs, as well as a data backup system) to practice recovering from disasters that can occur.
Documenting recovery procedures	Your disaster recovery strategy should include step-by-step procedures for recovering from different types of failures.

Recommendations

An effective disaster recovery strategy relies heavily on the steps you take before a disaster occurs. Waiting until you have a problem can be too late to figure out what information you're missing or whether you've backed up all data that needs to be preserved. To prepare a strategy, you should follow the five steps outlined in this lesson: prepare recovery systems, collect configuration and system information, test system components, test recovery systems, and document recovery procedures.

Example: Preparing the Recovery Systems for Coho Vineyard

Coho Vineyard is implementing a disaster recovery strategy to prepare for any disasters that might occur in its Web site. The company maintains a small Web site that hosts static content only and supports Anonymous access. The site uses two IIS server computers that are configured as a Network Load Balancing (NLB) cluster. As part of its disaster recovery strategy, Coho Vineyard is preparing the following recovery systems:

- **Windows 2000 Setup floppy disks**   Administrators prepare the Setup disks by using the MAKEBT32.EXE utility on the Windows 2000 Server installation CD-ROM. The MAKEBT32.EXE utility is located in the Bootdisk directory on the CD-ROM. The administrators create four disks: Windows 2000 Setup Boot Disk, Windows 2000 Setup Disk #2, Windows 2000 Setup Disk #3, and Windows 2000 Setup Disk #4.

- **Windows 2000 Startup floppy disks**   For each Windows 2000 Server computer, the administrators create a Startup floppy disk (or disks) by copying the NTLDR, NTDETECT.COM, and BOOT.INI files from the root directory to a floppy disk.

- **Windows 2000 ERDs**   For each Windows 2000 Server computer, the administrators create an ERD by using the Emergency Repair Disk Wizard in the Backup utility. The ERD contains information about the current Windows systems settings for the specific computer.

- **Backed-up data**   Administrators use the Backup utility to create backup jobs for each computer and define a backup schedule for each of those jobs. For each Windows 2000 Server computer, they back up everything on that computer, including the system state data.

Lesson Summary

A disaster is any situation that causes a serious disruption in your system's services. When designing a disaster recovery strategy, you should prepare recovery systems, collect configuration and system information, test system components, test recovery systems, and document recovery procedures. Recovery systems include the Windows 2000 Setup disks, Startup disks, and ERDs. Recovery systems also include the critical system state data, files, or other data important to your system that's backed up on a regularly scheduled basis. In addition to preparing the recovery systems, you should maintain a record of various types of information that will help you restore your system should a disaster occur, including information about hardware and software configurations; domains, computer names and IP addresses; local administrative passwords; and miscellaneous documentation. You should also test your internal and external components to try to predict failure situations and to practice recovery procedures. Once you've created your recovery systems, you should practice recovering from disasters that can occur. Your practice should include using the Setup disks, Startup disks, and ERDs, as well as Safe Mode and the Recovery Console. Finally, your disaster recovery strategy should include step-by-step procedures for recovering from different types of failures.

Lab 11.1: Designing a System Monitoring and Security Auditing Strategy

After completing this lab, you'll be able to

- Design a system monitoring strategy
- Design a security auditing strategy

About This Lab

In this lab, you'll design a monitoring strategy that uses the performance objects and counters in Windows 2000 and IIS. You'll also design an auditing strategy that uses events in Windows 2000 and IIS to log activity related to security and that uses IIS logging to log information specific to a Web site.

Before You Begin

Before you begin this lab, you must be able to

- Use performance objects and counters in Windows 2000, IIS, and other applications to monitor performance on Windows 2000 Server computers
- Use events in Windows 2000, IIS, and other applications to log events that occur on Windows 2000 Server computers
- Use IIS logging to log the activity of a Web site

Scenario: Northwind Traders Web Site

Northwind Traders maintains a small Web site that includes IIS on a front-end cluster and SQL Server on the back-end cluster. The site uses ASP applications on the front-end cluster to access data on the back-end cluster. The site supports Anonymous access for all Internet users. The front-end cluster includes three Windows 2000 Server computers, and the back-end cluster includes two Windows 2000 Server computers, as shown in Figure 11.12. Two firewalls are used to create a perimeter network that contains both clusters.

As the network administrator for this site, you must develop a monitoring and auditing strategy that uses Windows 2000 performance counters and events and IIS logging to provide performance and security data about your system.

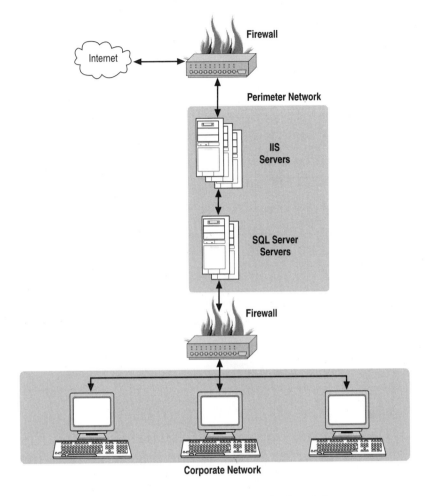

Figure 11.12   Northwind Traders front-end and back-end clusters

Exercise 1: Designing a System Monitoring Strategy

In this exercise, you'll develop a system monitoring strategy that uses the performance objects and counters in Windows 2000 and IIS. Currently, you plan to monitor the performance only on the three IIS computers. Your monitoring strategy will be the same for all three computers. You want to look specifically at each system's memory, processors, network I/O, and Web applications. Because users will be accessing the site anonymously, you won't be monitoring security overhead at this time.

1. The first step in your monitoring strategy is to collect performance data about memory. What five components of memory should you monitor?

2. Why should you monitor memory before monitoring any other components?

3. Next, you want to monitor the processors in your system. You plan to collect information about processor activity, IIS service connections, and IIS threads. What types of information should you collect about each of these categories?

4. The next step in your strategy is to collect data about network I/O. Specifically, you plan to collect data about transmission rates and TCP connections. What type of information should you collect about transmission rates and TCP connections?

5. Finally, you plan to monitor your Web applications. What components should you monitor?

6. Suppose that, during your analysis of the data, you discover periods of long, sustained queue lengths. What might be causing these long queue lengths?

Exercise 2: Designing a Security Auditing Strategy

In this exercise, you'll design a strategy to track the activities of users and services. You'll use two methods to log information about this activity: logging Windows 2000 security events (using the Security log) and logging site activity (using IIS logging).

1. The first step in your strategy is to configure audit policies that allow you to log specific events. How do you configure audit policies?

2. You're specifically concerned with auditing access to certain directories and files. You want to log events about successful and failed attempts to access resources. Which audit policy or policies should you configure and how should you configure that policy?

3. Once you've configured Group Policy, you decide that you want to audit the Inetpub\Scripts directory. What step do you need to take to configure auditing on that directory?

4. Once you've configured auditing on the Inetpub\Scripts directory, you want to be able to view the Security log regularly to view any events that might have been generated. How do you view the Security log?

5. In addition to auditing events, you want to log activity about your Web site. Specifically, you want to log date, time, client IP address, and username for each user who logs on to the site. At this time you don't want to log any other information about the site because you want to limit the size of your log files. How can you log this information?

6. Once you've logged data about your users, how can you view that data?

7. What log file formats does IIS logging support?

8. You decide that although you want to log activity to your Web site, you don't want to log activity on the Images directory, which is a part of the site. How do you disable logging on the Images directory?

Review

Answering the following questions will reinforce key information presented in this chapter. If you're unable to answer a question, review the appropriate lesson and then try the question again. Answers to the questions can be found in the appendix.

1. You want to monitor performance on your Windows 2000 computer. You want to first establish a baseline and then conduct ongoing monitoring. Which Microsoft tool allows you to establish a baseline and then measure the ongoing performance of your system?

2. You're the network administrator for your organization and you're monitoring performance on an IIS server. You discover that the Inetinfo working set often uses all the available RAM. In addition, during those peak usages of RAM disk activity is high. What's the most likely cause of the problem?

3. You're auditing logon events on your IIS server. You're interested only in failed logon events; however, the Security log shows successful logon attempts and failed logon events. As a result, your log reaches its maximum size too quickly. How can you log only failed events?

4. You're using IIS logging to log the activity on your Web site. You want to log all events to a SQL Server database. You create a database, a data source name (DSN), and a table within the database to store the logged events. Which log format should you use when configuring IIS logging?

5. You're developing a disaster recovery strategy for your IIS servers. As part of that strategy, you determine that you must prepare recovery systems to have in place should a disaster occur. You create the necessary Windows 2000 Setup disks, Startup disks, and ERDs. What other step should you take in preparing your recovery systems?

6. As part of a disaster recovery strategy that you're developing for your organization, you plan to test various system components to try to predict failure and to practice recovery procedures. Your tests will include internal and external components. What situations should you try to simulate when you stress test your system?

APPENDIX

Questions and Answers

Page 1

Chapter 1
Introduction to Designing Highly Available Web Solutions

Page 24

Review Questions

1. Define the following key terms: availability, failure, fault tolerance, manageability, reliability, and scalability.

   Availability is a measure (from 0 to 100 percent) of the fault tolerance of a computer and its programs. The goal of a highly available computer is to run 24 hours a day, 7 days a week, which means that applications and services are operational and usable by clients most of the time.

   Failure is defined as a departure from expected behavior on an individual computer system or a network system of associated computers and applications. Failures can include behavior that simply moves outside of defined performance parameters.

   Fault tolerance is the ability of a system to continue functioning when part of the system fails. Fault tolerance combats problems such as disk failures, power outages, or corrupted operating systems, which can affect startup files, the operating system itself, or system files. Windows 2000 Server includes features that support certain types of fault tolerance.

   Manageability is the ability to make changes to the system easily. Management has many facets, but it can be loosely divided into the following disciplines: change and configuration management, security management, performance management, problem management, event management, batch/output management, and storage management.

   Reliability is a measure of the time that elapses between failures in a system. Hardware and software components have different failure characteristics. Although formulas based on historical data exist to predict

hardware reliability, it's difficult to find formulas for predicting software reliability.

Scalability is a measure of how well a computer, service, or application can expand to meet increasing performance demands. For server clusters, scalability refers to the ability to incrementally add one or more systems to an existing cluster when the cluster's overall load exceeds its capabilities.

2. What are the key architectural elements of an *n*-tier business Web site?

Clients, which issue service requests to the server hosting the application that the client is accessing; front-end systems, which consist of the collections of servers that provide core services, such as HTTP/HTTPS and FTP, to the clients; and back-end systems, which are the servers hosting the data stores that are used by the front-end systems.

3. In the formula MTTR/MTTF, what do MTTR and MTTF refer to, how do they differ, and what's the purpose of this ratio?

MTTF (mean time to failure) is the mean time it will take for a device to fail, and MTTR (mean time to recovery) is the mean time it takes the device to recover from a failure. Downtime is determined by the ratio MTTR/MTTF.

4. What types of failures can cause system outages?

Software failures, hardware failures, network failures, operational failures, and environmental failures can cause system outages.

5. You're designing a highly available Web site. What are the three fundamental strategies that you should use?

Develop operational procedures that are well documented and appropriate for your goals and your staff's capabilities.

Ensure that your site has enough capacity to handle processing loads.

Reduce the probability of failure.

6. You're designing a highly available Web site and you're specifically concerned about preventing application failures. What techniques should you use to reduce the chance of failures?

Create a robust architecture based on redundant, load-balanced servers. (Note, however, that load-balanced clusters are different from Windows application clusters. Commerce Server 2000 components, such as List Manager and Direct Mailer, are not cluster aware.)

Review code to avoid potential buffer overflows, infinite loops, code crashes, and openings for security attacks.

Page 25

Chapter 2
Network Infrastructure

Page 49

Activity Questions

1. How should you design the network topology for the e-commerce site?

    The network topology should look similar to the design shown in the following illustration:

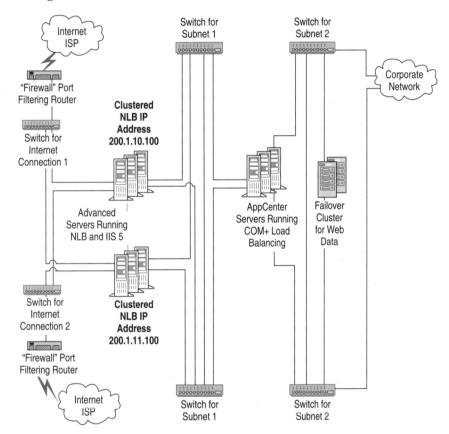

Lab Questions

Page 75

Exercise 1: Providing Redundant Components and Network Paths

1. What network elements can you make redundant for this topology?
    - **Switches**
    - **Routers**
    - **LAN paths**
    - **Internet connections**
    - **Services (through the use of clusters)**

2. On a piece of paper, sketch a design that builds on the design in Figure 2.18. Be sure to incorporate any network elements that can be made redundant. How should you modify your design?

Your design should be similar to the one in the following illustration:

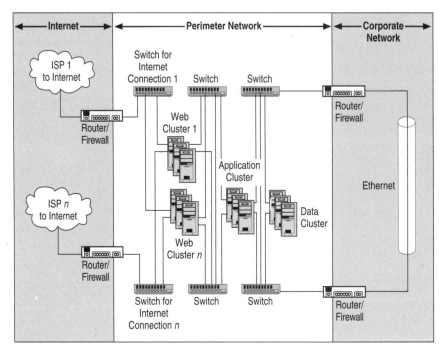

Notice that the design shown in the answer places the application clusters in a middle tier. Some topologies include only a front-end tier and a back-end tier.

3. Suppose a computer in the application cluster tries to communicate with the data cluster. What possible LAN paths can that communication follow?

■ **From the application computer to the first switch (top switch in the diagram) and then to the data cluster**

■ **From the application computer to the first switch, then to the second switch, and then to the data cluster**

■ **From the application computer to the second switch and then to the data cluster**

■ **From the application computer to the second switch, then to the first switch, and then to the data cluster**

Page 76

Exercise 2: Subnetting a TCP/IP Network

1. How many network segments will you use and where will you use them?

You will need to create four network segments:

- A network segment for the middle tier, which will bridge the Web clusters and the application cluster
- A network segment for the back-end network, which will bridge the application cluster and the routers to the secure network
- A network segment for the secure network
- A network segment for the management network

2. On your sketch of the network topology, label the four network segments and indicate the position of those segments. Your network topology should also indicate the position of the front-end network. How should you modify your design?

Your design should be similar to the one in the following illustration:

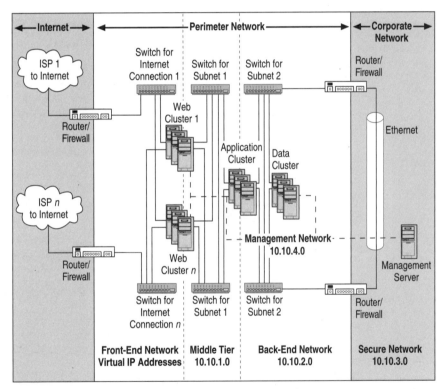

Notice that the management network is connected to each cluster and is on its own subnet. Also notice that in this topology the application cluster is connected to three different network segments: the middle tier (10.10.1.0), the back-end tier (10.10.2.0), and the management tier (10.10.4.0).

3. To which network segments do the Web clusters connect?

The Web clusters connect to the front end network, which is connected to the Internet; the middle tier (10.10.1.0); and the management network (10.10.4.0).

Page 77

Exercise 3: Designing a Namespace

1. How should you set up the internal and external namespaces?

   To simplify name resolution for internal clients, use a different domain name for your internal and external namespaces. You can use the same name internally and externally, but doing so causes configuration problems and generally increases administrative overhead. If you want to use the same domain name internally and externally, you need to perform one of the following actions:

   - **Duplicate internally the public DNS zone of your organization.**

   - **Duplicate internally the public DNS zone and all public servers (such as Web servers) that belong to your organization.**

   - **In the PAC file on each of your clients, maintain a list of the public servers that belong to your organization.**

2. You decide to use separate names for your external and internal namespaces: contoso.com for the external namespace and contoso-pvt.com for the internal namespace. On your sketch of the network topology, label how the namespaces are divided so the division between the two namespaces is clear. How should you modify your design?

   Your design should be similar to the one in the following illustration:

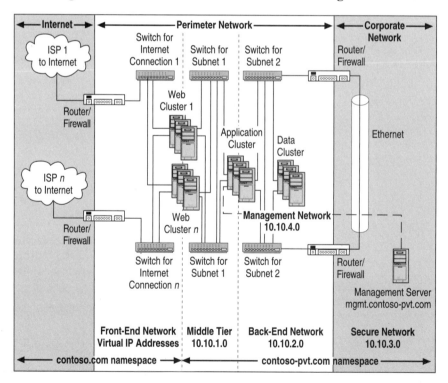

Notice that the management server is now labeled with an FQDN:
mgmt.contoso-pvt.com.

3. Suppose that one of the servers in Web cluster 1 is named Web1. What would be the FQDN for that server?

   The FQDN for the Internet side of the server would be web1.contoso.com, and the FQDN for the private side of the server would be web1.contoso-pvt.com.

4. Suppose that one of the servers in the application cluster is named App1. What would be the FQDN for that server?

   The FQDN for the server would be app1.contoso-pvt.com.

Page 78 ## Review Questions

1. The network topology for your organization includes a Web component that provides information and online registration for your company's training facilities. Figure 2.19 shows the Web component of your network topology.

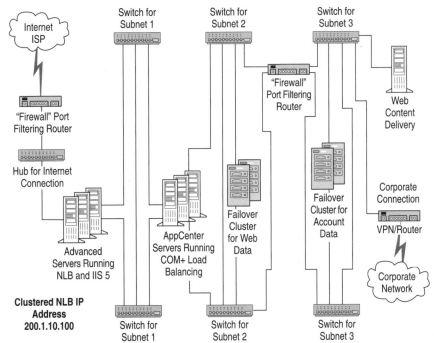

   Many users have been complaining that your site is often unavailable. You plan to modify the network topology to increase availability. What's the first step you should take?

   Add a redundant connection to the Internet.

2. When you subnet the network shown in Figure 2.19, you assign the network ID 10.10.1.0 to subnet 1, 10.10.2.0 to subnet 2, and 10.10.3.0 to subnet 3. What additional subnet should you add to this topology?

   You should add a management subnet (such as 10.10.4.0) that connects to each cluster.

3. You're planning the configuration of the DHCP Service for your network and want to ensure fault tolerance. However, you won't be implementing clustering. You set up a primary DHCP server and a backup DHCP server. How should you configure any scopes that you create?

   Use the 80/20 rule to divide scope addresses between the DHCP servers. The primary server should receive about 80 percent of the available addresses, and the backup server should receive about 20 percent.

4. Your company, Contoso, Ltd., plans to set up a Web site so customers can access services on the Internet. Until now, your company has had no Web presence. Your company has registered the name contoso.com with an Internet name authority and wants to use that name for both the internal and external namespaces. What actions must you perform to use the same name?

   You must perform one of the following actions:

   - **Duplicate internally your organization's public DNS zone.**
   - **Duplicate internally the public DNS zone and all public servers that belong to your organization.**
   - **Maintain a list (in the PAC file on each client computer) of the public servers that belong to your organization.**

Page 81

Chapter 3
Server Configurations

Lab Questions

Page 101

Exercise 1: Planning a File Server Configuration

1. How should you label the rest of the diagram?

   You should label the diagram in a way similar to that shown in the following illustration:

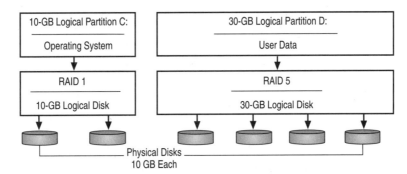

Notice that six 10-GB physical disks (60 GB) are used to store data, but the logical disks support only 40 GB of storage.

2. Why is there a difference in storage capacity between the logical disks and the physical disks?

    In a RAID-1 configuration the same data is written to each of the two disks. As a result, disk space usage is only 50 percent of the total for both disks. RAID-5 uses the equivalent of one physical disk to support its fault-tolerant configuration. In this case, one disk equals 10 GB, so 10 GB are used for parity information, leaving 30 GB for storage.

Page 102

Exercise 2: Planning a File Server and Operating System Configuration

1. How should you configure the data storage system for these servers?

    You should label the diagram in a way similar to that shown in the following illustration:

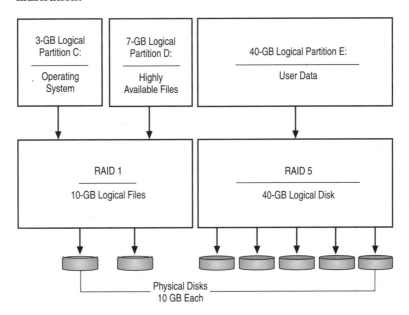

Notice that two 10-GB disks are used to support the RAID-1 configuration, but only 10 GB of storage are available on the logical disk.

2. Why is there a difference in storage capacity between the logical disk and the physical disks?

In a RAID-1 configuration the same data is written to each of the two disks. As a result, disk space usage is only 50 percent of the total for both disks.

Page 103

Exercise 3: Planning a Domain Controller and Services Configuration

1. Draw a diagram that provides a conceptual overview of how RAID will be implemented on these servers. Label the logical partitions, the logical disk, and the physical disks. Include the size of each partition and disk and their functions.

You should configure the data storage system in a way similar to that shown in the following illustration:

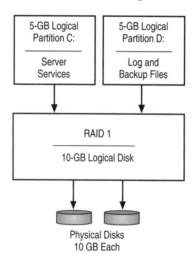

Page 104

Exercise 4: Planning a Relational Database Server Configuration

1. How should you configure the data storage system for these servers?

You should configure the data storage system in a way similar to that shown in the following illustration:

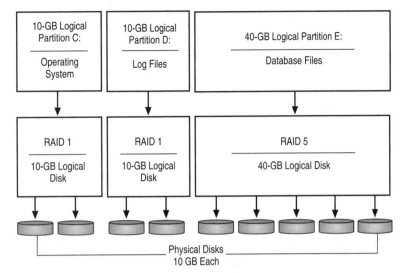

2. How much storage would the RAID-5 logical disk support if another 10-GB hard disk were added to the configuration?

50 GB

Page 105

Review Questions

1. You're designing a network infrastructure for the Baldwin Museum of Science, and you want to ensure that your servers are fault tolerant. One way that you plan to support fault tolerance is to use redundant components within your critical servers. What redundant components should you add to the servers?

   You should configure each server with the following redundant components:

   - **NICs**
   - **Cooling fans**
   - **Power supplies**
   - **Disk controllers**

2. Woodgrove Bank has been experiencing intermittent problems with their servers. The problems have included overheating, shorts, and unexpected restarts when an administrator touches one of the computers. Technicians have checked the computers, their components, and how they're configured and can't find an immediate cause of these problems. What other factors should be considered?

The servers' environment should be checked to make certain that the room temperature is about 70° F (21° C), that a proper amount of humidity is maintained, and that the computers and the computer room are kept clean.

3. City Power & Light stores a great deal of data in order to maintain their operations. At any one time, their storage capacity can exceed 6 TB. You're designing a data storage system for the company, and you want to ensure that the system is fault tolerant, the data is centralized, and backup and restores are easy to administer. What type of storage would you recommend?

Storage area network (SAN)

4. You're designing a data storage system for the Graphic Design Institute. The company maintains about 45 GB of data at any one time. The organization wants to ensure that the data storage system is fault tolerant, but they want to implement the least expensive solution available. Which storage solution would you recommend?

Recommend the software implementation of RAID-5 that's available in Windows 2000 Server.

Page 107

Chapter 4
Microsoft Windows 2000 Cluster Service

Page 132

Activity Questions

For each of the following steps, identify how your file server resource group will be configured:

1. List all the server-based applications.

   No server-based applications are running on these servers. However, examples of server-based applications are Microsoft SQL Server 2000 and Microsoft Exchange Server.

2. Sort the list of applications. Determine which applications can use failover.

   No server-based applications are running on these servers.

3. List all other resources.

   File Share, IP Address, Network Name, and Physical Disk

4. List all dependencies for each resource.

   The File Share resource type depends on the Network Name resource type, and the Network Name resource type depends on the IP Address resource type. The File Share resource type also depends on the Physical Disk resource type.

5. Make preliminary grouping decisions.

   You should create only one resource group because a resource and its dependencies must be together in a single group. In addition, a resource can't span groups.

6. Make final grouping assignments, and create any necessary dependency trees.

   You should create only one resource group. The dependency should look similar to the one shown in the following illustration:

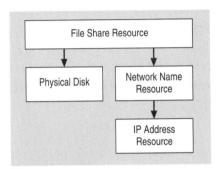

Lab Questions

Page 144

Exercise 1: Choosing a Server Cluster Model

1. What are the differences between the three configuration models?

   With a single-node configuration, you can organize resources for administrative convenience, use virtual servers, restart applications automatically, and more easily create a cluster later. However, this model can't make use of failover. If an application can't be restarted, it becomes unavailable.

   An active/passive configuration provides the maximum availability for your resources. However, this model also requires an investment in hardware that's not used most of the time. If the primary node fails, the secondary node immediately picks up all operations. This model is best suited for those applications and resources that must maintain the highest availability.

   An active/active configuration provides high availability and performance when both nodes are online and provides reliable and acceptable performance when only one node is online. Services remain available during and after failover, but performance can decrease, which can affect availability.

2. Which configuration best suits the needs of Wingtip Toys?

   An active/active configuration best suits the needs of Wingtip Toys because this configuration allows maximum use of hardware resources

while providing highly available services. Because performance degradation after failover isn't an overriding concern, an active/passive configuration isn't necessary.

Page 144   ## Exercise 2: Planning the Resource Groups

Listing the Server-Based Applications
1. What are those applications?

   SQL Server 2000 and Exchange 2000 Server

Sorting the List of Applications
1. Which applications will use failover?

   **Both SQL Server 2000 and Exchange 2000 Server can use failover and
   you should set up both to use it.**

Listing Other Resources
1. Which resources should you include?

   **You should include the following resources: Physical Disk, Network
   Name, and IP Address.**

Listing Dependencies
1. How are these resources dependent on each other?

   **Each service (mail and database) is dependent on the Physical Disk resource
   and the Network Name resource. Each Network Name resource is dependent
   on the IP Address resource.**

Making Preliminary Grouping Decisions
1. How will resources be grouped together?

   **You should create two groups: one for the database service and its related
   resource types (Physical Disk, Network Name, and IP Address), and one
   for the mail service and its related resource types (Physical Disk, Network
   Name, and IP Address).**

2. What are the advantages of this grouping strategy?

   **This grouping strategy allows the mail service to run on one node and the
   database service to run on another node, which supports an active/active
   configuration.**

Making Final Grouping Assignments
1. How would you create a dependency tree for each group?

   **In the database resource group, the database resource is dependent on
   the Physical Disk resource type and the Network Name resource type,
   and the Network Name resource type is dependent on the IP Address
   Resource type. The mail resource group has the same dependencies.**

Page 145

Exercise 3: Determining Failover Policies

1. How should you configure the Failover Timing setting?

   For each group, set the Cluster service to restart the group before failover occurs.

2. How should you configure the Preferred Node setting?

   Configure each group so it always runs on a designated node whenever the node is available. You should configure the database group so that one of the servers is set as the preferred node, and you should configure the mail group so that the other server is set as the preferred node.

3. How should you configure the Failback Timing setting?

   Configure each group to failback to its preferred node as soon as the Cluster service detects that the failed node has been restored.

Page 146

Review Questions

1. What objects does the Cluster service manage?

   Server cluster networks, network interfaces, nodes, resource groups, and resources

2. What are the differences between a resource group and a resource?

   Resource groups are logical collections of resources. Typically, a resource group is made up of logically related resources such as applications and their associated peripherals and data. A resource is any physical or logical component that can be brought online and taken offline, be managed in a server cluster, and be hosted (owned) by only one node at a time.

3. You're planning the resource groups for a cluster on your network. You've determined which applications will run on the servers and, of those, which can use failover. You've also determined the other types of resources that will be included in your list of resources, such as network names and IP addresses. What step should you take next?

   You should list the dependencies for each resource. The list should include all resources that support the core resource.

4. You're planning a cluster for your organization's network. The cluster will include two Windows 2000 Advanced server computers that will run a database application and a file and print services. You want the cluster configuration to support the maximum use of your cluster hardware. Which cluster configuration model should you use?

   You should use the active/active model because it supports the maximum use of hardware by placing resource groups on separate nodes. When the cluster is fully operational, the cluster provides high availability and performance.

Page 147   # Chapter 5
Network Load Balancing (NLB)

Page 172   ## Activity Questions

1. How should this configuration look?

   The network should be configured in a way similar to the configuration shown in the following illustration:

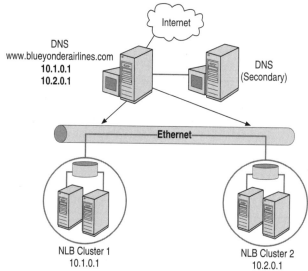

2. What option other than round-robin DNS can you consider to balance the load between clusters?

   When you have more than one cluster, you can use network switches to separate incoming traffic. However, if you use network switches and you deploy two or more clusters, consider placing the clusters on individual switches so that incoming cluster traffic is handled separately.

Lab Questions

Page 185   ### Exercise 1: Determining Which Applications to Run in the Cluster

1. What type of applications can you run on an NLB cluster?

   In general, NLB can scale any application or service that uses TCP/IP as its network protocol and is associated with a specific TCP or UDP port. In addition, the application must be designed to allow multiple instances to run simultaneously, one on each cluster host. You shouldn't use NLB to directly scale applications that independently update inter-client state data because updates made on one cluster host won't be visible to other cluster hosts.

2. Which application or applications will you run in the NLB cluster and why would you choose those applications?

IIS, because it uses TCP/IP as its network protocol and uses Port 80. In addition, IIS allows multiple instances to run simultaneously on different hosts.

3. Is there any application that shouldn't be run on the NLB cluster, and if so, why not?

You shouldn't run SQL Server and Exchange Server on the NLB cluster because these applications independently update inter-client state data. You should use the Cluster service to create clusters for these two applications.

Page 185

Exercise 2: Choosing an NLB Model

1. What are the advantages and disadvantages of each of these configuration models?

- **Single network adapter in unicast mode:**

  Unicast mode is the default configuration for NLB and works with all routers. However, ordinary network communication among hosts isn't possible, and network performance may be compromised.

- **Multiple network adapters in unicast mode:**

  Unicast mode is the default configuration for NLB and works with all routers. In addition, ordinary network communication among hosts is possible, and network performance may be enhanced. However, at least two network adapters are required.

- **Single network adapter in multicast mode:**

  Only one network adapter is required, and ordinary network communication among hosts is possible. However, this isn't the default configuration, network performance may suffer, and some routers may not support the use of a multicast MAC address.

- **Multiple network adapters in multicast mode:**

  Performance may be enhanced, and ordinary network communication among hosts is possible. However, this isn't the default configuration, at least two network adapters are required, and some routers may not support the use of a multicast MAC address.

2. Which configuration model should you use?

Each host in the NLB cluster should be configured with multiple network adapters, and the cluster should run in unicast mode. This model is easier to configure because it's the default mode, permits ordinary network communication among hosts, and works with all routers. The fact that at least two network adapters are required is not a problem because the hosts are part of a multitiered structure that requires at least two network adapters in each computer.

Review Questions

1. How does NLB work?

   NLB scales the performance of a server-based program, such as a Web server, by distributing its client requests among multiple servers within the cluster. With NLB, each host receives each incoming IP packet but only the intended recipient accepts it. The cluster hosts concurrently respond to different client requests or to multiple requests from the same client. For example, a Web browser may obtain the various images within a single Web page from different hosts in a load-balanced cluster. This speeds up processing and shortens the response time to clients.

2. What are the differences between Single affinity and Class C affinity?

   With Single affinity, NLB pins a client to a particular host without setting a timeout limit; this mapping is in effect until the cluster set changes. The trouble with Single affinity is that in a large site with multiple proxy servers a client can appear to come from different IP addresses. To address this issue, NLB also includes Class C affinity, which specifies that all clients within a given Class C address space will map to a given cluster host. However, Class C affinity doesn't address situations in which proxy servers are placed across Class C address spaces. Currently the only solution is to handle it at the ASP level.

3. How does NLB manage session state that spans multiple connections?

   When its client affinity parameter setting is enabled, NLB directs all TCP connections from one client IP address to the same cluster host. This allows session state to be maintained in host memory. However, should a server or network failure occur during a client session, a new logon may be required to reauthenticate the client and reestablish session state.

4. You're a network administrator at Trey Research. You're responsible for administering the company's Web site and its infrastructure. You want to implement an NLB cluster to run IIS. You've identified network risks and eliminated any single points of failure. The cluster will include four hosts, and each host will be configured to use RAID-5 for fault-tolerant storage. You'll determine the host's capacity requirements after you've planned the rest of the cluster.

   What other decision must you make?

   You must choose an NLB configuration model.

5. You're planning a small NLB cluster for your organization's network. The cluster will contain only two computers. Each computer will be configured with only one network adapter. You want the configuration to support ordinary network traffic between the computers.

   Which NLB configuration model should you use?

You should use a single network adapter in multicast mode. If the router doesn't accept an ARP response from the cluster, you should add a static ARP entry to the router for each virtual IP address.

Page 187

Chapter 6
Microsoft Application Center 2000

Page 212

Activity Questions

1. In the diagram, label the following components: client, Internet, Web-tier cluster, COM+ cluster, NLB, and CLB.

   The diagram should look similar to the following illustration:

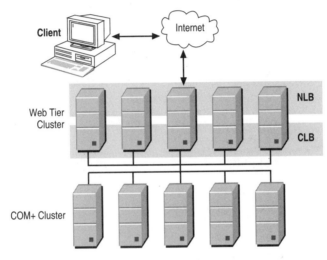

2. What are the different cluster types supported by Application Center?

   General/Web cluster, COM+ application cluster, and COM+ routing cluster

3. Which cluster type would you use to host Web sites and to support NLB and CLB?

   General/Web cluster

Lab Questions

Page 225

Exercise 1: Designing a General/Web Cluster

1. How should you draw your network design?

   Your design should look similar to the one in the following illustration:

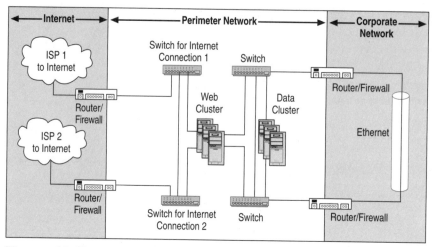

2. How would client requests be distributed to the hosts in General/Web cluster once those requests have passed through the firewall?

   Requests will be routed to the hosts through the use of NLB, which will be configured on each computer.

3. Based on the current network configuration, where would COM+ applications reside?

   COM+ applications would reside on the General/Web cluster.

Page 225   ### Exercise 2: Designing a COM+ Routing Cluster

1. How should you draw the network design?

   Your design should look similar to the one in the following illustration:

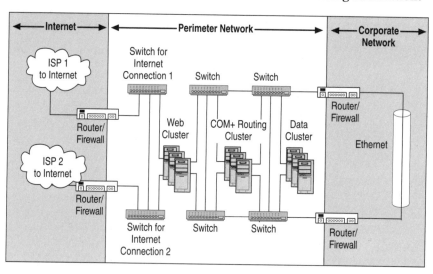

2. On which cluster or clusters would you now run NLB?

You would configure NLB on the General/Web cluster and the COM+ routing cluster.

3. What's the primary role of the COM+ routing cluster?

The primary role of the COM+ routing cluster is to route requests to a COM+ application cluster.

Page 226

Exercise 3: Designing a COM+ Application Cluster

1. How should you draw the network design?

Your design should look similar to the one in the following illustration:

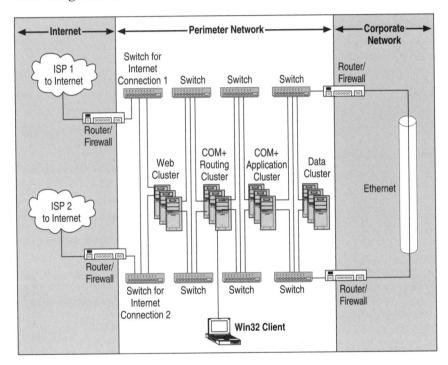

2. On which tiers should you run CLB and NLB?

You should configure CLB on the COM+ routing cluster and configure NLB on the General/Web cluster and the COM+ routing cluster.

3. How is network performance affected by running COM+ applications on a cluster separate from the General/Web cluster?

Calls over the network yield slower throughput than calls to software installed on the same computer. This is true in all software communication, whether it's through Microsoft software or something else. For this reason, CLB isn't an effective solution where throughput is absolutely

critical. In this case it's better to install the COM+ components locally on the Web-tier cluster members, thus avoiding cross-network calls. CLB support is lost, but load balancing is still available through NLB.

Page 227

Review Questions

1. How is NLB in Application Center integrated with NLB in Windows 2000 Advanced Server?

   NLB in Application Center is carried out by NLB in Windows 2000 Advanced Server or Datacenter Server. Application Center provides an interface that's integrated with NLB. The Application Center user interface serves to make load-balancing configurations for a cluster easier by removing much of the configuration detail and by reducing the number of user decision points.

2. In what scenarios should you consider using CLB?

   You should consider using CLB in the following scenarios:

   - **Security is a major concern and you want to segregate COM objects behind an additional firewall.**

   - **COM objects are relatively large and you want to run them on the fastest servers available.**

   - **Applications are partitioned into *n*-tiers, either for development or design reasons. If you're using NLB for your front-end servers and want to route component requests to a back-end COM+ server, the Application Center user interface lets you easily specify a target.**

   - **Scaling is important. A single cluster can use multiple COM+ clusters to service component requests.**

3. What are the three primary clustering scenarios?

   Single-node clusters, standard Web clusters, and COM+ applications clusters.

4. You're the network administrator at Graphic Design Institute, and you want to improve the availability of your company's Web site. You decide to implement an Application Center cluster to support the Web services. In planning the cluster, you decide to include three hosts, each of which is configured with enough resources to run Windows 2000 Advanced Server, Application Center, Event and Performance Logging, and IIS 5.0. You also plan to configure the cluster network adapters on a subnet separate from the back-end network adapters.

   Which cluster type and load balancing configuration should you use?

   You should use the General/Web cluster type and use NLB for your load-balancing configuration. The General/Web cluster type is used to host Web sites. NLB is recommended over other load balancing because it's inexpensive to implement and requires less administration.

5. Your company is implementing a Web site and is evaluating how to structure clusters and load balancing on your network. Throughput performance is critical to the operation and should be maintained at the highest possible level. In addition, management wants to keep network administration as uncomplicated as possible and to make full use of the hardware that they have available.

Which type or types of Application Center clusters (General/Web, COM+ routing, or COM+ application) should you implement in this site?

You should implement a General/Web cluster but not a COM+ routing cluster or COM+ application cluster. Using a separate tier for the COM+ applications will result in a degradation in throughput performance, in administrative complexity, and in difficulty in making full use of the hardware.

Page 229

Chapter 7
Capacity Planning

Page 253

Activity 7.1 Questions

1. Your first step is to determine the CPU cost per operation. In order to calculate this cost, you must first determine the CPU usage. How do you calculate the CPU usage for the Search operation?

You should use the following calculation:

$.9247 \times 3 \times 400 = 1109.64$

2. Now that you've calculated the CPU usage, you can use that calculation to determine the cost of the operation. How do you calculate the CPU cost for the Search operation?

You should use the following calculation:

$1109.64 \div 18.21 \times 2 = 121.87$

3. You can now use the cost per operation to figure out the cost per user. How do you calculate the CPU cost per operation per use?

You should use the following calculation:

$121.87 \times 0.00139 = 0.1694$ MC

Page 254

Activity 7.2 Questions

1. Your first step is to determine the cost per user for the Web server. How do you calculate that cost?

You should use the following calculation:

$0.003804 \times 4.297 = 0.01635$

2. Next you must determine the cost per user for the data server. How do you calculate that cost?

You should use the following calculation:

0.003804 × 119.36 = 0.45405

3. How do you calculate the total cost per user per second?

You should use the following calculation:

0.01635 + 0.45405 = 0.4704 KBps

Lab Questions

Page 269

Exercise 1: Identifying the User Base

1. How many concurrent users should your network support?

The network should support 6,000 concurrent users.

2. What's the first step you must take to calculate the CPU usage per user?

You must first calculate the CPU usage for the Default operation by using the following calculation:

.9615 × 3 × 400 = 1153.8

3. What's the next step that you should take to calculate the CPU usage per user?

Once you've determined the CPU usage for the Default operation, you should calculate the cost for that operation by using the following calculation:

1153.8 ÷ 96.98 × 1 = 11.897

4. What's the CPU cost for each operation?

The cost for each operation is as follows:

Default: .9615 × 3 × 400 ÷ 96.98 × 1 = 11.897

Add Item: .9208 × 3 × 400 ÷ 26.21 × 3 = 126.474

Listing: .9342 × 3 × 400 ÷ 29.29 × 2 = 76.548

Lookup: .9899 × 3 × 400 ÷ 82.08 × 2 = 28.944

5. Once you've determined the cost per operation, you can determine the cost per user per operation, and from there, determine the cost per user. What's the cost per user for each operation?

The cost per user for each operation is as follows:

Default: 11.897 × 0.00128 = 0.01523

Add Item: 126.474 × 0.00102 = 0.12900

Listing: 76.548 × 0.00329 = 0.25184

Lookup: 28.944 × 0.00121 = 0.03502

6. What's the total cost per user for CPU usage?

   The total cost per user for CPU usage is as follows:

   0.01523 + 0.12900 + 0.25184 + 0.03502 = 0.43109

7. What's the network cost for the Default operation?

   The network cost of the Default operation is as follows:

   (0.003682 × 1.845) + (0.003682 × 0) = 0.006793 KBps

8. What are the network costs of the remaining three operations?

   The network costs of the operations are as follows:

   Add Item: (0.000254 × 4.978) + (0.000254 × 127.756) = 0.033714 KBps

   Listing: (0.000523 × 26.765) + (0.000523 × 24.123) = 0.026614 KBps

   Lookup: (0.001134 × 25.678) + (0.001134 × 25.564) = 0.058108 KBps

9. What are the total network costs per user?

   The network costs per user are as follows:

   0.006793 + 0.033714 + 0.026614 + 0.058108 = 0.125229 KBps

Page 271   ### Exercise 2: Determining CPU Requirements

1. How much processing power does each server have and how much of that can be used?

   Each Web server is configured with three 400 MHz processors, giving each machine 1,200 MHz of processing power. However, the upper bound on each computer is 755 MHz.

2. What is the total cost per user for CPU usage?

   The total cost per user for CPU usage is 0.43109 MC.

3. How many concurrent users can the CPUs in each Web server support?

   The CPUs in each Web server can support the following number of users:

   755 ÷ 0.43109 = 1,751 users

4. Once you've determined how many concurrent users each machine will support, you should round down that amount to a whole number and use that fig-

ure to calculate the number of servers that you need. How many Web servers should your cluster contain?

The Web cluster should contain the following number of servers:

6,000 ÷ 1,751 = 4 servers

Page 272

Exercise 3: Determining Bandwidth Capacity

1. What's the network bandwidth and how much of that bandwidth should you utilize when planning your capacity requirements?

    The network is a 100-Mbps (12.5 MBps) Ethernet network. Normally, you should not push network utilization over 36 percent, which is 4.5 MBps.

2. How many concurrent users will your network support?

    The network will support the following number of concurrent users:

    4500 KBps ÷ 0.125229 KBps = 35,934 users

Page 273

Review Questions

1. You're a network administrator at Contoso Pharmaceuticals. Your network is connected to the Internet by a T1 line. You want to know the maximum transmission rate for a 5-KB page. With overhead, a page transmission runs about 55,360 bits. What's the maximum transmission rate over the T1 line?

    The maximum transmission rate is as follows:

    1,536,000 ÷ 55,360 = 27.7 pages per second

2. You're implementing new tools on your company's Web site. You want to find out how long it will take users to download a 90 KB page (including overhead) over a 28.8 Kbps modem and a 56 Kbps modem. How many seconds will it take each type of user to download the page?

    For the 28.8 Kbps modem, it will take the following amount of time to download the 90-KB page:

    720 kilobits ÷ 28.8 Kbps = about 25 seconds

    For the 56 Kbps modem, it will take the following amount of time to download the 90-KB page:

    720 kilobits ÷ 56 Kbps = about 13 seconds

3. Your company is implementing new services on their Web site. The new services include data access to a back-end SQL Server database. In testing and analysis, you discovered that the Add Item operation responds more slowly than you expected. You determine that the disk cost for the operation is 4.395

and the usage for that operation is 0.012345 operations per second. What's the disk cost per user per second for the Add Item operation?

The disk cost for the Add Item operation is as follows:

$4.395 \times 0.012345 = 0.054256$ KBps

4. You're planning your network's capacity requirements. The site will be a transaction site that will allow users to store and retrieve information. Content will be dynamic: ASP hitting a SQL Server database. You anticipate 5,000 concurrent users at peak usage. What other steps should you take?

    You should determine your hardware needs and your network bandwidth. You should also plan the site topology to take into consideration the capacity requirements. In addition, you should find potential bottlenecks and plan for future upgrades to the site.

Page 275

Chapter 8
Directory Services

Lab Questions

Page 296

Exercise 1: Defining a Site Structure

1. What criteria should you use when deciding how to structure your sites?

    You should create a site for each LAN or set of LANs connected by high-speed links, any perimeter networks separated from other network segments by firewalls, and any location reachable only by SMTP.

2. How many sites should you create for this site and where should they be located?

    You should create two sites: one for the perimeter network and one for the private corporate network.

3. Why have you chosen this site structure?

    The private corporate network can be all one site because it's one LAN that has fast and reliable connections. However, the perimeter network should be a separate site because it's connected to the corporate network through a firewall. A separate site for the perimeter network allows you to limit client authentication to domain controllers within that site, assuming the domain controllers are fault tolerant.

4. Assume that the private corporate network is spread across several physical locations connected by WAN links. How would that affect your site structure?

    You should create a site for each location that's connected by a WAN link because WAN links are traditionally slower and less reliable. Generally, a site shouldn't span across a WAN connection.

Page 297

Exercise 2: Placing Domain Controllers

1. What guidelines should you follow when determining where to place domain controllers?

   You should place at least one domain controller in each site and two domain controllers in the domain. Place additional domain controllers in a site when a large number of clients access the site; when intersite connections are relatively slow, unreliable, or near capacity; or when clients should be authenticated at a specific set of domain controllers.

2. In which sites would you include a domain controller?

   You should place at least one domain controller in the perimeter network site and one in the private network site.

3. How many domain controllers should you include in your network?

   You should place at least two domain controllers in each site to provide fault tolerance for the Active Directory services. That way authentication requests never have to pass through the firewall.

Page 297

Exercise 3: Defining an Intersite Replication Strategy

1. What guidelines should you follow when determining how to configure site links?

   You should configure your site links according to available bandwidth, network usage patterns, and type of transport—and if appropriate, configure additional site links to provide redundant replication paths.

2. What site links do you need to configure for the Northwind Traders network?

   You need to configure only one site link to connect the two sites.

3. What configuration information must your provide for each site link?

   You must provide the replication schedule, replication interval, replication transport, and link cost.

4. You decide that replication between the perimeter network and the private network should occur throughout the day at regular intervals. You want domain controllers on both sides of the firewall to remain relatively current, but you don't want to overwhelm the network. You plan to restrict directory replication to 12 times a day at regular intervals, every day of the week. How should you configure the site link?

   You should configure the replication schedule to permit replication at all times on all days of the week, because you want replication to occur every day at regular intervals throughout the day. You should configure the replication interval at two hours, which would equal 12 times a day. You should configure the transport type as IP, which is implied by the nature of the network and the connection through the firewall. Because you need

to configure only one site link, you don't have to be concerned with configuring the link cost. Link cost is the relative bandwidth of the connection as compared to other site links.

Page 298

Exercise 4: Placing Global Catalog Servers and Operations Masters

1. What guidelines should you follow when determining where to place global catalog servers?

   You should locate at least one global catalog in each site. Place additional global catalog servers in a site when a large number of clients access the site or when intersite connections are relatively slow, unreliable, or near capacity.

2. Where should you locate global catalog servers in the Northwind Traders network?

   You should configure all four domain controllers as global catalog servers. This provides fault tolerance within each site should a domain controller fail. If one does fail, the authentication process won't have to look outside the site (and through the firewall) for a copy of the global catalog. In addition, by configuring all domain controllers as global catalog servers, you don't have to be concerned about locating the infrastructure master on a domain controller that doesn't host the global catalog.

3. What guidelines should you follow when determining where to place operations masters?

   You should provide a standby operations master. In large domains, place the relative identifier master and PDC emulator on separate domain controllers. Don't assign the infrastructure master role to a domain controller that's hosting the global catalog unless all domain controllers in the domain are global catalog servers.

4. Where should you place the operations masters?

   You should locate the operations masters in the private network. Make one domain controller the operations master and make the other domain controller a standby operations master. You don't have to be concerned about assigning the infrastructure master role to a domain controller that isn't hosting the global catalog because all domain controllers in the domain will be hosting the global catalog.

Page 299

Review Questions

1. What are Active Directory objects and what's the purpose of the Active Directory schema?

   Active Directory objects represent the physical entities that make up a network. For example, users, printers, and computers are Active Directory objects. The Active Directory schema defines the types of objects and the

types of information about those objects that can be stored in the directory. There are two types of definitions in the schema: attributes and classes.

2. What are the components of the Active Directory logical structure and the physical structure?

The logical structure is made up of domains, trees, forests, and OUs. The physical structure is made up of sites and domain controllers.

3. What are the five operations master roles assigned to one or more domain controllers?

The five roles are schema master, domain naming master, relative ID master, PDC emulator, and infrastructure master.

4. You're planning the Active Directory physical structure for your organization. Your network is made up of three domains. Each domain is in a separate geographical location connected by a WAN link, and each location is a fast, reliable LAN with ample bandwidth. One of the LANs includes a Web site that's set up in a perimeter network, which is connected to the private network through a firewall. What's the minimum number of Active Directory sites that you should create for this network?

You should create at least four sites: one for each LAN and one for the perimeter network.

5. Your network is made up of two Active Directory sites. You're configuring a site link between the two sites. You configure replication to occur during non-business hours at intervals of 15 minutes. How often will the directory be replicated during business hours?

Replication won't occur between the two sites during business hours.

Page 301

Chapter 9
Application Integration

Page 313

Activity 9.1 Questions

1. What's the first step of your deployment strategy?

You should perform a single deployment from the staging computer to the Web cluster controller.

2. What's the second step of your deployment strategy?

After the application has been deployed to the controller, it should be replicated from the controller to member servers. You don't have to replicate the content manually if Application Center is configured for automatic synchronization. The replication will be automatic.

3. How will Web services be affected by this deployment strategy?

Web services shouldn't be affected because no ISAPI filters or COM+ components are being deployed. If they were, you'd have to reset the services.

Page 325

Activity 9.2 Questions

1. How should you set up the failover clusters?

   You should set up the clusters in a way similar to that shown in the following illustration:

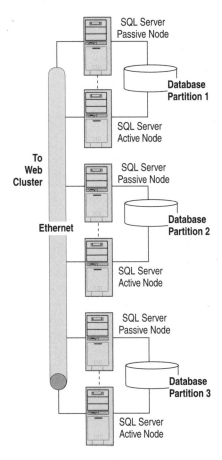

2. What methods can your application use to access the data?

   Your application can use distributed partitioned views or data-dependent routing.

3. How can you configure your failover clustering?

   You can create a four-node multiple-instance cluster that uses an N+1 topology. In this configuration, three of the servers contain an active instance of SQL Server, one for each partition, and the fourth node remains in standby mode and is configured as the primary failover computer.

Lab Questions

Page 335

Exercise 1: Designing an IIS Application Structure

1. How should you design the initial portion of the perimeter network?

   Your design should look similar to the one in the following illustration:

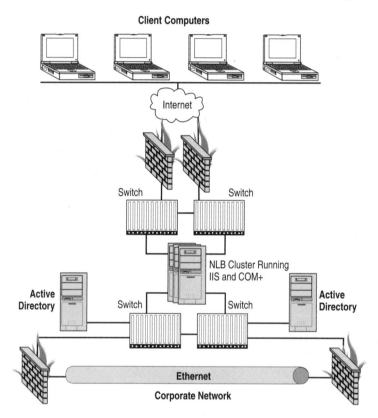

2. Which application layers will your design initially support?

   Your design should support the presentation layer and the business logic layer.

3. How will you deploy this content?

   You can perform a single deployment from the stager to the Web cluster controller. From there, Application Center will replicate the content automatically to the other member servers.

Page 335

Exercise 2: Integrating SQL Server into Your Application Structure

1. How should you modify your perimeter network's design to support the new applications?

   Your design should look similar to the one in the following illustration:

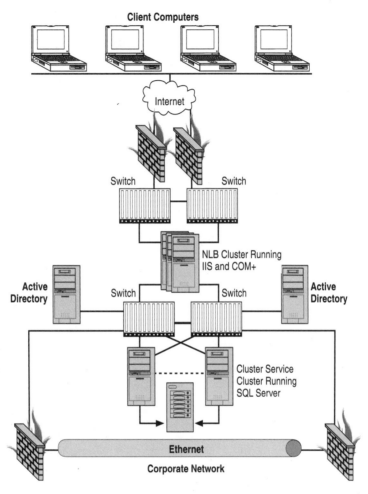

Client Computers

Internet

Switch   Switch

NLB Cluster Running
IIS and COM+

**Active
Directory**   Switch   Switch   **Active
Directory**

Cluster Service
Cluster Running
SQL Server

Ethernet

Corporate Network

2. You want to deploy the COM+ applications, but you don't want to take the Web services offline. How should you deploy the applications?

   To deploy the applications, you should take the following steps:

   1. **In the Web cluster, take the cluster controller and one member of the cluster out of the load-balancing loop.**

   2. **Deploy the applications to those two computers.**

   3. **After you've reset the services, bring the two servers back online for load balancing.**

   4. **Repeat the process for the third member computer.**

3. How should you set up permissions on the SQL Server computers?

   You must ensure that a guest account has been created that corresponds to the IUSR_*computername* account and that permissions have been granted to that account to allow it to log on to the SQL Server computers.

4. What methods can you use to optimize connections to the database?

   Change the threading model to Both, limit the connection time-out, close connections, share active connections, and increase the size of the record cache.

Page 336

Exercise 3: Integrating Exchange 2000 Server into Your Web Site

1. How should you modify your perimeter network's design to support the Outlook Web Access service?

   Your design should look similar to the one in the following illustration:

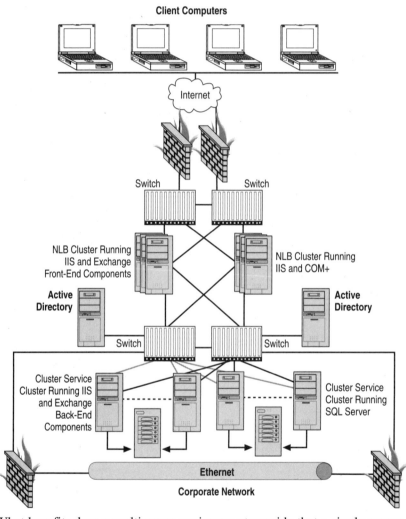

2. What benefits does a multiserver environment provide that a single-server environment can't?

   A multiserver environment has the following benefits:

- The multiserver model supports a unified namespace. You can disperse groups of users across back-end databases but allow them to connect to the front-end server by using a single server name.

- You can isolate back-end servers from attacks. You can locate back-end servers behind a firewall or on a different subnet. Front-end servers can each be configured with one NIC that connects to the Internet and another NIC that connects to the secure internal LAN.

- Multiple servers allow you to isolate processing tasks. Front-end tasks can be performed on computers that are separate from the computers that process data on the back end. For example, SSL processing can occur on the front-end servers only. From there, the front-end and back-end servers can communicate without the overhead of SSL.

- The multiserver model has the added benefit of being easier to scale out and make fault tolerant. You can use Windows 2000 NLB to set up a front-end cluster that's load balanced and use the Windows 2000 Cluster service to set up a back-end cluster that provides failover protection to the data store.

3. What authentication methods does Outlook Web Access support?

Outlook Web Access supports two authentication methods: Basic and Integrated Windows. Outlook Web Access also supports SSL encryption and Anonymous access.

4. Which authentication method would you recommend?

SSL (with Basic authentication) should be used. It provides the highest level of security and operability between clients and server because the entire communications session is encrypted.

Page 337

Review Questions

1. You're the network administrator for Trey Research. You're deploying a Web application that incorporates ActiveX controls, client-side scripting, ASP, server-side scripting, COM+ components, and stored procedures. Much of the content for the site will be stored in a SQL Server database. The COM+ components will be in an COM+ application cluster separate from the Web cluster. How should you deploy the application?

First deploy the COM+ components on the COM+ application cluster and then deploy the rest of the application to the Web cluster.

2. You're managing a SQL Server database that supports several applications on your Web servers. You decide to partition several of the tables in the database to improve performance. What two methods can you use to access the partitioned data?

You can use a distributed partition view or data-dependent routing to access the partitioned data.

3. After you partition the data in your SQL Server database, you decide to implement a fault-tolerant solution to ensure the data's availability. What two high-availability solutions can you use in conjunction with partitioning?

You can use failover clustering and log shipping in conjunction with partitioning to provide a high-availability solution.

4. You're configuring your Web site to support Outlook Web Access so that users can access their e-mail accounts through a browser. You're trying to determine how to set up the Exchange 2000 Server environment to support your users. You want the environment to support a unified namespace, and you want to isolate the data store from attacks. Which Exchange configuration model should you use?

You should use the multiserver model because it supports a unified namespace and back-end isolation. This configuration also allows you to isolate processing tasks such as SSL encryption and decryption.

5. You're setting up Outlook Web Access for your company's employees so that they can access their e-mail accounts through a browser. You plan to use a multiserver configuration and Windows clustering technologies to create a front-end NLB cluster and a back-end Cluster service cluster. You want to provide the highest level of security and operability between clients and servers by encrypting the entire communication session. Which protocol should you use?

You should use SSL along with Basic authentication to provide the maximum security.

Page 339

Chapter 10
Network Security

Page 358

Activity Questions

1. Why can't users access the Web site?

The IIS Read permission hasn't been granted to the site. Although the NTFS Read permission has been granted to the IUSR_*computername* account, the most restrictive permissions apply to the directory, which, in this case, are the IIS permissions.

2. Assume that the IIS Read permission has been enabled but that nonanonymous users would be accessing the account rather than anonymous users. How would you need to modify the permissions?

You should remove the IUSR_*computername* account from the DACL for the directory and add the appropriate users or groups to the DACL.

3. What steps in the access process occur when a user attempts to access a resource?

IIS verifies that the IP address, network, and domain name aren't denied access. IIS then authenticates the user and, assuming the user is authenti-

cated, authorizes the user. If a custom authentication application has been implemented, that application then authenticates the user. Finally, the user is authenticated by verifying the NTFS permissions set for that directory.

Lab Questions

Page 376

Exercise 1: Planning an Authentication and Encryption Strategy

1. What authentication models does IIS support and how do these models differ?

   IIS supports five authentication models: Anonymous, Basic, Integrated Windows, Digest, and client certificate mapping. This rest of this section discusses each of these models. IIS supports the following authentication models:

   - *Anonymous access*   Anonymous access allows all Web clients to access a site and works with most browsers. IIS uses the IUSR_*computername* account to provide anonymous users with the right to log on locally. Anonymous access provides no authentication. If password synchronization is enabled, Anonymous access can't access remote resources; however, if synchronization is disabled, Anonymous access can access remote resources.

   - *Basic authentication*   Basic authentication requires that a user provide credentials in order to log on to the system. Users must have local logon rights to the Web server in order to be authenticated. Most browsers support Basic authentication. In Basic authentication passwords are encoded, but not securely encrypted, so the authentication process isn't very secure. However, you can use Basic authentication along with SSL to establish a secure session.

   - *Integrated Windows authentication*   Integrated Windows authentication is more secure than Basic authentication, and it supports NTLM authentication and Kerberos authentication. Integrated Windows authentication can't be used through proxy server connections and has limited browser support.

   - *Digest authentication*   Digest authentication encrypts passwords before transmitting them from the client to the server, and it can be used through proxy server connections. However, Digest authentication is supported only for Windows 2000 domains, and only a few browsers, including Internet Explorer 5.0, support this authentication model. Digest authentication requires Active Directory.

   - *Client certificate mapping*   You can use certificate mapping in IIS to authenticate users by mapping certificates to Windows 2000 user accounts. When certificate mapping is enabled in IIS, Windows 2000 authenticates users and grants rights and permissions based on the mapped user account. IIS supports two types of certificate mapping: one-to-one and one-to-many. Certificate mapping is very scalable and secure, but not all browsers support it. In addition, certificate mapping can be cumbersome to configure.

2. Which authentication model should you use?

   You should use Basic authentication because it's compatible with most Web browsers.

3. What are the limitations on the authentication model you chose?

   User credentials aren't secure because they aren't encrypted.

4. In addition to authenticating users, you must ensure that all data transmitted between the users and the Web site is secure in order to ensure that data's privacy and integrity. One way to secure data is through encryption. What are several methods that you can use to encrypt data and how are those methods different?

   You can use the following methods to encrypt the data:

   - *SSL*   **SSL is an Internet standard commonly used to encrypt data. However, applications that use SSL must be SSL-aware, as most Web browsers and Web servers are. SSL requires considerable processor resources, compared to not encrypting and decrypting data. SSL supports authentication through the use of public key certificates.**

   - *IPSec*   **IPSec works at the IP layer of the TCP/IP protocol stack and is transparent to most applications. This offers a high level of protection for most applications, services, and upper layer protocols. IPSec supports authentication through Kerberos authentication, public key certificates, and preshared key values. However, to use IPSec, the computers on both ends of the communication link must be configured with Windows 2000 and have IPSec security policies defined. In addition, IPSec requires more processor power than SSL.**

   - *EFS*   **EFS can be used to protect sensitive data stored on a disk, but it doesn't protect data transmitted over a network.**

5. How can you make data transferred between clients and the Web servers secure?

   You should use SSL to secure the data. You can't use IPSec because not all browsers support it, and you can't use EFS to protect the data that's being transferred between the clients and the Web servers. However, you can use IPSec on the back end of your network to protect data transmitted within your private network, and you can use EFS to encrypt data where it's stored on a drive.

Page 377

Exercise 2: Planning an Authorization Strategy

1. Before you determine how users will be authorized, you decide to review the access process so that you have a complete picture of how users will access resources. What steps will the access process follow?

The access process will involve the following steps:

- IIS determines whether the client's IP address should be denied access to the Web site or virtual directory.

- If a user's IP address is accepted by IIS, the user is authenticated by one of the following authentication methods supported by IIS: Anonymous, Basic, Integrated Windows, Digest, or client certificate mapping. In this case, Basic authentication is used.

- Once a user is authenticated, IIS determines what permissions have been assigned to the resource that the user is trying to access.

- If custom authentication is used, users are authenticated after they've been authorized by IIS. Custom authentication isn't being used in this case.

- IIS uses the security context of the authenticated user to try to gain access to a specific resource, based on the NTFS permissions granted to that user.

2. IIS permissions apply to all users trying to access the Web site. How should you set up those permissions?

   Users should be granted the Read permission on the home directory and the Scripts Only execute permission.

3. Unlike IIS permissions, NTFS permissions apply to specific users and groups. How should you set up those permissions?

   In the related directories, remove all unnecessary users and groups, keeping only the required administrative users and groups. Grant these users the Full Control permission. Add the Customers group, and grant that group the Read & Execute permission.

Page 378

Exercise 3: Planning a Firewall Strategy

1. What are the two basic perimeter network topologies that you can use to set up your firewalls and how do these topologies differ?

   There are two basic perimeter network topologies:

   - *Single firewall*   **A single firewall is the simplest way to set up your perimeter network. In this configuration you use one firewall configured with three NICs. One NIC is connected to the private network, one to the Internet, and one to the perimeter network.**

   - *Back-to-back firewalls*   **In a perimeter network that's configured with back-to-back firewalls, a firewall is located on either side of the perimeter network. The front end of the perimeter network is connected to the Internet through one of the firewalls, and the back end of the perimeter network is connected to the corporate network through the other firewall.**

2. You want to maximize the amount of security that you provide your network through firewalls. Which configuration should you use?

You should use the back-to-back configuration.

3. You also want to protect your database as much as possible through the use of firewalls. How many firewalls should you use in your network?

You should use three firewalls—one in front of the Web servers, one between the Web servers and the data servers, and one between the perimeter network and the private network, as shown in the following illustration:

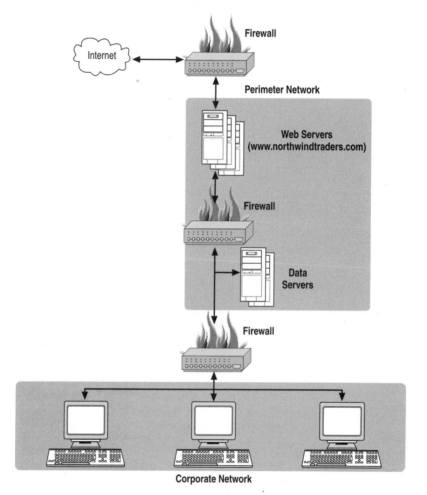

Page 379

Review Questions

1. You're the network administrator for Consolidated Messenger. Your organization is implementing an online tracking application that allows customers to

determine the status of packages that are being delivered. In order to check on the status of their orders, users must supply the tracking numbers that were provided when they shipped their packages. The tracking numbers aren't tied to any user accounts or authentication data stores, and users don't have to provide any information other than the tracking numbers. Which authentication model can you use for your Web site?

You can use Anonymous access for your customers because they aren't required to provide credentials in order to log on to the system.

2. Your company, Adventure Works, has implemented a Web site that allows users to access information about various locations around the world. The site uses ASP applications to access data from a SQL Server database. You configure the site with Anonymous access and configure IIS permissions on the Home directory with the Read permission and the Scripts Only execute permission. Next, you configure NTFS permissions on the Web directory. You add the IUSR_*computername* account to the directory and configure the account with the Read permission. When users try to access the Web site, they can read the static content on the home page but they can't execute any of the ASP applications. What is the likeliest cause of the problem?

You need to grant the Read & Execute permission to the IUSR_*computername* account.

3. You're setting up a Web site for Trey Research. Your customers must log on to the site and be authenticated in order to access resources on the site. Your customers use different types of browsers to access the site, and their computers are set up with different types of operating systems. You implement IPSec in order to protect data as it's being transmitted between the client computers and the Web servers; however, many clients are unable to establish a secure connection. What is the likeliest cause of the problem?

IPSec requires that both ends of the communication link be configured with Windows 2000.

4. You're the network administrator for a small organization that provides online Web services to its customers. The site contains only static content, which is all located on the IIS server. IIS is configured to allow Anonymous access. You want to implement a firewall solution that's inexpensive to implement, that's easy to administer, and that separates the perimeter network from the rest of the network so that the private network isn't dependent on the perimeter network's availability in order to access the Internet. Which firewall solution should you use?

You should use the single-firewall solution so that one firewall is configured with three NICs. One NIC is connected to the private network, one to the Internet, and one to the perimeter network.

Page 381

Chapter 11
Systems Monitoring and Disaster Recovery

Page 396

Activity 11.1 Questions

1. How can you log data about processor usage and then view that data?

   You can create a counter log in Performance Logs and Alerts to collect the data. You can then use System Monitor to view that data.

2. After you view the log data, you realize the processors reach maximum capacity a couple of times a day. You decide that you want to be notified whenever usage exceeds 80 percent. How can you be notified when usage exceeds the 80 percent threshold?

   You can create an alert in Performance Logs And Alerts. You can configure the alert with the Processor\% Processor Time counter and set the alert value to be over 80. When you configure the alert, you should configure the action so that you're notified when the threshold is reached.

3. Which counters, in addition to Processor\% Processor Time, should you consider monitoring in order to collect data about processor activity?

   You should consider monitoring the following counters: System\Processor Queue Length, Processor\% Privileged Time, Processor\% User Time, and Process\% Processor Time.

Page 404

Activity 11.2 Questions

1. Which method should you use to audit the Web site?

   You should use IIS logging to audit the Web site, and you should save your files in the W3C Extended log file format because this format allows you to specify which fields to include in your logs.

2. What tool can you use to view the logs?

   You can use a text editor such as Notepad to view the logs.

3. Why haven't the events been recorded in the Security log?

   Before one of these events can be recorded in the Security log, you must configure the Audit Object Access audit policy in Group Policy. You should configure the policy to log successful attempts and failed attempts.

4. Why haven't failed events been recorded in the Security log?

   The most likely cause for failed events not appearing in the Security log is that either the directory properties weren't configured to record failed events or the audit policy wasn't configured to record failed events.

Lab Questions

Page 413

Exercise 1: Designing a System Monitoring Strategy

1. The first step in your monitoring strategy is to collect performance data about memory. What five components of memory should you monitor?

   You should monitor available memory, paging, file system cache, paging file size, and memory pool size.

2. Why should you monitor memory before monitoring any other components?

   Inadequate memory can result in other parts of your system appearing as though the problems reside there. For example, what might appear on the surface as poor disk or processor performance can in fact be as a result of a memory problem. You should rule out memory performance problems before investigating other components.

3. Next, you want to monitor the processors in your system. You plan to collect information about processor activity, IIS service connections, and IIS threads. What types of information should you collect about each of these categories?

   Data about processor activity should include processor queue length and processor time percentages. Data about IIS connections should include the Web service and FTP service. Data about IIS threads should include thread count, processor time, and context switches.

4. The next step in your strategy is to collect data about network I/O. Specifically, you plan to collect data about transmission rates and TCP connections. What type of information should you collect about transmission rates and TCP connections?

   Transmission rate data should include bytes sent and received by the Web service, FTP service, and SMTP service. You should also collect sent and received data about TCP segments, IP datagrams, and the network interface. TCP connection data should include information about established, failed, and reset connections.

5. Finally, you plan to monitor your Web applications. What components should you monitor?

   You should monitor ASP requests and Web service GET and POST requests.

6. Suppose that, during your analysis of the data, you discover periods of long, sustained queue lengths. What might be causing these long queue lengths?

   A long, sustained queue length indicates that a processor can't handle the load assigned to it. As a result, threads are being kept waiting. A sustained queue length of two or more threads can indicate a processor bottleneck.

Page 414

Exercise 2: Designing a Security Auditing Strategy

1. The first step in your strategy is to configure audit policies that allow you to log specific events. How do you configure audit policies?

   To configure audit policies, you must configure your Group Policy settings in the Group Policy snap-in. For each policy, you can configure successful attempts, failed attempts, or both.

2. You're specifically concerned with auditing access to certain directories and files. You want to log events about successful and failed attempts to access resources. Which audit policy or policies should you configure and how should you configure that policy?

   You should configure the Audit Object Access policy to audit successful attempts and failed attempts.

3. Once you've configured Group Policy, you decide that you want to audit the Inetpub\Scripts directory. What step do you need to take to configure auditing on that directory?

   You must set up auditing in the properties of the Inetpub\Scripts directory. To access the auditing properties, click Advanced on the Security tab of the Scripts Properties dialog box. You can configure auditing on the Auditing tab of the Access Control Settings For Scripts dialog box.

4. Once you've configured auditing on the Inetpub\Scripts directory, you want to be able to view the Security log regularly to view any events that might have been generated. How do you view the Security log?

   You use Event Viewer to view the Security log.

5. In addition to auditing events, you want to log activity about your Web site. Specifically, you want to log date, time, client IP address, and username for each user who logs on to the site. At this time you don't want to log any other information about the site because you want to limit the size of your log files. How can you log this information?

   You can set up logging through the Internet Information Services tool. Open the properties for the specific site, and enable logging. You should use W3C Extended format for your log because this format allows you to specify which fields to log.

6. Once you've logged data about your users, how can you view that data?

   You can use a text editor such as Notepad to view data in a W3C Extended format.

7. What log file formats does IIS logging support?

   IIS logging supports the following log file formats: Microsoft IIS, NCSA Common, ODBC Logging, and W3C Extended.

8. You decide that, although you want to log activity to your Web site, you don't want to log activity on the Images directory, which is a part of the site. How do you disable logging on the Images directory?

You disable logging on the Images directory through the properties for that directory (on the Directory tab of the Images Properties dialog box), which you access through the Internet Information Services tool.

Page 416

Review Questions

1. You want to monitor performance on your Windows 2000 computer. You want to first establish a baseline and then conduct ongoing monitoring. Which Microsoft tool allows you to establish a baseline and then measure the ongoing performance of your system?

You can use the Performance tool in Windows 2000 Server to establish a baseline and then monitor performance on an ongoing basis.

2. You're the network administrator for your organization and you're monitoring performance on an IIS server. You discover that the Inetinfo working set often uses all the available RAM. In addition, during those peak usages of RAM disk activity is high. What's the most likely cause of the problem?

You don't have enough physical memory on your server.

3. You're auditing logon events on your IIS server. You're interested only in failed logon events; however, the Security log shows successful logon attempts and failed logon events. As a result, your log reaches its maximum size too quickly. How can you log only failed events?

Configure the applicable audit policies in Group Policy to log only failed attempts.

4. You're using IIS logging to log the activity on your Web site. You want to log all events to a SQL Server database. You create a database, a data source name (DSN), and a table within the database to store the logged events. Which log format should you use when configuring IIS logging?

You should use the ODBC Logging format.

5. You're developing a disaster recovery strategy for your IIS servers. As part of that strategy, you determine that you must prepare recovery systems to have in place should a disaster occur. You create the necessary Windows 2000 Setup disks, Startup disks, and ERDs. What other step should you take in preparing your recovery systems?

You should back up your data to ensure against the loss of any critical system state data, files, or other data important to your system. Your backup strategy should include regularly scheduled backup jobs so that the data is as current as reasonably possible if you should need to restore that data.

6. As part of a disaster recovery strategy that you're developing for your organization, you plan to test various system components to try to predict failure and to practice recovery procedures. Your tests will include internal and external components. What situations should you try to simulate when you stress test your system?

You should try to simulate heavy network loads, heavy disk I/O, heavy use of file and application servers, and large numbers of users simultaneously logged on.

Glossary

Numbers and Symbols

10Base-T A variant of Ethernet that allows stations to be attached by a twisted-pair cable.

A

access control list (ACL) A list that indicates which users or groups have permission to access or modify a particular file; the Microsoft Windows discretionary access control list (DACL) and system access control list (SACL) are examples of access control lists.

ACL *See* access control list (ACL).

Active Directory Service Interfaces (ADSI) A Component Object Model (COM)–based directory service model that allows ADSI-compliant client applications to access a wide variety of distinct directory protocols, including Microsoft Windows directory service and Lightweight Directory Access Protocol (LDAP), while using a single standard set of interfaces. ADSI shields the client application from the implementation and operational details of the underlying data store or protocol.

active hub A type of hub that uses electrical power to regenerate and retransmit network data.

active/passive configuration In the Cluster service, an active/passive configuration is a method that you can use to configure your cluster. In this configuration, one node acts as the primary node and another node acts as the secondary node. The secondary node is idle unless failover occurs.

Active Server Pages (ASP) A server-side scripting environment that can be used to create dynamic Web pages or build Web applications. ASP pages are files that contain Hypertext Markup Language (HTML) tags, text, and script commands. ASP pages can call Component Object Model (COM) components to perform tasks, such as connecting to a database or performing a business calculation. With ASP, the user can add interactive content to Web pages or build entire Web applications that use HTML pages as the interface to your customers.

ActiveX An umbrella term for Microsoft technologies that enable developers to create interactive content for the World Wide Web. A set of language-independent interoperability technologies that enable software components written in different languages to work together in networked environments. The core technology elements of ActiveX are the Component Object Model (COM) and distributed COM. These technologies are licensed to The Open Group standards organization and are being implemented on multiple platforms.

ActiveX Controls Reusable software components that incorporate ActiveX technology. These components can be used to add specialized functionality, such as animation or pop-up menus, to Web pages, desktop applications, and software development tools. ActiveX Controls can be written in a variety of programming languages including C, C++, Visual Basic, and Java.

ActiveX Data Objects (ADO) A high-level data access programming interface to an underlying data access technology (such as OLE DB), implemented by using the Component Object Model (COM).

administrative software In the Cluster service, the software that you use to administer the cluster.

ADO *See* ActiveX Data Objects (ADO).

ADSI *See* Active Directory Service Interfaces (ADSI).

agile model A type of threading model in which objects are specified as both-threaded.

alias A name that maps part of a Uniform Resource Locator (URL) to a physical directory on the server. In general, an easily remembered name used in place of an Internet Protocol (IP) address, directory path, or other identifier; also called a friendly name.

American National Standards Institute (ANSI) A voluntary, nonprofit organization of U.S. business and industry groups formed in 1918 for the development of trade and communications standards. It provides area charters for groups that establish standards in specific fields, such as the Institute of Electrical and Electronics Engineers (IEEE). ANSI is the U.S. representative of the International Organization for Standardization (ISO) and has developed recommendations for the use of programming languages including FORTRAN, C, and COBOL. Standards approved by ANSI are often called ANSI standards (for example, ANSI C is the version of the C language approved by ANSI). *See also* American Standard Code for Information Interchange.

American Standard Code for Information Interchange (ASCII) A coding scheme using 7 or 8 bits that assigns numeric values up to 256 characters, including letters, numerals, punctuation marks, control characters, and other symbols. ASCII was developed in 1968 to standardize data transmission among disparate hardware and software systems and is built into most minicomputers and all personal computers.

anonymous File Transfer Protocol (anonymous FTP) An FTP configuration that makes it possible for a user to retrieve documents, files, programs, and other archived data from anywhere on the Internet without having to establish a logon name and password.

ANSI *See* American National Standards Institute (ANSI).

API *See* application programming interface (API).

application A computer program, such as a word processor or electronic spreadsheet; or a group of Active Server Pages (ASP) scripts and components that perform such tasks. In Application Center 2000, an application can consist of any combination of Hypertext Markup Language (HTML) and ASP files, COM+ components, Microsoft Windows registry settings, and Internet Information Services (IIS) settings. In COM+, an application is a grouping of COM+ components.

application programming interface (API) A set of routines that an application uses to request and carry out lower-level services performed by a computer's operating system. Also, a set of calling conventions in programming that defines how a service is invoked through the application.

application state The data maintained by a server application on behalf of its clients.

ASCII *See* American Standard Code for Information Interchange (ASCII).

ASP *See* Active Server Pages (ASP).

Asynchronous Transfer Mode (ATM) A network technology capable of transmitting data, voice, video, and frame relay traffic in real time. Data, including frame relay data, is broken into packets containing 53 bytes each, which are switched between any two nodes in the system at rates ranging from 1.5 to 622 megabits per second (Mbps). ATM is defined in the broadband Integrated Services Digital Network (ISDN) protocol at the levels corresponding to levels 1 and 2 of the International Organization for Standardization Open Systems Interconnection (ISO/OSI) model. It's currently used in local area networks involving workstations and personal computers.

ATM *See* Asynchronous Transfer Mode (ATM).

auditing The process an operating system uses to detect and record security-related events, such as an attempt to create, access, or delete objects such as files and directories. The records of such events are stored in a file known as the Security log, whose contents are available only to those with the proper clearance.

authentication The process by which the system validates a user's logon information. A user's name and password are compared against an authorized list, and if the system detects a match, access is granted to the extent specified in the permission list for the user.

authentication certificate *See* certificate, authentication.

authorization In relation to computers, especially to remote computers on a network open to more than one person, the right granted to an individual to use the system and the data stored on it. Authorization is typically set up by a system administrator, Web master, or site owner and checked and cleared by the computer. This requires that the user provide some type of identification, such as a code number or a password, that the computer can verify against its internal records. Also called permission or privilege.

availability A measure (from 0 to 100 percent) of the fault tolerance of a computer and its programs. Availability measures whether a particular service is functioning properly. A highly available computer runs 24 hours a day, 7 days a week.

B

back end In a multitiered network environment, this term usually describes the portion of the network that resides behind the Web servers. For example, a SQL Server computer located on a data tier would be considered a back-end server.

bandwidth The capacity of the transmission medium stated in bits per second (bps) or as a frequency measured in hertz (Hz). Generally, a higher bandwidth number indicates faster data-transfer capability. In communications, the difference between the highest and lowest frequencies in a given range. In computer networks, greater bandwidth indicates faster data-transfer capability and is expressed in bps.

bandwidth throttling Setting the maximum portion of total network capacity that a service is allowed to use. An administrator can deliberately limit a server's Internet workload by not allowing it to receive requests at full capacity, thus saving resources for other programs such as e-mail.

Basic authentication An authentication protocol supported by most browsers, including Internet Explorer. It's a method of authentication that encodes user name and password data transmissions. Basic authentication is sometimes called clear-text authentication because the Base-64 encoding can be decoded by anyone with a freely available decoding utility. Note that encoding isn't the same as encryption. *See also* Integrated Windows authentication; encryption.

baud A measure of data transmission speed. Commonly used to refer to the data transmission speed of a modem.

bits per second (bps) The speed at which data bits are transmitted over a communications medium, such as a transmission wire or a modem.

bridgehead server In the Active Directory service, the bridgehead server is the point at which directory information is exchanged with another site.

browser Also called a Web browser. A client interface that enables a user to view Hypertext Markup Language (HTML) documents on the World Wide Web, another network, or the user's computer; follow hyperlinks among them; and transfer files. One example is Microsoft Internet Explorer.

C

CA *See* certification authority (CA).

cache A special memory subsystem in which frequently used data values are duplicated for quick access. A memory cache stores the contents of frequently accessed random access memory (RAM) locations and the addresses where these data items are stored. When the processor references an address in memory, the cache checks to see whether it holds that address. If it does, the data is returned to the processor; if it doesn't, a regular memory access occurs. A cache is useful when RAM accesses are slow compared with the microprocessor speed, because cached memory is faster than main RAM memory.

capacity planning The process of measuring a Web site's ability to deliver content to its visitors at an acceptable speed.

cascading failover In the Cluster service, cascading failover refers to a failover process in which a resource group may survive multiple server failures, each time failing over to the next server on its node preference list.

certificate, authentication *See* certificate, digital.

certificate, client A digital certificate that functions in a way similar to a driver's license or passport. Client certificates can contain detailed identification information about the user and organization that issued the certificate. *See also* certificate, digital.

certificate, digital An encrypted file, containing user or server identification information, that's used to verify identity; also called an authentication certificate. When issued to users, a digital certificate is called a client certificate. When issued to a server administrator, it's called a server certificate. *See also* certificate, client; certificate, server.

certificate revocation list A document maintained and published by a certification authority (CA) that lists certificates that have been revoked by the certification authority. *See also* certification authority.

certificate, server A unique digital identification that forms the basis of a Web server's Secure Sockets Layer (SSL) security features. Server certificates are obtained from a mutually trusted, third-party organization and provide a way for users to authenticate the identity of a Web site.

certification authority (CA) An entity that issues, manages, and revokes certificates.

CGI *See* Common Gateway Interface (CGI).

client On a local area network or the Internet, a computer that accesses shared network resources provided by another computer called a server. Also, an application or process that requests a service from some process or component. A client facilitates a connection to server computers and manages and presents information retrieved from those sources. In a client/server environment, the workstation is usually the client computer. When referring to Component Object Model (COM) objects, a program that accesses or uses a service provided by another component.

client affinity In Network Load Balancing (NLB), client affinity refers to a process that allows a client to be mapped to the same host during a session. After the initial client request, which is distributed like any other request, NLB looks at only the source Internet Protocol (IP) address and not the source port information. Therefore, a client with a given IP address will always map to a particular cluster host, and any session state that's maintained in that cluster host will persist across those connections.

client/server architecture A model of computing whereby client applications running on a desktop or personal computer access information on remote servers or host computers. The client portion of the application is typically optimized for user interaction, whereas the server portion provides centralized, multiuser functionality.

cluster Two or more computers connected for the purpose of providing services to the client. Microsoft Windows 2000 Advanced Server and Datacenter Server support two types of clusters: Network Load Balancing (NLB) clusters and the Cluster service clusters. NLB clusters usually operate on front-end systems to provide core services such as Hypertext Transfer Protocol (HTTP) and File Transfer Protocol (FTP). Cluster service clusters usually operate on the back-end to provide database and file storage services.

cluster adapter The network adapter in a Network Load Balancing (NLB) cluster that handles the network traffic for cluster operations (that is, the traffic for all hosts in the cluster). This adapter is assigned one or more virtual IP addresses and, optionally, a dedicated IP address.

cluster-aware application In the Cluster service, a cluster-aware application is one that supports the Cluster application programming interface (API). These applications can register with the Cluster service to receive status and notification information, and they can use the Cluster API to administer clusters.

cluster name In the Cluster service, the cluster name is the common name under which all members in the cluster are grouped. You can use the cluster name when accessing and managing the cluster.

Cluster service A service in Microsoft Windows 2000 Advanced Server and Datacenter Server that allows you to set up a cluster to support failover functionality. The Cluster service is made up of components on each node that perform cluster-specific activities.

cluster size In Network Load Balancing (NLB), cluster size is the number of hosts participating in the cluster, which can be up to 32.

clustered disk In the Cluster service, the clustered disk is an external disk storage system. Nodes in the cluster share access to cluster resources on the clustered disk.

clustering Connecting two or more computers for the purpose of sharing resources and request load. Each member computer of a cluster is called a node. The nodes in a cluster may either have their own storage devices or share a common device. Typically, clustering will involve support for load balancing, fault tolerance, and failover. *See also* failover; fault tolerance; load balancing.

clustering software In the Cluster service, clustering software is the software the makes the cluster run.

cluster-unaware application In the Cluster service, a cluster-unaware application is one that doesn't support the Cluster application programming interface (API). These applications can't register with the Cluster service to receive status and notification information, and they can't use the Cluster API to administer clusters.

COM *See* Component Object Model (COM).

Common Gateway Interface (CGI) A server-side interface for initiating software services; the specification that defines communications between information services, such as a Hypertext Transfer Protocol (HTTP) service, and resources on the server's host computer, such as databases and other programs. For example, when a user submits a form through a Web browser, the HTTP service executes a program, often called a Common Gateway Interface (CGI) script, and passes the user's input information to that program through CGI. The program then returns information to the service through CGI. Any software can be a CGI program if it handles input and output according to the CGI standard. CGI applications always run out-of-process.

Component Load Balancing (CLB) A service in Application Center 2000 that provides dynamic load balancing for COM+ application components. In CLB, the COM+ components are located on servers in a separate COM+ cluster. Calls to activate COM+ components are load balanced to different servers within the COM+ cluster.

Component Object Model (COM) The object-oriented programming model that defines how objects interact within a single application or between applications. In COM, client software accesses an object through a pointer to an interface—a related set of functions called methods—on the object. A COM component is a binary file containing code for one or more class factories, COM classes, registry-entry mechanisms, loading code, among others.

concurrency The appearance of simultaneous execution of processes or transactions by interleaving the execution of multiple pieces of work.

connected user A user who is currently accessing one of the services of a Web server.

connection pooling A performance optimization based on using collections of preallocated resources, such as objects or database connections. Pooling results in more efficient resource allocation.

content type The type of file (such as text, graphic, or sound), usually indicated by the file name extension (such as .txt, .gif, or .wav, respectively).

convergence In Network Load Balancing (NLB), convergence is a process in which the hosts exchange heartbeat messages to determine a new, consistent state of the cluster and to elect the host with the highest priority as the new default host.

cookie A means by which, under the Hypertext Transfer Protocol (HTTP) protocol, a server or a script can maintain information on the client computer. A cookie is a small text file that is stored in the user's browser by the Web server. Cookies contain information about the user such as an identification number, a password, how a user browsed a Web site, or how many times the user visited that site. A Web site can access cookie information whenever the user connects to the server.

CryptoAPI *See* Microsoft Cryptographic API.

cryptography A field science involving the transmission of information in an encoded form so that only an intended recipient can decode the information and reveal its meaning. Encoded information is commonly said to be encrypted.

D

Data Encryption Standard (DES) A specification for encryption of computer data developed by IBM and adopted by the U.S. government as a standard in 1976. DES uses a 56-bit key to protect against password discovery and playback.

data-dependent routing An application-based method that you can use to access partitioned data. Data-dependent routing uses code to determine where the target data is located.

datagram A self-contained, independent entity of data carrying sufficient information to be routed from the source to the destination computer without reliance on earlier exchanges between the source and destination computer and the transporting network.

data provider Software that implements OLE DB methods and interfaces.

data source The name that applications use to request a connection to an Open Database Connectivity (ODBC) data source. It specifies the computer name and (optionally) database that the data source name (DSN) maps to. A system data source is a data source that's available to anyone using the computer. Data sources that will be used with a Web server need to be system data sources.

Data Source Name (DSN) The logical name used by Open Database Connectivity (ODBC) to refer to the drive and other information required to access data. The name is used by Internet Information Services (IIS) for a connection to an ODBC data source, such as a SQL Server database.

data source tier A logical layer that represents a computer running a Database Management System (DBMS), such as SQL Server.

deadlock In operating systems or databases, a situation in which two or more processes are prevented from continuing while each waits for resources to be freed by the continuation of the others.

debugger A software tool used to detect the source of program or script errors, by performing step-by-step execution of application code and viewing the content of code variables.

default document Sometimes called a default home page. The file sent by a Web server when it receives a request for a Uniform Resource Locator (URL) that doesn't specify a filename. This document can be generated automatically by the server, or it can be a custom file placed in that directory by the administrator.

default gateway In Transmission Control Protocol/Internet Protocol (TCP/IP), the intermediate network device on the local network that has knowledge of the network IDs of the other networks in the Internet so it can forward the packets to other gateways until they're delivered to the one connected to the specified destination.

default host In Network Load Balancing (NLB), the host with the highest priority. It handles all client traffic for the virtual Internet Protocol (IP)

addresses that isn't specifically intended to be load balanced.

dependency In the Cluster service, a resource that depends on another resource to operate. Dependent resources are taken offline before their dependencies, and they're brought online after their dependencies. Also known as a dependent resource.

dependency tree In the Cluster service, a dependency tree is a series of dependency relationships. A dependent resource and all of its dependencies must be in the same resource group.

dependent resource In the Cluster service, a dependent resource is one that requires another resource, which is known as a dependency.

DES *See* Data Encryption Standard (DES).

DHCP *See* Dynamic Host Configuration Protocol (DHCP).

DHCP lease In the Dynamic Host Configuration Protocol (DHCP) Service, the DHCP lease refers to the allocation of Internet Protocol (IP) addressing information to the client computer. The DHCP lease process occurs when Transmission Control Protocol/Internet Protocol (TCP/IP) is initialized on the client, the client requests a specific IP address and is denied, or the client previously leased an IP address but then released it and requires a new one.

DHTML *See* Dynamic HTML (DHTML).

dial-up Of, pertaining to, or being a connection that uses the public switched telephone network rather than a dedicated circuit or some other type of private network. Also called a slow link.

Digest authentication An authentication method that sends user name and password information over the network as a hash value. *See also* authentication.

digital certificate *See* certificate, digital.

digital signature The part of a digital certificate that contains an encryption key that uniquely identifies the holder of the certificate.

direct dependency In the Cluster service, a direct dependency is a resource dependency in which no intermediary resources are between the two dependent resources.

directory browsing A feature that automatically provides a default Web page of available directories and files to browsers that submit a Uniform Resource Locator (URL) that doesn't specify a particular file.

directory service A network service that identifies all resources on a network and makes them accessible to users and applications. The directory service is the central authority that manages the identities of distributed resources and brokers the relationships between those resources.

disaster Any situation that causes a serious disruption to your system's services. A disaster can result in data loss or machine failure, making your system unavailable to users and applications.

disk duplexing The process of installing a second controller on a computer so that each disk in a mirrored volume has its own controller.

DLL *See* dynamic-link library (DLL).

DNS *See* Domain Name System (DNS).

domain In Microsoft Windows, a collection of computers that share a common domain database and security policy. Each domain has a unique name. In the Active Directory service, resources are organized hierarchically into domains.

domain controller For a Microsoft Windows 2000 Server domain, the server that authenticates domain logons and maintains the security policy and the master database for a domain.

domain, Internet The highest subdivision of a domain name in a network address, which identifies the type of entity owning the address (for example, .com for commercial users or .edu for educational institutions) or the address's geographic location (for example, .fr for France or .sg for Singapore). The Internet domain is the last part of the address (for example, www.microsoft.com).

domain name An address of a network connection that identifies the owner of that address in a hierarchical format. For example, www.whitehouse.gov identifies the Web server at the White House, which is a government agency. *See also* Domain Name System (DNS).

domain namespace The names in a Domain Name System (DNS) database that form a hierarchical tree structure.

Domain Name System (DNS) The system by which hosts on the Internet have domain name addresses (such as microsoft.com) and Internet Protocol (IP) addresses (such as 172.21.13.45). The domain name address is used by human users and is automatically translated into the numerical IP address, which is used by the packet-routing software. DNS is also the acronym for Domain Name Service, the Internet utility that implements the Domain Name System. DNS servers, also called name servers, maintain databases containing the addresses and are accessed transparently by the user.

domain naming master In the Active Directory service, the domain naming master controls the addition or removal of domains in the forest.

download In communications, the process of transferring a copy of a file from a remote computer to the requesting computer by means of a modem or network.

DSN *See* Data Source Name (DSN).

Dynamic Host Configuration Protocol (DHCP) A Transmission Control Protocol/Internet Protocol (TCP/IP) protocol that enables a network connected to the Internet to assign a temporary IP address to a host automatically when the host connects to the network.

dynamic HTML (DHTML) A set of innovative features in Internet Explorer 4 and later that can be used to create Hypertext Markup Language (HTML) documents that dynamically change their content and interact with the user. By using DHTML, authors can provide special effects on a Web page without relying on server-side programs.

dynamic-link library (DLL) A feature of the Microsoft Windows family of operating systems that supports executable routines—usually serving a specific function or set of functions—to be stored separately as files with the file extension name .dll and to be loaded only when called by the program that needs them. This saves memory during program execution and enables code reusability.

E

e-commerce Electronic commerce. The process of buying and selling over the Web—often based on software products such as Microsoft Commerce Server.

e-mail A system whereby a computer user can exchange messages with other computer users (or groups of users) through a communications network. E-mail is one of the most popular uses of the Internet.

encryption A way of making data indecipherable to protect it from unauthorized viewing or use, especially during network transmission or when it's stored on a transportable magnetic medium while it's being sent from computer to computer. Encryption can be either symmetric or asymmetric. Symmetric encryption involves the use of the

same key to both encrypt and decode the data. Asymmetric encryption uses one key to encrypt and another to decode.

Ethernet A 10 megabits-per-second (Mbps) standard for local area networks (LANs) initially developed by Xerox and later refined by Digital, Intel, and Xerox (DIX). All hosts are connected to a coaxial cable, where they contend for network access.

event Any significant occurrence in the system or in an application that requires an entry to be added to a log.

executable program A program, or collection of programs, forms, data, menus, and other files, that can be run.

exponential failure distribution A measure of how long it's likely to take a hardware component to fail under normal circumstances and after an initial phase.

F

failback The full restoration of a failed server node to its original state.

failover A process that takes place when one individual computer fails and another automatically takes over its request load. The transition is invisible to the user.

failover clustering Clustering functionality that provides failover service. In failover clustering, if one node fails, the other node takes ownership of its resources. Failover clustering assumes that an application can resume on another computer that's been given access to the failed system disk subsystem.

failure A departure from the expected behavior on an individual computer system or a system of associated computers and applications. Failures can include behaviors that are outside the defined performance parameters. System failure can be caused by software, hardware, operator and procedural error, and environmental factors.

fat client The client computer in a client/server architecture in which most of an application is run on that computer. Such a configuration yields good client performance but complicates administrative tasks such as software upgrades.

fault tolerance The ability of a computer or an operating system to respond to a catastrophic event or fault, such as a power outage or a hardware failure, in a way that ensures that no data is lost or corrupted. This can be accomplished with a battery-backed power supply, backup hardware, provisions in the operating system, or any combination of these. In a fault-tolerant network, the system has the ability either to continue the system's operation without loss of data or to shut the system down and restart it, recovering all processing that was in progress when the fault occurred.

file allocation table (FAT) file system The system used by MS-DOS to organize and manage files. FAT is a data structure that MS-DOS creates on the disk when the disk is formatted. When MS-DOS stores a file on a formatted disk, the operating system places information about the stored file in the file system table so that MS-DOS can retrieve the file later when requested. FAT is the only file system MS-DOS can use. *See also* NT file system (NTFS).

file encryption key (FEK) A symmetric bulk encryption key used by Encrypting File System (EFS) to encrypt the file. The FEK is then encrypted by using the public key taken from the user's certificate, which is located in the user's profile.

File Transfer Protocol (FTP) A protocol used for copying files to and from remote computer systems on a network using Transmission Control Protocol/Internet Protocol (TCP/IP), such as the Internet. This protocol also allows users to use FTP commands to work with files, such as listing files and directories on the remote system.

filter In Internet Information Services (IIS), a feature of Internet Server Application Programming Interface (ISAPI) that allows preprocessing of requests and post-processing of responses, permitting site-specific handling of Hypertext Transfer Protocol (HTTP) requests and responses.

filtering, host name Allowing or denying access based on the host name from which the browser is attempting access.

filtering, IP address Allowing or denying access based on the Internet Protocol (IP) address from which the browser is attempting access.

firewall A security system intended to protect an organization's network against external threats, such as intruders, coming from another network such as the Internet. A firewall prevents computers in the organization's network from communicating directly with computers external to the network and vice versa. Instead, all communication is routed through a proxy server outside of the organization's network, and the proxy server decides whether it's safe to let a particular message or file pass through.

forest In the Active Directory service, a forest groups together one or more domain trees. Although the trees have different naming structures, they share a common schema.

friendly name *See* alias.

FQDN *See* fully qualified domain name (FQDN).

front end In a multitiered network environment, this term usually describes the portion of the network that supports the Web services. For example, an Internet Information Services (IIS) computer that hosts a Web site would be considered a front-end server.

FTP *See* File Transfer Protocol (FTP).

fully qualified domain name (FQDN) A name that uniquely identifies a host's position within the Domain Name System (DNS) hierarchical tree. For example, a host named mycomputer in the microsoft.com domain would have an FQDN of mycomputer.microsoft.com.

G

gateway A device that connects networks using different communications protocols so that information can be passed from one to the other. A gateway both transfers information and converts it to a form compatible with the protocols used by the receiving network.

GIF *See* Graphics Interchange Format (GIF).

global catalog A central repository of information about Active Directory service objects in a tree or forest. It stores a full replica of all objects in the directory for its host domain and a partial replica of all objects contained in the directory of every other domain in the forest.

globally unique identifier (GUID) In COM, a 16-byte code that identifies an interface to an object across all computers and networks. Such an identifier is unique because it contains a time stamp and a code based on the network address hardwired on the host computer's local area network (LAN) interface card. These identifiers are generated by a utility program.

graphical user interface (GUI) A type of environment that represents programs, files, and options by means of icons, menus, and dialog boxes on the screen. The user can select and activate these options by pointing and clicking with a mouse or, often, by using a keyboard.

Graphics Interchange Format (GIF) A computer graphics file format developed in the mid-1980s by CompuServe for use in photo-quality graphic image display on computer screens. Now commonly used on the Internet.

GUI *See* graphical user interface (GUI).

GUID *See* globally unique identifier (GUID).

H

handshake A series of signals acknowledging that communication or the transfer of information can take place between computers or other devices. A hardware handshake is an exchange of signals over specific wires (other than the data wires), in which each device indicates its readiness to send or receive data. A software handshake consists of signals transmitted over the same wires used to transfer data, as in modem-to-modem communications over telephone lines.

home directory The root directory for a Web site, where the content files are stored. Also called a document root or Web root. In Internet Information Services (IIS), the home directory and all its subdirectories are available to users by default. Also the root directory for an IIS service. The home directory for a site typically contains the home page.

home page The initial page of information for a collection of pages, a Web site, or a section of a Web site.

host A Windows 2000 computer that runs a server program or service used by network or remote clients. For Network Load Balancing (NLB), a cluster consists of multiple hosts connected over a local area network (LAN).

host name The name of a specific server on a specific network within the Internet, leftmost in the complete host specifications. For example, www.microsoft.com indicates the server called "www" within the network at Microsoft Corporation.

hot link *See* hyperlink.

HTML *See* Hypertext Markup Language (HTML).

HTTP *See* Hypertext Transfer Protocol (HTTP).

hub A network-enabled device that joins communication lines at a central location, providing a common connection to all devices on the network. There are two kinds of hubs: passive and active. When a hub receives a transmission, it broadcasts traffic to all ports.

hyperlink A connection between an element in a hypertext document, such as a word, phrase, symbol, or image, and a different element in the document, another hypertext document, a file, or a script. The user activates the link by clicking on the linked element, which is usually underlined or in a color different from the rest of the document. Hyperlinks are indicated in a hypertext document by the use of tags in markup languages such as Standard Generalized Markup Language (SGML) and Hypertext Markup Language (HTML). Users generally can't see these tags. Also called hot link and hypertext link.

hypertext Text linked together in a complex, nonsequential web of associations in which the user can browse through related topics. The term hypertext was coined in 1965 to describe documents presented by a computer that express the nonlinear structure of ideas as opposed to the linear format of books, film, and speech.

hypertext link *See* hyperlink.

Hypertext Markup Language (HTML) A simple markup language used to create hypertext documents that are portable from one platform to another. HTML files are simple ASCII text files with codes embedded (indicated by markup tags) to indicate formatting and hypertext links. The formatting language used for documents on the World Wide Web.

Hypertext Transfer Protocol (HTTP) The client/server protocol used to access information on the World Wide Web.

I

ICMP *See* Internet Control Message Protocol (ICMP).

IETF *See* Internet Engineering Task Force (IETF).

indirect dependency In the Cluster service, an indirect dependency is a resource dependency in which a transitive relationship exists between resources. In other words, an intermediary resource is between the two dependent resources. For example, if resource A depends on resource B, and resource B depends on resource C, there's an indirect dependency between resource A and resource C.

infrastructure master In the Active Directory service, the infrastructure master updates the group-to-user references whenever the members of groups are renamed or changed.

inheritance Generally, the ability of a newly created object to automatically have, or inherit, properties of an existing object. For example, a newly created child directory can inherit the access-control settings of the parent directory.

in-process component A component that runs in a client's process space. This component is typically a dynamic-link library (DLL).

instance An object of a particular component class. Each instance has its own private data elements or member variables. Component instance is synonymous with object. An instance can also refer to the installation of an application that's completely separate from any other installations of that application.

instantiate To create an instance of an object.

Integrated Services Digital Network (ISDN)
Combines voice and digital network services in a single medium, making it possible to offer telephone customers digital data service and voice connection through a single "wire." A dial-up ISDN line can offer speeds of up to 128,000 bits per second (bps). A type of phone line used to enhance wide area network (WAN) speeds, an ISDN line can transmit at speeds of 64 or 128 kilobits per second (Kbps). An ISDN line must be installed by the phone company at both the server site and the remote site.

Integrated Windows authentication A method of authentication in which a server verifies user account information by means of a cryptographic exchange; actual passwords are never transmitted.

interconnect *See* network.

International Organization for Standardization (ISO) A voluntary, nontreaty organization founded in 1946 that is responsible for creating international standards in many areas, including computers and communications. Its members are the national standards organizations of the 89 member countries, including ANSI for the United States. *See also* American National Standards Institute (ANSI).

International Organization for Standardization Open Systems Interconnection (ISO/OSI) model A layered architecture (plan) that standardizes levels of service and types of interaction for computers exchanging information through a communications network. The ISO/OSI model separates computer-to-computer communications into seven layers, or levels, each building upon the standards contained in the levels below it. The lowest of the seven layers deals solely with hardware links; the highest deals with software interactions at the application-program level.

Internet Abbreviation for internetwork. A set of dissimilar computer networks joined by means of gateways that handle data transfer and the conversion of messages from the sending network to the protocols used by the receiving networks. These networks and gateways use the Transmission Control Protocol/Internet Protocol (TCP/IP) suite of protocols. Originally part of the Defense Advanced Research Projects Agency (DARPA), operated by the U.S. Department of Defense.

Internet Control Message Protocol (ICMP) An extension to Internet Protocol (IP), ICMP allows for the generation of error messages, test packets, and informational messages related to IP.

Internet Engineering Task Force (IETF) A protocol engineering and development organization focused on the Internet. The IETF is a large, open international community of network designers, operators, vendors, and researchers concerned with the evolution of the Internet architecture and the smooth operation of the Internet. It's now under the auspices of the Internet Society, a nongovernmental international organization for global cooperation and coordination for the Internet and its internetworking technologies and applications. For more information, see the Internet Society Web site at *http://www.isoc.org/*.

Internet Network Information Center (InterNIC) A coordinator for Domain Name Service (DNS) registration of names in the .com, .net, .org, .edu, .gov, and .mil top-level domains. To register domain names and obtain Internet Protocol (IP) addresses, contact InterNIC at *http://internic.net/*.

Internet Protocol (IP) The part of Transmission Control Protocol/Internet Protocol (TCP/IP) that routes messages from one Internet location to another. IP is responsible for addressing and sending TCP packets over the network. IP provides a best-effort, connectionless delivery system that doesn't guarantee that packets arrive at their destination or that they're received in the sequence in which they were sent.

Internet Protocol address (IP address) A unique address that identifies a host on a network. It identifies a computer as a 32-bit address that's unique across a Transmission Control Protocol/Internet Protocol (TCP/IP) network. An IP address is usually represented in dotted-decimal notation, which depicts each octet (8 bits, or a byte) of an IP address as its decimal value and separates each octet with a period. For example: 172.16.255.255.

Internet Server Application Programming Interface (ISAPI) An application program interface (API) that resides on a server computer for initiating software services tuned for the Microsoft Windows operating system. It's an API for developing extensions to Internet Information Services (IIS) and other Hypertext Transfer Protocol (HTTP) services that support the ISAPI interface.

Internet service provider (ISP) Public provider of remote connections to the Internet. A company or educational institution that enables remote users to access the Internet by providing dial-up connections or installing leased lines.

interoperability The ability of software and hardware on multiple computers from multiple vendors to communicate meaningfully.

intranet A network designed for information processing within a company or organization. Its uses include such services as document distribution, software distribution, access to databases, and training. An intranet derives its name from the fact that it usually employs applications associated with the Internet, such as Web pages, Web browsers, File Transfer Protocol (FTP) sites, e-mail, newsgroups, and mailing lists, in this case accessible only to those within the company or organization.

IP *See* Internet Protocol (IP).

ISAPI *See* Internet Server Application Programming Interface (ISAPI).

ISDN *See* Integrated Services Digital Network (ISDN).

ISO/OSI model *See* International Organization for Standardization Open Systems Interconnection (ISO/OSI) model.

ISP *See* Internet service provider (ISP).

J

Java An object-oriented programming language developed by Sun Microsystems. Currently, the most widespread use of Java is in programming small applications, or applets, for the World Wide Web.

JavaScript A scripting language developed by Netscape Communications that's syntactically similar to Java. JavaScript, however, isn't a true object-oriented language, and it's limited in performance compared with Java because it's not compiled. A JavaScript-client Web browser is necessary to run JavaScript code. Now an open standard that has been adopted by the European Computer Manufacturers Association (ECMA) and is known as the ECMA 262 language specification.

K

Kerberos protocol The basis of Microsoft Windows security, for both internal and intranet logon. The Kerberos protocol provides for the secure use of distributed software components.

L

LAN *See* local area network (LAN).

latency The amount of time a user has to wait for a page to load once a request has been made. In general, static content such as Hypertext Markup Language (HTML) pages doesn't contribute to latency nearly as much as dynamic content, such as Active Server Pages (ASP) pages.

LDAP *See* Lightweight Directory Access Protocol (LDAP).

Lightweight Directory Access Protocol (LDAP) A network protocol designed to work on Transmission Control Protocol/Internet Protocol (TCP/IP) stacks to extract information from a hierarchical directory. This gives users a single tool to search through data to find a particular piece of information, such as a user name, e-mail address, security certificate, or other contact information.

load-balanced adapter In Network Load Balancing (NLB), the network adapter on a computer in an NLB cluster that's used for front-end traffic.

load balancing A process in which a server cluster shares the information requests equally over all of its active nodes. This can be done either statically, by tying clients directly to different back-end servers, or dynamically, by having each client tied to a different back-end server controlled by software or a hardware device. The Network Load Balancing (NLB) feature of Microsoft Windows 2000 Advanced Server provides load balancing for Hypertext Transfer Protocol (HTTP) services.

local area network (LAN) A group of computers and other devices intended to serve an area of only a few square miles or less and connected by a communications link that enables any device to interact with any other on the network. Because the network is known to cover only a small area, optimizations can be made in the network signal protocols that permit data rates of up to 100 megabits per second (Mbps).

log file The file in which logging records are stored. This file can be either a text file or a database file.

log shipping The process of copying transaction logs from a primary SQL Server computer and applying them sequentially to another SQL Server computer. If the primary computer fails, you can direct your application to the backup server.

logging Storing information about events that occurred on a firewall or network.

M

Management Information Base (MIB) Software that describes aspects of a network that can be managed by using the Simple Network Management Protocol (SNMP). The MIB files included in Microsoft Windows can be used by third-party SNMP monitors to enable SNMP monitoring of the Web and File Transfer Protocol (FTP) services of Internet Information Services (IIS).

management-traffic adapter In Network Load Balancing (NLB), the network adapter on a computer in an NLB cluster that's used for back-end traffic.

MAPI *See* Messaging Applications Programming Interface (MAPI).

mean time to failure (MTTF) The mean time until a device will fail. By knowing the MTTF of a hardware device, you might be able to predict when that device will enter its failure mode.

mean time to recovery (MTTR) The mean time it takes to recover from a failure.

member scope In the Dynamic Host Configuration Protocol (DHCP) Service, a member scope is a scope that's added to a superscope.

Message Queuing A server technology that developers can use to build large-scale distributed systems with reliable communications between applications that can continue to operate even when networked systems are unavailable.

Messaging Applications Programming Interface (MAPI) An open and comprehensive messaging interface used by developers to create messaging and workgroup applications—such as e-mail, scheduling, calendaring, and document management. In a distributed client/server environment, MAPI provides enterprise messaging services within Windows Open Services Architecture (WOSA).

metabase A structure for storing Internet Information Services (IIS) configuration settings; the metabase performs some of the same functions as the system registry, but uses less disk space.

metadata Data used to describe other data. For example, Indexing Service must maintain data that describes the data in the content index.

MIB *See* Management Information Base (MIB).

Microsoft Cryptographic API An application programming interface (API) providing services for authentication, encoding, and encryption in Win32-based applications.

Microsoft Visual Basic for Applications (VBA) The development environment and language found in Microsoft Visual Basic that can be hosted by applications.

Microsoft Visual Basic Scripting Edition (VBScript) A subset of the Microsoft Visual Basic language, VBScript is implemented as a fast, portable, lightweight interpreter for use in World Wide Web browsers and other applications that use ActiveX Controls and Java applets.

middle tier The logical layer between a user interface or Web client and the database. This is typically where the Web server resides and where business objects are instantiated. Also known as application server tier.

middleware The network-aware system software, layered between an application, the operating system, and the network transport layers, whose purpose is to facilitate some aspect of cooperative processing. Examples of middleware include directory services, message-passing mechanisms, distributed transaction processing (TP) monitors, object request brokers, remote procedure call (RPC) services, and database gateways.

mirror A fully redundant or shadow copy of data. Mirror sets provide an identical twin for a selected disk; all data written to the primary disk is also written to the shadow or mirror disk. The user can then have instant access to another disk with a redundant copy of the information on the failed disk. Mirror sets provide fault tolerance.

mirrored volume A RAID-1 configuration in which the same data is written to a volume on each of two physical disks simultaneously. Each volume is considered a member of the mirrored volume.

mirroring In redundant array of independent disks (RAID), the process of providing fault tolerance by using a mirror.

modem A communications device that enables a computer to transmit information over a standard telephone line. Short for modulator/demodulator.

MTTF *See* mean time to failure (MTTF).

MTTR *See* mean time to recovery (MTTF).

multihomed host A host that has a connection to more than one physical network. The host may send and receive data over any of the links but won't route traffic for other nodes.

multihoming The process of installing multiple network interface cards (NICs) on a single server or configuring a single NIC with multiple Internet Protocol (IP) addresses. When multiple NICs are installed, each NIC is assigned a unique IP address.

multimaster replication The replication process used by the Active Directory service. In multimaster replication, all domain controllers for the domain can modify the zone and then replicate the changes to other domain controllers. Any domain controller can send or receive updates of information stored in Active Directory.

Multipurpose Internet Mail Extensions (MIME) mapping A way of configuring browsers to view files that are in multiple formats. An extension of the Internet mail protocol that enables sending 8-bit–based e-mail messages, which are used to support extended character sets, voice mail, facsimile images, and so on.

multithreading Running several processes in rapid sequence within a single program, regardless of which logical method of multitasking is being used by the operating system. Because the user's sense of time is much slower than the processing speed of a computer, multitasking appears to be simultaneous, even though only one task at a time can use a computer processing cycle.

multitier architecture A technique for building applications generally split into user, business, and data services tiers. These applications are built of component services that are based on an object model such as Component Object Model (COM).

N

N+1 failover A Cluster service cluster configuration in which the node preference lists of all cluster groups identify the standby cluster nodes to which resources should be made during failover. The standby nodes are servers in the cluster that are mostly idle or whose workload can be easily preempted.

name resolution The method of mapping friendly names to Internet Protocol (IP) addresses.

named pipe A high-level interprocess communication mechanism used by network computers to provide connection-oriented messaging.

network In the Cluster service, a network is an object managed by the Cluster service. A network can be private, public, private and public, or neither private nor public. Also called an interconnect.

network interface A card or other network adapter that connects a computer to a network.

network interface card (NIC) A type of network interface that connects a computer to a network. Can be an expansion card or another device. A NIC allows communication to occur between the computer and physical media, such as cabling.

Network Load Balancing (NLB) A service in Microsoft Windows 2000 Advanced Server and Datacenter Server that balances incoming Internet Protocol (IP) traffic across multiple cluster hosts. It automatically detects host failures and redistributes traffic to the surviving hosts. NLB enhances the scalability and availability of mission-critical services such Internet Information Services (IIS).

Network News Transfer Protocol (NNTP) The protocol used to distribute network news messages to NNTP servers and to NNTP clients (news readers) on the Internet. NNTP provides for the distribution, inquiry, retrieval, and posting of news articles by using a reliable stream-based transmission of news on the Internet. NNTP is designed so that news articles are stored on a server in a central database; thus users can select specific items to read. Indexing, cross-referencing, and expiration of old messages are also provided. Defined in RFC 977.

network sniffer A hardware and software diagnostic tool that can also be used to decipher passwords, which may result in unauthorized access to network accounts. Clear-text passwords are susceptible to network sniffers.

NIC *See* network interface card (NIC).

NNTP *See* Network News Transfer Protocol (NNTP).

node A computer that's attached to a network; also called a host. A node is also a junction of some kind. On a local area network (LAN), a node is a device that's connected to the network and is capable of communicating with other network devices. In the Cluster service, a node is a computer that's a member of the cluster.

NT file system (NTFS) A file system designed for use specifically with the Microsoft Windows operating system. It supports long file names, full security access control, file system recovery, extremely large storage media, and various features for the Windows Portable Operating System Interface for UNIX (POSIX) subsystem. It also supports object-oriented applications by treating all files as objects with user-defined and system-defined attributes.

NTFS *See* NT file system (NTFS).

O

Object Linking and Embedding (OLE) A set of integration standards that is used to transfer and share information among client applications. A protocol that enables creation of compound documents with embedded links to applications so that a user doesn't have to switch among applications in order to make revisions. OLE is based on the Component Object Model (COM) and allows for the development of reusable objects that are interoperable across multiple applications. The technology has been broadly used in business, where spreadsheets, word processors, financial packages, and other applications can share and link disparate information across client/server architectures.

octet Consists of 8 contiguous bits, or a byte. The term was created because some computer systems attached to the Internet used a byte with more than 8 bits.

ODBC *See* Open Database Connectivity (ODBC).

OLE *See* Object Linking and Embedding (OLE).

OLE DB Data-access interfaces providing consistent access to SQL and non-SQL data sources across the enterprise and the Internet. *See also* Structured Query Language (SQL).

Open Database Connectivity (ODBC) An application programming interface that enables applications to access data from a variety of existing data sources. A standard specification for cross-platform database access.

organizational unit (OU) In the Active Directory service, an OU is a container that can contain such objects as users, groups, computers, and other OUs.

OU *See* organizational unit (OU).

out-of-process component A Component Object Model (COM) component that runs in a process space separate from its client.

P

packet A transmission unit of a fixed maximum size that consists of binary information representing both data and a header containing an ID number, source and destination addresses, and error-control data. A piece of information sent over a network.

parity In redundant array of independent disks (RAID), parity refers to the mathematical method of determining the number of odd and even bits in a number or series of numbers, which you can use to reconstruct data if one number in a sequence of numbers is lost.

parity information In redundant array of independent disks (RAID), parity information is the data generated by the system to reconstruct lost information in case a disk fails.

partitioned In the Cluster service, partitioned refers to two nodes being unable to communicate with each other. After two nodes become partitioned, the Cluster service automatically shuts down on one node to guarantee data consistency.

partitioning The process of distributing data from one table into multiple, identical tables on different servers. Once the data is partitioned, you can use distributed partitioned views to access that data.

passive hub A type of hub that organizes wiring, but, unlike an active hub, it doesn't regenerate or retransmit network data.

PDC emulator In the Active Directory service, the PDC emulator acts as a Microsoft Windows NT Primary Domain Controller (PDC) if the domain contains computers operating without Microsoft Windows 2000 client software or if it contains Windows NT backup domain controllers.

Point-to-Point Protocol (PPP) A set of industry-standard framing and authentication protocols included with Microsoft Windows remote access to ensure interoperability with third-party remote access software. PPP negotiates configuration parameters for multiple layers of the Open Systems Interconnection (OSI) model. The Internet standard for serial communications, PPP defines how data packets are exchanged with other Internet-based systems using a modem connection.

Point-to-Point Tunneling Protocol (PPTP) A specification for virtual private networks in which some nodes of a local area network are connected through the Internet. PPTP is an open industry standard that supports the most prevalent networking protocols—Internet Protocol (IP), Internetwork Packet Exchange (IPX), and Microsoft Networking (NetBEUI). Companies can use PPTP to outsource their remote dial-up needs to an Internet service provider or other carrier to reduce cost and complexity.

port number A number identifying a certain Internet application. For example, the default port number for the WWW service is 80.

port rule In Network Load Balancing (NLB), a port rule is a configuration setting that describes which traffic to load balance and which traffic to ignore. By default, NLB configures all ports for load balancing.

PPP *See* Point-to-Point Protocol (PPP).

PPTP *See* Point-to-Point Tunneling Protocol (PPTP).

preferred node In the Cluster service, a preferred node is a preferred computer on which the resource is configured to run.

primary node In the Cluster service, a primary node supports all clients while its companion node (secondary node) is idle. If the primary node fails, the secondary node immediately picks up all operations and continues to service clients at a rate of performance that's close or equal to that of the primary node. *See also* secondary node.

process In Microsoft Windows, an object consisting of an executable program, a set of virtual memory addresses, and threads; in UNIX, a synonym for thread. A process is the largest component of activity in Windows 2000. *See also* thread.

process isolation Running an application or component out-of-process.

protocol The method by which computers communicate on the Internet. The most common protocol for the World Wide Web is Hypertext Transfer Protocol (HTTP). Other Internet protocols include File Transfer Protocol (FTP), Gopher, and Telnet. The protocol is part of the full Uniform Resource Locator (URL) for a resource.

provider In OLE DB, a provider is any component that allows technologies such as ActiveX Directory Objects (ADO) to access data in a uniform way through the OLE DB interfaces.

proxy A software program that connects a user to a remote destination through an intermediary gateway.

proxy server A firewall component that manages Internet traffic to and from a local area network and can provide other features, such as document caching and access control. A proxy server can improve performance by caching and directly supplying frequently requested data, such as a popular Web page, and can filter and discard requests that the owner doesn't consider appropriate, such as requests for unauthorized access to proprietary files. *See also* firewall.

public-key encryption An asymmetric scheme that uses a pair of keys for encryption: the public key encrypts data and a corresponding secret key decrypts it. For digital signatures, the process is reversed: The sender uses the secret key to create a unique electronic number that can be read by anyone possessing the corresponding public key, which verifies that the message is from the sender.

Q

quorum disk In the Cluster service, a single disk in the cluster storage system designated as the quorum resource.

quorum resource In the Cluster service, a special common resource that's a dedicated physical resource in the common cluster disk array that plays a critical role in the cluster operation.

R

RAID *See* redundant array of independent disks (RAID).

RAM *See* random access memory (RAM).

random access memory (RAM) Semiconductor-based memory that can be read and written by the central processing unit (CPU) or other hardware devices. The storage locations can be accessed in any order. Note that various types of read-only memory (ROM) are capable of random access but can't be written to. The term RAM is generally understood to refer to volatile memory that can be written to as well as read. Information stored in RAM is lost when the user turns off the computer.

redundancy The duplication of network components, paths, and services to provide fault tolerance and avoid any single points of failure in your network. The use of redundant hardware and software is the most effective way to ensure a Web site's availability.

redundant array of independent disks (RAID) A data storage method in which data, along with information used for error correction, such as parity bits, is distributed among two or more hard disk drives in order to improve performance and reliability. The hard disk array is governed by array management software and a disk controller, which handles the error correction. RAID is generally used on network servers. Several defined levels of RAID offer differing trade-offs among access speed, reliability, and cost. Microsoft Windows includes three RAID levels: Level 0, Level 1, and Level 5.

registry A central hierarchical database in Microsoft Windows used to store information necessary to configure the system for one or more users, applications, and hardware devices. The registry contains information that's constantly referenced during operation, such as profiles for each user, the applications installed on the computer and the types of documents each can create, property sheet settings for folders and application icons, what hardware exists on the system, and which ports are being used.

relative ID master In the Active Directory service, the relative ID master allocates sequences of relative IDs to each of the various domain controllers in its domain.

reliability A measure of the time that elapses between failures in a system. Hardware and software components have different failure characteristics. As a result, it's easier to predict hardware reliability than software reliability. With hardware, you can often predict when a component will fail and from there estimate that component's reliability.

Remote Data Services A Web-based technology that brings database connectivity and corporate data publishing capabilities to Internet and intranet applications.

remote procedure call (RPC) In programming, a call by one program to a second program on a remote system. The second program usually performs a task and returns the results of that task to the first program.

replication Copying from one server node to another of either content or the configuration metabase, or both. This copying can be done either manually or automatically by using replication software. Replication is a necessary function of clustering to ensure fault tolerance.

resource In the Cluster service, a resource is a hardware or software component within the cluster. A resource is any physical or logical component that can be brought online and taken offline, can be managed in a server cluster, and can be hosted by only one node at a time.

resource group In the Cluster service, a resource group is a logical collection of cluster resources. A resource group is usually made up of logically related resources such as applications and their associated peripherals and data.

root domain In Domain Name System (DNS), the root domain is the domain name that the zone is anchored to. A zone contains information about all names that end with the zone's root domain.

router An intermediary device on a communications network that expedites message delivery. On a single network linking many computers through a mesh of possible connections, a router receives transmitted messages and forwards them to their correct destinations over the most efficient available route. On an interconnected set of local area networks (LANs) using the same communications protocols, a router serves the somewhat different function of acting as a link between LANs, enabling messages to be sent from one to another.

RPC *See* remote procedure call (RPC).

S

SAN *See* storage area network (SAN).

scalability A measure of how easily a computer, service, or application can expand to meet increasing performance demands. A scalable system is one that can perform increasing work while sustaining acceptable performance levels. For server clusters, scalability refers to the ability to incrementally add one or more systems to an existing cluster when the cluster's load exceeds its capabilities.

scaling out The process of adding more servers to your network. Scaling out delivers high performance when an application's throughput requirements exceed an individual system's capabilities. Scaling out reduces contention for resources and improves availability.

scaling up The process of adding more resources to a system. Scaling up can include adding memory, processors, and disk drives to your computer.

schema master In the Active Directory service, the schema master controls all updates and modifications to the schema.

script A kind of program that consists of a set of instructions for an application or utility program. A script can be embedded in a Web page.

scripting engine A program that interprets and executes a script. *See also* script.

secondary node In the Cluster service, a secondary node is the companion node in the cluster that acts as a backup to the primary node. The secondary node is idle unless failover occurs. If the primary node fails, the secondary node immediately picks up all operations and continues to service clients at a rate of performance that's close to or equal to that of the primary node. *See also* primary node.

Secure Sockets Layer (SSL) A protocol that supplies secure data communication through data encryption and decryption. SSL uses Rivest-Shamir-Adleman (RSA) public-key encryption for specific Transmission Control Protocol/Internet Protocol (TCP/IP) ports. It's intended for handling commerce payments. An alternative method is Secure-HTTP (S-HTTP), which is used to encrypt specific Web documents rather than the entire session. SSL is a general-purpose encryption standard. SSL can also be used for Web applications requiring a secure link, such as e-commerce applications, or for controlling access to Web-based subscription services.

security descriptor The access control information associated with an object. Each object in Microsoft Windows 2000 contains a security descriptor. When a user tries to access the object, Windows 2000 examines the security descriptor to determine whether the user is allowed to access the object and what action the user is allowed to take with that object.

Security log A log, generated by a firewall or other security device, that lists events that could affect security, such as access attempts or commands, and the information about the users involved.

server A term that refers to any of the following: a computer on a network that sends files to, or runs applications for, other computers on the network; the software that runs on the server computer and performs the work of serving files or running applications; or, in object-oriented programming, a piece of code that exchanges information with another piece of code upon request.

server certificate *See* certificate, server.

server cluster A group of server computers that are networked together both physically and with software, in order to provide cluster features such as fault tolerance or load balancing. *See also* cluster.

server-side include A mechanism for including dynamic text in World Wide Web documents. Server-side includes are special command codes that are recognized and interpreted by the server; their output is placed in the document body before the document is sent to the browser. Server-side includes can be used, for example, to include the date/time stamp in the text of the file.

session key A digital key that's created by the client, encrypted, and sent to the server. This key is used to encrypt data sent by the client.

session state Client data that's visible to a particular client for the duration of a session. Session state can span multiple Transmission Control Protocol (TCP) connections, which can be either simultaneous or sequential.

shared-nothing model In the Cluster service, the shared-nothing model refers to how servers in a cluster manage and use local and common cluster devices and resources. In this model, each server owns and manages its local devices. Devices common to the cluster are selectively owned and managed by a single server at any given time.

Simple Mail Transfer Protocol (SMTP) A Transmission Control Protocol/Internet Protocol (TCP/IP) protocol for sending messages from one computer to another on a network. This protocol is used on the Internet to route e-mail.

Simple Network Management Protocol (SNMP) The network management protocol of Transmission Control Protocol/Internet Protocol (TCP/IP). In SNMP, agents, which can be hardware as well as software, monitor the activity in the various devices on the network and report to the network console workstation. Control information about each device is maintained in a structure known as a management information block. *See also* Management Information Base (MIB).

site In the Active Directory service, consists of one or more Internet Protocol (IP) subnets that are connected by highly reliable and fast links. A site often shares the same boundaries as the local area network (LAN), but a site isn't a part of the namespace.

slow link A modem connection, usually from 14,400 bits per second (bps) to 56,000 bps. Also called a dial-up.

SMTP *See* Simple Mail Transfer Protocol (SMTP).

snap-in A program hosted within Microsoft Management Console (MMC) that administrators use to manage network services. MMC provides the environment in which management tools (snap-ins) are hosted; snap-ins provide the actual management behavior necessary to administer network services such as Internet Information Services (IIS).

sniffer *See* network sniffer.

SNMP *See* Simple Network Management Protocol (SNMP).

socket An identifier for a particular service on a particular node on a network. The socket consists of a node address and a port number, which identifies the service. For example, port 80 on an Internet node indicates a Web server.

spoofing Impersonating another person or computer, usually by providing a false e-mail name, Uniform Resource Locator (URL), or Internet Protocol (IP) address.

SQL *See* Structured Query Language (SQL).

SSL *See* Secure Sockets Layer (SSL).

stager A server on which content is placed prior to being placed on a production server. A stager is also known as a staging computer or staging server.

stateful object An object that holds private state accumulated from the execution of one or more client calls.

stateful system A system (usually on the back end) that maintains data and state across sessions. Data can be stored in flat files, inside other applications, or in a database.

stateless object An object that doesn't hold private state accumulated from the execution of one or more client calls.

stateless system A system (usually on the front end) that doesn't store client information across sessions. If client information needs to persist between sessions, you can use techniques such as cookies to maintain the information.

static page Hypertext Markup Language (HTML) pages prepared in advance of the request and sent to the client upon request. This page takes no special action when requested.

sticky session A session in which a client request establishes a server-side state that's used in subsequent requests during the same session.

storage area network (SAN) A network comprised of one or more storage systems, each capable of providing terabytes of disk storage capacity at very high transfer rates. Most SANs use Fibre Channel technology and are capable of providing input/output (I/O) throughputs in the gigabits-per-second (Gbps) range.

stored procedure A precompiled set of queries that's stored on the database server. They control which operations are performed and which database fields are accessed.

stripe set Refers to the saving of data across identical partitions on different drives. A stripe set doesn't provide fault tolerance; however, stripe sets with parity do provide fault tolerance. *See also* stripe sets with parity.

stripe sets with parity A method of data protection in which data is striped in large blocks across all the disks in an array. Data redundancy is provided by the parity information. This method provides fault tolerance. *See also* stripe set.

Structured Query Language (SQL) The international standard language for defining and accessing relational databases.

subnet A subdivision of an Internet Protocol (IP) network. Each subnet has its own unique subnetted network ID, which is a subset of the original class-based network ID. Subnetted network IDs are created by using bits from the host ID portion of the original network ID.

subnet mask A Transmission Control Protocol/Internet Protocol (TCP/IP) configuration parameter that extracts the network ID and host ID from an IP address.

subnetting The process of dividing a Transmission Control Protocol/Internet Protocol (TCP/IP) network into subnets.

switch A computer or other network-enabled device that controls routing and operation of a signal path. Rather than broadcast to all ports (as a hub does), a switch establishes a direct path between two ports so that multiple pairs of ports can communicate without collision.

switch flooding In Network Load Balancing (NLB), switch flooding refers to the process in which the switch sends a client request, which contains the cluster media access control (MAC) address, to all ports because it doesn't recognize the MAC address in the packet.

symmetric encryption *See* encryption.

T

T1 A U.S. telephone standard for a transmission facility at digital signal level 1 (DS1) with 1.544 megabits per second (Mbps) in North America and 2.048 Mbps in Europe. The bit rate is with the equivalent bandwidth of approximately twenty-four 56-kilobits-per-second (Kbps) lines. A T1 circuit is capable of serving a minimum of 48 modems at 28.8 Kbps, or 96 modems at 14.4 Kbps. T1 circuits are also used for voice telephone connections. A single T1 line carries 24 telephone connections with 24 telephone numbers. When used for voice transmission, a T1 connection must be split into 24 separate circuits.

T3 A U.S. telephone standard for a transmission facility at digital signal level 3 (DS3). Equivalent in bandwidth to 28 T1s. The bit rate is 44.736

megabits per second (Mbps). T3 is sometimes called a 45-meg circuit.

TCP/IP *See* Transmission Control Protocol/ Internet Protocol (TCP/IP).

Telnet A protocol that enables an Internet user to log onto and enter commands on a remote computer linked to the Internet, as if the user were using a text-based terminal directly attached to that computer. Telnet is part of the Transmission Control Protocol/Internet Protocol (TCP/IP) suite of protocols.

thin server A client/server architecture in which most of an application is run on the client computer, which is called a fat client, with occasional data operations on a remote server. Such a configuration yields good client performance but complicates administrative tasks such as software upgrades.

thread The basic entity to which the operating system allocates central processing unit (CPU) time. A thread can execute any part of the application's code, including a part currently being executed by another thread. All threads of a process share the virtual address space, global variables, and operating-system resources of the process.

three-tier architecture Divides a networked application into three logical areas: the user interface layer, the business logic layer, and the database layer. Layers may have one or more components. For example, there can be one or more user interfaces in the top tier, each user interface may communicate with more than one application in the middle tier at the same time, and the applications in the middle tier may use more than one database at a time. Components in a tier may run on a computer that's separate from the other tiers, communicating with the other components over a network.

throttling Controlling the maximum amount of bandwidth dedicated to Internet traffic on a server. This feature is useful if there are other services (such as e-mail) sharing the server over a busy link.

time out A setting that automatically cancels an unanswered client request after a certain period of time.

traffic The interchange of incoming network requests and outgoing responses. In a Web environment, the request is sent by a browser on a client computer through a Transmission Control Protocol (TCP) connection with the server. The server sends out pages in response to the request.

Transmission Control Protocol/Internet Protocol (TCP/IP) A communications standard for all computers on the Internet. On the sending end, TCP breaks the data to be sent into data segments. IP assembles segments into packets that contain data segments, as well as sender and destination addresses. IP then sends packets to the router for delivery. On the receiving end, IP receives the packets and breaks them down into data segments. TCP assembles the data segments into the original data set.

tree In the Active Directory service, a hierarchical grouping of domains. You can create a tree by adding one or more child domains to the parent domain.

U

UNC *See* Universal Naming Convention (UNC).

Uniform Resource Locator (URL) A naming convention that uniquely identifies the location of a computer, directory, or file on the Internet. The

URL also specifies the appropriate Internet protocol, such as Hypertext Transfer Protocol (HTTP) or File Transfer Protocol (FTP). For example: *http://www.microsoft.com.*

Universal Naming Convention (UNC) The naming convention used for physical directories.

URL *See* Uniform Resource Locator (URL).

V

VBA *See* Microsoft Visual Basic for Applications (VBA).

VBScript *See* Microsoft Visual Basic Scripting Edition (VBScript).

virtual directory A directory name, used in an address, that corresponds to a physical directory on the server; sometimes called URL mapping.

virtual machine Software that mimics the performance of a hardware device, such as a program that allows applications written for an Intel processor to be run on a Motorola processor.

virtual server A virtual computer that resides on a Hypertext Transfer Protocol (HTTP) server but appears to the user as a separate HTTP server. Several virtual servers can reside on one computer, each capable of running its own programs and each with individualized access to input and peripheral devices. Each virtual server has its own domain name and Internet Protocol (IP) address and appears to the user as an individual Web site or File Transfer Protocol (FTP) site. Some Internet service providers use virtual servers for those clients who want to use their own domain names. In clusters, a virtual server appears as a single server to users.

W

W3C *See* World Wide Web Consortium (W3C).

WAN *See* wide area network (WAN).

Web application A software program that uses Hypertext Transfer Protocol (HTTP) for its core communication protocol and delivers Web-based information to the user in the Hypertext Markup Language (HTML).

WebDAV *See* Web Distributed Authoring and Versioning (WebDAV).

Web Distributed Authoring and Versioning (WebDAV) An extension to the Hypertext Transfer Protocol (HTTP) 1.1 standard that facilitates access to files and directories through an HTTP connection. Remote authors can add, search, delete, or change directories and documents and their properties.

Web farm A front-end cluster that provides core services, such as Hypertext Transfer Protocol (HTTP) and File Transfer Protocol (FTP), to the clients. *See also* cluster.

Web page A World Wide Web document. A Web page typically consists of a Hypertext Markup Language (HTML) file, with associated files for graphics and scripts, in a particular directory on a particular computer (and thus identifiable by a Uniform Resource Locator [URL]).

Web server In general terms, a computer equipped with the server software that uses Internet protocols such as Hypertext Transfer Protocol (HTTP) and File Transfer Protocol (FTP) to respond to Web client requests on a Transmission Control Protocol/Internet Protocol (TCP/IP) network.

wide area network (WAN) A communications network that connects geographically separated areas.

Windows Internet Name Service (WINS) server A server that uses the WINS protocol to map Internet Protocol (IP) addresses to user-friendly names. *See also* Domain Name System (DNS).

Windows Open Services Architecture (WOSA) Standards for creating cross-platform applications that use Microsoft Windows services.

Windows Script Host (WSH) A language-independent scripting host for ActiveX scripting engines on 32-bit Microsoft Windows platforms.

worker thread A thread that's created by a component or Internet Server Application Programming Interface (ISAPI) extension or filter to perform asynchronous processing. Using worker threads frees up Internet Information Services (IIS) input/output (I/O) threads to process additional requests.

working directory A term sometimes used to describe the directory in which the Web server software is installed.

working set The RAM allocated to a process in the Microsoft Windows operating system.

World Wide Web (WWW) The most graphical service on the Internet, the Web also has the most sophisticated linking abilities. It's a set of services that run on top of the Internet, providing a cost-effective way of publishing information, supporting collaboration and workflow, and delivering business applications to connected

users all over the world. The Web is a collection of Internet host systems that make these services available on the Internet using the Hypertext Transfer Protocol (HTTP). Web-based information is usually delivered in the form of hypertext and hypermedia using Hypertext Markup Language (HTML).

World Wide Web Consortium (W3C) Founded in 1994 to develop common standards for the World Wide Web, the W3C is an international industry consortium jointly hosted by the Massachusetts Institute of Technology Laboratory for Computer Science (MIT/LCS) in North America, by the Institut National de Recherche en Informatique et en Automatique (INRIA) in Europe, and by the Keio University Shonan Fujisawa Campus in Asia. Initially, the W3C was established in collaboration with the Conseil Européen pour la Recherche Nucléaire (CERN), where the Web originated, with support from the Defense Advanced Research Projects Agency (DARPA) and the European Commission. For more information, see *http://www.w3.org/*.

WOSA *See* Windows Open Services Architecture (WOSA).

WSH *See* Windows Script Host (WSH).

WWW *See* World Wide Web (WWW).

Z

zone transfer The process of replicating a zone file to multiple name servers. A zone transfer is achieved by copying the zone file information from the master server to the secondary server.

Index

A

MICROSOFT LICENSE AGREEMENT
Book Companion CD

IMPORTANT—READ CAREFULLY: This Microsoft End-User License Agreement ("EULA") is a legal agreement between you (either an individual or an entity) and Microsoft Corporation for the Microsoft product identified above, which includes computer software and may include associated media, printed materials, and "online" or electronic documentation ("SOFTWARE PROD-UCT"). Any component included within the SOFTWARE PRODUCT that is accompanied by a separate End-User License Agreement shall be governed by such agreement and not the terms set forth below. By installing, copying, or otherwise using the SOFTWARE PRODUCT, you agree to be bound by the terms of this EULA. If you do not agree to the terms of this EULA, you are not authorized to install, copy, or otherwise use the SOFTWARE PRODUCT; you may, however, return the SOFTWARE PROD-UCT, along with all printed materials and other items that form a part of the Microsoft product that includes the SOFTWARE PRODUCT, to the place you obtained them for a full refund.

SOFTWARE PRODUCT LICENSE

The SOFTWARE PRODUCT is protected by United States copyright laws and international copyright treaties, as well as other intellectual property laws and treaties. The SOFTWARE PRODUCT is licensed, not sold.

1. **GRANT OF LICENSE.** This EULA grants you the following rights:

   a. **Software Product.** You may install and use one copy of the SOFTWARE PRODUCT on a single computer. The primary user of the computer on which the SOFTWARE PRODUCT is installed may make a second copy for his or her exclusive use on a portable computer.

   b. **Storage/Network Use.** You may also store or install a copy of the SOFTWARE PRODUCT on a storage device, such as a network server, used only to install or run the SOFTWARE PRODUCT on your other computers over an internal network; however, you must acquire and dedicate a license for each separate computer on which the SOFTWARE PRODUCT is installed or run from the storage device. A license for the SOFTWARE PRODUCT may not be shared or used concurrently on different computers.

   c. **License Pak.** If you have acquired this EULA in a Microsoft License Pak, you may make the number of additional copies of the computer software portion of the SOFTWARE PRODUCT authorized on the printed copy of this EULA, and you may use each copy in the manner specified above. You are also entitled to make a corresponding number of secondary copies for portable computer use as specified above.

   d. **Sample Code.** Solely with respect to portions, if any, of the SOFTWARE PRODUCT that are identified within the SOFT-WARE PRODUCT as sample code (the "SAMPLE CODE"):

      i. **Use and Modification.** Microsoft grants you the right to use and modify the source code version of the SAMPLE CODE, *provided* you comply with subsection (d)(iii) below. You may not distribute the SAMPLE CODE, or any modified version of the SAMPLE CODE, in source code form.

      ii. **Redistributable Files.** Provided you comply with subsection (d)(iii) below, Microsoft grants you a nonexclusive, royalty-free right to reproduce and distribute the object code version of the SAMPLE CODE and of any modified SAMPLE CODE, other than SAMPLE CODE, or any modified version thereof, designated as not redistributable in the Readme file that forms a part of the SOFTWARE PRODUCT (the "Non-Redistributable Sample Code"). All SAMPLE CODE other than the Non-Redistributable Sample Code is collectively referred to as the "REDISTRIBUTABLES."

      iii. **Redistribution Requirements.** If you redistribute the REDISTRIBUTABLES, you agree to: (i) distribute the REDISTRIBUTABLES in object code form only in conjunction with and as a part of your software application product; (ii) not use Microsoft's name, logo, or trademarks to market your software application product; (iii) include a valid copyright notice on your software application product; (iv) indemnify, hold harmless, and defend Microsoft from and against any claims or lawsuits, including attorney's fees, that arise or result from the use or distribution of your software application product; and (v) not permit further distribution of the REDISTRIBUTABLES by your end user. Contact Microsoft for the applicable royalties due and other licensing terms for all other uses and/or distribution of the REDISTRIBUTABLES.

2. **DESCRIPTION OF OTHER RIGHTS AND LIMITATIONS.**

   • **Limitations on Reverse Engineering, Decompilation, and Disassembly.** You may not reverse engineer, decompile, or disassemble the SOFTWARE PRODUCT, except and only to the extent that such activity is expressly permitted by applicable law notwithstanding this limitation.

   • **Separation of Components.** The SOFTWARE PRODUCT is licensed as a single product. Its component parts may not be separated for use on more than one computer.

   • **Rental.** You may not rent, lease, or lend the SOFTWARE PRODUCT.

- **Support Services.** Microsoft may, but is not obligated to, provide you with support services related to the SOFTWARE PRODUCT ("Support Services"). Use of Support Services is governed by the Microsoft policies and programs described in the user manual, in "online" documentation, and/or in other Microsoft-provided materials. Any supplemental software code provided to you as part of the Support Services shall be considered part of the SOFTWARE PRODUCT and subject to the terms and conditions of this EULA. With respect to technical information you provide to Microsoft as part of the Support Services, Microsoft may use such information for its business purposes, including for product support and development. Microsoft will not utilize such technical information in a form that personally identifies you.

- **Software Transfer.** You may permanently transfer all of your rights under this EULA, provided you retain no copies, you transfer all of the SOFTWARE PRODUCT (including all component parts, the media and printed materials, any upgrades, this EULA, and, if applicable, the Certificate of Authenticity), **and** the recipient agrees to the terms of this EULA.

- **Termination.** Without prejudice to any other rights, Microsoft may terminate this EULA if you fail to comply with the terms and conditions of this EULA. In such event, you must destroy all copies of the SOFTWARE PRODUCT and all of its component parts.

3. **COPYRIGHT.** All title and copyrights in and to the SOFTWARE PRODUCT (including but not limited to any images, photographs, animations, video, audio, music, text, SAMPLE CODE, REDISTRIBUTABLES, and "applets" incorporated into the SOFTWARE PRODUCT) and any copies of the SOFTWARE PRODUCT are owned by Microsoft or its suppliers. The SOFTWARE PRODUCT is protected by copyright laws and international treaty provisions. Therefore, you must treat the SOFTWARE PRODUCT like any other copyrighted material **except** that you may install the SOFTWARE PRODUCT on a single computer provided you keep the original solely for backup or archival purposes. You may not copy the printed materials accompanying the SOFTWARE PRODUCT.

4. **U.S. GOVERNMENT RESTRICTED RIGHTS.** The SOFTWARE PRODUCT and documentation are provided with RESTRICTED RIGHTS. Use, duplication, or disclosure by the Government is subject to restrictions as set forth in subparagraph (c)(1)(ii) of the Rights in Technical Data and Computer Software clause at DFARS 252.227-7013 or subparagraphs (c)(1) and (2) of the Commercial Computer Software—Restricted Rights at 48 CFR 52.227-19, as applicable. Manufacturer is Microsoft Corporation/One Microsoft Way/Redmond, WA 98052-6399.

5. **EXPORT RESTRICTIONS.** You agree that you will not export or re-export the SOFTWARE PRODUCT, any part thereof, or any process or service that is the direct product of the SOFTWARE PRODUCT (the foregoing collectively referred to as the "Restricted Components"), to any country, person, entity, or end user subject to U.S. export restrictions. You specifically agree not to export or re-export any of the Restricted Components (i) to any country to which the U.S. has embargoed or restricted the export of goods or services, which currently include, but are not necessarily limited to, Cuba, Iran, Iraq, Libya, North Korea, Sudan, and Syria, or to any national of any such country, wherever located, who intends to transmit or transport the Restricted Components back to such country; (ii) to any end user who you know or have reason to know will utilize the Restricted Components in the design, development, or production of nuclear, chemical, or biological weapons; or (iii) to any end user who has been prohibited from participating in U.S. export transactions by any federal agency of the U.S. government. You warrant and represent that neither the BXA nor any other U.S. federal agency has suspended, revoked, or denied your export privileges.

DISCLAIMER OF WARRANTY

NO WARRANTIES OR CONDITIONS. MICROSOFT EXPRESSLY DISCLAIMS ANY WARRANTY OR CONDITION FOR THE SOFTWARE PRODUCT. THE SOFTWARE PRODUCT AND ANY RELATED DOCUMENTATION ARE PROVIDED "AS IS" WITHOUT WARRANTY OR CONDITION OF ANY KIND, EITHER EXPRESS OR IMPLIED, INCLUDING, WITHOUT LIMITATION, THE IMPLIED WARRANTIES OF MERCHANTABILITY, FITNESS FOR A PARTICULAR PURPOSE, OR NONINFRINGEMENT. THE ENTIRE RISK ARISING OUT OF USE OR PERFORMANCE OF THE SOFTWARE PRODUCT REMAINS WITH YOU.

LIMITATION OF LIABILITY. TO THE MAXIMUM EXTENT PERMITTED BY APPLICABLE LAW, IN NO EVENT SHALL MICROSOFT OR ITS SUPPLIERS BE LIABLE FOR ANY SPECIAL, INCIDENTAL, INDIRECT, OR CONSEQUENTIAL DAMAGES WHATSOEVER (INCLUDING, WITHOUT LIMITATION, DAMAGES FOR LOSS OF BUSINESS PROFITS, BUSINESS INTERRUPTION, LOSS OF BUSINESS INFORMATION, OR ANY OTHER PECUNIARY LOSS) ARISING OUT OF THE USE OF OR INABILITY TO USE THE SOFTWARE PRODUCT OR THE PROVISION OF OR FAILURE TO PROVIDE SUPPORT SERVICES, EVEN IF MICROSOFT HAS BEEN ADVISED OF THE POSSIBILITY OF SUCH DAMAGES. IN ANY CASE, MICROSOFT'S ENTIRE LIABILITY UNDER ANY PROVISION OF THIS EULA SHALL BE LIMITED TO THE GREATER OF THE AMOUNT ACTUALLY PAID BY YOU FOR THE SOFTWARE PRODUCT OR US$5.00; PROVIDED, HOWEVER, IF YOU HAVE ENTERED INTO A MICROSOFT SUPPORT SERVICES AGREEMENT, MICROSOFT'S ENTIRE LIABILITY REGARDING SUPPORT SERVICES SHALL BE GOVERNED BY THE TERMS OF THAT AGREEMENT. BECAUSE SOME STATES AND JURISDICTIONS DO NOT ALLOW THE EXCLUSION OR LIMITATION OF LIABILITY, THE ABOVE LIMITATION MAY NOT APPLY TO YOU.

MISCELLANEOUS

This EULA is governed by the laws of the State of Washington USA, except and only to the extent that applicable law mandates governing law of a different jurisdiction.

Should you have any questions concerning this EULA, or if you desire to contact Microsoft for any reason, please contact the Microsoft subsidiary serving your country, or write: Microsoft Sales Information Center/One Microsoft Way/Redmond, WA 98052-6399.

System Requirements

To use the electronic version of this book from the Supplemental Course Materials CD-ROM, you need a computer equipped with the following minimum configuration:

- 133-MHz or higher Pentium-compatible CPU

- Microsoft Windows 95, Windows 98, or Microsoft Windows NT 4 or later

- 16 MB of RAM

- 500-MB hard disk with 15 MB of available disk space

- CD-ROM drive

- Microsoft Mouse or compatible pointing device (recommended)

- Microsoft Internet Explorer 5 or later

To use the Evaluation Edition of the Microsoft Windows 2000 Advanced Server software included with this book, you need a computer equipped with the following minimum configuration:

- 133-MHz or higher Pentium-compatible CPU

- 256 MB of RAM

- 2-GB hard disk with a minimum of 1.0 GB free space

- CD-ROM drive

To use the Evaluation Edition of Microsoft Application Center 2000 included with this book, you need a computer equipped with the following minimum configuration:

- 400-MHz or higher Pentium-compatible CPU

- Microsoft Windows 2000 Server or Windows 2000 Advanced Server operating system, Microsoft Windows 2000 Service Pack 1 or later, and Microsoft Internet Information Services 5.0 must be installed as part of Windows 2000 installation

- 256 MB of RAM minimum recommended

- 100 MB of available hard-disk space to install services; additional space required for site content and databases

- CD-ROM drive

- Windows 2000-compatible video graphics adapter with 800x600 minimum resolution

- Microsoft Mouse or compatible pointing device

- One Network Interface Card (two recommended); if using Windows 2000 Network Load Balancing, two NICs are required